Americans
in a Splintering Europe

ALSO BY MARK STRECKER

*Shanghaiing Sailors: A Maritime History of
Forced Labor, 1849–1915* (McFarland, 2014)

*Smedley D. Butler, USMC:
A Biography* (McFarland, 2011)

Americans in a Splintering Europe

Refugees, Missionaries and Journalists in World War I

MARK STRECKER

McFarland & Company, Inc., Publishers
Jefferson, North Carolina

LIBRARY OF CONGRESS CATALOGUING-IN-PUBLICATION DATA

Names: Strecker, Mark, 1970– author.
Title: Americans in a splintering Europe : refugees, missionaries and journalists in World War I / Mark Strecker.
Description: Jefferson, North Carolina : McFarland & Company, Inc., Publishers, 2019 | Includes bibliographical references and index.
Identifiers: LCCN 2018047633 | ISBN 9781476676029 (softcover : acid free paper) ∞
Subjects: LCSH: World War, 1914–1918—United States. | Americans—Europe. | Civilians in war—Europe. | Civilians in war—United States.
Classification: LCC D570.1 .S77 2019 | DDC 940.3089/1304—dc23
LC record available at https://lccn.loc.gov/2018047633

BRITISH LIBRARY CATALOGUING DATA ARE AVAILABLE

ISBN (print) 978-1-4766-7602-9
ISBN (ebook) 978-1-4766-3451-7

© 2019 Mark Strecker. All rights reserved

No part of this book may be reproduced or transmitted in any form or by any means, electronic or mechanical, including photocopying or recording, or by any information storage and retrieval system, without permission in writing from the publisher.

Front cover image: The evacuation of Antwerp (Library of Congress Prints and Photographs Division. Red Cross Photograph Collection)

Printed in the United States of America

McFarland & Company, Inc., Publishers
Box 611, Jefferson, North Carolina 28640
www.mcfarlandpub.com

To Beth Little
This one has missionaries in it.

Table of Contents

Acknowledgments — viii
A Note on Geographic Names — ix
Preface — 1
Prologue: The Assassination — 3

1. American Refugees — 23
2. The Invasion of Belgium — 49
3. Into the War Zone — 76
4. The February Revolution — 89
5. The Ottoman Empire — 105
6. The Great Crime — 126
7. Persia — 143

Chapter Notes — 157
Bibliography — 179
Index — 185

Acknowledgments

A large number of people helped me in various ways while I researched and wrote this book, and it would be remiss of me to not give them some credit. I apologize for missing anyone. Thanks to Amy Garrett, Ph.D., Office of the Historian, U.S. Department of State; Tiffany H. Cabrera, Ph.D., Historian, Special Projects Division, Office of the Historian, U.S. Department of State; James Amemasor, Ph.D., Head of Research, New Jersey Historical Society; David A. Langbart, National Archives; Jerry Schmidt, Research Center Attendant, National World War I Museum; Professor George Hall, Department of Economics, Brandeis University; Paul H. Thompson, Hoover Presidential Library, who kindly forwarded me a copy of *American Bulletin*; Sara J. Keckeisen, Librarian, Kansas State Historical Society; Tom Edwards and Beverly R. Austin, librarians, Cleveland Public Library; David P Rosenberg, M.P.A., Reference Services Research Coordinator, Center for Jewish History; Dr. Beth Ann Griech-Polelle, Professor, Bowling Green State University; Emily Walhout, Librarian, Houghton Reading Room, Harvard University; Katherine Phillips, Imperial War Museum, UK; Lisa Jacobson, Senior Reference Archivist, Presbyterian Historical Society; Anita Sheahan Coraluzzi, a Philadelphia-based genealogist who did research job for me outside her usual specialty; Lisa Bors, Director of the Annual Fund, Ambrose Swasey Library, Colgate Rochester Crozer Divinity School; Terry Metter, Subject Department Librarian, Center for Local and Global History, Cleveland Public Library; Louis Adrean, Head, Research and Programs, Ingalls Library, Cleveland Museum of Art; and Mike Rose, Librarian, Geography and Map Reading Division, Library of Congress.

And a special thanks to Tracy Marr and Mark Hope. Tracy, the Adult Services Librarian at Bellevue Public Library, managed to get hold of all sorts of obscure out of system works for me. She is a valuable resource, as are all librarians and library personnel. Marc Hope was the guide for Leger Holidays' "The Old Contemptibles" historical tour in Belgium. He made that aspect of the war more real because of his limitless knowledge and excellent narrative. He also helped me crack a couple tough research questions.

A Note on Geographic Names

The world on a map looked quite different in 1914 than it does today. The nation of Poland, for example, did not exist because Prussia, Russia, and Austria had carved it up for themselves. The Ottoman Empire, which once spanned from Eastern Europe into western Asia and northern Africa, no longer exists. Nor do the maps of this era have the name of its capital right. Instead of Istanbul, they called it Constantinople, a name the city's inhabitants had not used since the fall of the Byzantine Empire in 1453! For that matter, many European cities, towns and villages had alternative names in 1914 because they now reside in different countries. The city of Tilsit in East Prussia, for example, is now Sovetsk in Russia. Belgium is even more confusing because it has both French and Flemish speakers, each with their own name for a given place.

In regions where the Latin alphabet gives way to others, Western cartographers transliterated names. A lack of universal standards for this resulted in place names being spelled a wide variety of ways. The city of Sarajevo, for example, is spelled "Sarajevo" in the 1911 atlas by William Shepherd, "Sarayevo" in the 1899 *Stanford's Compendium of Geography and Travel: Europe Volume 1*, "Saraievo" in the 1912 *Literary and Historical Atlas of Europe* by J.G. Bartholomew, and "Bosnia Serai (Sarajevo)" in a 1906 atlas published by W. & A.K. Johnston.

For the sake of consistency, I decided, with a few exceptions (such as using "Serbia" instead of "Servia"), to call places by the names used in 1914 rather than their present ones, which is why Iran is Persia and the Turkish city of Elazığ is Harput. I also removed obscure diacritic marks such as the one over the *g* in Elazığ because, with the exception of linguists, no one will have any idea how they change a letter's sound anyway. Readers will find modern or alternative names of places in parentheses on this book's maps.

Preface

When I began this book, I intended to write about two groups of American civilians during World War I: those who wanted to escape from Europe and those who headed there to cover the fighting. American refugees cared little for the politics behind why the war began or which side was in the right. They just wanted to get out of the danger zones and head to the safety of home. American journalists had the attitude that the first amendment applied to them no matter where in the world they went, prompting them to ignore the strict censorship and restriction of movement imposed by the belligerents. As a result, they published many stories in the United States that would never have seen print in Europe.

Trying to find accounts written by Americans in war zones outside of Europe initially proved difficult. Then I had an idea. Perhaps I ought to look at American missionaries because research for a previous project showed me that this well-educated group of people left behind a treasure trove of written materials both personal and official about their lives and activities. And sure enough, I found more material than I could possibly use in a single book. Better still, missionaries added a viewpoint different from that of refugees and journalists. Unlike the Americans who fled for home the moment war broke out or the journalists who stayed just long enough to get their stories, when the regions in which the missionaries worked became war zones, many had no intention of leaving their homes or abandoning their missionary vocations. Despite their neutral status, they sometimes intervened in local politics and even fought in skirmishes both to protect themselves and the locals among whom they worked. Not all of them survived the ordeal.

Prologue
The Assassination

Last of the Hapsburgs

The Treaty of Versailles, which officially ended World War I, infamously blamed Germany for starting this conflict and forced it to pay reparations, a terrible blunder that led to the rise of Adolf Hitler and World War II. Those who initiated the war—France, Austria-Hungary, Russia, Germany and Britain—share the blame equally. With the exception of a few to whom no one listened, most politicians and military personnel believed it would last just a few months and through it they could further their political and imperialistic goals. If responsibility for the war needs to be laid on a single nation, it has to be put at the feet of the Austro-Hungarian Empire in general and its emperor-king, Franz Joseph, in particular. His domestic policies so alienated the Serbs living in his empire's borders, it drove a group of them to carry out the assassination of Archduke Franz Ferdinand, heir to the throne, whose death sparked the war.

Franz Joseph came from the House of Hapsburg, a family that for hundreds of years ruled over large swaths of Europe that originated not in Austria but rather Germanic Switzerland where it ruled as counts. In 1250, Austria's reigning family, the Babenbergs, died out, giving the king of Bohemia, Ottokar II, the opportunity to make himself its overlord. An ambitious man, he took over neighboring Styria in 1261, then Carinthia in 1269. To his west stood the Holy Roman Empire, a hodgepodge of Germanic autonomous states that claimed descent from the empire of Charlemagne, whose rulers did not want an ethnic Czech in charge of Germanic Austria. In 1273, they elected a Hapsburg as their new emperor, Rudolf I, with the idea that he would take back Austria. Conflict ensued.[1]

On August 26, 1278, Rudolf defeated Ottokar at Marchfeld, an area just east of Vienna, making him the direct ruler of Austria. In 1282, he bequeathed his new holding to his two sons, Albert and Rudolf, whose descendants would rule the kingdom and later its empire for the next six and a half centuries. Although the office of Holy Roman Emperor was not hereditary but rather determined by a vote of German electors through means fair and foul (usually bribery), no one except for a Hapsburg held this title between 1438 and 1740.[2]

Over the centuries the Hapsburgs became lords of much of Europe more so because of their political prowess and a genius for marriage arrangements than military conquest, allowing the family to acquire most of the states that would one day make up the Austrian Empire, including Carinthia, Tyrol, Istria, and Moravia. In the fifteenth century, Holy Roman Emperor Maximilian I married Mary, the daughter and heiress of Charles the Bold,

Austro-Hungarian Empire. Map by the author based on one in the *Rand-McNally Indexed Pocket Map of Austria-Hungary*. Chicago: Rand, McNally & Co., 1906. LOC Map Collections.

Duke of Burgundy, and from her he gained control of the duke's lands, which included the Netherlands. Maximilian's descendants acquired the Spanish Empire, Bohemia, and Hungary among other places. Charles V, deeming this too much for one person to rule, divided his Spanish and Austrian lands in two, the latter becoming the Austrian Empire.[3]

Franz Joseph, born on August 18, 1830, became emperor because of the machinations of his mother, Sophie Friederike von Bayern. She forced his uncle, Ferdinand, to abdicate, then commanded her husband to let their son take the crown. By the time Franz Joseph became Austria's ruler on December 2, 1848, at the age of 19, his empire had reached a state of serious decay. It did not help that he saw himself not as a statesman but rather a soldier. And although he had worked his way up from the lowest to the highest of ranks during his army service and became an excellent horseman, he lacked a faculty for actual military leadership. During his reign, the Austrian army suffered a series of humiliating defeats, the worst of which came at the hands of the tiny nation of Serbia during World War I.[4]

Emperor Franz Joseph (left) and Archduke Franz Joseph Otto. Bain News Service. Taken between 1910 and 1915. Library of Congress Prints and Photographs Division.

That he had a troubled reign is an understatement. During his 68-year rule, he lost a staggering 18 close family members to tragedy, including his wife, Elisabeth, who died in 1898 at the hand of an Italian anarchist in Geneva. His brother, Maximilian, became emperor of Mexico in 1863 only to be executed his subjects in 1867, an event that drove Maximilian's wife insane. Empress Elisabeth's cousin, Ludwig II, King of Bavaria, also went "insane and finally drowned himself in the Lake of Starnberg during a violent paroxysm." Franz Joseph's sister-in-law, Sophie, died in a fire at the Bazar de la Charité in Paris.[5]

When the Holy Roman Empire fell in 1815, the Germanic states that had made it up, including Austria and Prussia, formed the German Confederation. This remained intact until 1866 when Prussia's prime minister, Otto von Bismarck, initiated a war with Austria designed to force it out of the coalition so he could forge a unified German state with Prussia at its helm. Austria's loss not only forced it out of the Confederation, it gave the Hungarians the political leverage they needed for more self-determination within the Austrian Empire.[6]

Needing Hungarian support to continue ruling over the mass of different ethnic groups under his rule, Franz Joseph approved the Hungarian Diet's Law XII in 1867, which removed Hungary from the Austrian Empire and gave it independent control over its domestic affairs. Franz Josef became its king with absolute power over foreign policy and defense. He could also dismiss Hungary's prime minister and its parliament. The new Austro-Hungarian Empire, which officially came into being on July 28, 1867, gave power to the Magyars at German expense, but did nothing to improve the lives of its ethnic minorities.[7]

Its Serbs, for example, wanted outright independence. They had long suffered under the yoke of Turkish rule, whose Ottoman Empire first tried to take over Medieval Serbia in 1389. Although a Christian coalition stopped the Turks at the Battle of Kosovo on June 28 in that year, they persisted and conquered Serbia in 1459. The Ottoman Empire kept a firm grip on this region until 1802 when a cadre of four Janissaries—elite Ottoman soldiers—took control of Belgrade. Two years later they tried to kill off as many Serbian leaders as they could to prevent a possible rebellion, motivating the Serbs to form a rebel force. After removing the Janissaries, the Ottomans continued to rule the country, but the Serb rebels never disbanded. In June 1876, they allied with Montenegro and together went to war to gain independence. The Serbs invaded Bosnia in the hope of taking control of it as well. Although an intervention by major European powers two years later granted Serbia the independence it desired, this same negotiation allowed Austria to temporarily occupy the Serb-dominated regions of Bosnia and Herzegovina.[8]

The Austrians entered these lands before the treaty took effect with a promise to allow qualified Ottoman officials to retain their positions. At the same time it abolished the Ottoman currency, placed the provinces under Austrian customs, issued Austrian passports to its people, and demanded military service from them. In other words, the Austrians had come to stay, formally annexing the provinces near the end of 1908, which increased the number of Slavs in Austria-Hungary by another 1.7 million for a total of about 22 million, causing their number to equal that of the Empire's ethnic Germans, Magyars and Romanians combined.[9]

Serbia was not the only former Ottoman territory to break away. All of its former Balkan provinces save for Macedonia and Kosovo had also done so, prompting the Russians, longtime adversaries of the Turks, to encourage Bulgaria, Montenegro, Serbia and Greece to ally themselves into what became known as the Balkan League with the aim of ousting the Turks from the Balkans altogether. An attack on the Ottoman Empire by Montenegro in 1912 prompted the former to declare war on the entire Balkan League.[10]

The Ottomans lost the short war that followed, which ended with the signing of the Treaty of London on May 30, 1913. Among other things, it guaranteed the independence of Albania. A month later, a disgruntled Bulgaria, feeling it had not gained sufficient territory, went to war against its former allies, encouraging the Ottomans to make a failed effort to retake Adrianople. This second conflict ended a month later with Bulgaria losing and the Ottomans no better off than before. These wars were the breeding ground for some of those who participated in or supported the conspiracy to assassinate Franz Ferdinand.[11]

Who, ironically, planned to treat the Serbs better than his uncle had. He wanted to give Serb nationalists the autonomy they desperately sought by creating a Slav confederation that would include Bohemia and Poland, each with its own kings. While sounding altruistic on the face of it, he had no intention of relinquishing Hapsburg control of them. If Serbia

Franz Ferdinand. Bain News Service. Creation date unknown. Library of Congress Prints and Photographs Division.

and Montenegro joined as he hoped, it would give Austria-Hungary power over them. Had he lived to rule, it is doubtful his scheme would have worked because the Serbs living inside and outside the Empire wanted total independence and nothing else would do.[12]

That anyone went to war over the death of Franz Ferdinand is outrageous when one looks at the man himself. Even after his assassination, few had anything good to say about him. Before reaching the age of 25, he had obtained the reputation of being Vienna's wildest nobleman with a taste for ballet dancers and an ability to consume vast quantities of champagne. His military career was rife with scandals. Known as a nervous fellow, he had a cold personality and thought little of those without noble blood. He strongly disliked Americans "whose women he particularly abominate[d] because of their lack of reverence for wifehood and maternity, and whose men he despise[d] for their lack of delicacy and pursuit of things material." He also hated Magyars, churchman, and the kingdom of Italy. With little money of his own, he was an infamous penny-pincher, although he did possess a massive collection of ancient weapons and art.[13]

The misfortune of his kin thrust him into the role of heir apparent. In 1889, Franz Joseph's only son, Rudolf, murdered his lover, Baroness Marie Alexandrine Freiin von Vetsera, at his hunting lodge in Mayerling. He then killed himself. This would have made the emperor's younger brother, Karl Ludwig, next in line for the throne had he not died in 1896, which left his son, Franz Ferdinand, as the heir apparent, who one commentator considered "a mere attache [sic] of the Austrian court, tolerated and but barely tolerated as the nephew of the emperor, disliked for his surly manners and selfish disposition and altogether the most unpopular man in Vienna…. Desperate efforts have been made to polish him up a little and reconcile his royal relatives, but with little success. While her son was alive, the empress would not allow … [him] to enter her presence."[14]

In 1892, he lost his appetite and some weight and came down with a low fever. His doctors feared he had inherited tuberculosis from his mother, Annunciata of Naples, who had died of the disease at the age of 28 in 1871. The archduke's doctors told him to seek warmer climates for at least six months. Although Franz Joseph, from whom the archduke had to receive permission to go on this trip, initially balked at the idea, he eventually gave in.[15]

Boarding the Austrian man-of-war *Kaiserin Elizabeth* on December 15, 1892, Franz Ferdinand departed from the Adriatic Sea port of Trieste on what would become a journey around the world. He and his entourage sailed into the Red Sea via the Suez Canal and from there visited "Arabia, Australia, India, China, Japan," then began a trip through America starting in San Francisco. He tried using the alias Count Franz Artolatten of Austria, but it fooled no one: American newspapers reported on him using his real name, although the *New York Times* gleefully noted that since he had registered at the Windsor Hotel in Niagara Falls under his assumed name, the staff could only call him that.[16]

His trip through the United States had no official status save for the vague purpose of promoting commerce and did not include an invitation to the meet President Grover Cleveland at the White House. Franz Ferdinand failed to endear himself to Americans, systematically insulting and otherwise annoying them from one end of the nation to the other. In Spokane, Washington, his first stop, the commander of local soldiers asked if he would review his men. Because he traveled incognito, he refused. He confided in his diary that Spokane reminded "him of obscure villages in Asia Minor!" His stop in Seattle induced the *Seattle-Post Intelligencer* to editorialize, "Archduke Franz Ferdinand d'Este, heir presumptive to the throne of Austria, who passed through Seattle last Friday, has all the bad qualities of Emperor William [Wilhelm] of Germany and none of his good ones." It characterized the archduke as "a hard drinker, an associate of lewd women, and [a man who] would have made a fine 'war lord' in the Middle Ages."[17]

At Yellowstone National Park he was irritated that he could not shoot any of the animals, nor did he like the cowboys at the Hot Springs Hotel who repeatedly spat tobacco juice. All across the West he became indignant that operators of hotels shook his hand and treated him like any other guest. In Chicago he visited the World Columbia Exhibition, the fair where, as Erik Larson chronicled in *The Devil in the White City*, a notorious serial killer operated. He annoyed the people of Chicago when he refused to let them treat him as a special guest and upset the Viennese working at the Austrian village Alt Wien on the fairway when he decided not to visit because too many people had gathered there to see him.[18]

Once back home, he began courting Maria Christina, daughter of Archduchess Isabella von Croy. While doing so he became enamored with one of Isabella's ladies-in-waiting, Sophie Maria Josephine Albina, Countess Chotek von Chotkowa und Wognin. The feeling was mutual. She helped improve his still precarious health and motivated him to curb many of his vices, including cards, betting on race horses, and taking on lovers. Sophie, who had six other sisters, came from an old Bohemian family. Her father had served as the Austrian ambassador to Britain. When she met Franz Ferdinand, both her parents were dead and she had no income save for what she earned working for Isabella.[19]

The two carried on a secret courtship right under Isabella's nose, even brazenly playing as partners in doubles tennis, although some evidence suggests Isabella knew of their affair but presumed he only kept Sophie as a mistress with the intention of marrying Maria Christina. In April 1889, after he departed from a tennis party at Bratislava Castle, a servant found his gold watch with an attached locket and gave it to Isabella. Opening it to see if he kept a miniature of her daughter there, she instead discovered one of Sophie. Outraged, she immediately dismissed her lady-in-waiting and informed the emperor of the courtship. She would never forgive Sophie for this perceived betrayal.[20]

With their affair exposed and Sophie now lacking an income, Franz Ferdinand decided to marry her. Except by law he could not without the permission of the emperor, and this Franz Joseph refused to give it because of Sophie's considerably lower rank in the aristocracy. Franz Ferdinand pointed out that if the royal family did not start marrying outside its own close blood, the line would produce nothing but "cretins or epileptics." It took the intervention of Franz Ferdinand's stepmother, Maria Teresa da Imaculada, to convince the emperor to consent.[21]

But this came with a price: no children from the union could ever ascend to the Austro-Hungarian throne, and Sophie would never take on the title of empress. The next in line to the throne would be Franz's Ferdinand's younger brother and his children. Sophie and Franz Ferdinand married on July 1, 1900. None of the latter's brothers attended, nor did the emperor or any of the higher ranking clergy in the realm. For the rest of their marriage, most of the royal family detested Sophie. The emperor himself warmed to her, even giving her the title of Duchess of Hohenberg.[22]

The Assassination of Franz Ferdinand

Gavrilo Princip, the young man who assassinated Franz Ferdinand, did not act alone. An entire conspiracy of young Serbian nationalists with aid from several low ranking Serbian officials plotted together. Princip came from the humblest of circumstances from the backwater village of Obljaj in the highlands of Herzegovina. He was born on July 13, 1894, and his village offered nothing but poverty, so his father sent him off to Sarajevo at the age of 13 for an education at the Merchant's School where his brother, Jovo, arranged for him to board at the residence of the widow Stoja Ilic and her son, Danilo, who was four years older than Princip. Despite this age gap they became fast friends, giving the former the opportunity to introduce the latter to Serbian radical literature.[23]

A voracious reader, Princip consumed works on anarchism, socialism, and especially about Serbian nationalism. In 1911, at the age of 17, he became radicalized. The next year when the First Balkan War broke out, he headed to Belgrade and enlisted with guerrilla force of the *Narodna odbrana* (National Defense) with which he did some training until illness forced him out. After this he stayed with Jovo in the village of Hadzici until March 1913. A good student for his first five years at school, he withdrew from the system in Sarajevo, then he headed to Belgrade in Serbia to further his formal education.[24]

Here he befriended Nedeljko Cabrinovic, an anarchist expelled from Austria-Hungary for five years because of his political activism. Having run away from home to escape his father, Cabrinovic had tried his hand as a locksmith, sheet metal worker, and, at the age of 14, a printer, eventually becoming a journeyman in this last trade. In Belgrade, he worked for the anarchist newspaper *Komuna* (*Commune*) at which he became an ardent follower

Belgrade. Bain News Service. Taken between 1910 and 1915. Library of Congress Prints and Photographs.

of that movement. No nationalist, he hated the Catholic Church and proclaimed himself an atheist. Ill health forced him to return to Sarajevo in 1912 for two months during which time he worked for the periodical *Narod (People)*. In 1913, he returned to Belgrade and there renewed his friendship with Princip.[25]

When Princip read in a newspaper that Franz Ferdinand would visit Sarajevo in June 1914, he came up with idea of assassinating him. A few days later in a park, Cabrinovic showed him a photo of the archduke and a newspaper clipping the upcoming visit. Killing Franz Ferdinand had not occurred to Cabrinovic, but when Princip proposed it, he consented with the caveat that they would not kill Sophie in the process. Another member of the conspiracy, Trifko Grabez, later claimed that both he and Princip had conceived of the idea together without Cabrinovic present and only invited him at Grabez's suggestion. The son of a Greek Orthodox priest who never lost his faith, Grabez had met Princip while attending school in Belgrade and even lived with him for a time. An official Austrian report agreed with Cabrinovic's and Princip's own recollections that Grabez joined the conspiracy only after the other two had formulated a loose plan.[26]

To carry it out, they needed weapons. In an effort to acquire them, Cabrinovic met Milan Ciganovic at a café, a man who wore a lice-infested suit and had fought as a guerrilla during the Balkan Wars. About a month later, Cabrinovic and Princip met with Ciganovic together to ask for bombs and guns. Although just a lowly railroad clerk, Ciganovic said he could acquire the bombs but they would have to get their own revolvers. Princip pointed out that their poverty made this impossible, so he agreed to get those as well.[27]

The 28-year-old Ciganovic took Princip and Grabez to Major Vojin Tankosic, his good friend and fellow Freemason. Tankosic asked the young men if they could handle a pistol. Grabez had never fired one, although Princip had during his training with the guerrillas on the Drina front. Tankosic handed them Browning pistols and told Ciganovic to teach them in their use. The three went to Topcider, then a forest outside Belgrade but now mostly gone save for a park. They did not use the firing range there because only members of a gun club had that privilege save for on Sundays, a day on which they had not come, so instead they fired at trees until a guard told them to stop. Princip, it turned out, had a better aim than Grabez. Cabrinovic later practiced at the gun club.[28]

Ciganovic possessed bombs left over from the First Balkan War, which he taught the young conspirators to operate and would later hand over for use in assassinating the archduke. These bombs, crude rectangles with 12-second fuses, came from the Serbian military depot at Kragujevac, a point the Austrians would later seize on as proof that the Serbian secret organization *Ujedinjenje Ili Smrt* (Union or Death) had had involvement with the plot.[29]

Most people know the Union or Death better as the Black Hand. Started in May 1911 by a cabal of military officers dissatisfied with a 1909 decision by the Serbian government to acquiesce to Austro-Hungarian demands that it stop protesting the annexation of Bosnia and Herzegovina and reduce the size of its military to 1908 levels, it had the goal of creating a Greater Serbia with Serbia itself in charge. Though it started its own newspaper, the *Pijemont*, to spread its propaganda, it preferred terrorist action to further its ends, something made pretty obvious by its logo, which consisted of a hand (not black) holding a skull and crossbones flag beside a dagger and vial of poison with the organization's name encircling it all.[30]

The man in charge of the Black Hand, Colonel Dragutin Dimitrijevic, known by his codename of Apis, was a lifelong officer in the Serbian military and the former head of the General Staff's intelligence service. In 1903 he infamously played a role in the plot that resulted in the assassination of the Serbian king and queen. During this venture he suffered from gunshot wounds from which no one ever extracted the bullets. The new king, Petar, helped to finance the Black Hand's newspaper. An 11-member Central Committee controlled smaller, isolated groups that could only communicate using the advertising section of the Belgrade newspaper *Trogvinski Glasnik*. Although in its early days mainly army officers joined, it later allowed professionals such as lawyers, journalists, university professors into its ranks.[31]

In April 1914, Ilic, who then lived in Sarajevo, received a letter from Princip explaining his plan to kill Franz Ferdinand, adding that he possessed the weapons to carry it out. In the time since Princip had departed from Sarajevo, Ilic had graduated from a teacher's school and briefly pursued that profession in Avtovac, then Foca, before resigning and returning to Sarajevo. There he worked for the Serbian National Bank for five months, departing for Serbia in July 1913 to look for different work. Unsatisfied with what he found, he returned home after just a month and a half. A stomach ailment that required a brief hospitalization kept him unemployed for several months. After this he became a journalist as well as a once-a-month proofreader.[32]

Ilic had often discussed using assassination as means of furthering political change with his Muslim friend Mehmed Mehmedbasic. Upon learning of Franz Ferdinand's upcoming visit to Sarajevo, Mehmedbasic had independently decided to kill the archduke and approached Ilic with the idea. Ilic replied that while they could not do so on their own for lack of available weapons, Princip had written to tell him he had taken care of this. Still another friend of Ilic's, Lazar Djukic, told him he knew others who wanted to kill Franz Ferdinand but lacked the means to do, so he introduced Ilic to Vaso Cubrilovic, an orphaned 17-year-old Serbo-Croatian who wanted to unite Croatia and Serbia into a greater Slav nation. Cubrilovic would have the opportunity to shoot the archduke but he lacked the grit to pull the trigger, excusing himself by claiming he had feared hitting Sophie. Cubrilovic recruited 16-year-old Cvjetko Popovic, a Slav nationalist who had Serbian citizenship but had never stepped foot in his homeland, who also wanted a united Slavic state, prompting him to agree to help despite not knowing Cubrilovic that well.[33]

On May 27, Ciganovic gave Princip, Cabrinovic and Grabez six bombs and four Browning pistols, glass tubes containing cyanide, 150 Serbian dinars, and "a small calling card in a sealed envelop" to be delivered to Captain Rade Popovic (no relation to Cvjetko), a friend of Major Tankosic's. They reached Sabac via the Danube on a steamboat and there found Captain Popovic in a cafe playing cards. They spoke with him in a quiet corner. Upon receipt of the calling card, he bought the three young men discount tickets for a private railroad using the forged names of revenue agents. Staying overnight, the next day they traveled to the Serbian village of Loznica to meet with a Captain Joca Prvanovic. After reading the letter from Captain Popovic, he phoned several sergeants at the watchtowers overlooking the Danube. Failing to get hold of anyone, he summoned them next day to ask what they considered the safest route into Bosnia. They said this would be at the post of revenue inspector Rade Grbic.[34]

The conspirators boarded the train for which Captain Popovic had procured tickets to reach the spa town of Banja Koviljaca along the Drina River. Here they bought postcards to send home as a ruse to mask their true destination. On his, Cabrinovic wrote on his a poem about crossing the border into Bosnia, which infuriated Princip, sparking a quarrel that resulted in Princip and Grabez deciding to travel separately from him. At the trial, Princip insisted their disagreement had nothing to do with this split. Rather, Princip gave his passport to Cabrinovic, who looked similar, so he could cross legally into Serbia at Mali Zvornik. Cabrinovic handed his weapons over to the his companions so they could smuggle them across the border.[35]

Princip and Grabez crossed to Isakovic's Island on which they went to the home of a peasant. Their next contact, Jakov Milovic, arrived in the evening and took them across the border into Bosnia between seven and eight that same night. They traveled the side roads into the mountains with their guns and bombs hanging from their belts. Upon reaching their next stop, the house of Obren Milosevic, they demanded bags for their weapons so passing gendarmes did not see them, then insisted Milovic and Milosevic to carry them, inferring if they did not comply, they would shoot them. Grabez later claimed at the trial they had no intention of doing them harm.[36]

The conspirators wanted Milovic and Milosevic to take them west to Tuzla, but neither man knew how to get there. Hiding in some bushes, Princip and Grabez sent the two Bosnians to Priboj to look for gendarmes. Milovic met an old friend, Veljko Cubrilovic (no relation to Vaso or Milan), riding a horse down the road. Milovic told his friend he had two people he wanted him to meet, so he followed him back. The conspirators asked Veljko to find a cart for his horse. Once acquired, they threw the guns and bombs into his horses' saddlebag, then told Veljko they planned to kill Franz Ferdinand. To this he wanted no part because he opposed assassination of any type, but the two implied they would revenge themselves on his family if he did not give his help. Indeed, they would do the same to anyone they met who hesitated to provide aid. They traveled for 21 hours straight, not stopping until they reached the house of the Kerovic family in the village of Lopare.[37]

Here Veljko went to a workshop ran by Mitar Kerovic. Veljko asked one of Mitar's sons, Nedjo, to take the two "students" he had with him to Tuzla using the family's cart and horses. Nedjo, whose hand was hurt, could not drive, so he recommended they have a young, illiterate farmer named Cvijan Stjepanovic to do this. He agreed. Nedjo went along so someone could look at his hand in Tuzla.[38]

Veljko tasked Nedjo and Stjepanovic to smuggle the conspirators' weapons into Tuzla, which they did by tucking them under their sashes. Princip and Grabez asked Veljko to recommend a contact in Tuzla in case they needed one. He wrote to Misko Jovanovic, a relation by god-parentage, to request that he offer them aid if necessary, although he did not know if Jovanovic would agree to help. Veljko told Nedjo to give the weapons to Jovanovic. Nedjo and Cvijan took the two conspirators in the cart as far as a Catholic convent at which they stopped to clean themselves up. Princip and Grabez continued to Tuzla where they met Jovanovic at Kavana Bosna, a cafe reading room. They asked him to take their weapons to Sarajevo, but he declined because of the risk involved, although he did agree to store them in his attic.[39]

A few days later Cabrinovic arrived in town. The reunited plotters headed for and arrived in Sarajevo three days before Franz Ferdinand. Once in the city, they split up again. Cabrinovic headed home, Princip went to Ilic's, and Grabez repaired to the town of Pale southeast of the city. Before their separation, they met with Ilic to discuss more details about their plan. By now Ilic had decided against going through with it. Although he still believed in assassination as a means of political change, he predicted killing the heir to the Austro-Hungarian throne would not benefit the Serbian cause. The others wanted to go ahead anyway, so he agreed to proceed. With the archduke's route published in the newspapers, it took little effort to decide where to ambush him. They chose Appel Quay, a wide boulevard in the center of Sarajevo that followed the northern bank of the river Miljacka and here chose a spot they expected to contain the thickest crowds waiting to see the archduke's car pass by, forcing it to go at its slowest. The crowd would also provide them with excellent cover.[40]

Ilic traveled to Tuzla to retrieve the weapons at Jovanovic's house. There he showed a pack of Stefanija cigarettes as the sign he had come for them. Ilic asked him to box the bombs and guns up and deliver them to the train station in the city of Doboj. The next day Jovanovic and two of his servants traveled to their destination carrying the weapons in a black sugar box wrapped in paper, which he took to the train station and, not seeing Ilic, left it there for awhile. Upon returning and still not seeing Ilic, he retrieved and gave it to an apprentice in a store, then returned to the station. When Ilic finally arrived, he took him to the store, handed the package over, and went to a restaurant for lunch.[41]

At eight on the morning on June 28, 1914—the day of Franz Ferdinand's visit—Grabez met up with Cabrinovic and Ilic at Vlajnic's sweet shop, then headed to Ilic's house. Here Ilic handed Grabez a bomb, doing so only after extracting a promise from him that he would not really make the attempt. Grabez agreed with no intention of honoring his pledge. He planned to throw his bomb to create a distraction while Princip shot the archduke with his pistol. Failing to find Princip in the crowd, Grabez feared the police had arrested him.[42]

The archduke and his wife rode through the city in a convertible with its the top down, the second vehicle in a line of four. This parade departed for the Town Hall at ten in the morning. Grabez resolved to kill the archduke if Cabrinovic failed to, and to that end repositioned himself at the Imperial Bridge where Franz Ferdinand's car would surely have to slow down for a turn. While waiting, he heard a bomb go off, which he suspected Cabrinovic had thrown because he doubted the others would have the courage to do the deed. Moments later he watched the archduke's convoy of cars pass with the man himself very much alive. From this new place he could not get at him, although had he stayed in his original position, the slow moving cars would have made an easy target.[43]

As Grabez suspected, Cabrinovic had indeed tossed his bomb at the archduke. He had wandered back and forth between Cumurija Bridge and the Austro-Hungarian Bank in an effort to avoid the many spies and detectives out and about looking for people just like him. Upon seeing the archduke's car, he smacked the bomb against a lamppost to arm it, then threw it only to watch it bounce off the auto's "rolled-down canvas top" and explode on the ground. It destroyed the back wheel of the next car in line and wounded one of those riding in it, Colonel Erich Edler von Merizzi. Cabrinovic jumped into the Miljacka and took a double dose of cyanide, but it did nothing more than make him so sick he could not eat for several days. When he learned that he had harmed innocent bystanders, he felt bad. He also later expressed great regret that the assassination sparked such an awful war.[44]

Princip had no idea who had thrown the bomb until he saw police take his friend away. He soon learned the explosion had failed to kill its target. Franz Ferdinand and his wife continued on for a meeting at the Town Hall. There, before Sarajevo's mayor could begin his speech, the archduke interrupted him: "Herr Burgermeister, it is perfectly outrageous! We have come to Sarajevo on a visit and have had a bomb thrown at us."[45]

Now the archduke's plans changed. Instead of taking Franz Joseph Strauss for a tour of the old city, he and he wife would skip that and just head to the main state hospital to visit the wounded Colonel von Merizzi. Appel Quay would take them straight there, so they intended to stay on this street instead of turning onto Franz Joseph Strauss at the intersection beside Moritz Schiller's delicatessen. The driver of the first car now made a terrible mistake: instead of going straight as planned, he turned onto Franz Joseph Strauss. The archduke's ignorant chauffeur followed. Informed of his mistake, he began backing

This is where Archduke Franz Ferdinand was assassinated. Keystone. Creation date unknown. Library of Congress Prints and Photographs Division.

up. At that moment Princip, who happened to be standing at the delicatessen just then, saw the car go by. He fired two shots. One hit the archduke in the neck, piercing his jugular vein, and the other slammed into Sophie's abdomen. Both targets quickly lost consciousness and neither survived long enough to reach the Konak, the governor's residence at which an army surgeon stood ready to receive them. The assassination notably did not occur on the day of their wedding anniversary as is often reported, but rather on the day Franz Ferdinand formally renounced the right of any future children to take the Austro-Hungarian throne.[46]

Some reports, including the court transcripts of the assassins' trial translated into English, state that Princip killed Franz Ferdinand with a revolver. He did not. Rather, he used a Belgian-made semiautomatic Browning FN Model 1910 that fired a .32 caliber round, the same type of gun the others had as well. This weapon eventually fell into the hands of a Jesuit priest named Anton Puntigam, who planned to open a museum using it as a centerpiece but died before ever doing so. It remained at the Jesuit community house in Austria for the next 90 years until interest caused it to resurface once more.[47]

After shooting Franz Ferdinand and his wife, Princip tried to kill himself with his pistol, but the police stopped him. During the struggle he swallowed his cyanide, but it failed to work: he threw it up. With its failure to kill either him or Cabrinovic, one wonders if Ciganovic really gave them poison. He probably had. Although spy novels and movies would have you think that biting on a cyanide pill immediately leads to death, it makes a poor choice for suicide. For it to kill, a person needs to ingest an exceptionally high dose. Though different forms of cyanide exist, Princip and his co-conspirators probably received pills filled with potassium cyanide. At too low a dose, it will do nothing worse than cause a headache, weakness, confusion, and sometimes vomiting and nausea.[48]

Grabez had not received cyanide because Ilic, having extracted a promise from him that he would not attempt to kill the archduke, had not given him any. Upon hearing the bomb set off by Cabrinovic and seeing the archduke still alive, Grabez went to his uncle's house. Here he hid his bomb in the bathroom and his gun under the roof. He returned to Franz Joseph Strauss for a time, then stayed the night in his uncle's house, fleeing the city the next day. He was soon arrested for not carrying a travel permit. Extradited to a Sarajevo jail, he planned to deny everything, but when he and Princip stood before a judge, he confessed all.[49]

Popovic had the chance to shoot the archduke but "didn't have the courage." He had stood at the corner of Appel Quay and Cumurija Strauss. Upon hearing about the duke's death a bit later, he hid his bomb and cyanide "in the basement of the *Prosvjenti Savjet* (Cultural Council)." He departed the city, but authorities caught up with him as he headed for Zemun, a town now part of Belgrade. Later he too expressed regret for the assassination because of the ultimate consequences.[50]

With the exception of Mehmedbasic, who escaped to Montenegro, Austro-Hungarian authorities arrested all the conspirators in their territory plus those suspected of giving them aid, detaining 25 people in total. Of those, the state could not seek the death penalty for Princip, Cabrinovic, Grabez, and Popovic because of their minority status. It could only execute those 21 and older. The trial for all 25 occurred in a military court in a Sarajevo garrison that lasted from October 12 to 23, 1914. All the core conspirators in custody admitted to their role in the assassination, so the court had little trouble finding them guilty. At the trial Princip showed no remorse in killing Franz Ferdinand, but he did express regret at accidentally shooting Sophie. He had hoped the assassination would spark a worldwide anarchist revolution, not the world war that resulted, something he had never imagined. He did not consider himself responsible for the war, a true enough assertion: those who began it had used his action merely as an excuse for what they wanted to do anyway.[51]

Princip, Cabrinovic, and Grabez received sentences of 20 years with a special order that on the day of the assassination's anniversary, they would be placed into solitary confinement in a dark cell with little food. Although Popovic had to suffer solitary confinement once a year as well, he only received a sentence of 13 years. The court condemned Ilic, Cabrinovic, Cubrilovic, Jovanovic, and Nedjo Kerovic to death by hanging, although Cabrinovic had his sentence commuted to 16 years hard labor plus confinement in a dark cell on the assassination's anniversary. The Austro-Hungarian state executed the other three on February 3, 1915.[52]

Princip's jailers chained him to a wall in a dank cell at the Small Fortress in the Bohemian town of Theresientstadt, now modern Terezín in the Czech Republic. Built in the late eighteenth century and named by the Austrian emperor Joseph II in honor of his mother Maria Theresa, it stood on "the confluence of the rivers Eger and Elbe as part of the northern defense perimeter of the Hapsburg empire." Having contracted tuberculosis of the bones, Princip died slowly of this disease. Sores covered his body, and he had to have his left arm amputated. He suffered from terrible loneliness and welcomed conversations with the well-known psychiatrist Dr. Martin Pappenheim, a professor in Vienna. Although Princip considered him a spy, he nonetheless spoke to him at length, giving historians the only real insight as to his motives and beliefs that we have. Princip died in terrible pain on April 28, 1918. He outlasted Cabrinovic, who died in 1916, but not Grabez, who died shortly after Princip but before the war's end. Cubrilovic and Popovic received their liberty after the collapse of the Austro-Hungarian Empire.[53]

Rather than admit to and address what had motivated the assassination of Franz Ferdinand, the Austro-Hungarian government blamed problems of its own making on Serbia. To that end, top Austro-Hungarian government officials, save for Hungary's premier István Tisza, developed a policy of retribution against Serbia approved by Franz Joseph. This despite the fact he and most of those behind the decision despised the man on whose behalf they made these plans. Germany upped the ante by agreeing to support Austria-Hungary's new policy, making a military expedition a certainty.[54]

Because Ciganovic gave the conspirators their bombs, pistols and cyanide, his loose connection with the Black Hand gave the Austrians all the "proof" they needed to link the assassination to the Serbian government. Yet, as David James Smith pointed out in his 2008 book *One Morning in Sarajevo: 29 June 1914*, no evidence exists to support the claim that the Black Hand in general and Apis in particular had anything to do with the plot. None of the conspirators ever admitted to belonging to the group or even receiving direct aid from it. The youngest conspirator, Vaso Cubrilovic, insisted upon this point when asked years later at a time when it no longer mattered to anyone but historians. Apis knew about the conspiracy but did nothing to stop it until the assassins had passed beyond his reach. No one could ask him to clarify his role after the war because he did not live that long. King Petar had him and others in the Black Hand arrested on the charge of plotting a coup. That such a plan did not exist mattered little: a court found nine of the 11 alleged conspirators guilty and sentenced them to death, although two had theirs commuted to 20 years in prison. Apis was killed by a firing squad on June 26, 1916.[55]

On July 23, 1914, Austria-Hungary sent Serbia an ultimatum that contained demands so onerous it was assumed the Serbians could never agree to it. The Serbian government, doubting it could hold out against an Austrian incursion for more than 24 hours, acceded to everything save for allowing Austrian officials to participate in its official inquiry into the matter. And even that it did not outright refuse, but rather asked for more information before proceeding.[56]

Austria-Hungary nonetheless deemed the reply unacceptable. It declared war on July 28, shelling Belgrade that night. When Russia called for full mobilization on July 30, the cascade effect of alliances became unstoppable. Germany declared war on Serbia. Russia mobilized. Germany demanded it demobilize. It refused. Germany mobilized the next day and declared war on Russia on August 1. France, obligated by treaty to fight Germany if it attacked Russia, began mobilizing on August 2, and the Germans declared war on it the next day. Britain had an obligation to defend Belgian neutrality but none to go to war otherwise, so at this point it committed to nothing.[57]

Belgium, only a nation since 1837, had become officially neutral in 1867 when it, France, Austria, Britain, Prussia, Italy, Russia, and the Netherlands signed a treaty declaring none of the signatories would violate the territory of Belgium and neighboring Luxembourg in exchange for a Belgian commitment to never going to war save for in self-defense. The Germans kept to this pledge until it became inconvenient. On August 2, 1914, they demanded the Belgians allow their army to march freely through their territory towards France. The Belgian king, Albert I, refused. The next day the United Kingdom pledged to go to war with Germany if it crossed into Belgium. When the German army did just that on August 4, the British fulfilled their promise. After crossing the border, the Germans posted proclamations falsely claiming the French had invaded, obligating the German army enter Belgian territory to remove them.[58]

Alfred Graf von Schlieffen, who served as Army Chief of the German Great General Staff from 1891 to 1905, had developed this plan as a solution to fighting a possible two front war against France and Russia. He figured the best way to attack France was to go around its border defenses by a flanking movement through Belgium, Luxembourg, and the Netherlands. Caring nothing about the political consequences, he gambled that the German army could reach and conquer Paris before the Russians mobilized, calculating this would take six weeks. Never implemented during his tenure and later modified, it still bore his name when the army used it in 1914.[59]

Although the Belgian government had no knowledge that Germany had plans to invade, it figured it was a possibility and to that end secretly began preparing. The chief of staff of Belgium's army held a secret conference with the British attaché in Brussels to discuss possible measures they could take. In 1906, the Belgian government secured the funding it needed to build a series of forts around Antwerp. In 1911, its premier, Charles de Broqueville, began a program to improve the army in five years that included compulsory military service. Despite all this, when war did come, the Belgian army still lacked all the armaments and training it needed.[60]

As they marched into Belgium, German soldiers faced the danger of coming under fire from the 12 Belgian fortresses that surrounded the industrial city of Liège. Designed by General Henri-Alexis Brialmont, the Belgians built these forts "between 1888 and 1892." Encircling the city, they were made of concrete with earthen reinforcement and could resist shells up to a 210 mm, the most powerful then available. Connected by underground tunnels and armed with cannons and machine guns, the Germans had not anticipated they contained a garrison of 40,000 reinforced by an army field division. Liège itself stood along the rivers Meuse and Ourthe, the former crisscrossed by a multitude of iron bridges. On Liège's left bank rose the main town, and on its right stood factories that manufactured a wide variety of materials and products, including cars, weapons, and zinc foundries. About the city one contemporary travel writer, Douglas Goldring, wrote, "It's a hideous and loathsome place, full of smoke and coal-mines and chimneys, and there's nothing to see there at all."[61]

German war planning had not taken into account the possibility that the minuscule and underprepared Belgian army would pose a serious danger. On the night of August 5 "two regiments of [German] cavalry attempted a night surprise of the Belgian position." In addition to a force of well-entrenched Belgians, the invaders had to contend with mines and barbed wire. The Belgians repelled the assault, then followed it up with a counteroffensive to sweep away those still lingering in the vicinity. According to one newspaper account, around 5,000 German soldiers died in the first three days of fighting. Surprised by the effectiveness of Belgian resistance, the Germans responded with a surprise of their own: they unleashed two newly designed secret weapons, the 420 mm Krupp howitzer and the Austrian-made Skoda 305 mm gun.[62]

Liège. Photographer unknown. Date unknown. Library of Congress Prints and Photographs Division.

"Austrian Skoda 305 mm Model 1911 Howitzer Siege Gun Used in Belgium." Bain News Service. Taken between 1914 and 1915. Library of Congress Prints and Photographs Division.

Both fired shells that first penetrated the bunker walls, *then* exploded. The forts held out for 11 days, the last one surrendering on August 16. The commander of the Liège forts, General Gérard Leman, ordered them to hold off the Germans as long as possible while he evacuated with a mobile defense force on the night of August 6. During the battle, the Germans flew a zeppelin overhead with the intention of bombing those below, but its low altitude allowed Belgian guns to knock it out of the sky. They did the same against German airplanes.[63]

Belgium's king, Albert I, took personal command of his nation's army. Born on April 8, 1875, no one had taught him how to rule the kingdom because too many heirs stood between him and the crown. A series of unexpected deaths plus his father's renunciation of the throne made him the heir apparent, forcing him to learn the art of being a ruling monarch much later in life than normal. Unlike his uncle, King Leopold II, he believed in interacting with the common people. He learned Flemish, "toiled in a coal pit at Seraing, near Liege [*sic*] [and] ... stoked the furnaces of a steel foundry." Wanting his country to have a world class merchant marine, he took on "the guise of a reporter, [and]

King Albert. Photographer unknown. 1918. Library of Congress Prints and Photographs Division.

representing a Belgian newspaper, he made a tour of Europe studying the shipping situation." In America, he traveled incognito, even becoming a reporter for a Brooklyn newspaper for a time.[64]

When he took the throne on December 23, 1909, he began his military training in a Liège regiment as a mere private, working his way up the ranks to commander-in-chief. In this capacity he injected a good dose of common sense when making decisions. He led the troops during the month-long Belgian resistance to the German invasion, refusing a bodyguard because he wanted to expose himself to the same dangers as his men. Though he would survive the war, he nonetheless met an untimely end. On February 17, 1934, at the age of 59, he drove by the Marche les Dames along the Meuse and decided on a whim to climb the roughly 100-foot-tall rocky pinnacle known as the Corneille. A keen rock climber, he left his one and only servant behind and never returned. Searchers found his body about two in the morning. He had fallen to his death.[65]

1

American Refugees

Opening Days

When Louise Townsend Nicholl handed over a traveler's check to pay for her lodgings in the French city of Rouen, it was refused. The banks would not cash it because of "la guerra" (the war). Nicholl, a "plucky" young American woman who would later become a poet and editor, had just come from Britain with a friend after a whirlwind tour of Scotland and England. During this sojourn she had lacked time and interest to read newspapers, leaving her ignorant about the war mobilization going on around her. Other Americans in Rouen told Nicholl she and her traveling companion would find it safer in Paris, where they could also cash their checks. Getting there was not easy: soldiers filled the trains because they had received boarding preference. Soldiers guarded all bridges and crossings.[1]

They arrived in Paris on August 1, 1914, four days after Austria declared war on Serbia and two days before Germany would declare war on France. They found Paris "hot, crowded, hectic, hurried, confused," and difficult to navigate because Nicholl spoke French poorly and her friend knew it not at all. When they checked into a hotel, its Russian proprietor asked, "How comes it that Americans still enter this city? It would be better not to come." They dropped off their bags and went to cash some checks at rue Scribe where, it turned out, hundreds of Americans had already gathered in anticipation of visiting various offices here including American Express and those of several steamship companies. At this point Nicholl and her friend had between them about 15 centimes, 100 of these equaling 1 franc with 5 francs equaling $1. A frugal traveler in France at this time would spend between 15 and 20 francs a day, and a better-off person such as Nicholl between 30 and 40.[2]

Nicholl had some checks from the Mercantile Marine and went to the American Line's office to cash them with plans to book passage on one of its ships home. Though its offices were closed, an English clerk speaking to her through a grate said she could not cash her checks for lack of funds. The *Philadelphia* would likely be the last ship to sail for home. He advised her to head to Southampton immediately to catch this vessel. Her friend found she could not cash her checks at the American Express office, either, although she might be able to on Monday.[3]

Money had become tight in France the moment Austria declared war on Serbia. One American woman in Paris, upon trying to make a purchase in the upscale department store Bon Marché, found her 100 franc bill refused because the philosophy now prevailed that "giving too much change ... in silver ... would be a greater evil than losing the entire sale." So she settled on buying 84.95 francs' worth of merchandise. At a candy store next door, she had to pay exactly 2 francs because the store had no change to offer. The next day she

Europe. Map by the author based on one in *The Rand-McNally New Library Atlas Map of Europe*. Chicago: Rand McNally, 1912. LOC Map Collections.

"Reservists Going to Gare de l'Est, Paris." Bain News Service. Taken between 1914 and 1915. Library of Congress Prints and Photographs Division.

and her companions attempted to cash checks at the American Express office, only to receive an insufficient amount of bills and silver pieces.[4]

American Express gave out a maximum of $10 worth of gold and silver coins to each person, which had become so scarce, Paris' cafes and restaurants posted signs declaring they would give no change. Although the French government tried to alleviate the situation by issuing bills with smaller denominations, these quickly became sparse as well. With no one taking them, larger bills did no good, either.[5]

The threat of a general war had periodically plagued Europe for years now, and every time it came, the French began hoarding gold and silver, stocking it away in their "old stockings" and "chimney-pieces," which inevitably caused its supply to dwindle for visiting tourists. At the time World War I broke out, "European statisticians estimated that [the] people of Germany, France, and Austria" had stashed away $350 million in gold. Americans without coins in the local currency were destitute because no one would honor their letters of credit or traveler's checks. Indeed, the entire European credit system effectively collapsed. For a week after the war broke out, almost everyone accepted nothing but gold.[6]

The monetary policies of the belligerents did not help, either. The day after the war's outbreak, the United Kingdom closed down its stock exchange, in part to keep hostile governments who owned British bonds from selling them. It took about £2 million of bank notes out of circulation, and had its central bank stop loaning to other ones. A fear that the Bank of England would not redeem gold for notes caused the British to hoard gold.

Germany faced this problem as well, so its government suspended payment of gold for its notes to avoid a bank run.[7]

Beyond the money situation, Americans in Europe in general and France in particular also found it difficult to get around. Raymond Weeks, a foreign correspondent for the *Nation*, watched in wonder at this fretful situation. Having arrived in Paris on August 1, he quipped, "Ten days ago, circumstances seeming to warrant, I bought a map of central Europe. To-day I need an atlas." On August 1, he saw "thousands of vehicles of all sorts ... transporting merchandise, and especially family furniture and heirlooms, to places of safety. Cabs were not to be found in sufficient numbers. Hundreds of people had to carry their own bundles, and one saw frequently a young wife and husband of the bourgeoisie carrying a trunk between them." By the afternoon all the buses had disappeared, the army having converting them into wagons. The next day France's armed forces mobilized, causing "thousands of men, especially officers ... [to leave] Paris before morning."[8]

In those first few days, French chauffeurs charged between 500 to 1,000 francs—about $96 to $196—for a one-way trip to a coastal city or town. This bit of price gouging ended when the French government seized nearly all the nation's gasoline and commandeered taxicabs as well as many autos for the general mobilization. Those Americans who brought over their own cars or hired ones found them confiscated along with everyone else's.[9]

A group of six Americans staying in the resort city of Vichy in southwestern France nonetheless managed to acquire one despite not having passports. To ease the difficulties created by this, they had their photos taken so Vichy's mayor could write "their names, descriptions, and a guarantee across the face of each photograph." They paid a staggering $1,000 for their hired car, which they drove nonstop for 60 hours to reach Dieppe. France's excellent roads made travel by auto easy, though they did have to stop for numerous checkpoints through which authorities let them pass upon seeing their autographed photos. They detoured around Paris for fear of getting caught in the mobilization efforts. In Dieppe, they took a boat for England and from there made their way home.[10]

The military confiscated most of Paris' horses as well. Only soldiers could use mechanized vehicles in the city, leaving everyone else to travel on foot. Tourists like Nicholl and her friend could only bring baggage they could carry. This was probably just as well because when they reached their hotel, they found most of its porters had left to fight in the war. With all hell seeming to break out around them, the two Americans felt very alone and quite afraid.[11]

On Saturday night at dinner, the Russian proprietor running their hotel said he would shut down at noon the next day so he could go home. Nicholl slept poorly because of her worry over how she would manage without any money and, it would seem, a roof over her head. When morning came, things did not turn out quite as badly as she had feared. The proprietor took the Americans' checks for food without bothering to look too closely at them, although his French wife had noticed they had been issued in the United States. After his departure, the propriety left an East Indian porter in charge of closing down. This man agreed to collect payment for the Americans' stay the next morning at which time Nicholl's friend hoped to get some money from American Express. The porter even offered to take them to another hotel on the Avenue des Champs Elysées from which one could see the Arc de Triomphe where even then a mad race of automobiles zipped dangerously about. The two women who ran this hotel spoke nothing but French, which helped Nicholl dramatically improve her command of the language in just a few days.[12]

She and her friend stayed on credit, charging as much as they dared, including meals when they could, although the stress of the situation caused Nicholl to have trouble eating. Monday morning they headed to the steamship office only to find it closed indefinitely. Nicholl's friend did get a bit of money from American Express, which she shared, and Nicholl cashed two of her Mercantile Marine checks. But even with badly needed money, they still had to find a way to get home. Because of the war, the French government now required all Americans to acquire a passport at their embassy, then get it signed at a police station.[13]

At this time U.S. citizens did not need a passport unless entering Turkey or Russia. Those who carried them to other destinations often used them as letters of introduction rather than a form of international identification. This changed in November 1914 when both the State Department and President Woodrow Wilson recommended but did not require Americans to carry passports to Europe. Nor did U.S. law require Americans to carry an exit document when leaving the States, although steamship companies demanded they do so when going abroad on their vessels.[14]

For an American to acquire a passport in France, the State Department required that he or she swear an oath to the United States in front of a consul, who would write "Good" on it, then sign and stamp it. After acquiring theirs, Nicholl and her friend went on a long and weary search for Paris' main police headquarters only to learn they had to go to the chief of the district in which their hotel resided so he could sign them. Deeming it too late to continue, they gave up and returned to their hotel.[15]

Nicholl's fears increased exponentially when she saw airplanes flying overhead that turned out to be German. She suddenly realized she could die in France, not an unreasonable fear. Although the first successful powered flight had occurred about 11 years earlier, the technology had already evolved enough for the Germans to send four planes to attack Paris on August 6, which a French air squadron headed off. Had the German planes gotten over the city, they would have faced anti-aircraft guns and powerful searchlights put in place by the French military in case of a night attack by zeppelins.[16]

During a speech to the Aero Club of America, aviation pioneer and inventor of the seaplane, Glenn H. Curtiss, predicted that people would soon see planes dotting the European sky doing reconnaissance work and dropping bombs. He believed the nations of Europe had foreseen this as well and had thousands of planes at their disposal. He doubted firing at one another in the air would bring any advantage because they would just shoot one another down.[17]

He went on to reveal what some might consider a military secret: the Russian Army Air Service had 360 planes, more than any one of its enemies or allies possessed. True enough, but those planes were obsolete and lacked standardized parts, making them pretty useless for military purposes. The Germans, in contrast, began the war with 246 aircraft and 254 pilots trained to fly them, and the British had 113 working aircraft with 197 pilots. The Austrians possessed 48 planes and the Belgians 12.[18]

One American, Gelett Burgess, who had come to Paris for a honeymoon with his new bride, Estelle Loomis, watched German planes drop their bombs. Rather than tremble in fear, he made light of it, not a surprising reaction from a professional humorist. A graduate of the Massachusetts Institute of Technology, he began working as a draftsman the Southern Pacific Railroad in 1891, and in that same year taught topographical drawing at the University of California Berkley. Offended by the campus' unattractive statue of Henry Cogswell, a local dentist known as a crusader for temperance, he smashed it. For this the university fired him. He went to San Francisco where he took up designing furniture. He moved to Russian Hill, one of the highest points in the city named as such because on it once stood a cemetery filled with Russians who had died while working for the Hudson Bay Company. According to *American National Biography*, it was from this residence that Gelett "puzzled his neighbors by appearing at odd hours with his 5'4" frame draped in vivid capes."[19]

As an outlet for his peculiar personality he started the *Lark*, a humorist magazine printed on bamboo paper purchased from Chinatown that has become a problem for collectors and preservationists because this material has a habit of disintegrating. Burgess and muralist Bruce Porter produced the first issue for $100 and doubted a second would appear. It did well enough to continue, eventually amassing a circulation of 5,000. Its success launched Burgess' writing career. After 25 issues he decided to end the magazine before it became stale, calling the finale issue *Epilark*. He moved to London for a year and while there borrowed "money for a lavish wardrobe, and pretended he was not seeking work" with the intended effect of causing editors to beg him to come write for them. This landed him a job as a staff member of the *Sketch*.[20]

On the night he came out to watch German planes flying overhead along with a crowd of Parisians, some of whom had opera glasses, the first bombs fell around the railroad station of Gare de l'Est but did little damage. A policeman wrote a ticket for littering to the pilot who dropped a bomb that had hit the rue de Vinaigriers. The threat of bombing from the air had caused the Parisian museums such as the Louvre to move their treasures to safer places belowground, placing, for example, the Venus de Milo in a fireproof vault.[21]

A single German Taube, a monoplane "designed by Igo Etrich" and built by the Austro-Hungarian Empire, flew around the Eiffel Tower and dropped a bomb on it, then casually dove towards the onlookers, scattering them. Burgess stayed put. From several places the French opened fire upon the plane. That prompted him to start running because, he wrote, "I would take my chance with a Prussian bomb, but when a thousand excitable Frenchmen began to pepper the sky, me for the tall timber!"[22]

Mobilizing for War

On Tuesday morning, Nicholl and her friend went to the local police station to get their passports signed only to learn they needed their identification cards, still back at the hotel. Later in the day an American woman Nicholl knew informed her that boats had started to cross the Channel to England once more, so she and her friend needed to pack their bags and catch a train for one of the ferry ports. They planned to leave the next morning.[23]

With no automobiles available, they had to rely on trains to get to the English Channel. Finding no porters, Nicholl moved the contents of one piece of baggage into the remaining ones and abandoned it. At the Saint-Lazare train station, she and her friend faced a long line. A family with an extra ticket for Dieppe offered to sell it to Nicholl if she wanted to go with them. This she snapped up. As she watched the family's luggage for a few minutes, a woman approached Nicholl's friend and offered to sell her two tickets for Le Havre. She considered buying one but hesitated because she had heard a rumor that ferries for England were not leaving from there. Nicholl did not mind chancing it, so she took a ticket for Le Havre and let her friend have the one for Dieppe.[24]

Arriving at the Parisian train station two hours before her 3:30 afternoon departure, Nicholl dedicated her time trying to exchange her *Philadelphia* ticket with one for the French steamer *La France*, which would sail out of Le Havre. On the latter she could get no berth, but if she waited for Saturday, she might book one on the American Line's vessel *Chicago*. A clerk for that company suggested she keep her ticket for the *Philadelphia* because she might still reach this vessel in time by taking one of two ferries leaving from Le Havre that night bound for Southampton, a city standing between the rivers Test and Itchen that served as a major port for steamship lines sailing to many points in the world. She decided upon the latter course. Her train took a grueling ten hours to reach its destination. Only about ten people boarded.[25]

As her ferry sailed into Southampton Harbor, torpedo boats surrounded and fired a shot over the boat's bow. Men boarded to look for Germans. Nicholl noted that as the ferry navigated through a maze of mines to reach the dock, the *Philadelphia* passed by "so near that we could almost have thrown our luggage to her decks." She implored the ferry's captain to stop, but because Southampton had come under martial law, vessels in its harbor could not signal one another.[26]

Nicholl and the thousands of other Americans arriving in the UK had to contend with its massive war mobilization effort starting with the hassle of obtaining British currency. On August 3, the UK had instituted a four day bank holiday that included American Express offices. One American who barely had a penny to his name had to pay for a cable home "partly with postage stamps." A policeman suggested this impoverished fellow join the British army because it, at least, would ensure he ate.[27]

Britain's trains ran 24 hours a day transporting troops to the coast. The civilian population remained calm and went about its business as best it could, not always an easy thing to do. The call up for military service caused businesses throughout the UK to lose both clerks and customers virtually overnight, a problem exasperated by the fact that trains and buses lost half their drivers. Many postal workers, telegraph operators, and police disappeared as well.[28]

The nation's horse power had also dwindled considerably. Certified government veterinarians began impounding horses with the exception of white and gray ones, those being exempted because of their cost (usually only high ranking officers could afford them), and the fact that they were easy to see at night. The British government, which seized about 165,000 horses in the first 12 days of the war, paid fair compensation for them. The Germans, also needing horses, seized 615,000. It was not enough. By war's end, all the belligerents had collectively used nearly two million horses for the cavalry alone.[29]

By October 1914, the stalemate on the Western Front had rendered cavalry obsolete, so the Germans transferred most of their units to the Eastern Front where they still could do some good. The French dismounted some cavaliers for use in their infantry, and both they and the British used those who remained as reserves to rush to trouble spots on the front. The British sent other units to fight in Palestine, where, in 1918, the last major horse cavalry action in modern war occurred.[30]

The Royal Army Veterinary Corps took care of sick or wounded animals for the British army, often up to 90,000 at a time, destroying those they deemed beyond help. Horses had more to fear from respiratory diseases and exhaustion than battlefield dangers. During the East Africa campaign, for example, the tsetse fly and other tropical pests caused in a staggering 290 percent equine mortality rate in 1916 alone. While Australia and South America provided some of the needed replacements, most came from the United States, which had such a surplus it did not even affect their prices.[31]

Historians often consider World War I the first industrialized war, but in reality the battlefield had changed little since the U.S. Civil War. A soldier from that conflict would see little he did not recognize on this new one: movement by rail or marching, trenches for protection from withering fire, and artillery pulled by horses set upon carriages with wooden spoke wheels. Although motorized vehicles appeared in combat zones, the closer they got to the battlefield, the less effective they became. Unable to negotiate the craters, mud, and other awful conditions caused by the fighting, horses and mules had to pull the supply wagons, move the artillery, bring in the ammunition, evacuate the wounded, and even deliver the mail.[32]

Just because British civilians went about their business calmly did not mean they endorsed the war. A reporter from the *Times* of London asked people in the Lancaster region what they thought. This area had suffered greatly during the Napoleonic and U.S. Civil Wars when the supply of cotton for its textile mills was severely reduced, so it came as no surprise that its people had little enthusiasm for the war here. It had already slowed down commerce in Manchester where all the vessels normally seen in the ship canal had disappeared. While much tension would exist between mill owners and weavers for the war's duration, they both agreed to work together for the greater good.[33]

That a British newspaper could print even a hint of dissent at all during a time of war in a nation that did not guarantee absolute freedom of speech might seem surprising, but this was in the war's opening days before the British government had a chance to get the censorship agency it created, the Press Bureau, ready. Established on August 7, it was headed by a civilian but run mainly by naval and army officers. It was tasked to ensure newspapers did not publish reports harmful to the war and to keep them from exaggerating successes. In time it became the sole source for information from the War Office and Admiralty. Those papers that defied the Press Bureau lost access to this. The government also suppressed newspapers whose opinions it did not like using Regulation 27.[34]

American journalist Richard Harding Davis, who will we meet in more detail later in this narrative, rushed to Europe when war broke out. There he discovered just how harsh British censorship could be. "Officers of the same regiment even with each other would not discuss the orders they had received. In no single newspaper, with no matter how lurid a past record for sensationalism, was there a line to suggest that a British army had landed in France and that Great Britain was at war." While a bit exaggerated, it nonetheless captured the atmosphere of the time.[35]

The Home Office, in charge of passports and immigration among other duties, threw up a mass of thick bureaucracy to deter British journalists from leaving the country to cover the war. When Robert Crozier Long, for example, tried to plan a trip to Russia, red tape made it almost impossible. He opined, "In the old days no freeborn Briton knew what the Home Office was. He thought it a sort of domestic-economy college. Now you find the

Home Office in full autocracy. In peaceful Roehampton, London ... the Home Office spies on my wife's foolish German maid: sends a constable to question her twice every day: and so worries her for her certified photograph that I have to cure her hysteria by vowing the constable has asked for her hand [in marriage]."[36]

Louise Townsend Nicholl's Journey Home

Nicholl's ferry, which had arrived in the morning, did not allow passengers to disembark until two in the afternoon. At the steamship office she learned there were no more ships bound for America leaving from this port. A clerk suggested she might be able to exchange her *Philadelphia* ticket for one for the White Star liner *Celtic,* departing from Liverpool at five the next afternoon. Going by train, she did not arrive until two in the morning. With the station hotel full, she went into Liverpool proper to find somewhere to stay. The city "was practically ... [an] armed camp. The harbor was full of transports, and between Liverpool and Seaforth were parked 1,200 motor trucks and automobiles, which were to be taken across to France to Belgium."[37]

She stayed at "a shambling old, black house" in which she and an American companion who had come with her from Southampton climbed up the stairs to reach their room. The drunken old man who took them to it advised them to lock their door. Nicholl got about three hours of sleep, her roommate none. Bags in hand, they made their way to the White Star Line's office at seven in the morning and waited for an hour until it opened. Both had tickets for the *Philadelphia*, which they exchanged for transport on the *Celtic*. They could only get berths in steerage (third class), the only thing left.[38]

Their small cabin contained six berths and one porthole, which shocked Nicholl. "I had never known anything about steerage conditions before. The word steerage, like the words emigrants and immigrants, had meant just the foreign peoples themselves, the colors of their strange customs [sic], the bewilderment of their faces when they reached Ellis Island, the odd, silent stories which they carried with them to the innermost parts of America." When she mentioned her dislike of steerage to the purser, he sneered, "Well, it wasn't intended for decent people. Those people don't want or expect any more. They are used to barns, most of them." A sentiment to which Nicholl agreed and an attitude that steamer lines of the day reinforced.[39]

The thinking went something like this: those who could pay for first class came from the elite and therefore expected exceptional food and service. When the American-Hamburg liner *Vaterland* sailed on her maiden voyage at two in the afternoon on May 14, 1914, for example, the first-class passengers enjoyed "a late luncheon in the dining saloon," and did not notice the ship departing. First class included heated cabins, a smoking room refreshed every morning with oxygen pumped into it, live palm trees in the aptly named Palm Court, a swimming pool in which passengers could play water polo, an orchestra on the upper deck, a barbershop, and a social hall filled with seventeenth century Flemish paintings from the Kaiser's own collection. One of its restaurants copied the New York Ritz and served gourmet fare including pork chops in jelly, smoked ox tongue, and roast beef or veal. First class encompassed three-quarters of the ship's space, this to accommodate 700 passengers. The other 3,350 souls had to share the remaining area.[40]

After two days, Nicholl and her companion upgraded to second class. Having only ever travelled first class, she did not much like this, either. "The beds were as hard as the boards on which they were made. The mattresses, if that was their name, were filled, or partially filled, with straw or cornhusks, and covered with some course material. There were no sheets, and the covering consisted of a black blanket," this one the same kind the immigrants used. She deemed seven in the morning too early for breakfast, and grumbled about a lack of butter and the stale bread, wondering that no one complained. Inconvenienced or not, she made it home.[41]

Fleeing to the Netherlands

Two American college students, Ernest Hamlin Abbott and a classmate, headed to Constance, Germany, for an ironically themed conference to discuss the peace plan proposed by American industrialist Andrew Carnegie as well as how to better improve relations between Germany and Britain. Carnegie's proposal hinged on the idea of convincing the United States, Germany, Britain, France, and Russia to agree to never again go to war. They would then create a league of nations designed to impose economic sanctions and create an international police force to keep other nations of the world from fighting one another. The Hague would host a powerful world court designed to arbitrate disputes between hostile parties.[42]

The seed money for the conference in Constance, scheduled to go from August 2 to 5, 1914, came from a $2 million endowment paid for with 5 percent bonds, this put into the hands of the Church Peace Union. An executive committee headed by the pastor of the Broadway Tabernacle, Dr. Charles E. Jefferson, would decide how to best use these funds to promote peace. Once the Church Peace Union, made up of representatives from 25 different denominations, achieved its goal, it would turn its attention to the "deserving poor," meaning those it deemed lazy would be excluded.[43]

Abbott and his classmate arrived at their Paris hotel late on Tuesday, July 28, and there heard of increasing tensions between Serbia and the Austro-Hungarian Empire. Although the next day such stories persisted, they considered "the chance of war ... remote" despite rumors to the contrary getting stronger by the day. As late as Friday they still planned on going anyway, possibly by taking a different route. Before committing to this course, Abbott called a prominent journalist as well as the American embassy for advice. Both convinced him to abandon the trip. Knowing if France mobilized for war it would tie up the trains, he and his classmate thought it best to immediately head to London, but their decision had come too late. Although France had yet to get into the war formally, civilians could no longer use the trains or send telegraphs. Despite this, they made their way to England without incident.[44]

Other Americans in France did not fare so well, such as Ona Brown of Dallas, Texas, and the "six young girls, five married women, and one small boy" she was chaperoning. Upon arriving in Paris on Sunday, July 19, her party checked into Hotel Regina by the Louvre overlooking Tuileries Garden. While out on a Wednesday night with some friends, Brown noticed that streets had become unusually congested. The next day she learned Austria had declared war on Serbia, though at the time she did not connect the two.[45]

While out shopping on Friday, she ran out of gold coins, leaving her with just paper money. A dressmaker told her rumors about the war had caused all the change to disappear, making the life of shopkeepers difficult. This prompted Brown to cash $300 worth of checks at American Express. Here she learned the extent of the crisis and decided it best to take her charges to The Hague in the Netherlands. When she arrived at the train station to purchase tickets, she found a long line full of others who had had the same thought. Fortunately she knew the head of the ticket department and acquired seats for her party on an express train leaving at noon the next day. She also called a hotel to ensure it had rooms when they arrived.[46]

Upon informing those in her care she had done this, some grumbled that they wanted to go to Switzerland instead, but Brown did not like that idea. They could get trapped there, and would be "at the mercy of Swiss hotel keepers." With doubt in her mind and not wanting to take entire responsibility for the decision, she went to the American consul for advice and news. The consul endorsed her idea of heading to The Hague, so when morning came, she went to the American Express office to get Belgian and Dutch currency. Her attempt to send a cable home to inform loved ones of her party's destination failed: the office had about 2,500 already, none of which would go that day. Once at The Hague, they stayed in a hotel "just across the way from the American Embassy and only a few blocks from the Peace Palace."[47]

Peace Palace (The Hague). Bain News Service. Taken between 1910 and 1915. Library of Congress Prints and Photographs Division.

The Hague began not as a city but as the hunting lodge of Count William II of Holland. Built in 1250, it did not become associated with peace until 1898 when young Queen Wilhelmina of the Netherlands dedicated it to that cause. A year later she hosted the First Hague Peace Conference at Noordeinde Palace, the royal residence in the city. The conference, organized by Tsar Nicholas II of Russia, sought to find a way to avert war, and out of this came the idea of establishing a permanent court designed to peacefully settle international disputes. Andrew Carnegie financed the construction of a new building to house it. On July 31, 1907, the Russian delegation at the Second Peace Conference laid down the new building's cornerstone. Completed on August 2, 1913, it became known as the Vredespaleis, or Peace Palace.[48]

Though the Netherlands had no intention of going to war, it mobilized its army just in case the Germans crossed the southernmost part of Limburg, a narrow strip of territory jutting between Germany and Belgium with just about three miles separating these borders. If the Germans went this way, they "would save some thirty or forty miles of weary marching" on the way to Belgium. The Dutch army did not occupy the part of Limburg the Germans might cross for fear of being bottled up there, but instead amassed a force to the north that would hit the Germans in the flank if necessary. The Dutch government deployed nearly the entirety of its army here. At the fortified city of Velno, which stood on the Meuse's right bank and had at this time about 17,400 inhabitants plus a garrison for two battalions, the army tore paving stones from its streets to make barricades that were reinforced with sandbags. It laid down "miles of barbed wire" and placed cannons in strategic locations.[49]

In 1907, the Dutch created a peacetime field army headquarters—the first European nation to do so—improved its reserves, and expanded the draft. In 1908, they started formulating a strategy to defend Limburg against a possible German intrusion, a plan that included destroying a bridge in Roermond. When the threat finally materialized in August 1914, the Dutch mobilized a force of 200,000 in three days. While impressive on paper, only 11,000 were career soldiers and 4,500 reservists. The other 180,000 had about four months' training. Even if all 200,000 were professionals it would not have remedied another problem: the Dutch army lacked sufficient armaments to stop the Germans.[50]

When American journalist Albert R. Williams arrived in the Netherlands, he set out to get a pass and hired a driver so he could examine this region. From a hill he could see the Belgian towns of Visé and Mouland that the Germans had set ablaze to warn others not to defy them. German soldiers marched across the plain below, their gray-green coats making them difficult to see. Behind them came their artillery, and in front the dreaded Ulhans, mounted lancers traditionally used as scouts and recognizable "by their square-topped hats." Consisting of 24 regiments at this time, in the war's opening days they served a useful purpose. Once trench warfare set in, most dismounted and became part of the cavalry rifle regiments.[51]

German planners knew the Dutch could not stop them but decided pushing through might delay their critical timeline. That and the Netherlands would serve Germany better as a neutral power rather than an occupied nation by giving it access to vital materials such as "cotton and grain from the United States, iron ore from Spain and Sweden, and copper from Norway, while manufactured goods from the east were shipped out to other continents." When the British began stopping ships heading into Dutch ports and confiscating any food they found in order to keep it out of the hands of the Germans, the Netherlands expanded its land into the Zuider Zee, an inlet of the North Sea, so it could increase its agricultural output and sell the surplus to Germany.[52]

All this made the climate in the Netherlands as fraught as elsewhere, and soon enough all the coins in the country disappeared. To counter this panic, the Dutch government made it against the law to refuse paper money. Here, like elsewhere, no one would take letters of credit, leaving wealthy Americans cash poor. Brown, who had wisely brought with her small denomination traveler's checks, had cash on hand because she always cashed them when she could.[53]

She had hoped to continue her group's tour of Europe into Switzerland and Italy, but England's entry into the conflict changed her mind. She tried to book berths on the Holland-American Line but obtained nothing more than a promise she might have anything that opened due to last-minute cancellations. In a Dutch newspaper, Brown saw an advertisement in English claiming that American Line ships would soon depart for New York. Cautious, she brought it to the American minister, Dr. Henry van Dyke, to get his opinion. He told her it was a fraud.[54] Van Dyke, a poet and essayist as well as a liberal Presbyterian minister, publicly supported President Wilson when he declared America's strict neutrality in this war, but privately urged him to side with the Allies. Born in Germantown, Pennsylvania, on November 10, 1852, he graduated from Princeton at the top of his class and served as a pastor for several years before moving to Princeton to teach literature. There he became friends with Wilson, who named him as minister to the Netherlands and Luxembourg primarily to help promote peace. Although van Dyke's open-mindedness led him to fight religious intolerance and for the conservation of birds, "he regarded jazz as 'invented by demons for the torture of imbeciles,' opposed 'immoral' art and stage production and was against writing that disparaged the United States." He would do much to aid American refugees in escaping and, later, with Belgian food relief efforts.[55]

Brown and five others in her party headed to Rotterdam, the largest city in the Netherlands at this time, with the hope of finding berths on a Holland-American liner there. At the shipping office they learned the Germans would allow the Dutch steamer *New Amsterdam* to sail unmolested providing the vessel took on no German subjects. Brown initially secured enough berths for eight people, reserved another two, and, before departing, learned she could purchase another three if she returned the next day, which she did. The whole party made it safety home.[56]

Escaping Germany

Americans trapped in Germany had far more trouble getting out of that nation than they did from France. To ensure its subjects did not escape the conscription, Germany made proving one's U.S. citizenship quite difficult, shutting down all its ports for good measure. Wellesley Harrington of Albany, New York, watched soldiers drag a man off a railroad car because he had supposedly tried escaping military conscription. During his trip, Harrington was trapped on a train for 30 hours without any food. Officials scrutinized his letters and cards. He watched the Germans detain another American with a Kodak camera because they suspected he was a spy, but after developing and viewing his film, they let him go. In Berlin, Americans learned not to speak English in public, and many

Henry Van Dyke. Photographer unknown. Taken between 1920 and 1921. Library of Congress Prints and Photographs Division.

took to putting small U.S. flags in their buttonholes so no one would mistake them for the British.[57]

When word of such troubles reached Secretary of State Williams Jennings Bryan, he went to Germany's Washington embassy to discuss it with the chargé de affaires, Edgar Haniel von Haimhausen, who insisted Germany had not purposely kept Americans within its borders, but rather had dedicated all its transportation to moving troops. Haimhausen had told the truth. On the first day of mobilization, August 2, the German military took control of all railroads. Passenger trains ceased to run, and, while some German civilians could ride if they had a military purpose, no foreigners could.[58]

Mobilization resulted in the shutting down of most factories save for those making war materials, and the shuttering of a number of shops. In Aachen, only a couple hotels remained open, and those were half-staffed with mostly old men serving as waiters and cooks. Few cabs operated, and those driving them had gray hair. Women carried their bundles from those markets and shops still open because delivery services no longer existed.[59]

Americans George von Lengerke Meyer and his wife Marion Alice Appleton began their odyssey out of Germany in Bad Kissingen, Bavaria, a town known for its medicinal waters. George came from a blueblood family in Massachusetts and had served in many government posts, including ambassador to Italy under President William McKinley. His inherent sense of superiority over the common person endeared him to European aristocrats, including Germany's Kaiser Wilhelm II. Meyer served as the ambassador to Russia in 1905, became U.S. postmaster general in 1909, and later in that year became the secretary of the navy, this post lasting until 1913 when Wilson took office.[60]

The Meyers had begun their trip to Europe on June 27 on the German liner *Imperator* along with their daughter Julia, a maid named Marie, and their valet Andrew. Although they learned about the assassination of Franz Ferdinand from a message received on the radio during the Atlantic crossing, they proceeded with their plans anyway. Julie headed off to Italy while her parents went to the aforementioned resort in Bavaria. War rumors drove many of those here to depart prematurely. The sight of troops marching and singing patriotic songs frightened Marion so much, she and her husband departed on June 30.[61]

Meyer had enough ready cash to pay for travelling expenses. The Meyers took a train to Stuttgart, the home of the Thirteenth German Army Corps and the state of Würtemberg's capital. This city of more than a quarter of million people stood in a valley close to the Neckar, a tributary of the Rhine. From here the Meyers planned to go on to Paris, but no train ran to that destination. The next morning they boarded one bound for Switzerland, then Paris.[62]

It was sidelined at Karlsruhe, an industrial city with a radial street layout from which the modern German style originated. When the train failed to start back up, George investigated,

George von Lengerke Meyer. Bain News Service. June 8, 1916. Library of Congress Prints and Photographs Division.

learning it would not take its passengers to Switzerland. His party switched to a train bound for the heavily fortified Prussian city of Cologne from which they planned to go to the Netherlands. Once there they would cross the Channel to England and meet Julia, who was already there.[63]

At the next station "a man dressed as a woman [was] ... shot nearby" as an alleged Russian spy. The Meyers boarded the last passenger train heading for the Hook of Holland, a small village that served as the ocean terminus for Rotterdam to which it was connected by a canal. As the train moved north, a couple got off at one of the stops, "and no sooner were they out of sight than" the Meyers saw police running after them. The chase ended with "a pistol shot,—another 'spy' gone."[64]

At 11 P.M. they arrived at Kleve, where they had to detrain and stay for the night. The Meyers hired a taxi to take them to a hotel in town, but it did not have enough room to carry both them and their remaining luggage—this *after* their trunks disappeared—they sent it to the hotel and awaited the taxi's return. Marion sat on a remaining piece of luggage and began whistling. A passing policeman took issue with this. When their taxi arrived, he told her and Mr. Meyer to get in, then had it take them to the police station. Officers put them into a small room and ordered them to empty their bags. Thinking they would find compromising documents in George's pouch, they instead discovered a card from Gottlieb von Jagow, Germany's foreign minister, who the Meyers had recently visited in Berlin. Now the police could not get these Americans back to their hotel fast enough, and one of them even offered a farewell salute. The next morning they took a trolley to the Netherlands, and from there to England, then home.[65]

Mrs. G.P. Waizfelder also experienced police detention. Upon seeing the German army mobilizing in Frankfurt, she and her husband decided to leave and to that end headed to the train ticket office. There the police detained her as a spy, taking her to the station where they had a female officer search her person in a detention room. Finding nothing of an incriminating nature, they released her.[66]

Reunited with her husband, the two boarded a train that stopped abruptly and ejected its civilian passengers shortly past Cologne. They walked to Belgium and stayed the night with two American physicians in a hotel in Welkenraedt, then hired a car to take them into Belgium, but their chauffeur refused to go any farther than the important textile city of Verviers along the river Vesdre. Another driver agreed to bring them to Liège, but the Belgian army forced them to detour about 12 miles out of the way, a good thing considering it then proceeded to blow the road up.[67]

The Waizfelders happened to enter the city just as the Germans began their march past. They escaped "on the last through train" heading to Brussels. Here Mr. Waizfelder got in serious trouble when a crowd, mistaking him for a German, surrounded, shouted, and even struck him. He spoke no French, making it impossible to communicate with his tormenters to correct their misperception. Fortunately, a woman who spoke English ascertained that he was an American and summoned a police officer for aid. When this official told the crowd that Waizfelder had come from the United States and pointed out its friendship with Belgium, the crowd began enthusiastically chanting, "Vive l'Amérique!" Waizfelder, when interviewed by a *New York Times* reporter, complained bitterly that the U.S. consuls in Germany had done nothing to aid American citizens.[68]

In another *New York Times* article that appeared the day after it quoted Waizfelder's grievance, S.W. Strauss of Chicago praised the help given by American consuls, who in any case were posted to give business advice to U.S. citizens in foreign countries, not help them get out of war zones. It is true that Wilson had appointed people who had no business working in the diplomatic service, such as a former brewer from Bohemia he made the minister to Lisbon who could not tell the difference between a legation and an embassy.[69]

Still, Wilson also named some very capable diplomats, none more so than James W. Gerard as ambassador to Germany. Born in Geneseo, New York, Gerard had no diplomatic experience, having spent most of his life as a lawyer, politician, sheriff of a New York county, and a judge on the State Supreme Court. In 1914, he defeated Franklin D. Roosevelt in the Democratic primary for U.S. senator in New York State but lost the general election. He fought in the Spanish-American War, serving first as a captain, then a major. Wilson picked him as an ambassador because he had raised vast sums of money for the Democratic Party in 1912. Gerard happily accepted because he had always wanted to be an ambassador.[70]

He had a blunt way of dealing with the Germans. When they resumed unrestricted submarine warfare in 1916, he went to the German foreign minister, Arthur Zimmerman, to protest. Zimmerman warned that the United States dared not go to war with Germany because it had at its call 500,000 German reservists in America ready to revolt. To this Gerard responded, "I told him that we had five hundred and one thousand lamp posts in America, and that was where the German reservists would find themselves if they tried any uprising."[71]

In early 1917, after America severed diplomatic ties with Germany, Gerard applied for his passports but did not receive them as requested. Returning to the U.S. embassy after taking a walk, he found Count Max von Montgelas waiting for him. Born in Petrograd in 1860 where his father served as the minister from Bavaria, this career army officer at this time headed the Foreign Office. Gerard asked him why he had not received his passports. Well, the count informed him, the German government did not know what had happened to Johann Heinrich von Bernstorff, the ambassador to America who had kept the United States from going to war over the sinking of the *Lusitania* in 1915. Monteglas had also heard rumors that the U.S. had confiscated German ships in its ports. Gerard assured him nothing had happened to Bernstorff and American had not taken any of Germany's ships.[72]

The count offered Gerard an updated version of a treaty signed by Prussia and the U.S. in 1799 that made it impossible for America to confiscate German patents and property if the two sides went to war. Montgelas insisted that if Gerard did not sign, those Americans still in Germany would find getting out very hard. Gerard said he had no authority to sign it, and in any case considered himself a prisoner because the Imperial government refused to give him his passports. He rounded this retort off with a parting and effective shot: "Even if I had authority to sign it I would stay here until hell freezes over before I would put my name to such a paper." Needless to say, he got his passports back without agreeing to a thing.[73]

In the days right before Germany declared war on France and invaded Belgium, thousands of Americans flooded the embassy in Berlin on Wilhelmstrausse. Most lacked passports and now needed them. Credit, too, became practically nonexistent, so Gerard asked the president of the Imperial Bank, Rudolf Havenstein, for relief for American travelers. He refused. What about the paper money the German government had just started printing? Again he refused. Fortunately the director of the second largest bank in Germany, Herbert

James W. Gerard. Harris & Ewing. Taken between 1915 and 1923. Library of Congress Prints and Photographs Division.

Gutmann, consented to honor American checks and letters of credit providing they had the embassy seal as well as one from an American consulate located outside of Berlin.[74]

With the help of volunteers, Gerard booked many Americans on special trains bound for Switzerland or the Netherlands. The embassy sold tickets to those who could pay and outright gave them to those who could not. Gerard bought several hundred steerage tickets for the Holland-American Line, "the only regular Dutch steamship line between the United States and [the Netherland's province of] Holland." Each week he had ladies resell them out of the embassy's ballroom because the company did not have a license to sell steerage tickets in Germany.[75]

Myron T. Herrick, ambassador to France, also did much to aid Americans as well as the French. Although exempt from the confiscation of motor vehicles, he nonetheless sold his car and put the money toward the American relief fund. When American refugees poured into the embassy, he treated both the wealthy and penniless equally, giving any Americans without a place to stay a room in which to sleep.[76]

Herrick's life gave fuel to the American myth of the self-made man. Born in Huntington Township, Ohio, in 1854, he began his career as a peddler of everything from rods to parlor organs to dinner bells. He became a lawyer but only practiced until 1886, the year in which he organized a national bank. Having not accomplished enough, he also started a hardware store, a railroad, and a life insurance company. When politics called, he ran for and won the nomination for Republican governor, then took this office in the largest landslide up to that date. He presumably did poorly, at least in the eyes of his constituents, because he lost his 1905 reelection bid. When President Taft offered him the ambassadorship of France in 1909, he accepted. He stayed until December 1914 at President Wilson's request.[77]

When it looked as if the Germans would take Paris, Herrick famously refused to leave, taking over the British and Japanese embassies when their diplomats fled with French officials to Bordeaux, this in addition to having already assumed the duties of the German, Austrian, and Turkish embassies plus several legations of still more nations. As the war progressed, he founded the American Relief Clearing House that cared "for widows, orphans, and the disabled." For all his work, the French awarded him the Grand Cross of the Legion of Honor.[78]

Finding a Way Back Home

James A. Patten, the former "wheat king of Chicago," and his wife began their difficult odyssey to England in Karlsbad, a city in Bohemia known for its mineral waters and mud baths. Patten, "born in Freeland Corners, Ill[inois]" in 1852, had made his millions by cornering the markets for oats, corn, cotton, and, most notably, wheat. Although a dedicated philanthropist, the way he made his fortune greatly offset any good he might have done. His manipulation of the cotton market nearly got him lynched by "indignant traders" when he visited the Cotton Exchange in Manchester, England. He eventually pled guilty to violating the Sherman Antitrust Act for which he paid a fine of a mere $4,000, not much for man of his wealth. When he retired at the age of 58, he had an estimated worth of $25 million.[79]

The Pattens made their way to Nuremberg via automobile on August 3. Here they stopped to submit to a thorough search at a guard house. They got on train for Ostend in

Myron T. Herrick. Harris & Ewing. 1914. Library of Congress Prints and Photographs Division.

the Netherlands but made it no farther than Cologne, where Germany's war mobilization caused them to stop. They took another train bound for the Belgian border, but this stopped prematurely in the Prussian town Herbesthal on the Belgian border, its customs house being known to delay trains coming from Belgium. Left out in a dousing rain at ten at night, the couple's first meal of the day consisted of nothing more than a slice of bread each.[80]

Here the Pattens took under their wing two penniless "lads" from New York, Jack

Yaras and Morris Rosenfeld. Another American joined them as well. The group hired "a horse and cart" to take them across the border to Verviers in which they hired another one to take them toward Liège. Along the way a team of Belgian engineers mining the road with dynamite told them to go a different way, which they did. The mine in question blew up about 3,000 Germans the next day. They arrived in Liège at about one in the afternoon of August 4. Before leaving on a train for Brussels about two hours later, the forts' cannons started firing at the Germans.[81]

The Patten party booked passage on the Red Star Line's *Finland*, a vessel that regularly sailed between Antwerp, Dover, and New York City. Boarding in Antwerp, Patten generously paid for the passage for "nine stranded Americans." Although Americans owned and ran this vessel and she flew a U.S. flag, Belgian military authorities looked at her with suspicion because the number of Americans in her crew amounted to less than five while her passengers were mostly Austrians and Germans who had been ejected from the country. Several Belgian military men boarded with the intent of cutting down her radio antennas, but her captain, Thomas J. Barman, compromised by promising to keep these down until the *Finland* entered the English Channel. The Belgians also refused to allow her to take on the food she needed for an Atlantic crossing.[82]

She sailed on August 8 but could not head through the usual route deep water vessels took, forcing Captain Barman to sail through the shallow East Gat using a Dutch pilot. To get through this, Barman released his vessel's water ballast to lessen her draft to keep her from grounding in the 21 to 27 feet of water through which she sailed. In the North Sea one could see from the *Finland's* decks a vast array of smoke coming from British battleships. As she headed into Dover, a torpedo boat came along her side to board and check her papers.[83]

The thousands of Americans who made their way to London all wanted to find a way home. In the first few days, panicked Americans piled onto what ships they could find. Cunard's *Mauretania* out of Liverpool brought 1,574 Americans to New York, 400 of them in steerage because they could not get better quarters. An American Line ship brought home 1,622. The charted Italian ship *San Guglielmo* out of Genoa carried still more. Because United Fruit owned 85 percent of the British shipping line Elder & Fyffes, the president of the former, Andrew W. Preston, offered to bring Americans home on the latter's ships *Montagua* and *Bayamo*, each taking on 200 passengers. That Americans willingly took berths on uncomfortable banana ships shows the desperation of those wanting to get home. While this venture would not make money, the company did charge standard transatlantic rates to pay for the charting of other boats used to continue its shipping business.[84]

A syndicate of 12 Americans bought the 8,500-ton steamship *Viking* for £80,000 to sail Americans home with a planned departure date of August 10. Operating as a private yacht, she could accommodate 400 passengers, each of whom would pay a staggering $500 for a first class cabin. One of the members of the syndicate, Grant Hugh Brown, admitted "that the object, in addition to patriotism, was financial profit." This did not endear him and his business partners to other Americans, who could do without this sort of patriotism. The *Viking* had trouble attracting enough passengers to make it economical to sail. The syndicate in any case had to delay her departure until August 22 because she had failed to receive a hoped for American registry. Nor did the *Viking* make it to America. Her name appears on a list of ships detained by the Germans that wound up in Rotterdam.[85]

Many of those Americans who did not have the means to pay for a passage home, or could not find a berth on the few ships still sailing the United States, headed to the American embassy in London for help. On one day alone, some 2,000 people stuffed themselves into the small space, all panicked and making demands for tickets for home or for an exchange of their British currency for American money. On that day, the embassy's staff worked until two in the morning. Visiting Americans wrote their names and London addresses down in a book with the hope the embassy would soon give them some aid. Then a clerk snatched the book away and informed them "there would be no more registration.... No explanation was vouchsafed except the simple one that the Embassy had no money to distribute, and therefore it was no use leaving names and addresses."[86]

Someone "in the crowd announced that the stranded Americans in London were to have a meeting at the Waldorf Hotel that afternoon." So everyone headed there. This location said much about those behind the gathering: only the wealthy could afford to stay here. When it first opened in 1883, *Life* had this to say about it: "It is a glad thought that at last we have a hotel where a person whose circumstances are easy can pay a thousand dollars a day for lodging, have his meals served on gold plates and stir his afternoon dinner coffee with a jeweled spoon, and sleep between real lace sheets, if he has in mind to pay a trifle extra.... We must look to induce our multi-millionaires to ease their congested treasuries at home rather than diffuse their surpluses over the continent of Europe."[87]

After someone called the meeting to order, New York banker Fred I. Kent proposed those in attendance nominate Theodore Hetzler as the chairman of an as of yet created committee dedicated to helping stranded Americans get home. Although "probably not one in a hundred of those present knew him," they elected him nonetheless. He, along with Kent and other prominent Americans in London at the time called this new organization the American Citizens' Committee.[88]

Hetzler, a lifelong banker, began his career at the Fifth Avenue Bank of New York in 1891 at the age of 15 as a messenger boy. He became its president in 1916, then headed its board of directors, taking time out to join and fight in Cuba with the First New York National Guard during the Spanish-American War. Like many wealthy bankers of that era, he had an expensive hobby: collecting etchings as well as supporting art and artists. To round out his portfolio, he also did philanthropic work, serving as vice president and a trustee of the Fifth Avenue Hospital, an institution that merged with the Flower Hospital.[89]

The Committee set its headquarters up in the Savoy, a hotel on the Strand that catered exclusively to guests belonging to that elite club of men and women who had more money than they could possibly spend in a lifetime. Aside from regular short-term rooms, it also offered more permanent residence in suites, or apartments, let for between £50 and £100 per year depending on the number of rooms one wanted. These contained such luxuries as hot and cold running water, heated halls and corridors, telephones, and "basic servants" such as porters, chimney sweeps, and page boys. Chambermaids, valets, and waiters cost extra.[90]

The Committee took over nearly an entire floor for its operations, making the White Room an office. The ballroom became a receiving area filled with tables and chairs and blank cards on which Americans could write their name, home address, foreign address, the ship supposed to take them home, and so forth. The Committee "immediately arranged that bank checks of the American Bankers Association," a group dedicated to ensuring people could redeem their paper money for specie, "should be paid. For several days these were the only checks on which coin was paid in London." Because most of those on the committee worked for or ran banks, they had little trouble getting American Express to also honor its checks.[91]

In its second week of existence, the Committee founded a daily newspaper, the *American Bulletin*. Possibly the most read periodical by Americans at the time, it found its way into hotels as well as the Committee's rooms. It contained mainly classifieds under headings such as "Information," "Personal Inquiries," "Luggage, Lost and Found," and "Who's Where." While it hardly makes for compelling reading today, it fulfilled its purpose quite well. To help pay for its production, it sold and ran commercial ads. The August 12 edition, for example, contained one for the up-market department store Selfridges.[92]

Business concerns forced Committee chairman Hetzler to resign and return home. Fortunately an even more capable man replaced him: Herbert Hoover. Because of his ill luck of being the U.S. president when the Great Depression hit as well as the one held responsible for debacle of General Douglas MacArthur's 1932 attack on the Bonus Army in Washington, D.C., he has a reputation of being heartless toward the common person. Until those events sullied his reputation, people around the world knew him as a great humanitarian. His first venture into this kind of work started here.[93]

He had made his millions as a successful civil engineer and at this time directed "eighteen mining and financial companies." He had come to Europe in March 1914 on the *Lusitania* as part of his effort to restructure the mining and land company Natamos Consolidated of California that involved British investment. His wife, Lou, and their boys followed on June 30, with the family planning to head home to California on the German ship *Vaterland* on August 13. The war killed that voyage and made any alternatives unlikely. And so, like many other Americans, he and his family were trapped in London.[94]

One destitute group that came to the Committee consisted of ten cowboys and 12 Native Americans along with their manager. An army had confiscated this Wild West troupe's ponies, leaving it with just a few animals not suited for the making of war, such as a tiger, an orangutan and a lion. They had left their inn in the middle of the night to escape paying the bill. In Hamburg they picked up an American boy wandering the streets who had come to Europe to visit his grandparents in Croatia. After giving them what money he had so they could eat, they pledged to get him home. Other entertainers suffered similar hardships. Nine Sioux working for a different Wild West troupe were arrested as spies in Trieste, Austria, then attacked by a mob.[95]

For the most part the Committee did not give anyone money outright but rather only offered loans. Out of the more than $1,500,000 distributed, Hoover reported in his autobiography that the Committee received repayment of all but about $300. He laid out a policy that anyone with no money whatsoever would travel home third class save for those with children, old age, or health concerns. If they wanted better accommodations, they could ask friends and relatives from home to send them additional funds. One upper class American woman without any money of her own demanded the Committee give her first class accommodations. When refused, she went on a hunger strike in the morning that lasted until about five in the afternoon when Hoover personally gave her four shillings to get a good meal with a reminder that she could have her third class ticket the next day.[96]

Richard Harding Davis viciously satirized this sort of person in his book *With the*

Allies: "Thousands of Americans were struggling in panic-stricken groups, bewailing the loss of a hatbox, and protesting at having to return home second-class. Their suffering was something terrible. In London, in the Ritz and Carlton restaurants, American refugees, loaded down with fat pearls and seated at tables loaded with fat food, besought your pity." He singled Judge Richard William Irwin, who served on the Superior Court of Massachusetts, for this stinging rebuke: "On leaving Switzerland for France they [he and his party] were forced to carry their own luggage, all the porters apparently having selfishly marched off to die for their country, and the train was not lighted, nor did any one [*sic*] collect their tickets," which they still possessed upon reaching Paris.[97]

Americans often complained to the Committee that the U.S. government would not provide them with the money for passage home, or that it appeared to do nothing at all. Like the grievance by G.P. Waizfelder that American consuls had done nothing to aid U.S. citizens in distress, this accusation had no truth behind it. President Wilson quickly went to Congress and asked for relief money. It duly appropriated $2.5 million for this purpose on August 4. Two days later the U.S. Navy's cruiser *Tennessee* headed to Falmouth, England, with private bankers providing $3 million in gold plus five of their representatives. Congress appropriated $1.5 million in gold and sent with it a large continent of military and government personnel that included five from the Treasury Department as well as 24 army officers. The cruiser *North Carolina* followed, reaching Cherbourg, France, on August 19. The relief representatives she carried headed for a variety of points throughout Western Europe with the purpose of exchanging checks and paper money for gold. Two officers took $25,000 to Vienna, then $30,000 to Rome, while others brought relief to Norway, Denmark, Sweden, the Netherlands, and Berlin, this last receiving $150,000. Because this effort had no official name, those running it began calling it the United States Relief Committee.[98]

The assistant secretary of war, Henry Breckinridge, arrived on the *Tennessee* as the relief effort's coordinator. Appointed to his position by Wilson in 1913, he had graduated from Harvard Law School a mere three years earlier. Although born in Chicago on May 25, 1886, he came from an old Kentucky family with a history of service to the country both in military and civilian capacities. When the United States entered the war in 1917, he went to officer's school, became head of a battalion, and saw action in France. After the war he joined the American Olympic Fencing Team and participated in the 1920 Olympics in Antwerp. As a lawyer he represented, among others, his friend Charles Lindbergh for whom he

Walter Hines Page. Bain News Service. Taken between 1910 and 1915. Library of Congress Prints and Photographs Division.

would unsuccessfully negotiate the ransom payment when someone kidnapped Lindbergh's 20-month-old son in 1932. Breckenridge later testified against Bruno Richard Hauptmann, the man accused of killing the child.[99]

The American Citizens' Committee quickly ran out of money. When Breckinridge arrived in London, he, Hoover, and Ambassador Walter Hines Page met to decide its future. The Committee would take over the distribution of funds brought over by the U.S. government and give them to those who needed aid. Hoover despised Breckinridge, criticizing him for travelling from one capital to another on special trains while ignoring the actual relief work.[100]

The U.S. government expected those who received aid to pay it back despite the fact many recipients had little money in the first place, especially naturalized citizens who had come to Europe to visit relatives. Many not only failed to pay what they owed, they had given false names and addresses. In October 1915, the Treasury Department released a list of 2,000 persons who still owned money with the hope of recouping these losses.[101]

Americans, in their hasty evacuation from Europe, abandoned thousands of pieces of luggage, 2,000 of which, mostly smaller ones, made their way back to a Wells Fargo warehouse in New York City. Few of the large, sturdy trunks favored by Americans made it home. In Germany alone the American embassy estimated that about 25,000 were left behind. Many abandoned along the Belgian-German border did not survive because both sides repurposed them as improvised barricades that became riddled by machine gun fire. One American, Edward Page Gaston, went to Europe in an effort to get lost luggage back home. He "found [much of it] at little taverns on lonely roads and carefully preserved in station masters' offices on the railways." In larger cities like Cologne, the police helped him round abandoned baggage up for shipment back to America via Rotterdam. The German government offered Gaston a surprising amount of cooperation and even allowed the use of trains to move what he recovered across the country.[102]

It did so in part because it did not want to antagonize the United States. As a neutral power, America had no problem selling belligerents materials, even those for war, which Germany desperately needed. Wilson wanted to forbid this, but his legal counsel, Robert Lansing, told him he lacked the authority to do so. Wilson nonetheless issued a statement that said in part: "The United States must be neutral in fact as well as name during these days that are to try men's souls. We must be impartial in thought as well as in action, must put a curb upon our sentiments as well as upon every transaction that might be construed as a preference of one party to the struggle before another." Many Americans found it impossible to abide by this.[103]

2

The Invasion of Belgium

Scrambling to Avoid the War

The German invasion of Belgium led to a clampdown on transport in the country. This made it difficult for foreigners to get around, even those with passports, which only established one's nationality but did not give them permission to move freely about. In some cities the police issued *permis de séjour* to those who had business there, but they were only good in the municipality that issued them. For full mobility, a foreigner needed the *laissez-passer* issued by the Ministry of Foreign Affairs. Foreign journalists who came to cover the war and wanted to follow the army in the field had to present, in addition to this, their journalist credentials and receive special permission.[1]

A lack of both did not deter Richard Harding Davis when he arrived in the country. He rose every morning from his Brussels hotel, rented an automobile that he shared with Gerald Morgan from the *London Daily Telegraph* and, carrying nothing but his *laissez-passer*, simply "joined the first army that happened to be passing." He had tried to get permission to accompany the British Expeditionary Force (BEF), but some other fellow had already gotten the only set of credentials issued to a U.S. citizen. Of all the American journalists who arrived in Belgium to cover the fighting, probably none had more experience as war correspondent than Davis. Certainly no one had as many eccentricities. Born on April 18, 1864, he affected a "foppish wardrobe, complete with fawn-colored kid gloves and cane." Known as a bit of a snob and prone to referring to himself in the third person, his outward confidence masked his propensity to suffer from crippling depression.[2]

He had begun his career as a newspaperman with the *Philadelphia Record*, but after three months the city editor fired him for being incompetent. Undaunted, he continued on his career path and soon made his name covering the Johnstown Flood that occurred in Pennsylvania on May 31, 1889. The disaster struck when a poorly constructed earthen dam collapsed and let loose the waters of the artificial lake it held back. This in turn created a flash flood that roared through a valley and destroyed everything in its path, including Johnstown, which lost 2,200 residents.[3]

Davis moved to the *Evening Sun* of New York City in 1889 and on the first day of work scored a coup when a notorious pair of con artists tried to fleece him. One called himself George Wanamaker and claimed to be the son of the postmaster general, and the other pretended to be a cattle king who had just sold $20,000 of his stock. Davis, who had immediately suspected something amiss, gave them the false name of Mr. Norris. Eventually the two confidence men engaged him in Three Card Monte, which started for low sums, then escalated it to $1,000. They wanted to know if Davis had that amount on him. No, but he

Belgium. Map by the author based on one in *Putnam's Handy Volume Atlas of the World*. New York: G.P. Putnam's Sons, 1921. Perry-Castañeda Library Map Collection.

did at the Astor House. The man calling himself Wanamaker said he would accompany Davis there. On their way, Davis placed him under citizen's arrest, holding him until a passing policeman took him into custody. Wanamaker, in reality the career criminal known as George "Sheeny Mike" Mortimer, was convicted for disorderly conduct for which he served six months in jail.[4]

Although terrified of women for much of his life, in the spring of 1889 Davis proposed to Cecil Clark of Chicago via telegraph from London. Clark, a sportswoman, painter, and lesbian, accepted with the condition that the two would not share a bed. Undaunted, Davis sent her an engagement ring by messenger service. The marriage did not satisfy Davis, and in 1912 he divorced her, remarrying in that same year to Elizabeth Genevieve McCoy. She would remain at his side until he died of a heart attack on April 11, 1916.[5]

Richard Harding Davis. Photographer unknown. Ca. 1901. Library of Congress Prints and Photographs Division.

After a stint writing fiction, he turned to covering wars beginning with the failed 1893 revolution in Honduras. Other conflicts included the Cuban Insurrection, the Spanish-American War, the Russo-Japanese War, the First and Second Balkan Wars, and the Mexican Revolution. All this experience prompted him to dress up in a homemade army uniform complete with "ribbons" for the wars he had covered complete with a Sam Browne belt, the type that goes around the waist that has a shoulder strap to give it extra support so one can hang heavy things such as guns and ammunition on the waist with less strain. Although against regulations, many British and French officers also wore these. The desire to look like a well-decorated soldier would later get him into trouble.[6]

He represented just one of an army of American journalists who had descended upon Belgium with "some of ... the most extraordinary credentials ever carried by a correspondent [or] ... no credentials at all." The Belgian provost marshal, head of the military police, stopped all sorts of people claiming to be journalists. One said he worked for the *Ladies' Home Journal*. Another that "he represented his literary agent," and still someone else produced a letter from his editor saying he would accept any articles the marshal might like to submit. A church minister from Boston had come to research "a series of sermons on the horrors of war."[7]

American journalists Irvin S. Cobb, Arno Dosch-Fleurot, John McCutcheon, and Will Irwin headed out of Brussels in search of combat despite the fact only one had experience as a war correspondent, and just Irwin could speak a little French. Brand Whitlock secured them passports and Ethelbert Watts, the consul-general, gave them supplemental ones affirming their American citizenship. Save for all being professional journalists, the four had little else in common. The corpulent Cobb, a Kentuckian by birth, did serious reporting but became better known for his humorous columns, short stories, novels, and, later, roles in movies. He had a photographic memory and glib pen. McCutcheon, who hailed from Indiana, worked as a cartoonist for the *Chicago Tribune*, a position he held for 43 years, winning a Pulitzer for the 1931 political cartoon "A Wise Economist Asks a Question." He began his career as a war correspondent after serving in Manila during the Spanish-American War. He covered a variety of other beats, including Theodore Roosevelt's post-presidential African safari during which he turned in illustrated articles.[8]

Dosch-Fleurot, born in Portland, Oregon, spent most of his career covering events in Europe. He would end his days in Madrid while at the *Christian Science Monitor*. During his time in Belgium he worked for the New York City newspaper *World*. In addition to this, the magazine *World's Work* commissioned him to write articles from the front. Irwin, born in New York but raised in the West, went to Stanford and spent his early days as a journalist working first in San Francisco then New York City as a reporter. He started writing for magazines beginning with *McClure's*. In 1917, he reduced his journalistic credibility by joining George Creel's infamous Committee on Public Information, the notorious propaganda arm of the U.S. government started after America entered the war. This entity helped to spark intense anti-immigrant and anti–German feelings in the country. Irwin later became Herbert Hoover's official biographer during the 1928 presidential race.[9]

Hiring a taxi, the four headed east straight into the teeth of the advancing Germans, who would occupy Brussels the next day. They went first to the village of Tervuren, home of King Leopold's Congo Museum, and from there towards the city of Louvain, Belgium's renowned center of learning. At first the road had no traffic, but about halfway there they encountered refugees from Tirlemont warning about oncoming Uhlans. The reporters heard the sound of cannon

Irvin Cobb. Bain News Service. Ca. January 22, 1916. Library of Congress Prints and Photographs Division.

Louvain. Photographer unknown. Taken between 1890 and 1900. Library of Congress Prints and Photographs Division.

from the direction of Louvain. A Belgian soldier asked them if they had seen the English or French, both of whom had pledged to help but neither had yet appeared, a question other soldiers repeated frequently. At the village of Leefdael, four miles away from Louvain, they saw the Belgian army readying to confront the oncoming Germans. Two English filmmakers in a car warned them not to go into Louvain, but because the Americans thought King Albert was still using the city as his headquarters (he had just moved it to Malines), they decided to go. Their cab driver, on the other hand, refused out of fear of the fighting and worry that the army would confiscate his car. The four walked the rest of the way, never again seeing their driver.[10]

In Louvain they visited a monastery at which they found someone who spoke English and insisted they drink some red wine. Next they stopped at an inn for a bit of food. As they readied to pay, a person burst in and warned that someone had seen eight Germans nearby. As the four headed toward the town square, a car filled with newsmen from Brussels rushed by, one of them yelling something. The only word they could make out was "danger." Moments later eight Belgian soldiers shuffled past, the first they had seen in the city.[11]

On their heels came German soldiers, one on a horse and the other on a bicycle. More Germans followed. The four evaded them. Realizing they needed to leave, they found their way back blocked by German soldiers. Although Irwin had taken nothing more than a high school course in French and could only read it, the stress of the situation brought his memory of it to the forefront of his mind, allowing him to ask a local where they could find the town leaders. He told them to go to the Hôtel de Ville.[12]

This did them no good. The Germans had already occupied it. For the rest of the day they tried to mingle with the crowd and look inconspicuous out of fear of being detained by the Germans as spies. With Irwin's limited French unable to cope, they went to the School of Languages for an interpreter but found none immediately available. There was no U.S. consulate in the city and the local police had no time for them, so they followed up on a rumor that the Spanish college handled American affairs. The head of that institution spoke no English and in any case only dealt with South American concerns.[13]

An interpreter from the School of Languages fluent in French, German and English arrived that night to help them out, obtaining for them rooms at the Hôtel des Mille Colonnes, which served the railroad line. Here they found beds but not food. They went to the hotel next door and explained to some German officers there that they had come to the city in a taxicab and could not get back to Brussels. The Germans thought going to war in a taxicab hilarious, an irony considering it would be this conveyance that later helped to save Paris from a German offensive.[14]

The next morning they went to the German adjunct in the Palais de Justice. He told them to confine themselves in their hotel save for when they went out for meals. They might have to go to Berlin but probably could stay so long as they made no trouble. A German major who became their minder had to listen to Cobb crying that he really needed to get back to Brussels not out of fear for his life but rather because the taxi's meter still ran at "fifty centimes every three minutes." They stayed for three days before being allowed to return to Brussels. During that time German soldiers bought goods and services just like everyone else, creating the illusion that all remained normal in the city and that commerce boomed. This détente would not last long.[15]

Upon returning to Brussels, Cobb and McCutcheon ventured out into the countryside once more along with a journalist name Lewis. With no cars of any sort available, they hired a cart and two bicycles. The corpulent Cobb perched himself atop the cart while the other two rode alongside. Later, at least according to Cobb, McCutcheon took to driving, but the horse pulling the cart gave out, so they had to rely on the bicycles. The Germans detained them as spies and sent them off to Aachen from which were eventually released.[16]

Saving Brussels

After refusing to allow the German army to pass through its territory, the Belgian government ejected the German minister. He sent his counselor to the American legation on 33 rue del la Science to ask its secretary, Hugh Gibson, if the Americans would take over the German legation so German subjects had a place to go for protection. Gibson could do no such thing and told him to formally request it from Washington via telegram. When the German minister himself stopped by later in the day and informed Gibson that he and his staff had to leave that afternoon, Gibson reluctantly agreed to temporarily take over their legation on humanitarian grounds and to that end went to there to make it official.[17]

He had tried to put off the Germans not just for legal but also practical reasons. The American legation only had a staff of three: Gibson, Minister Brand Whitlock, and one clerk. It had never needed more because nothing ever happened in Belgium. It was for this reason that Gibson, a career diplomat in the American Foreign Service who moonlighted as a noted illustrator, had requested a posting here the first place. He wanted to get away from the threats and rumors of war. Arriving in early July, that hope did not last out the month. Things became lively when the Austro-Hungarian Empire declared war on Serbia, and downright dangerous when the Germans invaded.[18]

Whitlock had also come to Belgium figuring a sparse official schedule would give him plenty of time to write a new novel. Born on March 4, 1869, in Urbana, Ohio, he moved to Toledo, Ohio, at the age of 15 and, upon graduating from high school, went to work for the *Toledo Blade*. Three years later he became the political correspondent for the *Chicago Herald*. He quit to become a clerk for Illinois' secretary of state, studying law the entire time. Never one to work at a single career for too long, he left this new profession in 1905 and moved back to Toledo, where he became its Progressive mayor with the mandate of championing the common worker. This brought him into conflict with the local clergy because they wanted him to stop prostitution and

Hugh Gibson. Bain News Service. Creation date unknown. Library of Congress Prints and Photographs Division.

shut down the city's saloons. Whitlock refused on the grounds that he would not take away the pleasures of the working man. During his time in office he wrote novels of no particular merit. In 1912, he campaigned for Woodrow Wilson and received as a reward the post of American minister to Belgium.[19]

American tourists from Germany, Switzerland, and France overwhelmed the legation with questions about where else they could safely go in Western Europe. German subjects who came sometimes created tricky diplomatic problems. Once, an American woman from Iowa arrived with her German husband and their young son and begged Whitlock to help them. Her husband had lived in America for several years and ran a business but had never gotten around to becoming a naturalized citizen. Now the Germans wanted to conscript him, which he desired to avoid, but without U.S. citizenship, he had no legal way to do so. Gibson got around this by taking the family to Cirque Royal and placing them onto a train for German refugees. A few days later Whitlock identified the husband as a German spy, learning that he had taken a room near Gibson's place to keep an eye on him.[20]

With the Germans getting nearer to the Belgian capital, Whitlock and the Spanish minister, Rodrigo de Saavedra y Vinent, Second Marqués de Villalobar, met with the Belgian minister of war, Charles Marie Pierre Albert, Count de Broqueville, to ask him to declare Brussels an open city so as to avoid unnecessary death and destruction. When the count

Brand Whitlock. Bain News Service. Taken between 1910 and 1915. Library of Congress Prints and Photographs Division.

rejected the idea, they approached Brussels' burgomaster, Adolphe Eugène Jean Henri Max, with the same suggestion.[21]

Max, a man with a small van Dyke and an inability to relax (he worked an average 18 hours a day) had trained as a lawyer and journalist. He was an eccentric lifelong bachelor

Adolphe Max. Bain News Service. Creation date unknown. Library of Congress Prints and Photographs Division.

who throughout his life always kept a pet terrier he named Happy. He saw resisting the Germans as a matter of honor and could not conceive of just letting them have the city. Whitlock and Villalobar countered that the Civil Guard, a militia composed of men who had to equip themselves and had little military training save for some on Sundays, had no chance against the Germans, and fighting would just result in the destruction of Brussels' priceless works of art. Max insisted he would defend the inner city and suggested the two diplomats relocate their legations to this area. Both refused. Fortunately King Albert ordered Max to open the city to the Germans, much to his disgust.[22]

Davis was in the city at this time, and on the morning of August 19 watched a stream of automobiles traveling up the boulevard du Régent at a good speed filled with the city's elite, all heading northeast for Bruges, Ghent, and the coast because of a rumor that the Germans had reached nearby Louvain. Later came a more sobering scene: peasants trudging down the streets either on foot or with their carts filled with what few goods they could escape with from the coming invaders.[23]

Despite the imminent arrival of the Germans, the majority of people in the city remained calm. They continued to fill its cafes and seemed little moved when two German airplanes flew overhead. This bravado evaporated when the Germans arrived on August 20. The streets emptied of people, shutters were closed, and posters from Burgomaster Max hung everywhere urging people to not commit hostile acts. The phone service ceased to work and the trains stopped running. At around 11 in the morning, Davis saw the German advance guard marching down the boulevard du Waterloo that consisted of "a captain and two privates on bicycles" followed by the Uhlans, infantry, and artillery pieces. It would take them three days to pass by Davis' hotel.[24]

By now the government in Brussels had departed. Per a military plan it had in place in case of invasion, both it and the army had retreated to Antwerp, the government going into the city and the army occupying a ring of forts surrounding it. There both planned to hold out until help came from France and Britain. King Albert had begun moving his men there on August 12. Another Belgian force held out at Namur until August 25, retreated across the French border from which it found transportation to Le Havre, sailed to Ostend, then joined with Albert on September 5.[25]

While Max had orders not to resist the Germans, this did not mean he could not make a nuisance of himself nor personally defy them. At their headquarters he greeted them wearing "the top hat and gold chain of his office." He berated the German commander, Major General Thaddäus von Jarotzky, for cutting down all the telephone and telegraph lines. He refused to shake the general's hand, then escorted the Germans into the city in a mocking way. He tore down the many military notices posted by the Germans, telling them they needed a permit to put them up. When the Germans banned all public meetings, he became a dedicated attendee of the Cathedral of St. Michael and St. Gudula as a pretence for gathering citizens together to promote "patriotism and fortitude."[26]

The Germans demanded 50 million francs (about $90 million) plus a large amount of food from the city within three days, warning that if it failed to do turn the latter over, it had to pay twice the market value of that not delivered. From the province in which Brussels resided, Brabant, the Germans demanded 50 million francs within a month. Max informed the Germans he could not pay. Fine, they would take what they wanted and not issue any receipts in return. Max replied he would not have given them the cash even if the city had it on hand. Irritated, the Germans issued an official proclamation stripping Max of his executive power on September 27, 1914, then arrested him the next day. He would spend the next four years as their prisoner.[27]

The Germans did not hesitate to loot during their conquest of Belgium. Between August 10 and September 20, for example, they stole from the National Bank's branches in Ath, Dinant, Mons, and Hasselt a total of 8,515,000 francs' worth of assets. The Belgians managed to keep the contents of the main branch, which held the majority of its securities and gold plus the plates used to print paper money, out of German hands by moving it to Antwerp. From here this 300 million francs' worth of assets went to the Bank of England for the duration of the war. The Germans demanded its return but the British refused. Upset that they could plunder no more, the Germans revoked the National Bank's power to issue paper money and gave this ability to Belgium's oldest banking corporation, the Société générale de Belgique, which had once done it anyway. The roughly 1.6 million Belgian francs then in circulation retained their value.[28]

The German seizure of Brussels' food supply threatened to cause mass starvation. Whitlock became furious when he learned they had shipped it to Germany rather than giving it to their troops in the city. Protesting, he got them to stop taking any more for at least a week. They ultimately confiscated the nation's entire 1914 harvest, at least that which had survived the fighting and not rotted in the fields due to a lack of manpower to reap it. This was a terrible blow because Belgium "imported three-quarters of its food." The German High Command decided to keep all food produced in Belgium and occupied France for itself so long as the war continued, which meant certain mass famine for the civilians living in areas under German control. The High Command blamed its action on the British, claiming it would not have done such a thing had the Royal Navy not set up a blockade that left Germany proper with little enough to feed its own people let alone those in occupied territories. Not all German officials agreed with this policy. Chancellor Theobald von Bethmann Hollweg warned Germany did not want a nation of hungry, rebellious people at its army's back.[29]

To alleviate the situation, a delegation from Belgium that included Gibson and the Belgian banker Émile Francqui headed to London to meet with Ambassador Walter Hines Page to see what they could do. Page asked Herbert Hoover to head up an organization to feed the people under German occupation. He agreed and, along with several others, created

Poster for the National Committee for Relief in Belgium. 1915. Library of Congress Prints and Photographs Division.

the Commission for Relief in Belgium (CRB) to coordinate the effort. Formed on October 22, 1914, it quickly raised money for thousands of tons of food and just as quickly exhausted its funds. Hoover estimated it would cost about $12 million a month to continue its work.[30]

He asked the British government for aid, but it initially refused for fear the food would get into the hands of the Germans rather than those for whom it was intended. When Hoover received assurances from Germany that they would not confiscate it nor molest CRB ships bringing it into Belgium, the chancellor of the exchequer, Lloyd George, agreed to help pay for the relief and to that end convinced other government ministers to go along with his decision. The British pledged $5 million a month and the French grudgingly gave an initial $7 million followed by $5 million per month. Thanks to Hoover and the CRB, the people of Belgium and occupied France did not starve.[31]

The Germans continued to loot the resources of Belgium for the rest of the war, including its manpower. On November 9, 1914, Belgium's foreign minister, Baron Eugène-Napoléon Beyens, issued "the first official charges" against Germany for deporting thousands of Belgian men to work in German factories. Out of Flanders alone, he asserted, the Germans had taken 15,000 men. They had also raided Belgian factories, appropriating from them things such as oil, copper, leather belting, and machinery.[32]

Moritz Ferdinand von Bissing, who became governor-general of Belgium on December 1, 1914, claimed he had done this in an effort to alleviate the mass unemployment caused by the British blockade, which kept raw materials from getting into the country, ignoring the inconvenient fact that Germany had confiscated them. He asserted that 30,000 Belgian subjects went to Germany voluntarily to work for lack of it in their own nation, and that by doing so they had reduced the amount of charity they otherwise needed. During the war the Germans would send 120,000 unwilling foreign laborers to work in the Fatherland.[33]

At Termonde, a Flemish town of 12,000 known for the manufacture of "rope and cordage," the Germans "demanded $200,000." But the town's council had already left, so they instead tried to shake down a local millionaire ironmaster. He had sent all his money to England. Furious, they seized several wealthy residents as hostages, gave the townspeople two hours to get out, then destroyed the place.[34]

With all this hardship one wonders if King Albert should have allowed the Germans to pass through his kingdom after all. Based on what they did to the neighboring Grand Duchy of Luxembourg, he had made the correct decision. Luxembourg gave the German army permission to pass unhindered, but instead of marching through as promised, it stayed, installing its headquarters at the government house, cutting off all telephone and telegraph communications, and seizing all lines of the Alsace-Lorraine Railway in the country with the claim that since Germany owned it, its army could use it. This despite the fact a treaty between the two nations signed on June 11, 1872, guaranteed Germany would never use the railway to transport its troops or war materiel. The Germans systematically looted the country, causing massive unemployment and inflation that sparked unsuccessful strikes and unionization efforts.[35]

Spy Fever

At 8:30 on the morning of August 6, Belgium's minister of justice, Count Henri Carton de Wiart, came calling at the American legation in Brussels. Dressed in a "top hat and frock coat," he had information that the Germans had set up a wireless station on top of their legation. Since the Americans had taken official charge of it, would they mind having the proper paperwork drawn up so a Belgian judge could investigate? Whitlock told the minister to find an expert in wireless communications, then they would all go together to look into it.[36]

Wiart returned with a telegraph lineman. Whitlock, Gibson, and the two Belgians went inside the German legation and headed towards the roof. To gain access one had to climb a ladder leading to a trapdoor. All save for the obese Wiart climbed up. No one saw a wireless device, although the lineman did clip a few wires for show. Perhaps German agents had one hidden away somewhere that they brought out only at night?[37]

Another rooftop trapdoor opened and out came a well-manicured, formally dressed man complete with a monocle in one eye and a cigarette in his mouth. Gibson and Whitlock immediately identified him as Señor Felix Cavalcanti de Lacerda, secretary of the Brazilian legation. The American-Belgian party had inadvertently strayed on top of his roof, so he had come up to investigate. Whitlock quipped, "If I'm violating Brazilian territory it's quite by mistake and unintentional, and I formally apologize." Everyone laughed. Then they heard it: the distinct sound of a wireless telegraph broadcasting Morse code. They quickly discerned the sound had originated from a squeaky *girouette*—a weathercock. More mirth ensued. Crisis averted.[38]

Although this ended well enough, the spy fever that swept through Europe at this time often had far more serious consequences. Belgian subjects started seeing foreign agents everywhere. When authorities found a wireless telegraph in a school at Antwerp's German

(Left to right) J.W. Thorne, A. Van de Vyere, Mme. De Wiart, Baron de Cartier and Count Henri Carton de Wiart. Bain News Service. Taken between 1910 and 1915. Library of Congress Prints and Photographs Division.

consulate, there for teaching purposes, they arrested the principal's two sons. A German national who worked at an aviation school with a wireless was arrested and punished for using it. Even the Belgian Boy Scouts got into the business of ferreting out spies. One, Georges Leysen, denounced 11 alleged German spies. He also successfully brought dispatches through German lines ten times for which the king decorated him and gave him a commission.[39]

The Belgians shot six spies in Antwerp and three in Louvain, four of them supposedly Germans wearing Belgian uniforms stolen from dead soldiers. This kind of accusation became a particular bugaboo for the Belgians. One report claimed they had caught and executed 100 spies for this kind of deception. War correspondent Martin H. Donohoe, a British journalist who worked for the *Daily Chronicle* and sometimes the *New York Times*, observed: "The superheated imagination of the Belgian peasant sees spies everywhere, and excess of patriotic zeal leads him to denounce the first stranger whom he comes across in the firm belief that thereby he is doing incalculable service to his country." This paranoia soon encompassed Red Cross workers and nuns, some of whom were arrested and one executed.[40]

A café owner in Brussels denounced Donahue and a companion, Dr. Charles Saroléa, as spies. The former was from Galway, Ireland, and the latter a Belgian native, although at this time he served as the "head of the French and Romance Languages Department of Edinburgh University." He also worked as a journalist in the city and had just become its Belgian consul. Police accused Donohoe and Saroléa of possessing forged Belgian military passes and thought little of Donohoe's English passport and French police pass despite the fact the latter even had his photograph. Detained for eight hours, authorities convinced themselves that Donohoe's "field glasses were some wonderful new-fangled kind of camera stored full of photographic impressions of Belgian positions." Fortunately a professor who knew Saroléa identified him, forcing the police to let him and Donohoe go.[41]

The Belgians gave German intelligence far more credit for its ability to successfully operate in foreign countries than it deserved. A day before the UK officially entered the war, a special unit detained 22 known German spies and began keeping tabs on another 200 individuals of interest. It took British intelligence a mere week to completely break up the German spy network in its home territory, and it had little trouble keeping track of agents working abroad and intercepting their messages.[42]

The Germans detained foreigners in Belgium who got too close to their lines, such as Dr. Nevil Monroe Hopkins, an American scientist and writer who had come to study the country in a time of war. Born in Portland, Maine, he had once taught chemistry. Between 1905 and 1908, he worked for the Department of the Navy developing weapons such as "a super-submarine designed to carry a 16-inch gun[,] ... various long-range naval and anti-aircraft guns[,] ... high-explosive anti-aircraft shells, and 'battle-ship wrecking bombs.'" A German officer near Malines detained him, his men confiscating Hopkins' car and making him empty his pockets. Out of these came items that would not help the paranoid think anything but the worst about his reasons for being in the area: papers, a camera, and a revolver.[43]

The Germans took him to a camp at which he stayed for two nights. Having spent time in Germany in his youth, he spoke the language fluently and during his incarceration told stories to the troops about his days in a German school as well as about Americans and German-Americans. The officer who had originally taken him prisoner brought him to a road with ditches on either side in which set several trucks and one ambulance abandoned by the Belgians. The Germans wished to use them but could not get them started. The officer had noticed among Hopkins' papers his "membership card in the American Society of Mechanical Engineers," so he asked Hopkins if he could get the vehicles running. Hopkins said he would try.[44]

With the help of a couple of German soldiers, he figured out and undid the Belgian sabotage that caused them to not work. The Germans offered to free him if he agreed to teach the others how to keep the vehicles operational and personally drive the ambulance to Contich. To this he agreed, so they returned his papers. After showing them how to keep their trucks going, he secretly sabotaged them once more. Knowing the downed telegraph lines he saw meant the Germans could not warn anyone ahead of his treachery, he took off in the ambulance and with it made it safety back to Antwerp.[45]

Davis had his own dangerous encounter with the Germans. On August 23, he and Morgan decided to take a taxi from Brussels to Hal, a city of over 14,000 inhabitants that stood along the Seine and Charleroit Canal to which pilgrims traveled to visit its cathedral of Notre Dame. Possessing *laissez-passers* issued by General Jarotsky, they took a cab to Hal past which they planned to walk to the British and French lines because they did not trust the Germans.[46]

During the ride to Hal, a German officer came alongside their vehicle "and pointed an automatic [pistol] at" them. Four enlisted men got into their cab, which went as far as the conditions allowed. After paying off the cabby, they marched with a German column. Although the officer had not placed them under arrest, he wanted to keep an eye on them all the same. Hitting the limit of their German-issued passes, Morgan decided to head back to Brussels. Davis continued.[47]

He stopped for lunch and, sandwich in hand, was accosted by four Germans, one of whom jabbed his stomach with the point of his pistol. They took him to their colonel, a genial fellow who wrote on Davis' *laissez-passers* that would allow him to continue on to Enghien two miles away. About 200 yards later two officers detained him and searched his knapsack. Finding nothing incriminating, they let him go. He received no welcome at the hotel in Enghien because its Belgian proprietor suspected him of a being a German spy, refusing to let him stay for that reason. The hotel's German guests, on the other hand, thought he was an English spy. The town's burgomaster gave him permission to remain in the hotel for the night, though it did not make its proprietor trust this strange American.[48]

Fearing his editors would berate him if he turned back, Davis continued past Enghien with the idea of getting the Germans to send him back to Brussels so he would have a legitimate excuse for returning. Soon enough a group of German officers did detain him, informing him they would take him to their general. They force marched him at double time for the next five hours. There an officer who Davis called Rupert of Hentzau, a villain in Alexander Hope's novel *The Prisoner of Zenda*, took Davis' papers and sent them forward to the front via an automobile. He returned and asked Davis to accompany him for a word with the general staff in front of which he accused him of being an out of uniform English spy, one who had "seen enough in this road ... to justify ... shooting" him immediately.[49]

Davis had mistakenly taken the road to Ath rather than Soignies, an easy enough thing to do because the Belgians had painted over all their road signs. He had stumbled into the midst of a gathering German force preparing to launch a major offensive designed to push the Allies out of Belgium. Known to history as the Battle of the Frontiers, it involved a joint force of more than a half a million men under the command of Generals Alexander von Kluck and Karl von Bülow. The British Expeditionary Force, meanwhile, marched north in columns. Unlike the German army, whose numbers had swelled thanks to a large influx of conscripts, the BEF was comprised of experienced professionals reinforced with reservists. Their commander, Sir John French, halted the latter at the Mons-Condé Canal and dug in despite a credible warning of three approaching German columns.[50]

At their first clash in and around Mons, the Germans learned they had underestimated the effectiveness of the British soldier: the BEF quickly showed its teeth when its men used their Lee-Enfield rifles to let loose between ten to 15 rounds a minute that quickly inflicted a steep number of German causalities, possibly up to 5,000. Despite doing so much damage, the British could not hold this position and began an orderly retreat the next day, which continued all the way to the Marne in France at which the BEF and French stopped the German advance and forced them into a retreat that ended with the Battle of the Marne, which is considered the starting point of the stalemate on the Western Front.[51]

The Battle of the Frontiers taught the Germans the value of superior camouflage: they had trouble seeing the British because they wore khaki uniforms. Although the Germans' gray-green ones worked satisfactory for this purpose, their leather spiked helmets, the *pickelhuabe*, did not. Snipers loved them, causing the German army to discard this piece of headgear and replace it with something better. It took the French a bit longer to see the value of good camouflage. When the war started, they wore bright red pants, and continued to do so until the French army finally issued its infantry blue-green uniforms and helmets in August 1915.[52]

A group of German officers questioned Davis from 11 in the morning until midnight. Rupert of Hentzau served as a sort of prosecutor, while other officers defended the American. Rupert accused him of being an English spy and presented as evidence Davis' passport photo in which he wore the coat of a British soldier complete with ribbons on his lapel. Davis had copied the coat eight years previously from the British West African Field Force, which he found "as cool and comfortable as a golf-jacket." As for the ribbons: no soldier from a single army could possibly have served in all those places, which represented the conflicts he had covered.[53]

Despite this show trial, the officers did not decide upon Davis' fate. They placed him in an auto and took him to a house in the village of Beloeil by which stood a château belonging to the Prince of Ligne where one could find gardens and a park designed by André le Nôtre, the man who had landscaped Versailles. The Germans locked Davis in a second floor room. He managed to get one of his guards, Major Alfred Wurth, to take a note to his "friend" Minister Whitlock, although in truth the two had only briefly met. He dearly hoped it would entice the Germans to put off arbitrarily shooting him. Wurth, who recognized Davis' American accent and therefore had doubts about his being an English spy, took it, then returned with news it could not be sent to Brussels. He had instead forwarded it to his general.[54]

Davis tried a different approach. He asked Major Wurth to give him a new pass stating his status as a suspected spy who had until midnight of August 26 to report to the military governor of Brussels. If found anywhere but on a major road going towards that city, or if his allotted time had passed, anyone catching him could execute him on the spot. Davis would try to catch a ride on an empty truck or ambulance heading to Brussels. Wurth liked this plan.

At midnight a guard carrying a flashlight woke Davis and took him to the Prince of Ligne's château. Here two guards brought him into a room filled with staff officers of a higher rank than those he had seen before. His guards sat him in a gilded silk chair at a table covered with maps, half-filled champagne bottles and burning candles set in silver candlesticks. Rupert of Hantzau appeared from the next room and presented Davis with a pass and the rules to go with as proposed to Wurth. When Rupert informed him he would depart at three in the morning, Davis exclaimed, "You might as well take me out and shoot me now!" He figured any Germans who saw him that time of day would kill him on the spot.[55]

He returned to the house but anxiety over the situation kept him from sleeping. At around three in the morning, its Belgian proprietor informed him that all the soldiers had left, so he could have a bed if he wanted it. Davis decided to just get on with the trip and headed out. Possessing nothing more than a box of matches he could to use to show his pass in the dark if the need arose, he began the 50-mile walk back to Brussels, a trek not made easy by the foot he had hurt during his forced march a few days earlier.[56]

Along the way, a German general passing by picked him up with the promise of taking him as far as Hal. Once there, the general received orders to continue to Brussels, so he took his new companion with him. Here Davis headed to the American legation and explained his situation to Whitlock, who suggested they go to the German headquarters at the Hôtel de Ville. There Whitlock cleared things up and got an officer to confirm Davis' identity and that he had checked in as ordered. Despite having covered six wars, Davis admitted nothing had scared him as much as this incident.[57]

Another American journalist, Albert Rhys Williams, was detained as a spy multiple times. This former Congregationalist minister who became a dedicated socialist and, after the overthrow of the tsar in Russia, an adamant defender of the Soviet Union, was arrested for spying in Antwerp by the Belgians on August 22, 1914. They interned him and about 200 other suspects at a train station. Of these, they picked him as one of about 20 candidates likely to be carrying out acts of espionage. They also strip searched him. Fortunately within two hours they realized they had made a mistake, apologized, and let him go. In another incident, the Germans detained him for spying near Louvain. The Dutch did the same in Eindhoven.[58]

These arrests paled in comparison to the scare he received in Brussels after its fall to the Germans. It began on his birthday, September 28, in his hotel room at the Metropole when a porter informed him an American gentleman wanted to see him. Bored because he could not get out of the city, he agreed. The man who greeted him did so in a very un–American way: he bowed. Despite this, Williams agreed to go this stranger's room, 502 on the fifth floor. There he told Williams that he worked for the German government. He charged Williams with paying a bribe for sensitive information.[59]

This man left the room, then returned wearing a military uniform. In his memoir, Williams called him Javert, the relentless police inspector in Victor Hugo's *Les Misérables*. The Germans took Williams to a hall filled with other detainees that served as a temporary holding area. Recognizing the trouble he now found himself in, he decided to rid himself of any potentially "incriminating" evidence on his person, including "a pass from the Belgian commander giving ... [him] access to the Antwerp fortifications" that he had kept as a souvenir and "cards of introduction from French and English friends." He ate them.[60]

At around six in the evening, an escort took him to a makeshift trial with Javert serving as the prosecutor. He presented several incriminating documents, such as a letter from the American vice-consul of Ghent, Julius van Hee, and a card of introduction from Henry van Dyke, the American minister to the Netherlands, which stated Williams worked for *Outlook*. This, Williams reflected, he ought to have destroyed because the magazine for which he currently wrote had taken a decidedly anti–German stance. It had originally started as a Baptist periodical called *Church Union*, transformed into a more a generalized religious paper called the *Christian Union*, then took on its present name in 1893 when it became a general family magazine with some religious reporting. It turned political around 1900 with its support of progressive causes in general and Theodore Roosevelt in particular, who it hired as a contributing editor when he finished serving his second presidential term. Williams pointed out his that his opinions did not necessarily conform to that of the magazine for which he wrote, but Javert did not believe him, and rightly so. Javert had in his possession Williams' shorthand notes neither he nor his men could decipher. This was just as well because Williams had written some unfavorable things about the Germans, but omitted these when he rendered it into longhand for his captors.[61]

He still had no idea why the Germans had arrested him. Finally Javert asked him point blank why he had offered someone money to learn about German troop movements. At first taken aback, this accusation triggered a memory: the day before his arrest, a Dutchman had approached him on a streetcar and offered to take him on an automobile tour via Liège to the Netherlands that would give him the opportunity to see troops and the destruction of war. Williams said he would pay to go on such a trip and gave the fellow his address at his hotel, not knowing this man worked for German intelligence.[62]

After the trial, if one could call it that, Williams was placed into a closet with six others for the night. He wrote a note to Whitlock appealing for help, but it never reached him. The American legation got wind of his detention anyway. An American representative appeared around five the next afternoon. He along with Williams met privately with several Germans, including a high-ranking officer Williams did not know. The Germans could not fathom why anyone would want to enter a war zone of their own free will. In the end they released him, forcing him to take a train via Liège into Germany and from there go to the Netherlands rather than allowing him to travel from Brussels directly to the border.[63]

The Germans had good reason to target Williams: since his arrival in Belgium, he had reported on a wide variety of German atrocities, something they certainly did not want made public. In mid–August, he left his hotel in the Netherlands and, with German permission, headed to Liège. Just half a mile into his trip he passed through the remains Mouland, a village he had seen burning the night before from afar in the Netherlands. In some areas only a few whitewashed walls of houses remained, their interiors charred ruins. Just a few artifacts of the lives of the people who had lived here survived: a blossoming geranium here, a rocking horse there. One newspaper reported that four of the village's inhabitants had died in the conflagration, and of its 132 houses, only 73 survived.[64]

Continuing along the road beyond, he saw dead horses, cows and dogs killed by bullets as well as flattened fields of grain. Fire had destroyed the village of Visé completely, displacing 4,000 people, at least eight of whom died. For several days, German officers plundered each house of its valuables, then directed soldiers to burn them using benzene. After rounding up the population, the Germans sent the men to Aachen as prisoners of war, although more likely they planned to use them as slave labor. Williams asked a German soldier what had happened. They had destroyed the two villages because civilians had fired upon them. A more detailed newspaper account reported that the Germans had burned Visé because civilians there had allegedly killed an officer, a sergeant, and four enlisted men plus wounded six others.[65]

The Germans repeatedly claimed civilians had attacked them to justify all sorts of atrocities. Although a civilian or two probably took a potshot at a passing German solider, for the most part this did not occur. The Germans unleashed violence against the civilian population as a means of retaliating against the Belgian army, which had dared to defy and inflict significant casualties upon them. Some German officers also thought terrorizing the civilian population would break the Belgian people's will to resist.[66]

The decision by the German High Command to tell its soldiers that the Belgians would greet them as liberators from the invading French had not helped, either. Imagine their surprise upon entering a village or town only to find Belgian soldiers firing at them in earnest. So ingrained did this lie become, when Donohoe interviewed several German soldiers wounded by Belgians, they expressed dismay: the Belgians were supposed to give them roses, and they simply could not understand why this resistance had occurred. Many of the inexperienced enlisted men who had never before seen combat believed that *franctireurs* had arisen to attack them, the legendary French irregular civilian fighters who had sniped against the Prussians during siege of Paris from October 1870 to January 1871. Fueled by paranoia, any stray shot fired by a departing Belgian soldier became one from a hidden civilian sniper. The holes found on the exterior walls of churches and houses became ports through which snipers poked their rifles to fire upon them rather than being used to hold scaffolding. In Liège, Williams saw a dead 20-year-old man lying on a stretcher who the Germans had just shot because he had gotten too close to a telegraph pole and looked suspicious about it.[67]

Williams decided finding lodging for the night in the city would prove too much trouble, so he started a 16-mile walk back to the Netherlands to ensure he arrived before dark because friends had told him not to cross the border at night. Along the way he saw the Germans rounding up about 10,000 Belgian cattle for their use. His feet now quite sore, he caught a ride on a farmer's cart that drove right into the midst of German soldiers. He boldly walked up to a group at a water pump and mimed a desire for water, which he received.[68]

Presuming he somehow belonged, they left him alone. He made it about 600 yards before being stopped and searched. Released, he walked several hundred yards more when someone else forced him to halt. This soldier began drilling him with questions, and the more answers Williams gave him, the louder and more excited the soldier became. Williams demanded to see his superior. This deflated his bluster, and he let him pass. He did not go very far before a tired solider overburdened by his gun and pack commanded him to halt. Seeing his distress, Williams offered to give him a hand with it, but the soldier refused. Williams gave him the last of his chocolate.[69]

He asked his new acquaintance: "Is it dangerous traveling along here so late?" The soldier answered, "Yes, it is very dangerous," adding that a Belgian had fired at a German soldier from the bluffs above, which had so angered them they cleared the road of civilians between this point and Mouland. The soldier advised, "Go straight ahead. Swerve neither right nor left. Be sure you have no weapons, and stop at once when the guard cries 'Halt!' and you will get through all right." Heeding this advice, Williams made it back to the Netherlands safely.[70]

Although his sober report of German-caused destruction gave his readers a glimpse at their wholesale pillaging, other journalists did not show such restraint. Many stories became tainted by atrocity propaganda often created by governments. The French, for example, were masters of faking photographs to "prove" atrocities had occurred. For the first time in warfare, propaganda spread across the world in a very short time because of instantaneous communication via the telegraph and telephone complemented by a high literacy rate and a healthy supply of newspapers.[71]

Not all Americans believed the atrocity stories. When James O'Donnell Bennet and four other American journalists investigated them, they visited a dozen Belgian towns in which they interviewed locals yet found no proof of one unjustifiable civilian death. Nor did they personally witness any atrocities, leading them to conclude none had occurred. The American consul at Aachen, Robert J. Thompson, wrote a report for the Associated Press in which he defended Germany's actions, seeing them as necessary because it found itself besieged by the Russians on one side and the French on the other. He dismissed stories of Germans cutting the hands off of babies and the amputation of a nurse's breast as well as tales of Belgians mutilating German soldiers. He found no evidence of wrongdoing. But because his report had defied Wilson's order that government officials stay neutral, the State Department dismissed him on November 5, 1914.[72]

The Belgian government asked American journalist E. Alexander Powell, who had arrived in the country in mid–August, to look into the stories. Powell, born in Syracuse, New York, was certainly a credible investigator. A soldier, diplomat, lecturer, and explorer, he had traveled all around the world. In 1909, the "Department of Agriculture sent him to Central Asia on a special mission, and later that year he" toured a variety of places around the world including Mexico, the Caucasus, and Sudan for *Everybody's Magazine.* During the war he wrote primarily for the London's *Daily Mail* and *Scribner's Magazine.* When the United States entered the war, he joined the U.S. Army and rose to the rank of colonel during his time on the front.[73]

The Belgian government loaned Powell a car and provided him with Marcel Roos for his driver, a grenadier who had given his own automobile to the Belgian army and was perfect for this venture because he could speak English, German, French, and Flemish. About him Powell recalled, "He was as big and loyal and good-natured as a St. Bernard dog ... [and] incidentally, he was the most successful forager that I have ever seen." After three weeks of traveling throughout Belgium tracking down reports of atrocities, the Germans contacted van Hee in Ghent to see if he would ask Powell if he would like to write about their side of the story. To this Powell agreed. General Hans Matthias von Boehn, commander of German Imperial Army's Ninth Corps and the official German "mouthpiece," arranged a meeting.[74]

For this Powell brought with him both van Hee and the eccentric American photographer Donald Thompson. While on their way out of Ghent, they came across two horse-mounted Germans who had strayed into the city and were being accosted by angry citizens.

The Americans' car had a siren, so Powell blasted it to open the lane. Van Hee told the Germans to jump in, hide their rifles, and take off their helmets. He said to the crowd: "I am the American Consul! These men are under my protection! You are civilians, attacking German soldiers in uniform. If they are harmed your city will be burned about your ears." One Belgian ignored this, jumped on the running board and pointed a pistol at the head of one of the Germans. Thompson wacked him away as Powell moved the car forward, knocking the potential assassin off.[75]

They drove at a high speed for five hours to meet Boehn at his headquarters. Along the way they passed into the midst of three columns of marching German soldiers, each issued with an incredibly detailed map of Belgium. The columns had with them "five gigantic howitzers, each drawn by 16 pairs of horses…. [These weapons] could tear a city to pieces at a distance of a dozen miles."[76]

After dinner with Boehn, Powell began his interview. He told the general that during his travels around Belgium, he had seen firsthand what the German army had done to the town of Aarschot, which he described as "a ghastly, blackened, blood-stained ruin." The town had stood between the advancing German army and Brussels. Upon reaching it on August 19, the Germans encountered well-entrenched Belgian soldiers who mowed their enemy down with machine guns. Although outnumbered about ten to one, the Belgians managed to hold out for two days despite heavy losses, and retreated in good order when the Germans began hitting them with artillery aimed with the help of airplanes.[77]

The Germans accused an Aarschot priest of firing a shot from the church's tower. He denied it, pointing out that many notices posted ordering the people not to molest the incoming soldiers had gone up. Keen on picking a fight with the civilian population and probably wanting a bit of retribution for the losses they had suffered taking the town, the Germans rounded up about 200 men—some of them invalids—as hostages until the townsfolk turned over all their firearms. When one person handed in a gun used for pigeon shooting, the Germans released their hostages. That night they herded the entire population out of town. After a night of looting, they spent the next three days destroying the town.[78]

They burned 386 houses, looted another 1,000, and killed around 150 people. Even the town's church, Notre Dame, did not escape damage: at first used to imprison the townspeople, the Germans soon destroyed much of it. A *New York Times* article reported, "[It] is partly burned, its floors are stained, its images bespattered with blood, and its altars befouled." So why, Powell asked Boehn, had the Germans done this? The general replied, "When we entered … [,] the son of the burgomaster came into the room, drew a revolver, and assassinated my chief of staff…. What followed was only retribution. The townspeople only got what they deserved." According to witnesses later interviewed by a sometimes dubious British investigation known as the Bryce Committee, the Germans knew the shots had probably come from the rifles of drunken German soldiers, but they nonetheless executed the burgomaster as well as his brother and son for it.[79]

Powell pushed Boehn: why had German soldiers taken out their wrath on women and children? The general denied this. Powell countered by saying he had seen their mutilated bodies, as had Hugh Gibson. Boehn dismissed this as an unfortunate consequence of war. Powell persisted, throwing in things that he probably did not witness but said to provoke the general: "But how about a woman's body I saw, with her hands and feet cut off? How about a white-haired man and his son whom I helped bury outside Sempstad, who had been killed merely because a retreating Belgian had shot a German outside their house? There were 22 bayonet wounds on the old man's face. I counted them. How about the little girl two years old who was shot while in her mother's arms by a[n] uhlan, and whose funeral I attended…. How about the old man who was hung from the rafters in his house by his hands and roasted to death by a bonfire being built under him?" While "taken aback," Boehn nonetheless insisted soldiers sometimes did such things without the knowledge of their officers. Indeed, he had personally sentenced two men to 12 years of penal service for assaulting women in Louvain, a city that would become the symbol of senseless German destruction.[80]

In 1425, Pope Martin V issued a paper bull establishing the University of Louvain here. It became a center of Renaissance learning, prospering until its closure in 1797 due to the French Revolution. Abandoned, it lay fallow until the University of Malines took over its grounds and buildings on December 1, 1835, at which point it became the Catholic University of Louvain since most of its funds came from a Belgian Catholic charity. The university's treasured library had its origins in 1627 when a former student, Laurentius Beyerlinck, gave the university 852 of his own books. Eight years later it received an additional 902 volumes from the university's professor of medicine, Jacques Romanus. These books served as the library's core, which officially opened on August 22, 1636.[81]

In 1914, the library housed "over 211,000 volumes" and contained manuscripts that dated as far back as the ninth century, including "a series of [handwritten] sermons by Thomas à Kempis," an important fifteenth century theologian who probably wrote the influential book (at least for theologians) *De Imitatio Christi* (*Imitation of Christ*). The library resided in the Old Guild Hall for cloth makers built between 1317 and 1345. Its collections became an important place for historians of Western Europe because of its rare books, including the priceless *Chronicle of Utrecht* and *Life of Charles V*.[82]

The Germans attacked and invaded Louvain on August 19 as part of their struggle for Aarschot. For six days they did nothing more than occupy it. That changed on August 25 when machine gun fire erupted in two places that resulted in wounded German soldiers. The shots probably came from the Germans themselves, but the paranoia over *franc-tireurs* and the anger that the Belgian army had the temerity to not only defy the German army but to inflict heavy casualties upon it led the soldiers to believe Belgian civilians had done this. One anonymous eyewitness later said drunken German soldiers had fired the shots at cows. Another stated that a captain in the military police burst into the house from which he thought the shots had come and burned it down using kerosene. This same witness alleged the Germans took 88 men out of town and shot them in retaliation.[83]

When the Germans decided to burn the library, they were unable to breach its doors, so they broke its main window and threw into it some sort of accelerant. The contents of old books, manuscripts and other documents made the perfect kindling. The fire reached the library's roof at 1:45 in the morning on August 26 and consumed the entire building by 2:15. The destruction of Louvain in general and the loss of its great library in particular gave the Allies the perfect propaganda tool to further their message about German barbarism.[84]

Someone in Berlin, aware of this, issued a diplomatic dispatch claiming several of Louvain's priests had armed civilians who used these weapons to fire upon and wound German soldiers. The Berlin dispatch denied the German army had burned or pillaged any-

The University of Louvain's library, destroyed by the Germans on August 25-26, 1914. Library of Congress Prints and Photographs Division. Red Cross Photograph Collection.

thing. When Powell asked Boehn about the destruction of the library, pointing out the importance of its contents, he simply said that he "regretted" it. He denied having purposely burned it down, asserting that when fire from nearby houses got there, they could not put the resulting conflagration out. But why give the order to burn the city in the first place? This question angered Boehn, causing him to pound the table and say, "Whenever civilians fire upon our troops we will teach them a lasting lesson. If women and children insist on getting in the way of bullets, so much the worse for the women and children."[85]

The Germans played up the "agent provocateur" priest story by taking some of them hostage, including one American, Monsignor Jules de Becker, president of the seminary at the American College. Belgian by birth and a canon lawyer by training, he had become rector of the college in 1898 and, in 1911, arranged for its integration into the University of Louvain. The Germans initially ejected him from the city, then arrested him when he reached Tervuren.[86]

One of the priests taken prisoner, a young Jesuit named Father Eugène Dupiéreux, had on his person a note he had written criticizing the burning of the Louvain library by comparing it an apocryphal story alleging that Caliph Umar I destroyed the Library of Alexandria and while doing so said if the Greek books within agreed with the Word of God, no one needed them, and if they contradicted it, they should be destroyed. Enraged by the comparison, the Germans decided to shoot Dupiéreux. Refusing him Last Rites, they forced 26 other priests, Becker and, unbeknownst to the Germans, Dupiéreux's own brother, among them, to watch.[87]

The Germans took Becker and the other priests in "a filthy cart" to Brussels as hostages. Whitlock and Villalobar, worried because a number of them were American and Spanish, tried to meet with the chief of staff of the Fourth Army, General Walther von Lüttwitz, to demand their release, but he refused to see them. Undaunted, they sent him their cards and waited. Eventually Major Hans von Herwaerts, once a military attaché in Washington, received them. He brought their concerns to General Lüttwitz behind closed doors, then returned to inform the ministers he would send orders to have the priests released immediately. To his surprise, when Becker returned to Louvain, he found the American College still intact.[88]

Gibson and his friend Daniel Lynds Blount, an American businessman, decided to personally inspect the American College. Before departing in Blount's car, the chargés affaires of the Swedish and Mexican legations asked to come along. As the four approached Louvain, cinders and heat from burning buildings forced them to put on goggles. Some houses still smoldered while others were blackened ruins. Bodies and horses littered the streets, as did other detritus, including "hats and wooden shoes, German helmets, swords and saddles, bottles, and all sorts of bundles." They parked at a train station used for freight.[89]

The German soldiers they spoke to, some of them drunk, insisted the whole thing began when civilians opened fire on them. One German lieutenant claimed an uprising of civilians had occurred in coordination with some British cavalrymen, the latter of whom killed 500 men when it fired two machine guns into two departing German regiments. This fantastic tale Blount did not believe. After interviewing eyewitnesses, he came to the conclusion that nervous German soldiers mistook one another for French ones and fired upon at each other in the town center's public square. This they blamed on civilians.[90]

Walking around, the visitors saw soldiers looting houses into which they piled furniture and combustibles to make these mostly stone houses burn. Gibson pointed out to one soldier that looting violated The Hague Convention, but the fellow did not care; he thought these "dogs" needed to learn to respect the superior Germans. Other soldiers echoed this sentiment. Here and there shots rang out. Upon returning to the freight station, their escort, a German lieutenant, offered them some champagne to calm their nerves. The sound of the popping cork appeared to have prompted someone to fire shots in return. Soon a firefight broke out. Gibson thought it had come from civilians in a nearby house, but more likely was Belgian soldiers. The lieutenant told them to take cover behind a platform. Beside them stood nervous horses stomping and kicking, which they feared would trample them. The skirmish lasted for about two hours. Because Blount's car stood on the line of fire, Gibson figured it would not survive the fight, but fortunately it did, taking them back to Brussels.[91]

After securing Louvain, or at least its remains, the Germans restored its train service, which brought with it battlefield tourists who wanted to see the death and destruction for themselves. People from all across the country not under German control came to see, many of them from Brussels. The Germans did not object, possibly because it would help spread the word of what happened to those who resisted.[92]

A merchant from Amsterdam who visited Liège as a disaster tourist regretted it: "I never want to set my foot upon another battlefield ... and I hope to God that there will never be another battlefield any place on the globe again!" He saw a boy gunned down by the Germans, then run over by an artillery piece. This because he had supposedly shot at them from his house. The boy survived, but the merchant gave him no aid, excusing his lack of humanity by claiming he had gone into shock. He also observed a field strewn with dead soldiers from both sides, bayonets having killed many. He told reporter Mary Boyle O'Reilly of *Day Book*: "I have been into hell—not of fire, but of macerated flesh and gore, of lingering agony and ghastly death. The flames of hell would seem pure, swift and sweet by comparison!"[93]

Fortunately, not all civilians had come to Belgium for such a gruesome purpose. The *Chicago Herald* sponsored an American venture headed by Rev. John B. de Ville to find Belgians with close relations in the United States and Canada with whom they could stay with for the duration of the war. Carrying several lists from the State Department, they arrived on August 31, heading first to the Brussels region where they found Anna, a beautiful Flemish woman affianced to Henry Fin of Chicago. Not everyone returned to North America with them. The son of Mr. Jansen of Chicago could not because the German military had conscripted him and refused to release him from service. A daughter whose American mother in Chicago wanted her brought home would not go because her grandparents refused to accompany her.[94]

The searchers spread across the nation, their investigation often frustrated by a lack of forwarding addresses. Although the Germans offered their aid, the Americans nonetheless had trouble getting into contested areas. De Ville, who in three months had personally traveled to "about fifty towns and hamlets," considered this a good start but figured it would probably take about a year to check everywhere. The Germans helped departing Belgians reach Rotterdam from which they boarded ships to North America. At this time de Ville and his group had already managed to get 315 people of all ages out of Belgium.[95]

Atrocities

The events at Louvain and elsewhere in Belgium and France did not help to improve American opinion of Germany, already soured because of its support of the Austro-Hungarian determination to punish Serbia and its invasion of neutral Belgium. Just four months into the war, many in the United States blamed Germany for starting it. In a letter to the editor of the *Nation*, a leftwing journal of opinion and news, Professor Paul Darmstaedter of Gottingen refuted this perception by pointing out what he considered the true causes of the war.[96]

He asserted that while it had begun because of Austria-Hungary's declaration of war on Serbia, this had served merely as a spark to ignite deeper tensions fueled by imperialist expansion. Germany had had nothing to do with the most recent imperial wars, the Boer and Russo-Japanese, neither of which benefited it and both of which involved Allied powers. Darmstaedter insisted that Germany had sought peace rather than war.[97]

Yet, despite what he wanted readers to believe, in the last nine years German actions had nearly sparked a war between it and France twice. The first occasion occurred when the Kaiser landed in Tangier on March 31, 1905, and there declared, "In an independent country such as Morocco, commerce must be free. I will do my best to maintain its political and economic equity." Translated from diplomatic speak, he had just told the French, who desired to make Morocco a colony, to keep its hands off or Germany might just interfere.[98]

He had decided upon this course of action when his minister in Tangier informed him Morocco's sultan did not seem keen on allowing the French to come into his country as the exclusive providers of economic development and reform. The Kaiser wanted, among other things, access to Morocco's reserve of iron ore, so he invoked a clause in the 1880 Treaty of Madrid that gave Germany the option of becoming a consultant whenever the status of a nation might change. The German government called for an international conference.[99]

Held in Algeciras, Spain, from mid–January to March 1906, it did not go as Germany had hoped. After six weeks, the talks stalled over the right of the French police to control Moroccan ports, something the Kaiser opposed because he feared they would use this power to keep German traders out of the interior. The British sided with the French, the Austro-Hungarians with the Germans. The sides asked a reluctant President Theodore Roosevelt to come to the negotiations as a mediator. Under his guidance, Germany got nothing it wanted. The French maintained their economic dominance. A joint force of Franco-Spanish officers that oversaw the Moroccan police remained in place. This crisis prompted Britain, France, and Russia to form the Triple Entente, one of the key ingredients for making the war between Austria-Hungary and Serbia into a worldwide affair.[100]

Two years later the Germans triggered a second crisis. In May 1911, French troops occupied the Moroccan city of Fes to help the sultan stamp out a revolt. Realizing this action likely served as a precursor for a French takeover of the kingdom and wanting to get some concessions, the Germans sent the warship *Panther* into the Moroccan port of Agadir on July 1 to provoke new negotiations, a ploy that worked.[101]

On June 27, German negotiators asked for control of the colonies of Gabon and the French Congo to balance France's plans to make Morocco a protectorate. The French agreed, giving up some of their African territory which Germany integrated into its colony of Kamerun. It withdrew the *Panther*. France formally made Morocco a protectorate in 1912. Germany's slice of the French Congo amounted to little, making the Germans feel humiliated. Darmstaedter spun these two losses with the claim that "Germany [had] renounced Morocco for the preservation of peace."[102]

As for the current war, he accused Russia of entering it to fulfill its goal of conquering Constantinople to give it unhindered access to the Mediterranean as well as creating a unified Slav state. France wanted to regain Alsace-Lorraine, territory it had lost in the Franco-Prussian War. True enough: Russia and France *did* have those war aims, although Darmstaedter probably did not know that the Schlieffen Plan had counted on the French desire to retake Alsace-Lorraine to lure its troops into a trap there.[103]

Darmstaedter justified German atrocities with a favorite trope used by German army officers: "The Belgians behaved like beasts and murdered and mutilated our brave soldiers in a treacherous way." Although false, Darmstaedter had nonetheless hit upon a grain of truth about the Belgians: some did have a record of committing atrocities, except instead of doing so against Germans, they, or least their proxies, had persecuted Africans in the Belgian Congo. Set up as the Congo Free State on August 1, 1885, under the pretext of stamping out slavery, the colony belonged solely to the Belgian king, Leopold II. He planned to use it to enrich his personal fortune, an idea that not only failed to ripen, it rotted on the vine, forcing him to spend vast amounts of his own money prop it up. No longer able to afford it, in 1891 and 1892 he implemented the infamous domain system, which confiscated all land the native population did not actively cultivate, forbade them from carrying out trade, and forced their men to pay taxes in the form of slave labor to the powerful companies that ran the colony's great plantations and other industries.[104]

The Congolese worked so much they had no time to grow food, causing rampant malnutrition that resulted in outbreaks of disease and famine. Some Congolese rose up in armed resistance, while others fled to areas in which authorities exerted little control. Companies sent gangs of men to take procure the workers owed to them from villages, using killing, flogging, maiming, and hostage-taking to force compliance. All this resulted in the depopulation of entire regions. One Belgian scholar estimated the entire native population dropped 40 percent between 1880 and 1920.[105]

Leopold and his partners in crime could not keep what they did here hidden forever. Two African Americans, George Washington Williams and Rev. William Henry Sheppard, publicized much of what was going on, as did Roger Casement, the British consul who worked in the Congolese port of Boma. This sparked a campaign for reform that attracted both the average and the famous, the latter including Mark Twain and Arthur Conan Doyle. King Leopold denied what he could, pled ignorance, and complained he could not control all that went on there. To salvage the colony's reputation, he launched a massive public relations campaign in the United States. By the time he died in 1909, Belgian officials admitted to atrocities, then claimed to have made improvements while doing no such thing.[106]

Darmstaedter pointed out that Allies had committed their own war atrocities. The Russians, for example, had done so in German East Prussia, yet this had not garnered the same attention. While inconsistent in their treatment of Germans there, the Russians had behaved badly. Fighting destroyed houses and fields, leaving the remaining harvest to rot away or become food for the Russian occupiers. Artillery pockmarked the land and destroyed countless buildings wherever battles raged. On August 30, 1914, the Russians began a three week occupation of Tilsit during which time they enacted a curfew, took hostages, and demanded a payment of 40,000 marks.[107]

When the Germans arrived to push them out on September 13, a Mormon missionary from America, Edward C. Hunter, found himself in the thick of it. While practicing a song for the upcoming Sunday service, he looked out the window and saw a cannon battle going on. As evening approached, the Russians, many badly wounded, began to retreat. An hour later the Germans marched down the streets. A crowd of civilians rushed out to greet them "with bread, beer, cigars, flowers and all kinds of fruit." Then came the crack of rifle fire. Bullets whizzed past, hitting the wall above Hunter's head. The German soldiers ordered the civilians to get off the street. A bloody firestorm between Russians who had stayed behind and the Germans erupted. The fighting continued until noon the next day. Hunter combed over the battlefield, taking a pistol from the hand of a dead soldier as a souvenir.[108]

3

Into the War Zone

A Road Trip to Antwerp

On Sunday, August 23, Hugh Gibson and Daniel Blount began what amounted to an exceptionally dangerous road trip to Antwerp where Gibson hoped to send telegrams to Washington. Armed with a pass from General Jarotsky and a letter from Burgomaster Max that gave them permission to go through German and Belgian lines, they took the legation's car. Gibson bought with him driving goggles, a wrist watch, and a teddy bear he tied to the radiator as a sort of mascot. He placed signs in French and German on the car's front and back proclaiming that it belonged to the American legation.[1]

On their way to Vilvorde—a city along the Seine infamous for being the place where the English arranged to have William Tyndale imprisoned for a year and a half, then executed for illegally translating the Bible into English—they were stopped by a mounted German officer and his staff. At first angry, upon realizing the men in the car had come from the American legation, they became far more cordial. Gibson showed them his pass and they let them go, advising them to avoid bullets and other dangerous flying objects. As they approached Malines, Belgian peasants warned them to go no farther because fighting had broken out ahead. Undaunted, they continued.[2]

As they passed through Eppegem, an officer in charge of cavalry escorting two carts of civilian prisoners being used as human shields halted them. He cared little about the Americans' diplomatic status, pointed his gun at Blount's head a couple of times, and initially refused to honor their passes. About this incident Gibson wrote in his diary: "I was glad to get out of his range, for I verily believe that if somebody has shouted *boo!* he would have let that gun off with a bang."[3]

In Malines a Belgian flag flew atop the town's cathedral. The fighting had ended with little damage done. This would not last. Two days later the Belgian army launched a sortie out of Antwerp to attack German trenches in an effort to help take pressure off of French forces between Malines and Brussels. The Belgians leveled part of the town in order to give their fort a clearer shot at the Germans. Later fighting would result in the destruction of 1,500 houses. In the country beyond came the contested area between German and Belgian lines where the Belgians had laced some of the roads with landmines, which were probably artillery shells armed with special fuses. To allow traffic to get through until the Germans arrived, they marked them with red flags.[4]

While passing a small house, someone stopped Gibson and Blount to ask if they could take a wounded man to Antwerp, now about 12 kilometers away. To this they agreed, and once in the city they dropped him off at a military hospital. They tried to get a room at the

Hôtel St. Antoine only to be refused by the proprietor because he believed they were German spies with forged papers. Fortunately a British diplomat staying there knew Gibson and verified his identity, easing the proprietor's mind. Gibson sent his telegraphs, then went to the Grand-Hôtel near the central railroad station to meet with the king's Council of Ministers to whom he reported all he could about German activities in Brussels as well as the overall conditions there.[5]

Gibson and Blount stayed in the city for several days. Early in the morning on August 25, powerful explosions woke them, one of which nearly rocked them out of their beds. They figured the Germans had starting firing artillery at the forts surrounding the city, but E. Alexander Powell, also staying in the hotel, knew better. Just a few minutes earlier the chime from a nearby cathedral clock had woken him. The sound of "a million bumblebees" outside caught his attention, so he went to the window through which he saw a cigar-shaped black object sailing through the sky that turned out to be a German zeppelin.[6]

It dropped bombs, ten by Powell's count and eight by Gibson's. Morning revealed the destruction these had wrought. About 200 yards from the hotel a bomb had fallen onto the stock exchange that disintegrated its top three floors and blew out all the windows of nearby structures. Shrapnel from the destroyed buildings left those still standing with pock-marked facades. Another bomb had hit the Poids Public (the public weight house), leaving a hole large enough for a horse to walk through. This blast had killed a nearby policeman and blew the legs off another. Six others sleeping in a nearby house died as well, with one women being blown into pieces, and at least a dozen more suffering wounds.[7]

Powell reported that this bombing was the first attack from the air ever to occur. This is incorrect. This event had happened on August 6 when an L6 German zeppelin flying out of Cologne dropped its deadly cargo on Liège. To counter the effectiveness of airships, Antwerp's authorities ordered all the city's lights doused at eight each night as well as the silencing of the cathedral clock. Big guns lined the streets and searchlights brightened the sky. No more bombs fell here before Gibson and Blount's return to Brussels on the 27th.[8]

The Belgians protested the attack, asserting it violated one of the Fourth Hague Convention's articles of war. Otto Wislecenus, a reservist in the German Engineering Corps in America at the time, placed the blame for the attack on the Belgian king. Since he was a legitimate target of war, he should never have gone into Antwerp because his presence endangered it, a reasonable point. The Germans *had* targeted the royal palace, although their bombs only struck its grounds. Wislecenus also took the Belgian army to task: it should have stored ammunition and food in its outlying forts rather than in the city center.[9]

The zeppelin had a limited usefulness as a weapon of war despite the fact the man who had invented it, Count Ferdinand von Zeppelin, dedicated much of his life and fortune to develop it as one. Born in 1838 near Friedrichshafen, he first took to the air in an observation balloon during the U.S. Civil War in his capacity as a military observer for the Prussian army. A few years later he participated in the Franco-Prussian War and during the siege of Paris saw Parisians using hot air balloons to escape the city with communications.[10]

While still an active officer, Zeppelin tried to get the German army interested in this new air technology, but no one paid much attention. In 1890 at the age of 52 he was forced to retire after receiving a failing grade for his part in joint maneuvers. The next year he began investing in the creation of a dirigible, different from the hot air balloon in that it had a supporting frame, which Zeppelin built using aluminum, an idea first developed by an Austro-Croatian inventor named David Schwarz. To create the power needed to propel it through the sky, Zeppelin used an internal combustion engine.[11]

The dirigible's frame ensured it retained its shape no matter what pressure its air bags contained. Schwartz tried to make his dirigible float with hydrogen-filled goldbeater's skin, which is made out of cattle bladders, but too much hydrogen leaked from these for them to work effectively. Zeppelin's use of treated silk overcame this issue, though he had his own problems, chief among them steering. His first four prototypes were either scrapped or destroyed by accidents. The fourth, for example, blew up when sparks from static electricity ignited its hydrogen gas. It would take a few more years to overcome all these troubles, though he solved them before the outbreak of World War I.[12]

The Germans used zeppelins as a terror weapon rather than a practical way of winning battles. They dropped bombs on the United Kingdom in an effort to demoralize and terrorize its civilian population. Being difficult to see at night, airplane pilots had trouble finding them. And even when they did, they could not shoot them down because their bullets poked holes through the zeppelins' air bladders but failed to ignite the volatile hydrogen within. They tried incendiary bullets, but these, too, did not work because the airbags contained no oxygen. The British developed an explosive bullet capable of blowing holes large enough in the bags to allow sufficient amounts of oxygen for combustion, but this failed to work as well. It was only when pilots starting alternating the two types of rounds did zeppelins start going down in flames.[13]

No doubt the Germans would have switched to inert helium to counter this had they possessed the means to extract it in sufficient quantities. Although science had verified the existence of this element in 1868, it was not until two chemistry professors, David F. McFarland and Hamilton Perkins Cady at the University of Kansas, found it in natural gas that it was thought to be potentially useful. It took university researchers until 1917 to figure out how to extract it. Because the only known natural gas reserves in the world were in America's central plains, the United States retained a monopoly on its production long enough to keep it out of the hands of the Nazis. Had the Germans possessed it, the *Hindenburg* disaster may well never have happened.[14]

The Germans armed their zeppelins with machine guns to fend off attacking airplanes, then retrofitted them to fly at exceptionally high altitudes to avoid detection, sometimes over 16,000 feet. At these heights the crew had to use oxygen masks to avoid falling unconscious. The noise of the engines made it impossible for them to hear one another, so they relied on hand singles for communication. Pilots navigated using landmarks, explaining why one zeppelin bombardier thought he had dropped his load on London only to later learn it had fallen some 60 miles southeast on the Royal Military Canal.[15]

Germany Advances

American journalist Arthur Ruhl, writing for *Collier's Weekly*, traveled to the French commune of Crépy-en-Valois and here he stayed in the Hôtel de la Banniere along the railroad. Within two weeks, its coffee room and small bar filled with English soldiers retreating from the Battle of Mons. Following them were Germans expecting to take Paris in just days. They returned a few weeks later during their retreat from the Marne, taking the time to burn and loot a house from which the owners had fled, then demand 100,000 francs from the town. Ruhl thought it ironic they executed this barbarity in such a disciplined and polite manner.[16]

He had begun his coverage of the war in Ostend, at the time considered Belgium's second seaport because of its high Channel traffic to and from London as well as its fine beach that attracted about 40,000 visitors a year. Ruhl found the railway station nearly abandoned. The trains had no set schedule and at first appeared to not move at all. Finally one did with the promise of going to Bruges and possibly as far as Ghent. This he took.[17]

He arrived in Ghent just after it had suffered from a panic caused by a rumor that the Germans would soon arrive, prompting some of its civil guards to throw their uniforms into the canal to avoid being shot by Germans who might mistake them for regular soldiers. Ghent, home of Jan van Eyck's famous altarpiece *The Adoration of the Lamb*, had a population of over 165,000. It was linked to the Scheldt River by a canal large enough to accommodate seagoing vessels.[18]

Ghent had a close connection with the United States because here American and British diplomats had signed the treaty that ended the War of 1812. With this history in mind, Major Louis L. Seaman, a reservist in the U.S. Medical Corps, and Ghent's burgomaster, Baron Émile Braun, penned a letter to President Wilson asking for aid. The letter incorrectly claimed the Treaty of Ghent included a clause committing the United States to protecting the city's treasures if threatened. Wilson ignored the plea, although Seaman got into trouble for violating Wilson's prohibition that active members of the army and navy "refrain from discussing the war."[19]

On September 8, Braun met with the German commander of an approaching force and begged him not to molest his city. The officer agreed to march around if Ghent disbanded its civil guard and provided a number of supplies, including benzene, mineral water, oats, bandages, and 100,000 cigars. This tentative peace nearly collapsed. About an hour after establishing it, a pair of German officers looking for medical supplies became lost and wound up in the city. A Belgian armored car carrying three men and a machine gun saw them and opened fire, unaware of the burgomaster's agreement. The Germans tried to escape, but the Belgian driver, William van Calck, rammed the Germans' car, stopping it. Luckily this incident occurred right outside the American Consulate, allowing its vice-consul, Julius van Hee, to witness the whole thing. He immediately placed the survivor under his protection, asserting this man would not become a prisoner of war. He tracked down Braun and insisted he go with him to explain the situation to the Germans. At first Braun refused, fearing the Germans would make him a hostage, but in the end he went to smooth things over.[20]

Boehn was furious and threatened to destroy Ghent. Van Hee pointed out America had a long association with the city and ruining it would surely sour American goodwill for Germany. The general relented after securing a promise from van Hee that no more such incidents would occur. Van Hee also received permission to send wounded Belgians to Brussels.[21]

Born in South Bend, Indiana, on January 26, 1875, van Hee had come to Ghent in 1895 and there stayed for much of his diplomatic career. American journalist Horace Green described him as "a hair-trigger politician and live wire if there ever was [*sic*] one." The

German war machine did not intimidate him in the least. At his hotel, he warned, "If you send any spy prowling into my room, I'll take off my coat and proceed to throw him out of the window." When the German commandant refused to allow him to take three Belgian women through their lines, he took out a packet of captured German letters and dangled them before him, telling him if he did not get a pass, the Germans would not get the letters. The commandant gave in.[22]

A month later, the Germans threatened the city again. Two Red Cross nurses tending to 12 badly wounded Belgian soldiers at the Hotel de la Poste needed to get their charges out of the city but had no way of doing so. Just about every vehicle here had already left carrying the wounded, leaving doctors and stretcher-bearers with more wounded soldiers in the local military hospital. Because of his diplomatic status, van Hee still possessed his car and began using it to ferry them from the hotel and hospital to the railroad station from which most of them escaped on a train. The Germans broke through the Belgian defenses at Melle and occupied the Ghent on October 12, 1914.[23]

The city became the focal point of a German attempt at divide and conquer. Wanting to exacerbate existing tensions between the French and Flemish-speaking parts of the Belgium, the governor-general reopened the University of Ghent on December 31, 1915, as a purely Flemish institution with classes taught in that language. To reinforce the idea, he placed a German in charge and brought in some Dutch professors. Offers of generous scholarships and beer permits enticed few to sign up. In the 1916–1917 academic year it had a mere 138 students, all of whom would later have their degrees voided and be banned from returning.[24]

From Ghent, Ruhl headed to the still unoccupied city of Antwerp, arriving there on September 26. That night he "awoke to the steady clatter of hoofs on cobblestones and the rumble of wheels." Looking out the window, he saw the Belgian army retreating across the Scheldt followed by civilians loaded with what worldly goods they could carry. At the time of the war's outbreak, no bridges crossed the river in Antwerp itself, but knowing they might need them during a crisis, the Belgian army had enough materials on hand to quickly build four. The bridges could only handle so much traffic, forcing many to cross the river using ferries. When a rumor that two of these planned to head to Ostend, 40,000 people gathered at the quay hoping to board. It turned out to be untrue. Others caught rides on a dozen to 15 tugboats heading to the Netherlands. Belgian soldiers who made their way to that country found themselves interred for the rest the war. The army would destroy the bridges after their usefulness ended to keep them out of enemy hands.[25]

The Belgian government had designated Antwerp the national redoubt during a time of war. It and the army planned to make their last stand here. A ring of forts surrounded the city, the farthest of which stood 15 miles away and the closest five. In preparation for the oncoming Germans, the Belgian army leveled Antwerp's suburbs, replacing them with wood spikes, landmines and mantraps consisting of buried barrels with their tops removed and replaced with collapsible camouflage. They cut down all the trees on either side of the roads coming into the city for several miles. Sandbags lined canal banks on city's southern side, while sappers placed dynamite on bridges and in viaducts for a quick destruction. Barbed wire covered the ground and machine gun nests stood ready.[26]

All this self-inflicted destruction was futile. The Germans never attempted to negotiate these obstacles. Instead they fired upon the forts with their long range guns. Once softened up, they quickly took the first and second ring, the latter falling on October 2. This same attack destroyed the city's waterworks as well as much of its southern portion. In addition to the shelling, German planes dropped bombs that, among other things, hit and ignited oil tanks that spat flames 20 to 30 feet high and spewed billows of black smoke at least 200 feet into the sky.[27]

The booming of artillery fire awoke Ruhl around midnight on the first night of the attack. Getting up, he headed to the street and there saw flashes and fire in the distance, although no shells came near his hotel. He along with several others headed towards the fighting outside the city. After stopping at a château serving as a field hospital, they drove on until shells began falling near them, one smashing through a house about 50 yards ahead.[28]

Returning to Antwerp, Ruhl walked back to his hotel through the deserted streets, hoping no shells fell upon his head, which had destroyed houses seemingly at random. Along the way he stopped at a couple of hospitals to give what aid he could. At his hotel, an American reporter, two American photographers, a British intelligence officer, and a Belgian family planned to take a boat to out of the city the next morning for fear of becoming prisoners of the Germans. This spooked Ruhl so much he decided to leave as well. In the morning, as he gathered up his luggage, the hotel shook from an explosive concussion.

"Evacuating Antwerp: British Marines and Belgian Soldiers on the Outskirts of Antwerp During the Evacuation of the City by the Allies." Library of Congress Prints and Photographs Division. Red Cross Photograph Collection.

At first he thought it had taken a direct hit, but it turned out the retreating Belgians had just blown one of their improvised bridges.[29]

Many in Antwerp complained bitterly to visiting journalists like Ruhl that the English had failed to show up with their promised help. This changed on October 3 when a force of 2,000 British infantrymen arrived under the direction of Winston Churchill. When it became apparent their presence would not be enough to stop the Germans, they retreated. Albert and his foreign minister left the city. Although Antwerp surrendered on October 9, some of the untaken inner forts continued to fight on to keep the Germans occupied in an effort to give the Belgian army time to escape and retreat to Ostend.[30]

Photographing the Fighting

None of the armies on the Western Front wanted anyone photographing or filming the fighting for fear it would destroy morale among the civilians at home. Those few allowed in the lines had to submit their images to the censors who decided which photographs the public could see. Few journalists defied this restriction for fear of losing their jobs or facing arrest. Getting uncensored images out of the war zone required much nerve and a good dollop of guile, two traits exhibited with much gusto by the American photographer and filmmaker Donald C. Thompson, the man who had accompanied Powell when he interviewed General Boehn.[31]

Born in Topeka, Kansas, probably on January 19, 1885, Thompson's appearance hid an ambition and audacity unmatched by few others. A mere five four in height with an average weight of about 120 pounds, he had a clean shaven face and a "sunflower smile." He showed an uncanny coolness when under fire. Even after suffering a major wound, he went right back to the fighting after recovering. Usually seen chewing or puffing on a cigar, when Powell first met him in Ostend, Thompson "blew into the [U.S.] Consulate ... wearing an American army shirt, a pair of British officer's riding-breeches, French puttees [a single length of cloth wrapped around each leg], and a Highlander's forage-cap, and carrying a camera the size of a parlor phonograph."[32]

Thompson had begun his career as a photojournalist in 1903 when he went to work for the Topeka newspaper *Capital*, supplementing his income with an occasional bit of fraud. In 1909, the Secret Service arrested him in Norfolk, Virginia, for impersonating two different army officers, Lieutenants D.C. Huffman and Earl McFarland, in whose names he had written a series of bad checks across the country. Thompson had posed as the latter in Los Angeles despite the fact the genuine man was stationed in the Philippines. When caught, he confessed to all, serving two years in Leavenworth for his crimes. Upon his release on June 6, 1911, authorities arrested him the moment he walked outside the prison gates, this time for fraud he had allegedly committed in Columbus, Ohio. Imprisonment did not deter him from trying it again. In 1923, he passed bad checks in the names of naval officers. During this crime spree, he even had the audacity to pose as Franklin D. Roosevelt.[33]

Thompson's experience as a confidence man would serve him well during his coverage of the war: he did not hesitate to lie, cheat or steal to get what he wanted. When the Germans offered him money to spy on their behalf, he took it, then claimed, "Their dastardly work

I did not do. The money I spent in cafés in many a capital in Europe.... I am only sorry they didn't give me more." When asked how many languages he spoke, he replied, "Three ... English, American and Yankee." His inability to speak any foreign tongues did not deter him from plunging alone into areas in which no one spoke English.[34]

He was living in Montreal and working for the newspaper *Cartier Centenary* when the war broke out. Gambling it would present a photographer like him the chance of a lifetime, he sold off all his possessions, pawned his watch, and used the proceeds to buy three large cameras plus a ticket on a steamship, leaving him with about $15. Knowing he would need credentials, he solicited his friend Sir Sam Hughes, the Canadian minister of the militia, for letter of introduction. Hughes, born in Ontario and descended from Ulster Orangemen (militant Irish Protestants who wanted Ireland to remain part of the United Kingdom), he would recruit about 40,000 army volunteers in the war's first two years, but later come under fire for his autocratic tendencies. He tried but failed to keep the Canadian Expeditionary Force independent from the British.[35]

Thompson brought to Europe with him both still and motion picture cameras. For the former, he always used Kodaks, possibly the Autographic model. For the latter, usually made out of wood in this era, he probably did not employ the common hand crank model but rather relied on one that used battery power. He arrived in Liverpool in August 1914 and from there made his way to London where he foolishly spent the remainder of his money by staying in the Savoy. Penniless, he nonetheless made his way to France with dubious credentials: a passport, his letter from Hughes, and card saying he belonged to the Benevolent and Protective Order of the Elks. Told he could go to the front as soon as permission to do so came through, after two days he gave up waiting and headed for Paris anyway. There he met with Ambassador Herrick and from him procured an introduction to French War Office. Those working there told him he could go to the front when the British War Office gave him permission. Realizing they would never allow a photographer there, he left for it anyway, pawning his last piece of jewelry to raise the funds.[36]

Here his skills as a con artist served him well, starting with his claim of being a captain in an unnamed branch of an unknown military service. French authorities arrested him a number of times, but his excuses usually secured his freedom. Once he told them he needed to get to the Belgian front to rescue his wife and children. One of the French officers who heard the tale, greatly moved, gave him a lift in his car. On another occasion, he presented his letter from Sir Hughes and said he needed to catch up with the Canadian Expeditionary Force, an interesting tale considering its first wave of soldiers did not sail until October 2 and would not arrive in Liverpool until October 14.[37]

He reached the front by taking a train as far as it would go, then walked the rest of the way. At Mons, the Belgian town at which the first battle the BEF fought on the European continent occurred, he embedded himself with a Highland regiment. For 18 hours he took photos and filmed them while under continuous German fire. He made his way to the French trenches and there met a lieutenant who had once arrested him. He put Thompson on a train for Amiens with guards to ensure he transferred to one in Boulogne that would go nonstop to the coast. Once there, Thompson was ordered to go straight to England.[38]

To escape his minders, he dove through an open window into a first class compartment reserved for a Russian countess who had decided to leave Paris and return to her homeland. Just outside of Boulogne, the train stopped to allow officials from Scotland Yard to search foreign passengers for contraband. Having had his film confiscated once before, he asked the countess to hide it on her person, gambling authorities would leave her alone. She said she would if he loaned her the 1,000 francs she needed to get home. He only had 250 on his person, so he handed these over, then said he would give her the rest in American money. Having an insufficient amount of this, he threw into the bargain all his coupons from the United Cigar Stores, a chain started in New York City owned by George J. Whelan. Known for banning the placement of Indian statues in front of his stores, within his establishments men could exchange coupons for items such as fishing rods and pipe cases for themselves and cut-glass dishes and silk stockings for wives or girlfriends.[39]

The police, mistaking Thompson for a spy, took him off the train and strip searched him in front of a gathering crowd. Finding nothing, they allowed him to get back on. In London, he found the Russian countess at her hotel. She not only gave him his precious film, she also returned his money and coupons. He sold his work to the *World* and *Daily Mail* for $5,000.[40]

He returned to the continent in October, this time landing in Ostend, where he met the American vice-consul. This official introduced him to Powell, who had secured a permit to embed himself with the Belgian army and who had a car he planned to take to Antwerp. Thompson talked his way into accompanying him despite the fact the Belgian army allowed no photographers. After arriving at their destination, Powell offhandedly remarked during a dinner that King Albert resided just a few doors down from their hotel at the Place de Meir. Thompson excused himself and headed there.[41]

Although a guard stood at its entrance, he just passed him by and, once inside, got into a strange argument with a servant in which he spoke in English and the other in French. The first secretary to the minister of foreign affairs came downstairs and asked in English what Thompson wanted. He desired to chronicle German atrocities on film, which would give the Belgians irrefutable proof of this. Ten hours later he met with the king himself and, although a bit shy at first considering only a few years earlier he has shucked corn in Kansas, he told his majesty what he wanted. The king agreed, handed him a *laissez-passer*, and said his people would help in any way possible.[42]

During the siege of Antwerp, Thompson appropriated an abandoned house at 74 rue de Peage and from it hung a large American flag. Several others, including a couple of journalists and the former Dutch vice-consul, stayed with him. Dubbing it "Thompson's Fort," he plundered the surrounding neighborhood for supplies. Fellow American journalist Horace Green stopped by and invited everyone to stay at the Queen's Hotel, which stood along the Scheldt, but the house's inhabitants decided to stay put. Half an hour after Green's departure, a white-faced Thompson and the others arrived at the hotel. A shell had destroyed the top two floors of their house and burned the rest down.[43]

Thompson sold his photos and films to a variety of newspapers, including the *World*, the *Chicago Tribune*, the *Illustrated London News*, and the *Daily Mail*. The owner of the last of these periodicals, Lord Northcliffe, hired Thompson to report from Germany. Northcliffe, whose full name amounted to quite the mouthful—Sir Alfred Charles William Harmsworth, 1st Viscount Northcliffe of St. Peter-in-Thanet and Baron Northcliffe of the Isle of Thanet—owned a number of newspapers but loved the *Daily Mail* the most, a paper he personally edited that had a daily circulation of 900,000 when the war broke out. Despite coming from noble stock and having many titles, he grew up impoverished (at least for an aristocrat), an experience that made him embrace the working class.[44]

He founded the *Daily Mail* on May 4, 1896, and with it transformed the newspaper industry with innovations such as heavy use of cables and the employment of popular writers. During the war he used his paper to affect British politics. With it he drove Lord Horatio Herbert Kitchener, the minster of war, out of office by critiquing his failure to keep the British army sufficiently stocked with shells and bullets, and forced the government to address the issue. Some found this criticism unpatriotic and burned copies of the paper in public as a protest.[45]

Going to Germany would be dangerous for Thompson because the Germans had posted notices to apprehend him out of the mistaken belief the British military had used his photos as a source of intelligence. Northcliffe had the fake Brooklyn newspaper, the *Daily Observer*, printed up that included an interview with Thompson in which he said nice things about the Germans. At the border, the Germans detained, beat and incarcerated him. When his jailors searched his person and found the clipping from the *Daily Observer* from his billfold, they let him go, a reprieve that did not last long. A German spy working at the *Daily Mail* informed his handlers of the deception. While at his hotel, a chambermaid warned Thompson that German authorities had come for him, so he departed by sliding down a fire escape. He promised a local girlfriend he would elope with her in exchange for her obtaining a passport made for him by her brother. Once safely across the border, he told her he did not love her after all.[46]

Next he went to Antwerp. The moment he got off his train, a German lieutenant arrested and took him to the German headquarters at City Hall. There this young officer admitted to having mistaken Thompson for an Englishman. Thompson received an apology. The commanding general asked him to lunch. To this he readily agreed. He told the general and several others at the meal that his wife lived in Ostend and he very much wanted to see her. They would happily motor him there. Knowing this might result in the discovery of his lie, he said he planned to stay in Antwerp for a few days before heading there. The Germans loaned him a motorcycle. Having never rode one before, he learned how to operate it on the fly, making a considerable bit of noise (and annoying the locals) while he figured it out. He went to Malines to retrieve a trunk he had left there during one of his earlier trips. All the villages between it and Brussels were "in ruins" with the dead still lying in fields.[47]

Upon his return to Antwerp, he asked for permission to head to the coast, where he heard fighting had broken out. Refused, he dug out a letter from the vice-consul in Ostend and pretended he needed to deliver it to him as a special American envoy. Still using the motorcycle, he made his way to Bruges, showing his American passport when necessary. In Dixmude, "a quiet little town on the Yser" the Germans had taken, lost to the Belgians, then reoccupied, he convinced a German captain that he had personal permission from the Kaiser to photograph German troops. He embedded with a detachment of soldiers heading north.[48]

He arrived just in time for the Battle of the Yser, itself a small part of what would become known as the Race for the Sea, the last great maneuver of the war on the Western Front before the stalemate. Having lost their opportunity to take Paris in a quick swoop, the Germans now made a desperate attempt to outflank French, Belgian, and British forces by heading around them to the north. To slow them down, King Albert ordered the dike gates opened in Nieuport to flood the lands to the south with seawater so as to create a natural barrier between the Germans and Belgians. The gates stayed open between October 28 to 31.[49]

The Germans countered by opening other dikes. Not only did both sides have to contend with marshy territory, a northern gale had brought with it mist, rain and fog that prevented British battleships from getting close enough to shore to shell German forces along the coast. Across the Yser itself, both sides dug in and began flinging artillery shells at one another at close range. The fighting resulted in untold carnage. One journalist reported, "Nieuport and Dixmude are literally cities of the dead.... Shells have battered down the walls and buildings and all that either the Germans and allies may hold in occupying either post is a pile of shattered[,] crumbling ruins."[50]

At the coast, Thompson joined the Germans in trenches dug out of the sand into which enemy batteries and British battleships fired. He made himself a sort of cave away from the main line for added protection. At some point the Germans retreated using underground passages without Thompson realizing it. He became lost in the maze of them and did not emerge until night. Trenches along the coast such as these became the northernmost part of a system that would stretch south all the way to the Swiss border. After the Race for the Sea ended, King Albert, never captured, retired to the village of La Panne, one of the few remaining parcels of Belgium soil under his control.[51]

Thompson returned to Dixmude. While dining with General Boehn and some of his officers here, a British shell hit the house in which they ate. Two inhabitants died instantly and another later succumbed to his wounds. Wooden splinters pierced Thompson's back and nose while other flying debris bruised his body. He awoke in a field hospital alongside wounded Germans, then returned to Antwerp in an ammunition cart. He thought he had lost his nose because he could not feel it, but it remained. He went to London to recuperate, then returned to America in mid–November, arriving in Topeka in January 1915. Here he showed about 1,000 feet of his film at the Novelty Theater.[52]

He received an invitation from Robert R. McCormick, publisher of the *Chicago Tribune* as well as one of its war correspondents, to cover the Russian front after its government invited him to do so. McCormick also owned the *New York Daily News* and *Washington Times-Herald*, but of these papers, the *Tribune*, started in 1847, did the best. It reached a circulation of 410,000 in 1918, an impressive feat considering McCormick did not get into the newspaper business until 1910 when he and partner, Joseph Medill Patterson, took it over rather than allow a rival to buy it out. McCormick and Thompson headed for Russia in February 1915.[53]

One of the fiercest battles these two men covered was at the Austro-Hungarian fortress city of Przemysl. It was located in the province of the largely unindustrialized Galicia, an area that had once belonged to the kingdom of Poland before it ceased to exist after Russia, Prussia, and the Austrian Empire carved that nation up for themselves between 1772 and 1795. The Russians had to take Przemysl if they wanted to successfully invade Austria-Hungary, and to that end attacked it on September 26, 1914. Capturing it on October 10, they abandoned it several weeks later. Undaunted, they returned and began a siege at the beginning of November.[54]

This city of 50,000, founded in the eighth century and inhabited mainly by ethnic Poles, stood along the river San and served as the seats for both Roman Catholic and Greek Orthodox bishops. On November 4, the Austro-Hungarian army garrison ejected the city's

Przemysl forts after their destruction. Bain News Service. Taken between 1914 and 1915. Library of Congress Prints and Photographs Division.

civilian population, although many returned for lack of anywhere else to go, leaving the city with about 18,000 civilians and 127,000 soldiers. The Russians laid siege for six months, attacking from all sides and shooting down any planes attempting to bring in supplies. Not an animal save for the horses that belonged to army officers remained in sight.[55]

The Austrians reluctantly surrendered on March 22, 1915, only doing so when their garrison threatened to mutiny because its men had grown tired of starving and suffering from disease. The Russians offered generous terms: officers received parole, enlisted men would not be sent to Siberia, the wounded could return to Austria, and civilians could either stay or go as they pleased. Some footage of this struggle later appeared in Thompson's *Tribune*-produced 1915 movie *With the Russians at the Front*.[56]

After his tour of Russia, during which he met the notorious Rasputin, Thompson headed to Bucharest. The next day—May 23, 1915—neutral Italy joined the Allies in exchange for a promise of new territories carved out of the Austro-Hungarian Empire. Thompson moved on to Bulgaria where he was arrested and jailed for a week for reasons he claimed to never understand. It ejected him into Serbia, where he purportedly filmed Austro-Hungarian atrocities against the Serbs, although whether he saw these firsthand or just heard about them remains questionable. Certainly such atrocities did occur. George Macaulay Trevelyan, an American historian, visited Serbia in the opening days of the war. He reported that in the middle of August 1914 near the city of Sabac, the Austro-Hungarian army killed about 3,000 civilians, including burning some to death, and forced millions more into flight.[57]

Next Thompson headed to Constantinople where he visited the nearby Gallipoli front, a peninsula at the entrance of the narrow Dardanelles Strait along which Ottoman fortifications prevented both British and Russian navies from passing, blocking access to the Black Sea. After attempts to destroy its fortifications from sea failed, Winston Churchill, then the First Lord of the Admiralty, concocted a plan for an amphibious landing on the beaches of Gallipoli that would take possession of the entire Strait and from there Constantinople itself. Begun on April 25, 1915, the operation failed spectacularly despite an influx of reinforcements in August. The Allies began withdrawing from this disaster in December.[58]

In 1916, Thompson went to France as an official cinematographer of that government and there filmed the first Battle of the Somme, an area in which virtually no fighting had occurred since 1914. This lack of activity had given the Germans time to dig advanced trenches complete with well-placed machine guns and other implements of death. General Douglas Haig of the British army came up with the idea of bombarding German positions with a weeklong artillery barrage of over a million shells that would, he believed, kill all the Germans, allowing the British army to move into the open country beyond.[59]

In mid–May German airplanes flying overhead saw Haig's preparations for a massive offensive, and although the German General Staff had no idea when it would begin, it nonetheless began preparing. When the Allies began setting up large artillery pieces on June 22, the Germans knew the attack would come soon. Before sending their troops "over the top" into no man's land, the Allies fired off a barrage of poison gas. Neither this nor the weeklong bombardment did any good. Of the 100,000 men on the Allied side who attacked that first day, 20,000 died and another 40,000 returned wounded. The Allies managed to take some front line trenches and forced the Germans to pull back from a few French villages, but beyond that no other gains occurred. Thompson became a casualty of the battle as well: he received a cracked skull.[60]

He included some the footage he had taken in his 1916 documentary *War as It Really Is*, a deceptive title considering it showed nothing of the sort, possibly because the French supposedly censored about 70 percent of what he had filmed. It also included parts of the 1914 Battle of Yser in Belgium. For most of it, one sees little but troop movements, shots of generals, and a spectacular view of the battlefield from 10,000 feet above in an airplane. The sixth and seventh reels show actual fighting, although the shots of the dead at the film's end are strictly stills. Despite being a sanitized version of events, it was a box office hit.[61]

It showed abandoned German trenches, an attack from enemy artillery while in a trench at night, and, most interesting, sappers in Yser mining underground to reach the German trenches. Although the trenches of both sides zigzagged to make it harder for shells or grenades to easily penetrate them from above, this did not lessen their vulnerability to miners digging beneath where they placed massive amounts of explosives.[62]

So prevalent did mining beneath one another's trenches become, both sides had to create stations dedicated to listening for the sound of digging and the stockpiling of explosives. In 1916 alone, the British blew up some 750 mines and the Germans 700, leaving behind a landscape of pockmarks or, for some of the bigger ones, giant craters. In 1915, for example, the British blew a mine near the hotly contested Hooge Château near Ypres. So deep and significant did this crater become it not only exists to this day, a museum well worth visiting stands next to it.[63]

4

The February Revolution

Unrest in Petrograd

A cracked skull did not lessen Donald Thompson's lust to film and photograph the war. On November 14, 1916, his doctor said he could return to work. The next day he phoned John Sleicher, publisher of the magazine *Leslie's Weekly*, for an assignment. Sleicher asked him to cover the Romanian front. Thompson doubted much action would occur there due to the intrigues of German spies in Budapest, but said he would go anyway. Sleicher arranged for him to travel with one of his staff writers, Florence MacLeod Harper. Instead of trying to reach Romania by travelling through the many war zones of Europe, they decided to go via Asia. To that end they boarded the *Empress of Russia*, a steamer bound for China that sailed on November 30 out of Vancouver.[1]

During a stop in Yokohama, Thompson learned the Germans had taken over Budapest, making the reason for going there pointless. He and Harper decided to cover the war from Petrograd, then the capital of Russia. During his stay in Yokohama he interviewed a local Russian officer who alleged the ammunition being made in Japanese factories was not going to its nearby ally of Russia but rather being kept by the manufacturer. The Japanese had also refused to send troops to France unless the British sold all its Elizabeth-class battleships to them. Thompson swallowed these lies, writing to his wife, Dorothy (whom he called "Dot"): "I fear Japan is getting ready for another war against some other nation than Germany."[2]

The British had in fact asked the Japanese government to sell *them* battleships after heavy Royal Navy losses, an offer it had rebuffed. Nor could Japan in any practical way send troops to France. Even if it wanted to commit the desired 250,000 men, it lacked the transport ships necessary to get them there. And if it had possessed the needed vessels, the logistics of moving soldiers such a vast distance would prove difficult to readily overcome and probably take a year to a year and a half to complete. The Japanese did give the Royal Navy badly needed aid by sending their own ships to the Mediterranean to help with operations there.[3]

After stops in Manila and Hong Kong, Thompson and Harper disembarked in Shanghai. From here they planned to take a train to Peking from which they would switch to one for Harbin in Manchuria, a city that stood along the Songhua River and served as the junction for the Chinese Eastern and Trans-Siberian Railways. First class passengers on the latter had two berths and private bathrooms, while second class sleepers had four berths with public bathrooms. Both first and second class passengers could take up to 50 pounds of luggage before being charged for extra (which Thompson exceeded). Trains consisted of six cars: two first class, two second class, one sleeper, one dining, and one baggage. Passenger cars contained compartments rather than rows of seats such as one would find on American trains. Theoretically the cars had electricity and heat, but when Thompson and Harper rode, they found neither in the sleeper.[4]

The Russian government had built the Trans-Siberian Railway without the participation of private investors to avoid becoming accountable to them for profits and loss. The main line ran from Petrograd along the Baltic Sea to Vladivostok on the Sea of Japan. Deeming completion more important than building it right, the Russian government constructed it on the cheap with the inevitable result: it started falling apart the moment trains began rolling down its tracks. All but the largest of its bridges quickly decayed. A 1918 U.S. Army Intelligence report noted that its main line had good rails but suffered from poor grading and excessive curves.[5]

Thompson and Harper arrived at the Harbin station in late February, allowing them to experience firsthand the extreme winter cold known to this part of Asia. Temperatures could and did fall as low as −22° Fahrenheit. With some hours to spare, the two took a sleigh into the Harbin proper, where they discovered a cosmopolitan city inhabited by people of many nationalities, including Chinese, Russians, Mongolians, and even a couple of Japanese military officers. Someone had told Harper that if one spoke French and English, communication in Russia would not present a problem, but it took her little time to realize she needed to learn Russian if she wanted to talk to anyone, and to that end she began studying it.[6]

Their train arrived past its advertised time at around midnight. Passengers brought with them large cuts of meat that they hung from the ceiling to take home to Petrograd because it was suffering from a major food shortage. Neither Thompson nor Harper found the ride particularly pleasant. They arrived in Petrograd on February 25 during a blizzard. After detraining, they walked to the Astoria, "the largest and most modern hotel in the city," only to find it had no rooms available. On board the train Harper had made a friend named Bolton. Being able to speak Russian, he managed to procure rooms for both her and himself, but not for Thompson. The hotel would not even let him sleep in a chair in the lobby. So out into the blizzard he went. He tried to sleep at the train station but a guard refused to let him in. Policemen moved him along when he huddled in doorways. With the help of a local woman walking about in the middle of the night, he finally booked into a lower class hotel.[7]

The next day he secured a room in the Astoria. Needing an interpreter, he found a young man named Boris in a local hospital recovering from wounds he had received on the Romanian front. Boris spoke excellent English because he and his family had moved to Brooklyn after the Russian Revolution of 1905 where he went to school for a few years. After returning to Russia, he worked for the American embassy until 1915 when the Russian army drafted him.[8]

Without Boris, Thompson might have had a harder time navigating the chaos erupting in the city because of its food shortage, which was not due to a lack of food but rather the weather. The trouble was blizzards had stopped incoming trains while the extreme cold prevented the transport of food into the city on carts. A lack of fuel and flour caused bakeries to shut down. The fact that the army still got fed regularly infuriated many of Petrograd's inhabitants, especially since they had to queue up for hours to obtain necessities such as bread, vegetables, sugar, and milk, often in temperatures of 20 below zero or more.[9]

Fuel shortages forced the closure of factories, putting tens of thousands of men out of work. On International Women's Day (March 8), men in munitions factories went on strike protesting the food shortages. At the same time mostly poor and working class women took the streets for this cause. Protesters began breaking into bakeries to take their bread, and some even stormed a factory in which the workers had refused to strike. The departure of Tsar Nicholas II for the front did not help matters. His minister of the interior, Aleksandr Dmitrievich Protopopov, sent him whitewashed reports about the severity of the riots and protests.[10]

The nervous Russian government brought into the city 13,000 armed Cossacks in case an uprising occurred. The Cossacks, an equestrian people who lived on the Steppes primarily north of the Caspian and Black Seas, had long served the tsars, who had used them to expand the Russian Empire all the way to the eastern edge of Asia. Geography determined whether Cossacks belonged to the Roman Catholic, Greek Orthodox, or some other Christian denomination. In theory their military units, called Hosts, only had Cossack officers, although in practice a Cossack could rise no higher than subaltern in some of them.[11]

A day after taking to the streets, the protesters became more political. In the city's main square, the Znamenskaya, they began yelling slogans such as "Down with the autocracy!" and "Down with the war!" When a fur-clad wealthy man riding in a sleigh ordered his man to plow through the crowd, several striking workers dragged out and beat him. He tried to escape into a street car but they followed and smashed in his head with an iron bar.[12]

When the crowd refused to disperse after being ordered to do so, someone commanded the Cossacks to fire into it. This they refused, mostly because they were young with little

Russian Cossacks. Bain News Service. Taken between 1914 and 1915. Library of Congress Prints and Photographs Division.

military experience and had no desire to kill a crowd consisting mainly of women. Their lack of cooperation did not stop the Pavlovskii Guard Regiment, the tsar's personal force, from firing at these civilians. This ruthless act, which killed 40, sparked the February Revolution of 1917, which actually occurred on March 8 but, because the Russians still stilled used the Julian rather than Gregorian calendar, for them it fell on February 24. The violence spread to the railroad station where machine guns came into use. This so disgusted the Cossacks that they attacked the police in an act of retaliation. The next day several of their regiments defected and took over the Fortress of St. Peter and Paul.[13]

On Sunday, March 11, Thompson and Harper ate at a French restaurant with an English friend. Afterward the Americans took a walk with him down Nevsky Prospekt, Petrograd's main thoroughfare. When they reached Anichkov Palace, an edifice built by Peter the Great in 1714 for his daughter that at this time served as the primary residence for the dowager empress, a crowd singing the Marseillaise passed by them, then turned onto the street of Sadovaia. At a little after three in the afternoon, mounted police armed with sabers charged down a sidewalk and began cutting people down.[14]

As the panicked crowd ran away down Nevsky Prospekt, police standing on the bridge that crossed the Fontanka Canal beside Anichkov Palace began firing on them. Thompson and Harper dropped flat to the ground. After the initial slaughter, policemen walked down the street and shot those lying on the ground. Thompson broke the window of a nearby glove shop so he and Harper could take refuge within, Thompson's fear making him feel so weak he could barely walk. Other bystanders followed their example. When the police on the bridge started shooting at the store, its owner, armed with a revolver, returned fire. Realizing they would find no safety here, Harper and Thompson departed.[15]

Back in the street, they had to lie in the snow and hope for the best. From this vantage

"Bridge Over the Fontanka Canal in Petrograd." James Maxwell Pringle. Taken between 1917 and 1918. Library of Congress Prints and Photographs Division.

they watched a small girl about 60 feet away get shot in the throat while running towards them. A policeman shot off the kneecap of a woman when she stood up, possibly to go to the girl. Thompson had never before heard such terrible screaming. About an hour and 15 minutes later, ambulances came, but those who stood to reach them were fired upon. Thompson told Harper to pretend she was wounded so the stretcher bearers would pick her up. Once tucked into the ambulance, she kept her eyes closed for fear of seeing the dead around her. Thompson played dead and, when night fell, made his way back to the hotel, getting there at around seven. Here he found Harper, who had arrived about an hour earlier. When she told people living in the hotel what had happened, they refused to believe it.[16]

Angry soldiers and civilians went after the police, killing or arresting about 4,000 in one day. During this they discovered police had hoarded food, some even keeping "live hens." As a result of this action, the police force disintegrated. The protesters, now outright revolutionaries, stormed the Ministry of Interior, released criminals from the prisons, and broke into arsenals for weapons. Late in the afternoon, a crowd broke into the headquarters of the Okhrana, the secret police dedicated to investigating political crimes, and began destroying its records. By the end of the day armed peasants had taken control of the city. Half of its 160,000-man army garrison mutinied and the other half remained neutral.[17]

Tsar Nicholas ordered the dissolution of the Duma, the Russian parliament, on March 11, but it ignored him. His time as the autocratic leader of the Russian Empire did not last long past that. He abdicated on March 15 upon realizing other cities had also revolted, leaving him with no place to take refuge. His commanders concurred: he must do this else the war effort would collapse. He named his brother Grand Duke Michael Aleksandrovich his successor, but he never wielded power. The revolutionaries arrested all the tsar's ministers. A red flag replaced the old imperial one. In Petrograd the last defenders of the old regime retreated to the roofs of St. Isaac's Cathedral and the Astoria, both in the same square. The latter housed a number of Russian officers and their wives. A crowd of armed men consisting of seamen, soldiers, and civilians surrounded the hotel and demanded their surrender. A Russian general responded by firing his gun at the gathered revolutionaries, this followed by a machine gun attack from the roof.[18]

Thompson, in his room at the time, broke a window so his camera had a clear view for filming. Boris wisely lay flat on the floor, but when a Russian woman came into the room screaming that the police had started firing from the roof with machine guns, she ignored Thompson's warning to keep away from the window and instead pushed a curtain aside to look outside. A bullet hit her in the throat. In a letter to his wife, Thompson heartlessly reported, "I carried her back to the bathroom, where she died about fifteen minutes later. I lost a lot of my film, thanks to this woman's damn foolishness."[19]

The revolutionaries, infuriated by the bullets raking their ranks, stormed the hotel and began struggling with the Russian officers within. Although blood spilled, the invaders left the hotel's English officers and their families alone. When the Russian officers surrendered, the revolutionaries took some out to the square and shot them on the spot; others they detained. They dumped the body of the general who had fired the first shot into a canal. In the hotel's basement they discovered the stores of alcohol, which proved too much a temptation for many and resulted in much drunkenness.[20]

With the tsar deposed, two separate and not always complementary governing bodies took power: the Provisional Government headed by Georgii Evgevevich Lvov, and the Petrograd Soviet, which consisted of workers and enlisted soldiers. The more formal Provisional Government, officially called the Provisional Committee of Duma Members for the Restoration of Order in the Capital and the Establishment of Relations with Individuals and Institutions, consisted mainly of liberals, mostly Constitutional Democrats (Kadets) complemented by a number of moderate socialists, especially the Mensheviks, who joined in April.[21]

The Petrograd Soviet inspired others throughout Russia to create their own for specific groups such as soldiers, workers, sailors, and so forth. Because soviets represented large numbers of people directly, they effectively became more powerful than the Provisional Government. Each soviet had a council of leaders with both executive and legislative powers. The soviets worked with the Provisional Government, and to that end, the new minister of justice, 36-year-old Aleksandr Fedorovich Kerenskii, became a vice president in the Petrograd Soviet and thus the de facto liaison between the two bodies, making him the most powerful of all government officials.[22]

Kerenskii, born in Simbirsk (now Ulyanovsk) along the Volga River, came from a privileged family. His father served as the superintendent of a local gymnasium, or high school, at which he taught Vladimir Ilich Ulianov, known better by his later alias, V.I. Lenin. With the latter being 11 years Kerenskii's senior, it seems unlikely that the two met at the time. Kerenskii went to the University of St. Petersburg where he studied law. He became a noted defense lawyer who worked to exonerate the oppressed with an emphasis on putting a stop to the persecution of Jews. A democratic socialist, he became a member of the Duma in 1912.[23]

The Petrograd Soviet inspired the city's downtrodden to become openly hostile to the wealthy. While in a working section of the city covering the revolution with Thompson and Boris, Harper was mistaken for a member of the Russian elite because she wore a seal fur coat. This happened all too frequently. In one case, two women who once named the tsarina a friend tried a bit of subterfuge to make their way through the city unmolested. They placed two Red Cross flags on their automobile and dressed up as Sisters of Mercy, a secular order of nurses working for the Russian Red Cross. A crowd stopped the imposters and asked them to assist a man who had suffered terrible wounds. To keep up their masquerade they tried to help but at the sight of blood both fainted. The crowd spared their lives but took their car and uniforms.[24]

Thompson benefited from the change of government in an unexpected way. He had gotten to know the new minister of foreign affairs, Pavel Nikolaevich Miliukov, a few years earlier when this man worked at the University of Chicago. Miliukov offered Thompson any help he could to enable him to send his photographs abroad and thus ensure knowledge of the current revolution reached the whole world. Thompson did not get to enjoy this newfound access for long. A few days later appendicitis forced him to go to a hospital him in which, much to his annoyance, a Russian Orthodox priest visited him to administer the Last Rites. Thompson stayed for a week.[25]

The American Doctor in Charge of a Mobile Russian Field Hospital

Harper struck out on her own. To get the front, the whole reason she had come in the first place, she needed a permit but could find no one willing to issue one. Then she met

Dr. Eugene Hurd, a six-foot-three, 250-pound American surgeon from Seattle who had just arrived in the city from a field hospital he ran for the Russian army. He offered to take her back with him if she could leave within 24 hours. To this she readily agreed.[26]

Hurd came from a family with a tradition of serving in wars, so the moment the current one broke out, he wrote to the tsar offering his services as a doctor. In response, a representative from the Russian consulate stopped by his office to hand him money and ticket to Petrograd. Hurd immediately quit his prosperous practice and headed to Vancouver to catch a steamer for Vladivostok. The Russians made him a colonel in their army and put him charge of a field hospital as the chief surgeon. Here he would treat an estimated 31,000 soldiers and win five citations for bravery, three of which came from the tsar himself. In 1920 he married a German baroness, Nella von Hochstetter, a California native whose first husband had died on the front during the war.[27]

Hurd joined the Twenty-Ninth "Grodno Nobility" Flying Column, a mobile surgical unit active mainly in Belarus and Lithuania and so named because aristocratic families from the city of Grodno had funded it. Usually working about a mile behind the trenches, Hurd and his outfit barely escaped capture or death a number of times. Once, for example, the German cavalry passing through the Russian lines went right by his hospital with the idea of rounding him and the others up upon their return. Having instilled great discipline in his camp to ensure it could move at a moment's notice, he hurriedly harnessed his horses and escaped.[28]

Hurd gave Harper papers saying she worked for the Red Cross and arranged for her to travel in a first class carriage on a military train to the front, a ride she did not much like in part because of the fleas. She and Hurd detrained in at a station Harper called Broussi. They boarded a horse-drawn troika that followed a railroad spur used for an evacuation train, which connected to the roughly 155 miles of track that followed along the Dvinsk Front in Galicia. It took three hours to reach the hospital. Along the way a German plane flew over and attempted to bomb the tracks, missing their troika by about 50 yards and frightening their horses so badly they frantically galloped across the fields. A plane dropped another bomb on the other side of some trees, which Hurd feared had hit his hospital, something that had happened the year before. Fortunately this was not the case.[29]

Hurd's hospital consisted of nine tents, each flying a Red Cross flag, as well as portable frame buildings, a barn, bath, meat and ice houses, a blacksmith's shop used to repair ambulances, and sleeping quarters for the doctors and nurses. It even had some of the few working automobile ambulances on the front. A Sister of Mercy greeted them. The Sisters' matron mistook Harper for a volunteer and proceeded to give her a tour in the expectation she would soon offer her services as a nurse, a notion Harper did not correct because the soviet representing enlisted men working at the hospital, the Soldiers' Committee, had decided during Hurd's absence that, with the exception of patients, none could stay who did not work. Harper gave her name as Sister Florencia Williamovna. The Sisters consisted mainly of aristocratic women who received at least four months training before going to the front. Headed by the Dowager Empress, in 1915 the organization had 70 stationary and 40 field hospitals with 30,000 beds available and another 20,000 in reserve.[30]

At first Hurd got along well with the Soldiers' Committee, which followed his orders without question. When a second committee replaced it, the same occurred. A third one proved more radical, causing Hurd no end of trouble. It decreed that hospital staff would receive a mere half glass of milk a day. The rest produced by the hospital's 14 milk cows would go to the soldiers. Something similar occurred in George Orwell's *Animal Farm*, an allegory for the Bolsheviks' takeover of Russia. During the day while most of the farm's animals are out harvesting, all the milk disappears. It turns out the pigs, who represent the communist leadership, had taken it for themselves. They also snatch up all the apples, claiming they need both for the good of their health, which will benefit the workers.[31]

One morning the hospital's male waiters stopped serving the nurses food in the dining room. Free men such as themselves simply could not perform such an undignified act. After finishing his breakfast, Hurd called the Committee. It had promised him it would to do nothing that interfered with running of the hospital and yet had gone back on its word. He planned to leave the hospital for good that day. The soldiers and nurses conversed and presented Hurd with a promise that no more obstruction of operations would occur. This satisfied him enough that he agreed to stay.[32]

On Harper's first day of work, a sister who disliked her handed her a bandage and told her to bind up a soldier's dirty foot. She had never in her life done such a thing. Fortunately Hurd had witnessed the incident. Using English, he instructed her how to proceed. She did not do as well when witnessing an amputation in the surgery. From this she fled, although realizing she had no other choice, she returned. She would work at the hospital for several months, even heading to the front to minister to the wounded.[33]

In May, a fully-recovered Thompson made his way to the Russian front to do some filming and take photos. There he saw the effects of a German poison gas attack on Russian soldiers. Because most of them had either lacked masks or possessed crude ones unable to protect against newer types of gas, a large number had died. One photo Thompson took showed a man with a foaming mouth. The very first time the Germans used poison gas as a weapon against the Allies occurred not at Ypres as is usually reported, but rather on January 31, 1915, at Bolimów, now in modern Poland. Here they lobbed shells filled with liquid xylyl-bromide at the Russians. When exposed to the air, it should have turned into gas, but the below-zero temperatures froze it. This failed attempt convinced Fritz Haber, the German scientist responsible for developing the new weapon, to switch to chlorine delivered from gas cylinders. The Germans first tried this at Ypres on April 22, 1915, killing around 1,000 and wounding another 4,000. Not foreseeing such a success, they failed to follow up with an infantry attack that would surely have gained some significant ground.[34]

By 1916, the British had developed gas masks capable of filtering out most poisons, although French versions had less success, but by 1917 better masks made chlorine and other inhaled poisons useless, so the Germans tried something new: mustard gas. Fired via artillery shells, at first it seemed to do nothing. Then, after about an hour, any exposed skin started to blister severely. Although it blinded many, only prolonged exposure made the damage permanent. Soap and water could wash it off, leading to the introduction of bath trucks containing showers. If not washed quickly enough, eyes exposed to it could contract conjunctivitis. It did its worst damage if it got into the lungs because no effective way of removing it existed.[35]

On the morning of June 7, Thompson arrived at Hurd's hospital. Hurd made sure the starving photographer got a good breakfast, which consisted of ham and eight eggs along with coffee containing sugar and cream plus white bread. He found the last a real treat because for most of his time in Russia he had eaten black bread, which he disliked. He washed it all down with whiskey still in a corked bottle. He somehow got around the Committee's edict that no one could stay without working. Hurd even gave him a place he could use as a dark room.[36]

Thompson did not stay long. He headed back to the front and here witnessed the last major Russian offensive of the war, the only one after the February Revolution. Kerenskii, at the time the minister of war and the navy, ordered the attack to begin on June 1. Although General Aleksei Brusilov had overall command, Kerenskii climbed into the front line trenches and gave the order to charge. At first things went quite well. In the first ten days, Russian soldiers supported by heavy artillery fire crossed two major rivers, captured a number of towns, cities, and villages, and took thousands of prisoners consisting of Austrians, Germans, and Turks. They even managed to threaten the Galician capital, Lemberg, but never took it.[37]

The offensive petered out when it encountered the extensive defenses put up by General Erich Ludendorff. By late July, Russian troops had abandoned their recently taken positions along the Dvinsk-Vilna Railroad. The Germans launched a successful counteroffensive that spanned from the Baltic to Black Seas. Retreating Russians burned their magazines at Tarnopol to keep the enemy from taking possession as well as destroying any supplies they could not carry with them. Their retreat fell into disarray, many of the men throwing down their arms and some shooting officers who insisted they fight on. In his memoir, Kerenskii claimed he never intended for the offensive to succeed. Rather, he wanted to tie up German forces to give the Americans time to arrive at the Western Front. He also saw it as a matter of Russian pride to see their army succeed once more.[38]

General Erich Ludendorff. Bain News Service. Creation date unknown. Library of Congress Prints and Photographs Division.

During the offensive the Russians bolstered their forces by adding regiments of women soldiers, an effort organized by Maria Leontievna Bochkareva, a peasant born in 1889 in a small village along the Volga. She married a butcher but when he became abusive left him for a member of the Russian intelligentsia. She followed the latter into exile in Tomsk, Siberia, the largest town in that region in which stood "a huge, ugly prison" and "a flourishing university." In 1915, she petitioned the tsar to allow her to serve as a volunteer in the Russian army. Accepted, she trained with the Twenty-Fifth Tomsk reserve battalion for two months, then headed to the front to join its regiment, which had served there since the war's beginning. She considered herself the first women to serve as a soldier in the war.[39]

She fought in the trenches near the Lithuanian capital of Vilna during an offensive launched on March 19, 1916, by Russian generals Alexei Evert and Alexei Kuropotkin, during which troops had to move through "knee-deep slush." While initially a success, it bogged down when the Russians failed to take high ground positions occupied by the Germans. Here Bochkareva showed her fighting mettle, so impressing her male counterparts, they nicknamed her Yashka. On July 23, she suffered a wound to the spine.[40]

Sent to Moscow to recover, nine months later she returned to the front at the Styr River in Austria complete with a promotion to officer. She participated in the July 4, 1916, offensive to drive the Austrians out of Galicia and back into the Carpathian Mountains. Its mastermind, the brilliant General Brusilov, came up with the strategy of attacking all Austrian positions at once to look for weaknesses in their lines, then exploit them. In three days the Russians captured about 300,000 prisoners. The offensive nearly destroyed the Austrian Fourth Army. During the fighting the Germans captured Bochkareva and around 700 of her fellow soldiers. Claiming to be a Sister of Mercy, the Germans let her return to the Russian lines.[41]

When the February Revolution broke out, she cared nothing about the politics involved but was dismayed at the number of men who threw down their arms and refused to fight. Kerenskii asked her to come to Petrograd. He along with Mikhail Vladimirovich Rodzianko—a monarchist and conservative who was president of the Duma when the tsar unsuccessfully tried to shut it down, then a founding member of the Provisional Government—asked her to form and command a women's battalion with the hope it would shame men into fighting. Promoted to colonel, she became a hard taskmaster. She forbade "giggling and flirting, encouraged smoking, and swore at her recruits 'like a cabdriver.'" She forced them to crop their hair military style and wear men's uniforms, at least those who could get them. She refused to allow a soldiers' committee to form because she believed it hurt discipline, a point of contention that got her into yelling matches with her superiors. Her force became known as the Battalion of Death because its women planned to go down fighting.[42]

Put off by her brutal command style, many deserted from her battalion, although other women found inspiration in the idea and formed ones of their own, including a second one based out of Petrograd and another from Moscow. Their formation failed to stop the Russian military from crumbling. After the Bolsheviks took power, Bochkarev could not handle the new committee system imposed by the military and resigned, her battalion disbanding. She headed to the United States to drum up support for the White Russian forces that opposed the Bolsheviks in the civil war that had erupted after they took power. Arrested on Christmas Day in 1919, she was tried and convicted "as an enemy of the workers' regime." A firing squad executed her on May 16, 1920.[43]

During her time in Petrograd, Thompson and Harper interviewed her. A photo Thompson took shows her as a stout, plain, well-built woman with obvious strength who clearly had the physique to handle any combat situation thrown at her. Thomas liked her. Harper did not. Disapproving of women as soldiers, she wrote, "She walks and talks like a man, and she has the face of a man." Harper considered the Battalion of Death a failure.[44]

The Kronstadt Revolution

Enemies wishing to invade Petrograd from the sea had to sail into the Gulf of Finland and there pass the fortified island of Kotlin, known as Petrograd's "water gate." On it stood the city of Kronstadt, which served as home for the Russian Baltic Fleet and had at this time a population consisting of roughly 12,000 seamen, 20,000 soldiers, and 50,000 civilians, a good number of this last group working in the dockyards. For those serving in the Russian armed forces, only officers could patronize the city's many tea houses, parks, taverns, markets, and theaters. Enlisted men were fed subpar food and treated with harsh discipline. In October 1905, the enlistees mutinied against this. Although unsuccessful, the dissatisfaction continued to simmer.[45]

When Vice-Admiral Robert Nikolaevich Viren became the head of the naval garrison as well as Kronstadt's governor in 1909, things did not improve. It ought to come as no surprise, then, that when the enlisted men learned of the revolution taking place in Petrograd, they mutinied en mass. They murdered 51 officers, Viren among them, and arrested the rest, who they sent to the Naval Investigation Prison for safekeeping. When Thompson visited, he saw two of them by match light whom he described as "the worst wrecks I ever saw in all my life; both of them had gone mad."[46]

Seven military men and three civilians formed the Kronstadt Committee of the Movement to act as an executive body of a larger group of elected officials called the Assembly of Delegates that had formed to act as the legislature. Military men created the Soviet of Military Deputies and civilians formed the Soviet of Workers' Deputies. To effectively rule, both sent representatives to a newly formed Executive Committee chaired by former chemistry student Anatoli Lamanov, who one contemporary newspaper article described as "a smooth faced, dark haired, soft eyed man in a student's uniform ... [who] is magnetic and ready of speech." This same writer unfairly declared that Lamanov "aims at being a Napoleon and a Rousseau at the same time, combining a resolute government with the propagation of novel political and social ideas." In truth he deeply believed in direct democracy on a small scale. He belonged to a group called the Non-Party that wanted no factions in the soviets and, although a radical on the left, he never belonged to the better known Bolsheviks.[47]

In mid–May, the Kronstadt Soviet, unhappy with the Provisional Government, declared itself an independent republic. Thompson and Harper determined to see for themselves. The roughly 18-mile trip to reach it took an hour by boat. They arrived on a hot, sunny day in July to this pine tree-covered island that had a harbor with well-maintained docks. Harper figured the customs people would never let them step foot on land. Thompson sent Boris to shore to tell authorities about his intention to make a movie about the leaders of Kronstadt's revolution. Flattery got him everywhere: he received permission to come to shore with his cameras.[48]

He and Harper went to the headquarters of the city's Executive Committee and there explained to two sets of guards why they had come. The second pair escorted them to the commissioner of the city's gendarmerie, Tovarish Parchevskii, then brought them to see Lamanov and the Executive Committee. Harper took a strong dislike to Parchevskii, who before now had served as a low-level naval officer and had survived the mutiny because the trust his men had in him and his distrust of fellow officers. On the day Harper met him, he had made himself look more like a peasant than a well-educated person from the upper classes. No radical and certainly no Bolshevik, he nonetheless did believe in the revolution. About him Harper opined, "This man was one of the few I met in Russia who was willing, for the sake of saving their own lives or for a little temporary power, to forget birth and position and go over body and soul to the Bolsheviki [sic]. I have seldom met a man whom I hated so thoroughly at first sight as I did that man."⁴⁹

To her annoyance, he brought around two cars and offered to serve as one of their guides for a tour of the city. At first she road in a small back seat in Paracheviskii's car, but, disgusted by him, refused to stay in the same vehicle, preferring to take the one carrying the camera equipment. She and Thompson visited the Naval Cathedral of Saint Nicholas, a beautiful white neo-Byzantine edifice with a copper-gilded dome, which Harper mistook for gold, prompting her to ask why the revolutionaries had not stolen it since they had no qualms about murder. The whole day she had a sour attitude, remarking, "It isn't pleasant to be an imperialist in a hot-bed of socialism."⁵⁰

Her manner did not improve when she returned to the Astoria. Its staff had gone on strike demanding equality. The idea that the serving class had suddenly aspired to become her social equal horrified her. She cried that she had not eaten since noon, and upon returning in the evening could get no food. The next morning she made some tea with sugar on a hot plate she had brought with her. Fortunately Thompson had fewer qualms about scavenging, and much to her relief, he and Boris brought some loaves of bread for lunch. The kitchen staff had consented to work to keep guests from starving, although they would not deliver it. Harper went to the kitchen and procured tea, sardines, and strawberries but no cutlery or plates. After her dinner she found and washed some of her own, then stashed them into a cupboard in her room.⁵¹

The city's hotel and restaurant workers refused to live solely on their tips any longer. They demanded and received 15 percent of the total profits per month, this shared equally among them. Despite this concession, some still insisted on receiving tips anyway. Much to her disgust, Harper's hotel maid demanded she hand over some of her extra shoes among other things. Harper refused, but while out, the staff came into her room and took what they wanted. She tried locking up her jewelry, but they just forced the lock or used a key. The hotel manager could do nothing about it. If he dismissed someone, the entire staff would go on strike. Frustrated, she moved to a different hotel but had difficult experiences there as well. The city's domestic servants also organized and set rules for themselves in the Duma that included a scale for wages, a day off each week, and a limit to how late they had to work into the night. Harper could not conceive of doing without servants altogether and therefore decided she would just have to put up with it.⁵²

Both she and Thompson blamed the Germans for the current troubles, something with some truth behind it. They certainly dropped propaganda pamphlets onto Russian positions as well distributed posters and newspapers filled with words blaming the food and coal shortages on the Americans and British. One message claimed that all peasants and workers would receive land because of the revolution, but they had to better get back home before they lost their opportunity. This prompted entire regiments to throw down their weapons and rush home, only to discover they would be given no such thing.⁵³

Harper believed that Russian Jews living in America had returned to their homeland in large numbers because it had become "ripe" for their taking. While many Jews living in the Russian Empire did indeed join the revolution, they did so because it gave them a chance to reverse their second-class status and institutionalized ill-treatment. Few if any Jews from America came to participate in the Revolution. This idea probably originated in pro-tsarist newspapers and other sources of anti–Semitic propaganda.⁵⁴

The tsarist government had a long tradition of blaming the country's Jews for its shortcomings rather than admit to its own failures. As the war progressed and Russia's losses mounted, it began blaming Jews for the army's military failures. In East Prussia, where some of the hardest fighting occurred, the Russian army plundered Jewish property and sold it for far below its value. The official Russian telegraph "agency spread rumors to the effect that Jewish soldiers whom the Germans had captured were appointed overseers of the Christian prisoners and were torturing them." Russian newspapers printed anti–Semitic propaganda to stir peasants into starting pogroms against their Jewish neighbors. The Russian Red Cross stopped allowing Jews to join its ranks.[55]

Although the Russians had censored reports of these activities, news nonetheless got out and made its way beyond the borders to places like the United States. When American journalist Herman Bernstein contacted the Russian premier about this, he denied it, although he did admit to executing a few Jews as spies when Poles denounced them. Four days after the Germans smashed through the Russian Third Army on April 19, 1915, Russian Army Headquarters began issuing the first of several orders to governors in mostly Polish provinces to expel their Jews who numbered between one-half to one million. Placed on trains, many died of outbreaks of typhus before ever reaching their destination. In time the army gave up this effort. Instead it let the majority go home, taking hostages to ensure they remained "loyal."[56]

During the deportation phase of its anti–Semitic operations, the Russian army used Kiev as a hub to bring all its prisoners for shipment into other parts of the empire. Ruth Pierce, an American from Boston living in Bulgaria with her husband, saw thousands of Jews from Galicia here when her train arrived in the city. In letter to home she reported, "The men looked about them with quick, furtive movements, a bewildered, frightened look in their dark eyes. The women held their shawls over their faces, and pressed against their skirts were little children. A stale, dirty smell came from them all." The Russians had them in chains and used whips to hurry them along.[57]

Pierce had gone to Kiev with a friend, Marie, and this women's son, Janchu. Pierce never revealed in her published letters what possessed her to travel into a nation then involved in the biggest war the world had ever seen, but went she did. She, Marie and Janchu stayed in a boarding house. For the first few weeks she did not dwell on what she had seen at the railroad station. Then one morning a noisy crowd below her bedroom window awoke her. It consisted of a line of worn out Jews guarded by soldiers armed with bayonets. The stench of this unwashed group wafted through the window. Marie, unmoved by this terrible scene of human suffering, suggested with indifference: "Let's shut the windows and keep out the smell."[58]

Although both women had strong anti–Semitic beliefs, for Pierce, seeing their suffering humanized them. At the invitation of the French consul's wife, she visited a detention camp on a hot day. Here she saw starving Jews dependent on food from the Jewish Ladies' Benevolent Society. Jews with money could bribe the overseer to leave them alone and even stay in the camp rather than continue on the trip to Siberia. But when that ran out, so did their luck. One Jew had American citizenship, but it did him no good. When he showed his proof to the overseer, the man ripped it up. Pierce came to the conclusion that they had become victims of a terrible injustice: "They say the Galician Jews turn traitors and act as spies for the Austrians. But surely not these. What could these broken creatures do? How near death they seemed!" All this and more she reported in a letter to her parents in the United States.[59]

A few days later, at around four in the afternoon, six men, two of them in police uniforms, came for her and Marie shortly after they finished dinner and just hours before their planned departure for Odessa. The intruders, members of the Okhrana, took them down to their boarding house's salon in which the Russians had also detained a friend of theirs, Panna Lolla. Two matrons strip searched the three women, which distressed Panna so much she tried to cover herself up with a curtain. Back in their room, the secret policemen examined their possessions, dumping them onto the floor.[60]

Unaware of what they had done wrong, Marie asked why the men had come. One of them produced the letter Pierce had written home describing what she had seen in the Jewish detention camp. The sight of it made her break out into a cold sweat. The chief of the city's Okhrana, a loyal tsarist despite being a German by birth, placed her and Marie under house arrest.[61]

Because no American consul resided in the city at this time, the British one gave what aid he could. Sometime in September, he agreed to accompany Pierce to an interview with the chief of the secret police, which opened like this[62]:

> CHIEF: Are you a Jew?
> PIERCE: No.
> CHIEF: Is your mother or father Jewish?
> PIERCE: No. There is no Jewish blood in our family.
> CHIEF: Then why have you such sympathy for them?
> PIERCE: Because they are suffering.[63]

Later the chief came to the whole crux of why Pierce had found herself in such trouble: "This letter makes your case a very serious one. Of course, we can't have such things as that published about us." He asked if she reported for any journals. She did not. The interview concluded with the chief informing her that he now had to report what he had found to the Chief of the General Staff. The military would decide her fate, not him.[64]

As is wont to happen when something in one's life goes catastrophically wrong, other events caused Pierce's fears to increase. First came a rumor that a German drive into Russia would result in their occupation of Kiev in just two days. The Germans had initiated this offensive with the hope that they alongside their Austro-Hungarian allies could knock Russia out of the war for good. To that end, they attacked Rivne Fortress in Ukraine, which they had to take if they wanted Kiev. Having heard what the Germans had done in Belgium, Pierce found the idea of their arrival horrifying. The Okhrana chief informed Pierce that she and other political prisoners would be sent to Siberia, so she ought to ready herself for that. Fortunately the Russians stopped the German advance and she managed to stay put. In November the Russians returned her and Marie's passports and allowed them to depart for Bulgaria.[65]

Fall of the Provisional Government

On July 16, Thompson's interpreter, Boris, informed him that the next day V.I. Lenin, the notorious Bolshevik, planned to overthrow the Provisional Government. Boris had learned this from his brother, who belonged to a workers' organization that had warned its members to keep off the streets. Thompson prepared his cameras to capture the action. At 11 the next morning, an invasion of sorts launched from Kronstadt arrived on a steamer and several tugs that carried ten to 12,000 armed sailors, soldiers, and workers. They had come not to do violence but rather make known their desire that they wanted the Central Committee of Soviets to take complete power, dismissing the Provisional Government. Their march toward Taurida Palace, where the Duma met, began at the corner of Nevsky and Sadovaia streets. Some members of the army regiments stationed in Petrograd found this message inspiring and joined their ranks.[66]

No one at the time understood just who had initiated this protest. One American newspaper blamed it on the Maximalists, a political offshoot of the Revolutionary Socialists that had organized during the 1905 Russian Revolution and wanted to make pure socialism an immediate reality even if that meant carrying out assassinations, economic terrorism, and other types of violence to achieve it. Thompson and Harper both thought the Bolsheviks had started the protest. Although their ignorance of local politics ranged from the naïve to the outright laughable, in this case they had more or less gotten it right. While radicals in Kronstadt's First Regiment of Machine-gunners—who had Maximalists in their ranks—had organized the march, it was the Bolsheviks, Lenin among them, who stirred them up.[67]

Kerenskii and Thompson both believed the rumor that the Germans had sent Lenin to the city to overthrow the Provisional Government and, once in power, make an immediate peace. Here some truth exists. Lenin lived in Zurich when the February Revolution broke out. The Kaiser, knowing Lenin wanted to overthrow the existing Russian government and end the war, sent German agents to aid him in getting home. At Germany's behest, the Swiss arranged to release Russian emigrants in exchange for interned Germans. The freed Russians would travel home on a train from Switzerland. Lenin wisely avoided contact with any Germans on board so no one could accuse him of collaborating with them. While the train did have diplomatic status, no one had sealed it as legend purports.[68]

The demonstrators from Kronstadt did not reach Taurida Palace without incident. Someone fired a shot, prompting many trigger-happy people in the crowd to do the same. The leaders of the movement calmed them down enough to get them to their destination. A few went inside and presented their petition to the Duma. The protesters outside nearly lynched one politician, Viktor Mikhailovich Chernov, when he came out to explain the Provisional Government's coalition with the Petrograd Soviet. Two Bolsheviks leading the crowd, Fedor Raskolnikov and Leon Trotskii, talked their fellow protesters into letting this well-intended but foolish man to go free. Another one of the Bolsheviks, Grigorii Eveevich Zinovev, told the crowd to go home. Most did.[69]

A few radicals, unsatisfied with the outcome, caused trouble for the next few days. The Provisional Government responded by bringing some Cossacks in from the front to restore full order. The resulting skirmishes left 56 dead and 650 wounded. It also forced the head of the Provisional Government, Lvov, to resign as premier. Kerenskii replaced him. He promptly had Trotskii and other Bolsheviks arrested. Lenin went into hiding in Finland.[70]

Up until this time, the Provisional Government had done its work well. Democratic in nature and filled with competent leadership, it had enacted freedoms of the press and assembly, removed restrictions on civil rights due to ethnicity or religion, and even abolished the death penalty. But after this failed overthrow, it faced one crisis after another. The war effort continued to falter. Over two million men deserted. Inflation ran rampant. The Provisional Government found itself paralyzed by opposition from both the right and left.[71]

The man Kerenskii had appointed as the army's commander-in-chief, General Lavr Georgievich Kornilov, turned on his benefactor in late August when he initiated a failed attempt to create a military dictatorship. Desperate to keep his hold on things, Kerenskii released Trotskii and his compatriots with the hope they could help him restore order. Upon hearing of Kornilov's arrest, Harper resolved to leave Russia immediately because the Bolsheviks had openly declared their intention to take over and she did not wish to see that. Thompson started for home in early August by retracing the route that had brought him to Petrograd. Harper made her way across Europe to London and, from there, home.[72]

On November 6 and 7, the Bolsheviks overthrew the Provisional Government, this being known to history as the October Revolution because on the Russian calendar it fell on 24th and 25th of that month. It was a coup that succeeded only because the Bolsheviks had taken control of the military. No popular movement of the masses had demanded they take power. Kerenskii fled Petrograd in an automobile. A few Provisional Government holdouts barricaded themselves in the Winter Palace, but a short attack against them motivated their surrender.[73]

Lenin immediately declared an armistice. Russian troops responded by going home. Lenin did not want to formally surrender because it meant agreeing to Germany's demands that Russia give up its Polish territory. Tired of waiting for Russia to acquiesce, Germany broke the armistice on February 17. With no way to stop them, the new Bolshevik government signed a treaty that gave the Germans 460,000 square miles of territory.[74]

Kerenskii went into hiding for a time, then escaped Russia on a British destroyer. He made his way to England, joined there two years later by his wife and children. They stayed in Czechoslovakia and Germany for a time before settling in France, where they lived until 1940 when the Nazi invasion forced them to flee to the United States. Here Kerenskii died at the ripe old age of 89.[75]

5

The Ottoman Empire

The Coming War

In September 1914, a high ranking Ottoman official told American doctor Clarence D. Ussher that he might requisition medicine and supplies from the missionary hospital in Van. Ussher, who ran it, pointed out that the "premises were extraterritorial by treaty right as well as by Irade [decree] of the Sultan," so the official could not do that. Yet he did. "A few days later" Ussher found eight policemen led by a captain accompanied by a physician taking supplies from the hospital's dispensary in the cellar. This Ussher put a stop to. When the captain ordered his men to bring a barrel of Epsom salts up, Ussher, a large blond-haired man with an intimidating presence, blocked the trapdoor entrance. The police captain ordered his men to do it anyway, but they found this a difficult task to execute because Ernest A. Yarrow, a large American missionary who had once played football for Wesleyan College and now ran the Boys' School, had arrived to assist Ussher. The captain called for reinforcements.[1]

Ussher knew if he allowed Ottoman officials to violate his dispensary, they would likely begin intruding into the rest of the mission compound. In an effort to diffuse the situation, another American missionary, Grace Knapp, hurried to the Russian consul for aid. He chased the police away, then complained to the *vâli* (governor), who apologized to Ussher in person and ordered the police to stay out of the American compound without special permission. Ussher made the hospital an official Red Cross facility to give it added protection.[2]

Ussher, an American citizen born in Canada, had attended a theological seminary in Philadelphia with the desire of working as a doctor for the Foreign Mission Board of the Reformed Episcopal Church in India. With no openings available, he headed to Boston to visit the American Board of Commissioners for Foreign Missions, the organization that oversaw all Congregationalist efforts around the world. It was established in Massachusetts in 1810 when four seminary students got it into their heads that they wanted to become foreign missionaries. Ministers and prominent layman gathered at Andover Theological Seminary and there created the nine member American Board to oversee the students' venture.[3]

The Congregationalist religion traces its origins to the Puritans and Pilgrims who had come to America for religious freedom—at least their own. Although intolerant of competing Christian denominations, each congregation ran its affairs as it saw fit with the proviso that only a well-educated minister and not a layperson lead it. Because this church's interpretation of Christ's teachings derived from a harsh version of Calvinist doctrine, their

Ottoman Empire. Map by the author based on one that appeared in *Turkey in Asia (Asia Minor) and Transcaucasia: Keith Johnston's General Atlas, Oct. 1911*. Edinburgh: W. & A.K. Johnston, 1911. David Rumsey Historical Map Collection.

5. The Ottoman Empire

missionary work excluded charity, a sentiment Ussher's father-in-law expressed as such: "To give indiscriminately ... to the very poor, while nothing is required in return, is always destructive of the better aims and purposes of the recipients."[4]

The American Board ran missions scattered all across the Ottoman Empire including Harput, Constantinople, Merzivan, Anitab, Smyrna, and Van. Here missionaries worked primarily with Armenians, a Christian people who belonged to the Armenian Apostolic Church, which was similar to but independent from the Greek Orthodox faith. Because Armenian dogma and theology did not conform to the Congregationalists' view of faith as a pathway to Heaven, they tried to steer it in a direction more to their liking. Although they had not originally intended to do so, when reforms failed, they created a new Armenian evangelical church. The missionaries also hoped that when local Muslims saw their success, they themselves would convert, but most showed little interest. It was in any case against the law for missionaries to proselytize to Muslims, and the Ottoman state punished those few who converted on their own.[5]

American Board member Dr. James L. Barton asked Ussher if he would like to do mission work in the city of Harput. Ussher agreed, then departed for Constantinople on May 12, 1898, on board the *Armenian*. Upon arriving, he was infuriated that "any ignorant native quack might practice unmolested ... [while] diplomaed [sic] physicians from other countries ... had to pass an examination by the Imperial Medical College in Constantinople before the lives of the subjects of this paternal government could be entrusted to their care." The law, recently revised, required those who took the exam do so in Turkish or French without an interpreter, which Ussher planned to use. Having learned some French while spending two summers in "a French-Canadian village," he opted to try it in that language despite not having spoken it for 13 years and lacking knowledge of its medical nomenclature. After navigating a thick stream of bureaucracy, he paid to take the test, the fee being split among those who administered it. This he figured must have served as a bribe because he passed it with no trouble. Ottoman customs stole about $140 worth of his equipment, confiscated his dictionary because it contained such words as "revolution" and "liberty," and cut maps out of his Bible because several had the word "Armenia" on them. It confiscated his horsehair mattress, telling him he could only have back if he could prove that its place of manufacture, Boston, had no horse diseases at the time of its assembly.[6]

He spent the next year working in Harput, learning the Armenian language during that time. When the missionaries in Van asked him if he would relieve their current doctor, George C. Reynolds, for six months, he agreed. During this time Reynolds died, so Ussher stayed on permanently. Just ten days after arriving, he received a telegram from a William W. Peet, "treasurer of the American missions in Turkey," asking him to escort two new missionaries, Virginia Wilson and Elizabeth Freeman Barrows, from the mountain city of Erzerum to Van. Wilson, an Englishwoman, planned to assist with the orphanage, while Barrows would take charge of the Girls' School.[7]

Beth Barrows, born in the middle of Anatolia in the city of Kaisariel, lived her first seven years in the Empire until her brother's poor health forced her family to move to New England. Educated at Northfield Seminary and Women's College, she became a teacher but really wanted to be a missionary. Her father, Rev. John Otis Barrows, thought her unsuited for work in a foreign place because she lacked the ability to readily learn new languages. He tried to steer her towards writing, but she wanted none of that and decided to pursue her calling, ignoring her parent's disapproval of a young unmarried lady traveling with an escort only as far as Constantinople. Upon arriving, she found that she understood Turkish far better than expected.[8]

High walls surrounded Erzerum and snow buried it for six months every year. When Ussher arrived and passed through one its tunnel-like gates, he picked up an unwanted escort of four soldiers. Here, in addition to Barrows and Wilson, he found Miss Louise Bond, an Englishwoman who would serve as the superintendant of the American hospital in Van. Wilson decided to stay in Erzerum, leaving Ussher with just Bond and Barrows. The presence of Bond caused him no end of trouble because local officials had gotten it in their heads that she and Wilson had come as revolutionaries to stir up trouble.[9]

After waiting three weeks for permission to depart, Ussher decided they would just leave. He hired men and sleds for transport. The American consulate's dragoman and acting vice-consul, Vital Ojalvo, would serve as their interpreter and guide through the thick mountain snow. Ussher, accompanied by servants and a personal guard he had brought with him, took the ladies' baggage on sleds to a village about 15 hours' travel away and there waited in a house for the rest of his party. The English and American vice-consuls in the city, meanwhile, arranged for the women to depart, but trouble with guards and thick snow delayed them for a day. After reuniting with Ussher, they traveled another four hours to the next village in case Turkish soldiers followed.[10]

Which they did, catching up with the Ussher party at a house in which it had stopped to rest. When a Turkish colonel entered, Ojalvo pretended to be an old friend from Constantinople. Not wanting to offend the old "friend" he could not remember, the colonel went along with this ruse and ultimately took tea with him and Ussher. The colonel volunteered to use his men to open the road ahead. For the rest of the trip local Ottoman authorities made multiple attempts to stop the Ussher party from reaching Van. Once, for example, when gendarmes keen on apprehending the "fugitives" from Erzerum tried to do so, Ussher whipped out his notebook and took their names with the implied threat he would report them to an important Ottoman official who would not be pleased that someone had molested him. He often used this technique to bluff his way out of tight spots or to intimidate locals.[11]

Christian missionary or not, he did hesitate to threaten violence when the need arose. In another incident during this trip, he saw four gendarmes loading their rifles as they galloped towards his party. Whipping out his empty Remington rifle and opening his pistol holster, he pointed the former at one of the gendarmes, which so startled him that he dropped his weapon. His companions followed suit, making the four Ussher's prisoners.[12]

Six months after their arrival in Van, Ussher and Barrows married. They would have three homeschooled children. In addition to her other duties, Beth started a lace factory. Slave to the belief that God only helps those who help themselves, she hired poor women and children to do the work, paying them piece rate, rejecting shoddy work and ensuring no one got paid for work they did not do. Her father, in his memorial biography of her, insisted these women were grateful for receiving low wages.[13]

In July 1914, Ussher and several other missionaries hired horses for a trip to Harput. During the 12 days it took to return home, they noticed that many of the towns and villages through which they passed had lost the majority of their Armenian men between the ages of 20 and 40. The Ottoman army had conscripted them in anticipation of entry into the

European war. In the villages and small towns through which the missionaries passed, neither Turks nor Armenians could afford to pay for a deferment. Wealthy Armenians capable of doing so lived primarily in cities, so many that the number of Armenians of a fighting age who remained behind exceeded that of Turks, a situation the Ottoman government considered dangerous.[14]

Since its establishment, the Empire had always contained a polyglot of ethnic groups who had more or less lived in harmony. That began to change on July 23, 1908, when its autocratic sultan was forced by civil unrest and the rebellious Third Army in Macedonia to recall the Turkish parliament and restore the 1876 constitution. Another factor in this uprising was the Young Turks, a political movement that began in 1894 as an umbrella term for a variety of groups all with the aim of overthrowing the sultan. One of these was the Committee of Union and Progress (CUP), which, in addition to desiring the removal of the sultan, wanted to make the Empire a place ruled by and for ethnic Turks. A year later it absorbed into its ranks the Ottoman Freedom Society, which shared the same aims with the added advantage having a membership that included important military men. After the Ottoman parliament's restoration, the CUP sent the Committee of Seven to influence events in Constantinople.[15]

Despite being politically weakened, the sultan nonetheless got involved with war in the Balkans that resulted in the loss of most of the Empire's European territory. On January 23, 1913, Ismail Enver Pasha, once a major in the Third Army and a leader in the CUP, burst

The Sublime Porte. Abdullah Fréres. Taken between 1880 and 1893. Library of Congress Prints and Photographs Division.

into the chambers of the sultan's cabinet with a contingent of soldiers and there shot and killed Hüseyin Nâzim Pasha, the war minister, then forced the resignation of Grand Vizier Mehmed Kâmil Pasha. While the sultan would remain as a figurehead, the Empire's real rulers would be Enver along with two others from the CUP, Mehmed Talaat Pasha and Ahmed Djemal.[16]

At this time the Ottoman Empire still encompassed all of modern Turkey plus parts what are now Iraq, Syria, Yemen, and Iran. Central power resided in Constantinople, a city whose name did not officially change to Istanbul in the West until 1930. Djemal, Enver, and Talaat secured their power in part by appointing *vâlis* loyal to them to rule over the Empire's *vilâyets* (provinces). They along with other ministers resided in the Sublime Porte, a collection of buildings located in Constantinople that served as the Empire's administrative center.[17]

To fulfill their goal of making the Empire more Turkish, these hardliners filled all ministerial and other important government positions with Turks. Turkish became the official language of the government and Ottoman schools. Knowledge of the language was a prerequisite for anyone taking a government post, creating a real burden for the millions of Arab-speaking people under Ottoman rule who spoke not a word of Turkish. The Albanian population was forced to replace the Latin letters used for their alphabet with Turkish ones. CUP leaders considered the Armenians the biggest obstacle to making the Empire a truly Turkish place because this ethnic minority was its largest and most prosperous.[18]

Some high ranking CUP officials saw entering the war as an opportunity to give them to chance to regain lost territory and increase Turkish prestige, though the Empire did not enter it immediately despite the fact it had signed a secret treaty of alliance with Germany on August 2. Enver wanted to but the rest of the cabinet members opposed this on the grounds that the Empire was not prepared for a full scale conflict. The Germans sent over matériel as well as officers to lead the Ottoman army and navy. They also promised the return of Egypt, which the Empire had lost to the British in 1882.[19]

Public opinion in the Empire at this time favored the British because throughout the nineteenth century they had often been an ally, which was one of the reasons the treaty with Germany had been kept secret. Positive sentiment about the British soured when Winston Churchill, in his capacity as First Lord of the Admiralty, ordered the confiscation of two dreadnaughts built for the Turks at the Armstrong-Whitworth yards in Newcastle-upon-Tyne in England just as the Turkish crews were heading there to man them. Not long after this, the Royal Navy chased two German warships, the *Goeben* and *Breslau*, into the Dardanelles. Because of the Empire's neutrality, the Brits could not go after them, though nothing prevented the Royal Navy from waiting for them to come out. To counter this, Germany sold the Turks these ships. German sailors exchanged their caps for fezzes.[20]

To entice the Turks to get into the war sooner rather than later, the German ambassador to the Porte, Baron Hans Freiherr von Wagenheim, arranged for Germany to give the Empire an infusion of money in the form of a large loan in gold. The Turks entered the war on October 29 with a surprise naval attack on the Russian cities of Odessa and Theodosia in the Black Sea. At first the Porte denied it had ordered the attacks, but the Russians did not swallow this lie and declared war four days later, its allies following suit. In his capacity as caliph, the Ottoman sultan, Mehmed V, declared the war a jihad.[21]

Things did not go well for the Ottoman military. Enver personally led the Third Army, then consisting of 90,000 men, into the Caucasus on December 21, 1914, with the aim of taking the strategically important town of Sarikamis in Russian territory. At first unseasonably warm temperatures aided the offensive, but soon enough brutal cold (an issue Enver had been warned about but ignored) and a Russian counteroffensive pushed the Third Army out. The Ottoman army would never fully recover from this disaster, nor would it make any more headway into Russian territory until the Bolsheviks signed an armistice with the Germans.[22]

Ottoman leadership blamed the offensive's failure on the Armenians, claiming they had defected to the Russian army en masse. Perhaps this idea came from their own attempt at a similar scheme. At a meeting in Erzerum that occurred before the war broke out, they had promised the Armenians an autonomous state in return for enticing their relatives in Russian territory to rebel in coordination with an uprising by Muslims living there. The Armenians instead recommended a policy of neutrality, which only fueled Ottoman worries about their loyalty.[23]

The Russians had the same idea. They gave their Armenian subjects a disingenuous promise of a homeland carved from Ottoman territory, which prompted the Armenian National Bureau—an organization representing a variety of social, political, and philanthropic societies—to begin recruiting Ottoman Armenians to fight against their Turkish masters. Only about 10,000 volunteered, many refusing out of a fear the Ottomans would attack their relatives at home if they did so. About 100,000 Armenians living under Russian rule joined the Russian army, but most were sent to the Eastern front in Europe to keep them from being affected by the Armenian nationalism the Russian government had stirred up.[24]

Siege of Van

In February 1915, the Porte installed Jevdet Bey, Enver's brother-in-law, as Van's new *vâli*, a man Ussher knew well because he had been his family's physician. He considered Jevdet a "past-master of the art of concealment and dissimulation." The American ambassador to the Porte, Henry Morgenthau, characterized Jevdet as "a man of unstable character, friendly to non–Moslems one moment, hostile the next, hypocritical, treacherous, and ferocious according to the worst traditions of his race. He hated the Armenians and cordially sympathized with the long-established Turkish plan of solving the Armenian problem."[25]

Van had at this time about 30,000 inhabitants. It stood beside Lake Van on "a plateau bordered by magnificent mountains" and served the capital of a *vilayet* of the same name. The original one-square-mile walled city stood beneath the shadow of a high cliff upon which rose the fortress known as Castle Rock. To the east sprawled the city's residential areas split into quarters. The Armenians lived primarily in Garden City, so named because most of its houses had gardens and vineyards. Perched at its southeast corner on a hill was the walled American mission compound in which stood schools, the hospital, four missionary residences (including the one belonging to the Ussher family), and a church.[26]

Jevdet disliked the American missionaries and harassed them when he could. Having control of a contingent of soldiers known as the "Butcher Regiment," he insisted the Americans allow him to post 50 soldiers plus cannons and supplies in the mission compound on the pretext of protecting them. The missionaries asked, "Against whom?" He answered, "These despicable Armenians." But, the Americans insisted, they had nothing to fear from them. Jevdet replied with a warning that if the Armenians got into a fight with the Kurds, the Americans might get caught in the crossfire. Over the next few days Ussher, with the assistance of the Italian consul, tried to negotiate with Jevdet over this point, especially since the Armenians warned that they would not allow 50 Turkish soldiers in their quarter of the city. Ussher told Jevdet that if he sent that many men, violence would surely erupt. Jevdet insisted it would be 50 or none, and if the Americans refused his protection, they had to sign a statement that they had done so. Fearing he would use this as a legal pretext to take over the compound, Ussher agreed, but promised if a Turkish soldier there fired a single shot, he would personally shoot that man for violating American neutrality. The Ottoman soldiers never came.[27]

In the spring, Jevdet called for 3,000 Armenian soldiers. He invited four prominent Armenian leaders of the socialist political party known as the Dashnaktsutyun (Armenian Revolutionary Federation) to discuss the matter. Three of them agreed to go, but when they arrived, he had them murdered, a repeat of what he had earlier done to four Armenian representatives in the village of Shattakh south of Lake Van. Angered, the Armenians told him they would give him just 400 men for his army and pay exemptions for the rest.[28]

Tensions further escalated when Turkish soldiers attacked an Armenian orphan girl and several village women trying to leave the city's German mission. Several Armenians responded by firing upon the soldiers, who at dawn on April 20, 1915, escalated this situation by shooting a cannon and rifles into the Armenian quarter. Having anticipated something like this might happen, the Armenians had barricaded 80 houses and connected them with mud walls and shallow trenches in an area about one square mile in size. They possessed a limited supply of rifles, grenades, and pistols, though an Armenian professor began making crude smokeless black powder cartridges brought to the soldiers by women and children. Ussher's 14-year-old son, Neville, and his Boy Scout troop offered aid by "extinguishing fires, reporting and carrying sick and wounded[,] and enforcing sanitary regulations among 4000 [sic] Armenian refugees" who had come to the American compound for protection.[29]

Van presented the Armenians with a no-win situation: if they resisted, the Turks would point to this as proof of Armenian disloyalty and rebellion, and if they complied, the Turks would just massacre them, an event that had occurred periodically throughout Ottoman history. One of the worst massacres spanned from 1884 to 1896 when Sultan Abdul Hamid II organized and sanctioned attacks against his Armenian subjects by sending his personal Kurdish regiments under the command of Turkish officers, the Hamidiyé, to kill them and take their lands and houses. Between 100,000 and 300,000 Armenians died, and so much blood ran that Hamid became known as the Red Sultan.[30]

Jevdet accused the missionaries of allowing armed men to enter and leave their compound as they pleased, and warned he would destroy it if so much as one shot came from there. Bullets from both sides flew across its grounds, wounding several bystanders in the process. To keep American neutrality in tact, Ussher allowed no wounded Armenians into his hospital for treatment, instead setting up a separate one up for them outside the compound's walls.[31]

Problems only increased when several hundred Armenians were driven by the Turks from their mountain village. The refugees flooded the compound on April 25, many of them wounded. Of those who had been mutilated, 60 needed immediate surgical attention. More refugees followed. Ussher realized that only intervention by the Russians would save the city's Armenians from slaughter. Although he had no way of knowing it, the Russians had already begun working toward that end via diplomatic channels. Their ambassador to Washington had met with Secretary of State William Jennings Bryan and requested he use American influence with the Porte to aid non-combatant Armenians, which Jennings promised to do.[32]

In early April, the Ottoman force cut all of Van's communication by burning its telegraph and post offices. The mission compound, now in serious danger, desperately needed to get a message out. Ussher and Yarrow handed copies of the following plea to a dozen who volunteered to deliver it by crossing Ottoman lines:

> Van, April 27, 1915.
>
> To Americans, or any Foreign Consul.
>
> Internal troubles in Van. Government threatens to bombard American premises. Inform American Government American lives in danger.
>
> (Signed)   C.D. Ussher
>   E.A. Yarrow
>
> Reward messenger.[33]

Four of those who made the attempt returned after failing to penetrate Turkish lines, while others died or went missing. Word of the fighting had nonetheless reached Ambassador Morgenthau in Constantinople by other means. Talaat, then minister of the interior, assured him the Ottoman army had only targeted combatants, promising to punish anyone who molested innocents, especially women and children.[34]

On May 15 and 16, the Turks shelled the mission compound, which caused one death, that of an Armenian child. When the Armenians attacked the army barracks from which the shells had come, they found the Turkish force had abandoned it. They had fired at the compound as part of a diversion to mask their retreat from the city, executed in order to evade an oncoming Russian offensive. The Russians occupied Van on May 19.[35]

Jevdet's Butcher Regiment of 8,000 men moved south out of Russian range where it continued to live up to its name. It massacred Christians in Sairt, then went to Bitlis where it demanded a ransom that equaled £5,000. Jevdet had 20 Armenian leaders hanged, then surrounded the town to cut off its communications. Rounding up all able-bodied men, he made them dig their own graves before having them shot. He gave his men any women and children they wanted, then sent the remaining townsfolk southeast where they were drowned in the Tigris.[36]

The Turkish women, children, and old men left behind in Van by the Ottoman army had no protection from vengeful Armenians. To keep them safe, the missionaries reluctantly took them into their compound. Ussher disliked them. In his memoir he claimed they stole, hoarded food, and would do no work to help the common good. He unfairly characterized them as "filthy beyond description in person and habits." They did unintentionally bring with them cholera, influenza, and measles, which in such close and unsanitary conditions resulted in an average of eight deaths per day. Food became scarce and expensive, forcing the missionaries to dole out a bit of milk to women and children plus two pieces of bread a day. They served meat when they could get it. In contrast to her husband, Beth Ussher had a far more sympathetic view of the Turks: she realized they were just more victims of the war.[37]

The missionaries tried to convince Major General Nikolaev, the Russian officer in charge of the city, to remove the Turkish refugees from their compound, but he did no such thing. Then came Countess Alexandra Tolstaya. When she arrived in Van, she brought with her aid that she gladly gave the refugees living in the mission compound. Born in 1884 as the 13th of 14 children and called Sasha by her family, she was the daughter of legendary Russian writer Leo Tolstoy. At the age of 17 she became his personal secretary and for many years refused offers of marriage to remain as such. After his death in 1910, she took on the role as his executor and in this capacity used the funds from an edition of her father's last works to buy his estate in full so she could give the land to peasants. When the war broke out, she became a nurse and went to the front lines. For a time she took command of a number of medical units operating along the Turkish-Russian lines. When the relief money she brought with her to Van ran out, she convinced General Nikolaev to remove the Turkish refugees in the compound to Ottoman-controlled territory.[38]

Typhus broke out in the city, a disease spread by body lice that usually becomes epidemic when a large number of people live closely together in unsanitary conditions. Symptoms include exhaustion, aches, fever and a rash covering the upper body and limbs. In June, all of the Ussher children save for Neville, who had gone to America for schooling, came down with a different communicable disease, whooping cough. In July Beth took them to their summer home in the Van suburb of Artamid to the south for recovery and too get away from the typhus outbreak. Although the Turks had looted their summer house the month before, killing the family's caretaker and chopping off his wife's hand when she tried to protect him, it still stood intact.[39]

Ussher followed his family there, but by then it was too late: both he and Beth had come down with typhus. Fellow missionary Grace Highley Knapp, one of the few American missionaries still healthy, nursed them both. Beth died of the disease on July 14. No one told her husband for nearly two weeks because they wanted to wait until he had sufficiently recovered before giving him the bad news. His bout of typhus caused complications. He contracted pneumonia, then developed a parotid abscess, an infection of the largest salivary gland in the body that causes the production of much pus.[40]

On July 30 General Nikolaev recommended that all Armenians and foreigners leave the city at once because his force would soon depart after a mere six weeks of occupation. The Turks had begun pushing them back at Erzerum. Nikolaev sent out two ambulances to take ill missionaries back to the compound. The missionaries decided to flee for their lives, believing the Turks would kill them when they reoccupied the city. Their party consisted of 15 Americans, eight Armenians, and a friend of Ussher's who would bring with him his children and ill wife.[41]

Two Russian Red Cross doctors, believing the missionaries had already left, came to the compound to take supplies from the hospital dispensary. When they found the missionaries still there, they promised to get them safely to Igdir, the first village in Russian territory, in exchange for the medical supplies they wanted. The Russian doctors procured "a litter hung between two horses ridden by Red Cross orderlies, and for the rest of the party two ambulances, springless, two-wheeled carts with canopy and Red Cross insignia." In addition to this, the missionaries had two carts of their own. Those who could "took turns walking."[42]

They started for Russian territory on August 3 as part of an exodus of roughly 250,000 refugees who had to traverse between 100 and 150 miles through "a waterless and trackless country ... under the burning August sun, smothered in dust and overcome by thirst and fatigue." North of Lake Van they forded the deep and swift Bendimahi River near the town of Bergri. On its far side rose a steep bank beyond which was a narrow gorge. At its top stood Turks and Kurds who opened fire upon those below. The Cossacks guarding the refugees galloped away to safety, leaving their charges behind. Members of the Russian Red Cross stayed to help those left behind.[43]

As the refugees crossed the river under fire, many girls and women threw themselves in it rather than allow the Turks to kill or capture them. Entire families got pushed into it by others rushing past in a panic. The Kurds killed the children and sick left behind. Ussher estimated that about 7,000 died that day. Although the missionaries survived this gauntlet of death, Mrs. Reynolds broke her leg below her knee, leaving her helpless for the remaining journey and forcing her to ride in an ambulance.[44]

A lack of food and water killed many children. One mother wrapped her dead child in a shawl, gave it once last hug, set it alongside the road, then went on. Another carried two children in her arms while a third clung to her skirts crying to be picked up. The weeping mother detached the walking girl and moved too quickly for her to keep up, ignoring her cries and not looking back even when others asked who had lost their child.[45]

In Igdir none of the five military hospitals would take in Ussher because they feared he might cause an epidemic of typhus, prompting one of the Russian doctors who had

Tiflis. Photographer unknown. Taken between 1890 and 1900. Library of Congress Prints and Photographs Division.

accompanied him to telegraph F. Willoughby Smith, the American consul in Tiflis, for help. Smith arranged for an automobile to take Ussher to an ambulance train bound for Tiflis. When it arrived, his dragoman transported Ussher to a hospital in the consulate's car. By now Ussher had, in addition to all his other medical problems, come down with a terrible case of dysentery, causing him to became "a nervous and physical wreck…[,] a ghost of himself." But at least he had survived. The trip proved too much for Mrs. Reynolds. She passed away on August 27. From Tiflis the missionaries made their way to Petrograd, where Ussher recovered his health.[46]

Ambassador Henry Morgenthau Receives Unsettling News

In early April 1915, the Porte revoked Ambassador Morgenthau's use of a telegraphic cipher for communications with American consuls throughout the Empire as well as censoring letters coming from them. It had done so in an effort to keep Morgenthau from learning about what its forces were doing to the Armenians and other ethnic minorities. Yet he could hardly fail to notice the deportation of 200 prominent Armenians from Constantinople starting on April 24, 1915, with whom he had frequent contact. When he asked Talaat about this, the minister claimed they were enemies of the state, and that he had evidence these men had corresponded with the Russians. After this another 1,000 were deported, all of whom died during their journey into the eastern desert.[47]

The Porte's attempt to keep Morgenthau in the dark failed. Accurate intelligence from the Empire's interior reached him, including what had happened in early April to the Armenian town of Zeitoun. Here 25 to 30 men refused to be conscripted on the ground that the Turks had raped 30 of their women. The Ottomans proclaimed them "outlaws." Making their way to a high point in the rocks between Zeitoun and Marash, the "outlaws" took up an easily defended position fortified with plenty of ammunition, food and water. The first Ottoman military force that tried to dislodge them lost 300 men. A larger one followed, occupied Zeitoun with the promise it would withdraw if the townspeople gave the rebels up.[48]

This they did, but the Turks reneged on their pledge. On April 9 they gathered the town's most prominent families at the local government house and informed them they had to go to Marash without the opportunity to retrieve any belongings at home, gather up their children, or tell their friends and family about their departure. More deportations followed. The Ottomans also removed Armenians from the surrounding towns and villages, replacing them with ethnic Turks from Thrace who took their houses, lands, livestock, and possessions.[49]

The journey for the Zeitoun migrants did not end in Marash as promised. Instead they combined with the Armenians native to the city and together journeyed onward to an unknown destination. The American consul, J.B. Jackson, estimated that the number from the Zeitoun-Marash area amounted to "between 4,300 and 4,500 families," or around 28,000 people. Wealthy Armenians had less of a struggle because they could afford carts and beasts of burden, but the rest experienced utter misery. Those on foot had to put up with the constant harassment of their escorts.[50]

They continued to the outside of Taurus, birthplace of the Saint Paul and a city located on a lush plain covered with gardens and orchards. Despite this plenty, little food made its way to the refugees because the local soldiers refused to allow them to enter the town for supplies. Desperate, they sold their belongings at bargain prices. Valuable livestock such as mares, goats, and donkeys sold for just a few piasters, one of these equaling about 44 cents. The local Christian missionaries tried to give aid but their resources proved too meager to make much difference.[51]

After a month of travel with little food and no utensils with which to prepare and eat it, the refugees reached Konya, one of the oldest cities in the world. They thought their journey would end here, but the Turks had other plans: they sent them east into the desert on foot. When confronted by this wave of human suffering, Dr. William S. Dodd, an American missionary who helped to run a Red Cross hospital in the city, asked the chief of police for permission to see the refugees. The chief told Dodd that he would have to wait for the *vâli* to arrive because only he could give it. The *vâli* outright refused even after Dodd pointed out that two years earlier the Red Cross had given aid to Muslim refugees. The *vâli* replied that Ottoman "soldiers needed clothing more [than the] … Armenians."[52]

More refugees poured into Konya from Ada Bazar via the railroad. The Turks had stuffed this group into box cars, each containing about 40 to 45 men, women and children, healthy and sick. Furthering their indignity, the Ottomans charged each passenger 180 piasters, forcing them to sell what possessions they had to local Turkish women for about a tenth of the value to raise the money. Soon enough local Turks started outright robbing them. Their guards as well as local policemen saw this but did nothing to stop it.[53]

Over a few months, between 5,000 and 10,000 Armenians camped here. The Turks gave them no food, leaving those without money to starve. Many succumbed to dysentery, malaria, and heat exposure. The total lack of sanitation created a terrible stench. Women began giving their children away. Dodd accepted some but soon had to stop after being overwhelmed. When the Turks learned what he had done, they demanded he cease. Women must turn their children over to Turkish families.[54]

Both Dodd and fellow missionary Wilfred M. Post did not sit idly. They mailed letters to Morgenthau. Dodd sent one in August via special courier to ensure it remained uncensored. Upon receiving it, Morgenthau forwarded it to Secretary of State Robert Lansing, the man who had replaced Bryan after he resigned on June 19, 1915, over differences in foreign policy with the president. Although Morgenthau had no diplomatic experience and had only received the ambassadorship as a reward for his work as chairman of the Democratic Finance Committee that had raised the money that helped Woodrow Wilson become president in 1912, he nonetheless had a natural talent for this sort of work. Officially presenting himself to the Porte in 1913, he never liked the Turks, considering them "dull-witted and lazy."[55]

Born in Mannheim, Germany, on April 26, 1856, Morgenthau moved to Brooklyn along with the rest of his family in 1865. He had a long and varied career before taking up public service. Graduating from Columbia Law School in 1877, he set up a successful practice with two partners in 1879, only to leave it in 1899. He founded and became the president of the Central Reality Bond Company, left that in 1905, then formed the Henry Morgenthau Company, serving as its president until 1913. A noted philanthropist, among other projects he helped to found the American Red Cross. A Reformed Jew who believed in promoting community service over religion, in 1907 he and several others started the Free Synagogue in Manhattan to further this philosophy.[56]

Reacting to the pleas of assistance from missionaries, he secured for Konya's approximately 20,000 Armenian citizens an exemption from deportation. Authorities shut down their businesses to kill off their livelihoods. By the end of October about 500 of them were so destitute, they had to go to the missionaries daily for food.[57]

American consuls living throughout the Empire sent Morgenthau reliable and uncensored eyewitness accounts of other atrocities. Leslie A. Davis, stationed in Harput, provided the most detailed and disturbing intelligence. Born on April 29, 1875, in Port Jefferson, New York, Davis became an attorney and practiced law for several years before joining the U.S. Foreign Service in 1912. His first posting took him to Batumi, Russia, where he learned the local language. His boss, A.L. Gottshalk, disliked his subordinate's love of the outdoors and gave him a poor review, recommending that the State Department post him somewhere remote. It made Davis the consul in Harput because that city stood in the middle of Anatolia in rough, mountainous country unconnected to the outside world by railways or modern roads. Davis formally took over on May 31, 1914, then left for home the next day to visit his ill father. The war broke out during this trip, and in Egypt he received orders to return to his post. He never again saw his father alive, nor would see his wife, who had gone to America due to poor health, for another three years.[58]

During his absence from Harput, the Porte replaced the *vâli* with a new one, Sabit Bey, who Davis considered ignorant yet shrewd. Like many Ottoman officials, he made many promises he had no intention of keeping. On the plus side, he had little interest in persecuting the Armenians. When the order came to deport of them from the *vilayet*, he allowed several thousand to flee to Russian territory and others, mostly Roman Catholics, to remain in Harput for a time. He announced a moratorium on deportations, then unexpectedly reversed this on November 4 when he directed the police to round up all the rest in the city.[59]

Because Harput served as a main point of transport for Armenians being deported from the region, Davis described the refugees from Erzerum and Erzingan as such:

> A more pitiable sight cannot be imagined. They were almost without exception ragged, filthy, hungry, and sick. This is not surprising in view of the fact that they have been on the road for nearly two months with no change of clothing, no chance to wash, no shelter and little to eat. The Government has been giving them some scanty rations here [in Harput]. I watched them one time when their food was brought. Wild animals could not be worse. They rushed upon the guards who carried the food and the guards beat them back with clubs hitting hard enough to kill them sometimes....
> The Turks have been taking their choice of these children and girls for slaves, or worse. In fact, they have even had their doctors there to examine the more likely girls and thus secure the best ones [as slaves]. There are very few men among them, as most of them have been killed on the road. All tell the same story of having been attacked and robbed by the Kurds.[60]

When Sultan Mehmed declared a holy war against all enemies of Islam in 1914, this served as a signal to the three million or so Kurds living in the Empire and the lands bordering it that they now had permission to attack non–Muslims. One newspaper reporter who knew his history pointed out that the Ottomans had often used the "savage" Kurds as their "licensed assassins." Both in the Empire and in neighboring Persia *some* Kurds raided non–Muslims, and they certainly played their part in what would become an outright genocide against Armenians. Yet to vilify an entire ethnic group for the actions of a minority does them a great disservice.[61]

The Porte controlled the Kurds by exploiting their social structure, which consisted of two classes: serfs who did the bidding of their lords, and warriors who constantly fought among themselves for supremacy. Kurds had no homeland of their own, although not far lack of trying. They had periodically rebelled against their Turkish masters and on several occasions attempted to create an independent state. Unification proved difficult because loyalty to the tribe superseded loyalty to all other things, even God. Each tribe had as its head a chief, the *agha*, who owned great swathes of land upon which worked the lower classes of peasants and serfs. The tribes fought with one another as often as they formed alliances, and so long as each one swore fealty to Constantinople, the Porte showed little interest in their internal affairs. Tribes also paid customs' dues and taxes. To keep the Kurds unbalanced and unable to unite against the Empire's rulers, the Porte played tribes against one another. In the nineteenth century, they became subject to conscription into the Ottoman army. Despite their disunity, they frequently rebelled, prompting to the Porte to dissolve all principalities in 1867 and replace them with *vilâyets* ruled directly by its loyal proxy governors.[62]

In the Empire the Kurds took on the social role of feudal warriors while Armenians and other Christians living in the area alongside the Jewish population tended to be its merchants and manufacturers. Although the Armenians and Kurds usually got along, Kurds often resented Armenian money lenders when these individuals called in their loans. This antipathy explains why the two people never united to oppose the Empire in any significant way. CUP leaders inflamed Kurdish hostility towards this Christian minority by promoting the stereotype of "rich but immoral Armenians." When the war broke out, the Empire moved the bulk of its Kurdish forces to the *vilayet* of Van. Unknown to the Kurds, it planned to deport them as well once they had finished helping remove all the Armenians. In this future scheme, Kurds would not exceed more than 1 percent of the population, nor would their leaders be allowed to remain with them, this to ensure they could not unify their people. Morgenthau disliked the Kurds as much as he did the Turks, although he recognized that they attacked Armenians because of orders originating from Constantinople.[63]

At the Porte he frequently dealt with Talaat, then the minister of interior. Born in 1874 in Adrianople as the son of a Turkish farmer and Roma mother, Talaat had helped to plan the 1913 coup that made the CUP absolute master of the Ottoman Empire. Opposition to and plots against the sultan had resulted in his imprisonment between 1895 and 1898. After the restoration of the constitution in 1908, Talaat became a member of parliament and later its president. He became grand vizier in 1917.[64]

Until the war, he remained incorruptible in a nation known for an excess of corruption. During it he made a fortune by speculating in sugar and buying the homes of wealthy Armenians for a third of their price. A correspondent for the *Times* of London called him "an engaging villain." When this reporter arrived for a dinner with Talaat in 1913 during Ramadan, the holy month of Islam during which the faithful must fast until sundown, he saw Talaat breaking this prohibition because he could not wait any longer to sate his thirst and hunger. He swallowed "a pound of caviar … washed down by three tumblers of *raki*, or Turkish brandy. Then he began his dinner—a mighty feast. Two bottles of claret disappeared as rapidly as the *raki*, and afterwards he drank as many bottles of champagne." Good Muslims also do not drink alcohol.[65]

Morgenthau found Talaat difficult to deal with. Once, for example, when he tried to intervene on behalf of a mistreated British subject, Talaat told him: "He's English, isn't he?

Mehmed Talaat Pasha. Bain News Service. Creation date unknown. Library of Congress Prints and Photographs Division.

Then I shall do as I like with him!" to which Morgenthau suggested, "Eat him, if you wish!" Talaat replied, "No, … he would go against my digestion." Talaat stubbornly clung to his determination that the Armenians had to go from the Empire despite impassioned arguments by Morgenthau that this was inhumane, and the removal of such a wealthy minority would harm the economy.[66]

Talaat once asked Morgenthau for a list of recently dead Armenians who had taken out American life insurance policies with New York Life and Equitable Life of New York. He believed the payouts should go to the Ottoman state. Morgenthau angrily replied, "You will get no such list from me." It turned out New York Life had no more scruples than Talaat. The family of Martin Marootian, a pharmacist in California, tried for 75 years to get the company to pay out the benefits owed for his uncle, Setrak Cheytanian, killed by the Ottomans on June 21, 1915. New York Life repeatedly refused to pay out or deny the claim, so Cheytanian's family along with 11 others sued in a Los Angeles court. New York Life tried to get the case dismissed on the grounds the statute of limitations had passed, but when members of the California legislature who represented a sizeable Armenian-American constituency heard this, they pushed through a special law extending the statute of limitations so the suit could go forth.[67]

At first the insurer claimed it lacked any records of these policies, but in the end it all came out. Of the roughly 3,600 policies sold to Armenians living in the Ottoman Empire before 1914, the company had dropped or paid out just 300 before the war's outbreak and a mere 1,100 after it, leaving 2,200 cases unresolved. New York Life lost the trial, and although most of the original policies paid not more than $1,000, it agreed to pay families ten times their original value.[68]

Morgenthau sometimes met with Enver, the man who had bungled the invasion of the Caucasus in late 1914 and who now served as the minister of war and commander in chief of the army. Born in Constantinople in 1881, he liked to get his hands dirty, preferring to do his killing himself rather than leaving it to others. Although trained by the Germans in military science, he had no head for tactics or strategy, which he demonstrated with aplomb by nearly losing the entire Third Army against the Russians. He showed scant competency in politics either, a point the writer of his *New York Tribune* obituary made plain: "As a statesmen he was a mere swashbuckler."[69]

Enver blamed the Armenians for the military setbacks of the Ottoman army. He told Morgenthau that they had "had a fair warning" not to join with the Empire's enemies. When Morgenthau pointed out that the Armenians removed from Zeitoun had received no food whatsoever, Enver promised they would get what they needed. Morgenthau suggested Americans could give them aid, but Enver refused on the grounds that it would just encourage other Armenians to rebel. At a meeting on August 5, 1915, Morgenthau gave Enver a list of demands to help the Armenians, but the minister refused listen to all of them and rejected those he had heard.[70]

Realizing the futility of convincing anyone at the Porte to stop the massacres, Morgenthau tried applying diplomatic pressure. To this end he attempted to enlist the aid of the ailing German ambassador, Wagenheim, the man who had done more than any other to forge the existing Turko-German alliance. Though Wagenheim did not deny the Ottoman treatment of the Armenians, he believed they were rebels and therefore deserved their fate.[71]

In a report he sent to Theobald von Bethmann Hollweg, imperial chancellor of Germany, he speculated that the Russians had armed the Armenians in Van else they never would have had a sufficient number of explosives and weapons to hold off the Ottoman force as effectively as they had. The Ottoman claim that many of the Armenians killed in the fighting had worn Russian clothes—the implication being they had betrayed the Empire—was proof enough for him. Still, he did present a note of protest about their treatment to the grand vizier on July 5, 1915, but the man who then held that position, Said Halim Pasha, had no power to do anything about it.[72]

Wagenheim wanted to hear nothing that contradicted this. When Paul Weitz, a correspondent for the *Frankfurter Zeitung* who had lived in Constantinople for 30 years, tried to tell him what he knew about the massacres, Wagenheim twice threw him out of the room. Nor did going over Wagenheim's head do much good. Four German missionaries running a school in Aleppo wrote to the minister of foreign affairs in Berlin about the horrors they had witnessed, reporting that "out of 2,000 to 3,000 peasant women from the Armenian Plateau who were brought here in good health, only forty or fifty skeletons are left. The prettier ones are the victims of their gaolers' lust; the plain ones succumb to blows, hunger and thirst (they lie by the water's edge, but are not allowed to quench their thirst)." Local authorities forbade Europeans from giving them bread. The missionaries finished their letter with an appeal to German pride: surely if the German government failed to act, this would stain the people's good name. It did nothing.[73]

Morgenthau next approached Lieutenant Commander Hans Humaan, the German embassy's naval attaché in Constantinople who was a close friend of Enver's and thus had

Ismail Enver Pasha. Photographer unknown. Creation date unknown. Library of Congress Prints and Photographs Division.

his ear. Born in Smyrna, Humaan's father had worked in the Empire as an engineer and archeologist, one of the reasons Humaan was a Turkophile. Morgenthau tried appealing to this man's humanity, but he had none. He believed even more firmly than Wagenheim that the Armenians had rebelled and therefore deserved their fate.[74]

Frustrated, Morgenthau telegraphed Secretary of State Lansing with a recommendation that the Wilson Administration demand the Porte immediately stop its oppression of the Armenians and allow survivors to go home if they could. In not, they should receive "proper treatment." If this approach was not feasible, perhaps the Administration could contact

Abram Elkus (left) and Henry Morgenthau. Bain News Service. 1916. Library of Congress Prints and Photographs Division.

Kaiser Wilhelm and ask him to put pressure on his ally. Morgenthau suggested that the U.S. government should in any case demand that the Turks allow Americans and other foreigners to give the Armenians aid. Lansing cared little for the Armenians and figured the Ottoman treatment of them was justified, though the State Department did object to the brutal way the deportations were being executed. Save for instructing Morgenthau to tell the Porte that America was concerned for the Armenians' welfare, the Administration did nothing else about it until the United States entered the war in 1917.[75]

Morgenthau's wife, Josephine, became so disgusted by the whole thing she abruptly left for home in September 1915 after having lived in Constantinople for about a year and eight months. Her route home took her through Bulgaria. While in its capital of Sofia, she met with Tsarina Eleonore Reuss-Köstritz, a compassionate woman of German birth who had spent much of her youth in Petrograd. During the Russo-Japanese War she worked for the Red Cross, and amid the Balkan wars founded a hospital in which she served as a nurse.[76]

Mrs. Morgenthau reported all she knew about the treatment of the Armenians to the tsarina with the hope she could intervene on their behalf. Now that Bulgaria had committed to the Central Powers, it might be able to get some concessions from the Turks since it served as an important land bridge for communications between Europe and the Empire as well as a means to ensure Serbia fell. In return, the Central Powers promised to give it part of Macedonia. Mrs. Morgenthau's meeting had its desired effect. Bulgaria formally protested the Ottoman treatment of the Armenians, but this changed nothing other than temporarily straining Talaat's relationship with Ambassador Morgenthau.[77]

Near the end of April 1916, Morgenthau resigned his post. Realizing he could do nothing more for the Armenians in this capacity, he decided face to face conferences with officials in America might work better. He also wanted to work on Wilson's reelection campaign. The president replaced Morgenthau with Abram I. Elkus, a 45-year-old Jewish lawyer who at the time was the president of the Hebrew Technical School for Girls in New York City. Elkus accepted the appointment and headed to Constantinople with his wife and three children. By the time he arrived in August, the Armenian deportations had pretty much run their course, although those who had survived still suffered from Ottoman oppression and needed much aid. Wilson chose Elkus because he wanted "a trained lawyer" to navigate the international implications of the crisis. Elkus served until the Ottoman Empire broke diplomatic relations with the United States on April 20, 1917, although he did not depart immediately because he had contracted typhus.[78]

6

The Great Crime

Sex Trade in Armenian Girls and Women

The American missionary station in the city of Merzivan could not prevent its 350 Armenian teachers, students and staff from being deported despite American diplomatic pressure and the bribes they had paid to the Ottoman to prevent it. The children forced to leave the safety of the compound faced the very real danger of being kidnapped and sold into slavery, which become so prevalent during the war that after it ended, the League of Nations set up the Rescue Movement to liberate those still in bondage and aid those who had escaped. Students at the mission's Girls' School faced an elevated danger because they often became sex slaves. The staggering number of girls and women taken for this purpose glutted the market, allowing Dr. George E. White, head of all mission operations in the city, to purchase the freedom of three enslaved girls for 1 lira, or about $4.[1]

In the rural areas of the Empire, Kurds, Arabs, and Turkish military officers had a long tradition of selling girls and boys to brothels and orphanages. Sometimes they took them into their own households where a girl or young woman might become a second wife because she came with no bride price and had no family to protect her. A boy, on the other hand, might become a low ranking servant but more often was put to work as a farmhand or shepherd. Ottoman officials in the slaving business sold their chattel to wealthy and middle-class Turkish families. Prominent males of the household sometimes used the girls (and probably a few boys) strictly for sex. The neutrality of American missionary schools did not necessarily prevent slavers from raiding them. At one such school, an eyewitness reported seeing Turkish officers take the prettiest girls for themselves, give the lesser ones to the enlisted men, then sell the rest at auction.[2]

In the Syrian Desert, the final destination of most Armenians who survived the terrible trek from the west, many girls and young women were auctioned off "like cattle" to Arabs in tents. They remained "naked for months" and suffered repeated beatings and sun blisters from exposure to the relentless desert sun. Some converted to Islam to survive. Their captors "bound and forcibly tatooed [sic] [them] on the forehead, lips and chin to mark them as Moslem women." Those old enough often became pregnant. Contemporary newspaper accounts estimated that during the Armenian massacres, the Ottomans and their proxies sold between 500,000 and 600,000 girls and women into sexual slavery.[3]

On August 12, 1915, Ottoman officials ordered the girls in the American mission school in Merzivan to go to Sivas. Dr. White decided to accompany them on horseback as far as Amasia, a town about 25 miles to the southeast as the crow flies that stood alongside a gorge through which flowed the river Iris. To ensure their safety he brought a contingent of mounted guards. Two others Americans, Charlotte Webb and Frances C. Gage, the latter the head of the Young Women's Christian Association in Anatolia, planned to travel with them all the way to Sivas, but in Amasia local officials refused to recognize their travel papers, forcing them to return to Merzivan. By the time they convinced the *vâli* to give them permission to continue, the girls had gotten six days ahead of them, although their wagon was still under guard from hired gendarmes.[4]

In the town of Yenikhan, a place known for its vibrant rug industry, Gage pretended to look into purchasing a rug while Willard followed up a rumor that the girls currently resided in an old factory. In a letter to Henry Morgenthau, Gage wrote, "We found no rugs and no girls. The former had been confiscated by the Government, and the latter had gone two hours before toward ... [Sivas], five hours away." A friend in the town warned her that the girls were in grave danger. Rushing ahead, Gage and Webb finally caught up with them, though

George E. White. Harris & Ewing. Taken between 1905 and 1945. Library of Congress Prints and Photographs Division.

some of them had been taken elsewhere and one converted to Islam and married. In Sivas, Gage and Webb asked the *vâli* to give them permission to take the girls back to the school. To this he agreed.[5]

Without this protection, their students might have suffered the same fate as Arshaluys Mardiganian, whose experiences during this period typify what happened to young girls who fell into the hands of slavers. On the Easter Sunday of April 1915, the military commandant of her district, Hussein Pasha, came to her house in the city of Chimishguezek demanding her father, a banker by trade, sell her to him. Despite her age—just 14—Hussein wanted her for his harem. Although defying a powerful Ottoman military officer would mean persecution, her father refused three times. Hussein warned that all Armenians would soon face deportation and only by giving away Arshaluys could he save the rest of his family, which included 16-year-old Lusanne, 15-year-old Paul ("who wanted to be a priest") plus three younger sisters and one younger brother.[6]

As promised, soldiers rounded up the town's men and older boys, including Arshaluys' father, plus Paul when he dared to follow him. Held locally for a time, those not killed outright were marched to the nearby village of Gwazim in which half went into a building used as both a barracks and prison and the other half were taken across a river and killed. Arshaluys and Lusanne traveled there to see their father and brother, but never got the

Arshaluys (Aurora) Mardiganian. Ca. 1919. Wikimedia Commons.

chance. Instead they found an old Armenian woman, Fatimah, who had converted to Islam when she became part of a harem but continued to practice her Christian faith in secret. She told them not to give up hope, though had she revealed her real plan, the girls would not have found it a pleasant prospect.[7]

Allowed to visit the prisoners and take them water, Fatima told them that the Turks had murdered those who not been locked up with them, and this surely would be their fate as well. She smuggled into the prison heavy rocks hidden in her water buckets. With these the younger men killed the older ones. Arshaluys's father used one to kill Paul. The next time Fatimah came, she had in her buckets coal oil, which those still living used to burn themselves to death. Realizing what she had done, the guards threw her into the burning building to suffer the same fate.[8]

In Chimishguezek, notices went up throughout the city informing its population of 18,000 Armenians that they had to leave in three days. When the day of departure arrived, soldiers offered to place weaned babies and old women in ox carts to make their journey easier. About three hours later, these stopped and the soldiers executed them. That night Turkish civilians purchased the refugees' goods at prices far below their value.[9]

The next morning a raiding party of Kurds came. Their leader, Musa Bey, ripped off the veil Arshaluys wore to hide her face and, seeing her youthful beauty, threw her onto the back of his horse. He took her and several other captives to the castle of Kemal Effendi, a Young Turk who asked his new acquisitions to convert to Islam. Those who refused would suffer. Arshaluys told him she would do so only if he agreed to save her family. Otherwise she preferred to die.[10]

Kemal agreed to her proposal. The next day he rode out on horseback to find them. Arshaluys walked along. As they skirted the top of a cliff-like bank along a river running red with the blood of hundreds of slaughtered Armenian men and boys, Arshaluys jumped into the water below, swimming to the other side, which had a much lower bank. Soon she found her family. Kemal ordered his men to punish them in retaliation for Arshaluys' escape, but her mother bribed them to go away.[11]

Days later their guards began robbing them, forcibly stripping those who they suspected had valuables hidden on their persons. That night soldiers came to take pretty young women. When one grabbed Lusanne by the hair, Arshaluys tried to pull her away. The guard became so infuriated at Lusanne's resistance "he drew his knife and buried it in … [her] breast," the blade slicing into Arshaluys' cheek and leaving a permanent scar. Lusanne died in her sister's arms. She and several others used their hands to dig a grave.[12]

While camped outside of Arabkir, a city known for its weaving, a Kurdish raiding party came. It took Arshaluys along with a dozen or so other girls and young women "into the desert beyond," where the Kurds stripped off their captives' remaining clothes, then raped them en masse. Afterwards the Kurds tied them to their horses and left them in that state for the night. The next morning they untied and fed them, then took their prisoners on horseback north to the city of Egin. As they approached, Arshaluys watched Turkish convicts bury the bodies of slaughtered Armenians.[13]

The Kurds paraded the girls naked through the city's crowded streets to a building's courtyard into which about 400 young Armenian females unwillingly assembled. They were divided into groups of about 20. Their captors took Arshaluys' group into a room to display them to a pasha from Constantinople and a bey who served as the emissary of Talaat and Enver. The bey told them if they converted to Islam they would receive imperial protection and go to schools that would teach them how to become good Muslim wives. Soldiers whipped Arshaluys and the others who refused. Arshaluys's unrelenting spirit of survival and depth of her Christian faith prompted to her hold out, one of just 25 to refuse apostasy.[14]

Four days later she and several other captives merged with a larger group of about 1,000 comprised of small children and middle-aged and elderly women. They walked to Malatia, which English travel writer Mark Sykes called "a miserable place" consisting of nothing but mud houses. Here gathered about 20,000 refugees. Along the road the captives passed 16 deceased, naked Armenian girls hanging from crosses. The Turks had crucified them because of their refusal to submit to their new masters.[15]

On the second night in the city, Arshaluys, covered in rags, crept out to look for members of her family. Becoming lost, she could not make it back to her quarters before morning came and, fearing punishment if caught returning, did not do so. Coming across a house over which flew an American flag and knowing that the United States had befriended the Armenian people, she knocked on the door. Several Turks saw her and, because of her attire, easily indentified her as an Armenian. As they came towards her, she "screamed and pushed at the door." A woman opened it and brought Arshaluys into her arms. The Turks demanded she turn the girl over, but she refused, saying they had no authority over an American citizen. She was Miss Grisell Mclaren, an American missionary who had once been one of Dr. Ussher's students. Unfortunately Mclaren lacked Ussher's influence and cunning, so by the end of the day she tearfully gave up her new ward.[16]

In late June, Arshaluys joined with about 15,000 young and old Armenian women for a journey to the city of Diarbekr, a settlement surrounded by dark basalt walls that stood along the Tigris and served as the nexus for several key trade routes. Along the way a Kurdish raiding party took her and other girls to the house of Hadji Ghafour, a man known for his deep Islamic faith. He offered them relief from their miseries if they agreed to become Muslims and entered his harem. To show his resolve and to break theirs, he had the first girl who refused whipped to death in front of the others. They all agreed to convert.[17]

Stripped naked and put into a room for the night, morning light brought still one more horror: outside the window they saw the body of the girl that Ghafour had ordered killed for refusing to convert hanging upside-down. He had sex with a different girl each night, who he called his "betrothed," and on the fifth called for Arshaluys. The morning after being raped, she decided to escape. She and another Christian girl even younger than herself, Arousiag Vartessarian, got away through a window and headed west in the hope of finding refuge in a Dominican monastery in that direction.[18]

The walk to reach it involved a harrowing trek across sandy land in the heat, but it paid off: the monks took them right in. After a brief prayer in the chapel, they escorted them to a building with about 200 other refugee girls and women who had escaped from the Turks. Two weeks after settling into this sanctuary, Chechen bandits attacked one night, climbing the monastery's walls to gain entry and killing the monks when they refused to give up their Armenian wards. The bandits killed all but 23 of those under the monks' protection, including Arousiag.[19]

They took Arshaluys and the other captives to Diarbekr in which Arshaluys hoped to find her remaining family. The Chechens sold her and seven others to some Germans soldiers in the city. One of their officers, Captain August Walsenburg, took a fancy to Arshaluys, finding her resistance to his advances amusing. Two weeks later the soldiers received orders to go to Harput, so they abandoned their slaves.[20]

For three days the freed slaves women cowered in the house, sure local gendarmes in search of loot would find them, which they did. Arshaluys snatched up a knife and hid it on her person. When one of them took her to a room to rape her, she stabbed and possibly killed him, then fled to the street where a Turkish woman motioned for her to enter her yard. Wary but desperate, Arshaluys complied. This woman, who did not like way the Armenians were being treated, hid Arshaluys there until the night. When it came, she gave Arshaluys some food, three liras, and told her to go out the city's north gate and join the refugees in the morning. She snuck through the gate easily enough, but upon seeing some guards, screamed, calling attention to herself.[21]

Rather than kill herself with her knife as she had planned, she tossed it away and told the guards she wanted to join the refugees. She told them they would be paid if they took her to the camp, inferring the money would be coming from other Armenians rather than that she had on her person because she did not want them to rob her. The refugees, who had come from Erzerum, gladly took her in. That morning they began the 200 mile trek towards Urfah, a terrible walk during which they did not receive water for four days in one stretch. On the 23rd day after leaving Diarbekr, their escorts herded them into a gorge and began slaughtering them. Of the roughly 2,000 who had started on this journey, only about 160 still lived the next day, most of them young like Arshaluys.[22]

At Urfah they settled in by an artificial lake along with other refugees who had arrived. The Urfah Turks came out to take the newly arrived Christian girls, but their guards refused to part with them without being well paid. That night the Urfah Turks flooded the lake to force both the refugees and guards out of their camps, then swarmed into the resulting chaos to snatch up little girls whom they took to a school for the conversion to and teaching of Islam. For once Arshaluys escaped.[23]

One day a company of refugees riding ponies and donkeys escorted by Kurdish cavalry arrived. Among them Arshaluys saw her mother, two of her surviving sisters, and her younger brother. Rushing to embrace them, the Kurds allowed her to travel with them. Her uncle, Ipranos Mardiganian, lived in the city. He had converted to Islam in 1895 to save his life during a state-sponsored Armenian massacre. Taking the name Ibrahim Agha, he secretly practiced Christianity. He took Arshaluys and her family into his house in which he had also hidden four Armenian girls plus openly hosted and protected a few older women in his cellar. They stayed for a month until a high Ottoman official, Haidar Pasha, informed her uncle that he could no longer safely keep his family here. Her uncle paid to give those under his protection a military escort to Chimishguezek. They went to a small village not far from Mush and there stayed in an Armenian church while waiting for their escort to arrive.[24]

Before it did so, 1,000 mounted and armed Kurds on their way to Mush rode in. Their leader, Sheik Zilan, decided to use the church for a stable and within his men found the Mardiganian party. Arshaluys' mother handed them a pass written out by Haidar. Zilan pointed out that it only specified protection for her family, not the four young women with them. Deciding Arshaluys belonged to the latter group despite her mother's protests to the contrary, he took her as well. He bound his prisoners' hands and linked them together with a rope, then took them into Mush the next morning.[25]

He sold them to the notorious Kurdish slave dealer Bekran Agha, who received the equivalent of 85 cents for Arshaluys because of the glut of Armenian girls on the slave market. He in turn sold her to a servant representing none other than Jevdet, the notorious *vâli* of Van, who gave her away to Ahmed Bey as a present. This man placed her into his harem of 24 girls and young women, directing his two sons to impregnate as many of them as they could. Ahmed demanded she become a Muslim, but she refused outright, angering him greatly. He called in one of his sons, Nazim, to break her spirit.[26]

She would never become a Muslim, never become his "bride" unless he saved her mother and the rest of her remaining family. She gave him their location so he could retrieve them. Slaves, she was told, had no bargaining power. Hours later a guard brought her outside to the road into the front of the house. There stood her family whom Nazim's men killed. In her memoir she wrote, "My eyes see them now, every day and every night—every hour, almost—when I look out into the new world about me. I must keep them closed for hours at a time to shut the vision out." She cried for two days straight, which she believed caused her to have poor eyesight.[27]

Three days later, Ahmed and Nazim tried to force her to convert to Islam and submit to their will, but she refused, insisting she wanted to die. They threw her into an empty room with a single barred window. There she stayed for many days, stubbornly declining to surrender. Then a remarkable thing happened. Outside the window she heard a shepherd bringing in a flock of sheep. To command their movements, he used a whistle unique to those from around her home. She jumped up, briefly caught the bars of her window, and repeated the whistle to attract this person's attention. It was an old man named Vartabed who had once worked for her father and loved her dearly. Having survived the Armenian deportations by pretending to convert to Islam, he promised to free her.[28]

A few nights later he pried out the old iron bars in the window with a steel bar to effect her escape, an act for which Ahmed would later have him killed. Vartabed took her to a hut in which lived a family of Kurdish shepherds friendly to Armenians. Although they said she could stay, she feared their close proximity to Ahmed's house would pose too much danger for them. The family gave her woolen socks, a blanket, a loaf of bread, and a jug of water for her journey. She headed into mountainous "highlands of grass and sand" of the *vilayet* of Dersim and there spent over a year wandering about, sometimes serving as the temporary slave for farmers. In time she headed toward Erzerum with the hope of finding the Russians, a trek during which she often lacked sufficient amounts of food and water and was in a state of near nakedness.[29]

She arrived in the city just as the Ottomans surrendered it to the Russians. Wandering about aimlessly, she came across a house from which flew an American flag. Fearful at first, she approached "and fell at the feet of a tall, kindly-looking man," this being Canadian missionary Dr. F.W. (Frederick William) MacCallum. He had come with the Russians as part of an effort to buy thousands of Armenian slaves back for $1 a piece. He picked her up and took her inside.[30]

Armenian Genocide

In the fall of 1914, a German colonel visited the American missionary school in Sivas, one of the smallest of the American missions in Anatolia, to hint that its mostly Armenian staff and students faced great danger. Mary Louise Graffam, principal of its schools, did not want to help the Ottomans, but she decided it best to ingratiate herself with them and to that end agreed to become the matron of the Red Crescent hospital in Erzerum where a typhus epidemic had broken out. Having graduated from Oberlin College in Ohio with a degree in teaching, she had no medical training, but nonetheless did well, in part because she spoke fluent Turkish and thus did not need a translator.[31]

Upon her return to Sivas in March 1915, she began hearing rumors that the Ottomans planned to deport the city's Armenians. When the police started raiding Armenian houses, she went directly to the *vâli*, Mora Bey, to protest. He claimed they were being sent away because they had rebelled against the state. Some of the deportees entrusted their jewels to the missionaries, who buried them in spots all across the city to keep them well hidden. Then came the order that all Armenians in the city had to go to Urfah, which included her mission's Armenian staff and its 50 students. She planned accompany them so she could help them establish themselves at their final destination. For the trip she secured "two ox carts, two horse arabas [Turkish carriages], five or six donkeys, and a supply of medicine, food and money."[32]

Between 2,000 and 3,000 deportees trekked southeast. Locals living along their route robbed them as they passed through their villages. Graffam's party hired a special escort to keep them safe, though they extorted another 45 liras for continued protection against both thieving villagers and marauding Kurds. Hardships increased the farther they went. Although Graffam's party had the means to buy water, those lacking it often died of thirst. On the third day out, the guards watching over the refugees took all the adult males aside on the pretext of sending them to Kangal, leaving Graffam's party with just a couple male teachers and the school's boys. She later heard the Turks had shot all them, though she could not decide if she should believe it or not.[33]

Her part of the journey ended when she received an order to meet the *vâli* in Malatia. The Turks foisted upon her an old woman as an "escort" whose real mission was to spy on her. She stayed in Malatia for three weeks in an upper room from which she watched thousands of Armenians pass by to their deaths. Then she was placed in a horse-drawn wagon bound for Sivas along with a party of several Ottoman officials and their escort of gendarmes, the last being useless when actually needed. When a raiding party of Kurds surrounded them, they, the cart's driver, and the officials ran, leaving Graffam and her companion to fend for themselves. Terrified, Graffam had the presence of mind to tell her companion to get into the wagon, then she grabbed the horses' reins and took off at high speed. The Kurds yelled but did not pursue.[34]

Officials in Sivas prevented her from returning to the American mission, so "she rented houses and barns for destitute refugees coming from all directions. She started a factory for the manufacture of flannels and sweaters for the Turkish Army" and employed a number of Armenians to do it. When officials questioned this, she pointed out they worked for the Ottoman government, which kept them safe. Local officials did all they could to make her life miserable, at one point threatening to try her for treason. She also leased a farm owned by Kaiser Wilhelm. After the war, the farm's caretaker, no friend of hers, unexpectedly gave her its deed on orders from the Kaiser himself. Another surprise came from the Turkish government: it decorated her for the selfless humanitarian work she had done during the war.[35]

Not all Americans handled the stress of the Armenian deportations and massacres nearly as well as Graffam had. One was Walter Mackintosh Geddes. Not long after finishing his education from Yale Forestry School and attending Harvard to study landscape architecture, he joined his father's firm McAndrews and Forbes as superintendent of harvesting licorice root throughout Asia Minor. He settled in Smyrna, learned Arabic, began wearing the local garb, and often traveled using Arabian stallions. When the war broke out he sent his wife and two-year-old son home to Pittsburgh.[36]

On September 16, 1915, he left on an extended trip for Aleppo. At Afium Karahissar, he saw a huge encampment of perhaps 10,000 Armenians living in "deplorable" conditions. In Konya, an Armenian man was forced to board a train without being able to bring with him his wife and baby. At a camp in Osmanieh, Turks whipped men, women and children. The starving Armenians sold what meager possessions they had to buy food.[37]

The closer to Aleppo the Armenian refugees got, the dryer and hotter things became. Hundreds died daily from thirst and hunger. In Aleppo, survivors of the journey crowded into Armenian churches, houses, courtyards, and even open lots. Those who could afford it buried their relatives in coffins, but most were just thrown into two-wheeled carts that took them to mass graves. Many Armenians refused to accept alms, preferring death by starvation over prolonged misery.[38]

After a month here and in Damascus, Geddes began his return trip to Smyrna on

This photograph of an Armenian woman and a deceased child was taken near Aleppo. Photographer unknown. Creation date unknown. Library of Congress Prints and Photographs Division.

October 26. During this trek he saw thousands more Armenians heading towards Aleppo, many so starved they had become mere skeletons. Dead Armenians littered the side of the road. Stopping to eat lunch one day, a crowd of emaciated, filth-covered children surrounded him to beg for bread. It all proved too much for him. He shot himself on November 7 in a hotel room. Possibly motivated by the wishes of the family, the obituary that appeared in *Yale Forest School News* reported he had died of a heart attack rather than by his own hand.³⁹

Rev. Francis H. Leslie was an American missionary originally from Michigan who had come to Urfah four years earlier to oversee one of the more out of the way missions in Asia Minor, which included an orphanage, a school for the blind, a variety of shops, and a lace and handkerchief factory. Things started going wrong on August 19, 1915, at around 4:30 in the afternoon when town criers began calling for Turks who owned arms to come out with them. Once assembled, authorities incited them to beat and kill Armenians regardless of age or sex in retaliation for an alleged incident in which policemen were killed by Armenians hidden in a well. When the vigilantism began, most Armenian men had just left work for the day and therefore had no sort of weapons on their persons with which they could defend themselves or their kin. This orgy of violence lasted two days before calm returned.⁴⁰

When told to turn over their personal weapons to the authorities, the Armenians in Urfah refused because they still remembered the Turkish massacres of their people in 1895. Many also vowed to die rather than be removed from their homes after seeing the terrible treatment of their brethren from Zeitoun who had marched through the city. The order to depart was issued on September 29. Those who decided to remain barricaded themselves in their quarter of the city and dug tunnels to connect with other ones. Armed with rifles,

Aleppo. The American Colony (Jerusalem). Photo Department. Taken between 1900 and 1920. Library of Congress Prints and Photographs Division.

ammunition, and a few French machine guns for defense, they had enough food to hold out for awhile. In the first week of October, an Ottoman force of about 6,000 arrived and began firing artillery at these "rebels." During the fighting, the Turks tied their prisoners together in groups ranging from 50 to 100, marched them up a hill, and threw them into a ravine. Those who survived the fall did not live for long. Soldiers killed them using bayonets and swords instead of guns to save bullets.[41]

Amidst the siege, several Armenians took over the American mission by force and held those within hostage, including Leslie. The Turks dislodged the Armenians by bombarding it, causing all its inhabitants to flee. Ottoman authorities charged Leslie with aiding the Armenians because he had taken some of their valuables for safe keeping. Upon seeing a gallows designed to hang 60 of them, fear overcame him, so he killed himself by drinking an entire bottle of carbolic acid, leaving a suicide note that professed his innocence.[42]

Another American persecuted by Ottoman officials, Ethel Marston Agazarian, never took her life, but she certainly suffered greatly. Born on October 8, 1884, in Gray, Maine, she married an Armenian-American born in the Ottoman Empire named Bagdasar Agazarian with whom she had a son. In 1913, they decided to visit Bagdasar's hometown of Harassa. Arriving in September, they learned that Bagdasar's father had died, so they used some of

The Red Cross produced this photograph of Armenians being killed after the Armistice. February 1919. Library of Congress Prints and Photographs Division.

the money set aside for their trip home to pay off his debts. To earn enough to get back to America as well as help his stepmother and brother, Bagdasar began working on the farm.[43]

When the war came, he paid for an exception from conscription, but sometime at the beginning of June 1915, the police chief of a nearby village summoned him. He left on a Wednesday and never came back. Ethel feared the Ottoman army had decided to ignore his deferral and drafted him after all. On Sunday, Bagdasar sent a boy to retrieve his wife. She found him crying. The police had promised to let him go home Tuesday, but he did not believe it. He said his goodbyes. Ethel never saw him again. She heard he wound up imprisoned in nearby Harput where the Turks drowned him.[44]

A week after Bagdasar went missing, the police came to Harassa on a Saturday night ordering all its inhabitants to travel to a nearby village where they placed about 39 men into one room, and forced more than 50 women and their children into another. The police brought the men to the river and drowned them, even taking the time to track down and shoot two who had run off to avoid being detained. They moved the women and children back and forth between Harassa and another village for a time, then drowned all save for Ethel and her son, exempted because of their American citizenship.[45]

For the next three months, she and her son lived with a Turkish man in Harassa who had taken an Armenian as his wife. Then they went to Harput to stay with the American consul. In July 1916, they headed to Constantinople. Arriving on August 29, they sought the aid of Ambassador Abram Elkus. He wanted to give her an American passport, but one of his secretaries warned him that because she had married an Armenian born in the Ottoman Empire, it made her one of its subjects.⁴⁶

Elkus knew if the Ottomans sent her back into the interior that she would die, so he issued a passport under her very American-sounding maiden name of Marston. His defiant secretary considered this a "grave offense," mainly because he was an Ottoman subject and feared this deception might cause him problems. Elkus pointed if he did not help, she would surely die, making him an accessory to murder. The secretary complied but warned Elkus that the Porte might remove him as ambassador if he proceeded. Elkus could happily live with that. The secretary made a formal protest to the State Department to protect himself. When Talaat, now the grand vizier, confronted Elkus about it, he said he could justify it on the grounds that her husband had died. Talaat insisted this man still lived, so Elkus told him if he could prove it, he would recall her and apologize. Talaat never brought it up again.⁴⁷

Fall of the Ottoman Empire

Many of the Armenians who survived the journey into Syria took up residence in small villages and camps around Damascus, a sparse, forbidding land. Others settled outside of Aleppo. Ottoman officials offered them neither shelter nor clothes nor food, and their guards continued to rape and otherwise molest them. Deaths occurred daily. Slavers swept up what viable women had not yet escaped. Whether by outright murder or neglect, Ottoman policy killed an estimated 1.5 million Armenians out of a population of 2.3 million.⁴⁸

Realizing the Empire was going to lose the war, top Ottoman leaders resigned en masse on October 8, 1918. To keep the British and French from detaining them, many boarded the German torpedo boat *Lorelie*, when it sailed on November 8 for the Crimea. Here Talaat, Enver, and Djemal went their separate ways. To distance itself from them, the new Ottoman government charged the three exiles with everything from

This photograph shows a "widowed Armenian woman and her children in the aftermath of the Armenian Massacres of 1894 to 1896." Bain News Service. 1899. Library of Congress Prints and Photographs Division.

profiteering to subverting the constitution to massacres against the Armenians. It prosecuted them in absentia via courts martial, found them guilty and condemned them to death, although it never had an opportunity to carry these sentences out. The new government also signed the Ottoman Empire's death warrant by agreeing to the Armistice of Mudros on October 30, 1918. Much of its territory went to the allies and the Greeks. The Empire officially ended on March 3, 1924. Out of its ashes rose modern Turkey.[49]

As a condition for peace, the Turks formed the Ottoman War Crimes Tribunals. Starting in the spring of 1919 and ending in 1922, these yielded little justice. Of those found guilty, the state executed just three minor officials for "crimes against humanity." Many others that the courts had found guilty never served their sentences. Justice had failed in part because America wanted nothing to do with the trials and the British had left too few soldiers in Turkey—just 320,000—to effectively force the issue.[50]

During the war, Djemal, after leading a failed attack on the Suez Canal, served for a time as the minister of the marine, then as the military governor of Syria during which he oversaw the Armenian massacres. He died violently at the end of July 1922 when two Armenians assassinated him and his aids. Enver lasted just a month longer. After the war he first went to Germany, then returned to Asia Minor where he began operating in the Caucasus region with the hope of rebuilding the lost Ottoman Empire. To that end he became an agent of the Soviet Union, and when that failed to get him anywhere, turned against it and tried to carve out a new nation of his own. He died on August 4 in a battle in Baldzhuan, now modern Tajikistan. About his death his obituary in the *New York Tribune* said, "Good riddance."[51]

Talaat escaped to Switzerland, then went to Germany where he lived under a variety of assumed names. It did him no good. On March 15, 1921, as he walked with his wife along a street in the Berlin suburb of Charlottenburg, a young man tapped him on the shoulder on the pretence that he knew him. When Talaat turned around, the man shot him point blank in the head, killing him instantly and wounding his wife. The assassin tried to escape but witnesses to the murder caught and nearly beat him to death before the police intervened.[52]

This man, an Armenian student named Soghomon Tehlirian, came from the small village of Nerkin Pakarich in the *vilayet* of Erzerum. During the war

Ahmed Djemal Pasha. Photographer unknown. Taken between 1910 and 1922. Library of Congress Prints and Photographs Division. George Grantham Bain Collection.

he had gone to Tiflis to fight with the Russians. While serving with the medical corps, he saw the aftermath of massacres against his people, which unsettled his mind. During his trial he claimed that for two weeks the ghost of his mother, whose head had been split open by an ax, had haunted his dreams. She called for him to avenge her. A German psychiatrist testified that Tehlirian "could not be held responsible for his act." Eyewitnesses of the Armenian massacres told the court about the horrors they had seen. The jury found Tehlirian not guilty by reason of insanity. He may have bamboozled them. In the book *Operation Nemesis: The Assassination Plot That Avenged the Armenian Genocide*, writer Eric Bogosian convincingly argues that Tehlirian had acted on behalf of a conspiracy that formed in the United States with the single goal of killing the architects of the Armenian massacres.[53]

The Armenians called what happened to them during the war the *Medz Yeghern* ("Great Crime"), which served as a prelude for the Holocaust. In a 1939 speech, Hitler said, "I have placed my death-head formations [special SS mass execution units] in readiness—for the present only in the East—with orders to them to send death mercilessly and without compassion, men, women, and children of Polish derivation and language. Only thus shall we gain the living space (*Lebensraum*) which we need. Who, after all, speaks today of the annihilation of the Armenians?"[54]

The fate of the Armenians inspired Raphael Lemkin, a Polish Jew, to become a lawyer dedicated to punishing those who destroyed groups of people. In one of life's ironies, he nearly became a victim himself. When Germany invaded Poland in 1939, he fled to the United States and there taught law at Yale and Duke. Many of his family members who could not escape died in the Holocaust. During the war he knew about the death camps in Europe but could find no word that sufficiently described their purpose, forcing him to create his own, "genocide," which he constructed by merging the Latin word *cide* (the act of killing) and the Greek word *genos* (tribe or family). It appeared for the very first time in his 1944 book *Axis Rule in Occupied Europe*.[55]

To this day the nation of Turkey officially refutes that Ottoman leadership committed willful genocide against the Armenians, although it does admit to the deportations. At the time of this writing, Turkey's Ministry of Foreign Affairs had on its official English language website an entire page dedicated to this denial by questioning the number of Armenians who died as well as the veracity of witnesses, this despite the overwhelming evidence to the contrary. A staggering number of credible eyewitnesses left behind testimony, including Leslie Davis, who saw an estimated 10,000 slaughtered Armenians just five miles outside of Harput. And he took photographs.[56]

The planned genocide of the Armenian people unfolded in phases, each one worse than the next. In 1914, Ottoman forces crossed into Persia and Russian territories to plunder Armenian settlements. The Ottoman army conscripted Armenians en masse, sweeping up those between the ages of 15 and 60 to get as many of them as it could under its control. The Porte blamed the Armenians and not Enver Pasha for his failed offensive into the Caucuses in the winter of 1914–1915 by claiming the Armenians in his army had defected en masse to the Russian army, making them all traitors. In February 1915, Ottoman army commanders received a secret order to disarm all Armenian soldiers in combat roles and transfer them to special labor battalions that amounted to nothing more than a way to gather them up for mass executions by their former Turkish comrades.[57]

In May 1915, authorities arrested 1,200 mostly Armenian men and women in the *vilayets* of Diarbekr and Mamuret-al-Aziz and placed them on 13 barges that would travel down the Tigris to Mosul with a guard of 50 gendarmes. Not long into the trip, their guards stripped them of their money and clothes, executed them, then threw them into the river. During this slaughter about half the guards walked along the river's banks to ensure no one escaped. In June, Ottoman authorities began looking for weapons held by the Armenians as evidence of their disloyalty to the state. Some Armenians confessed under torture. The possession of arms as well as certain books and images were made illegal as a pretext for more arrests.[58]

Upon his return to the United States, Morgenthau decided one way to aid the Armenians was to create charities for relief, an idea he suggested to the Board of Foreign Relations. In November 1915, three such charities merged to become the American Committee for Armenian and Syrian Relief and headed by James L. Barton, the same man who had asked Ussher if he wanted to go to Turkey. This organization changed its name to the American Committee for Relief in the Near East and began operating under a Congressional charter starting in 1919. Americans gave generously. The organization raised $116 million from 1915 until its end in 1930.[59]

In 1918, it brought Arshaluys to California so she could star as herself in a film version of her tale. She had arrived in the United States from Oslo on November 5, 1917, with the idea of tracking down an older brother who lived somewhere in the country. She was met at Ellis Island by an Armenian-American couple who placed ads about him in the papers. This attracted the attention of reporters from the *Sun* and *Tribune*, which brought her to the notice of the author Henry Leyford Gates, who wrote as H.L. Gates. He took down a sanitized version of her story and published it first as a newspaper serialization, then as the book *Ravished Armenia*. It sold half a million copies. He Americanized her first name to Aurora, which she used from then on.[60]

The film was called *The Auction of Souls*. She suffered much during the filming. Upon seeing actors dressed as Turks, she screamed out of real fear and possibly tried to kill one with a knife. While sliding down a makeshift rope made of two rugs, she fell and shattered her ankle. To top all this off, she came down with the often fatal Spanish flu. Despite these obstacles, she completed the filming. Its eight reels showed the Armenian massacres with such realism the Carrick Theater in Los Angeles refused to admit anyone under the age of 16, a sound decision considering it included a scene showing Turks flogging an Armenian woman who refused to enter a harem, Turkish slave markets, and naked girls hanging from crosses with at least one nipple showing on screen. The movie sparked sympathy for the Armenians and a great hatred for the Turks.[61]

It did very well both in America and abroad, so much so that studio executives wanted to make Aurora a Hollywood star. Not that she had personally gotten much out of it. The studio paid her $15 a week and, though the American Committee took credit for the movie's production, a producer named Colonel William N. Selig owned the rights. Having accomplished her goal of getting her story out, Aurora refused to do any more pictures. Instead she found an uncle to live with, Steve Long (an Anglicized name), who had moved to America many years ago. Although she would remain in the safety of the United States for the rest of her life, she never found peace. She married and had a son who later abandoned her. In her last years she became so worried about Turkish soldiers coming for her she had a woman deliver her food through a window. When she died at the age of 93 in 1994, no one claimed her body, which wound up in a mass grave with no headstone. *The Auction of Souls* fared little better. Only one 15-minute reel found in 1994 survived.[62]

It seems ironic that American sympathy went so far for a people persecuted on a far-off continent while at the same time did not extend to the United States' indigenous people, who in many ways had suffered a fate very similar to that of the Armenians. From the "1780s to the 1840s," the southern states in cahoots with the U.S. government systematically removed the native people living within their borders, taking the land for themselves to make it into plantations. President Andrew Jackson, who had a slave plantation in Tennessee, orchestrated one of the most notorious Indian Removal incidents when he force marched the Cherokees to unsettled territories to the west. This people lived mainly in Georgia as well as the eastern portion of Tennessee and the western parts of North and South Carolina. In an effort to avoid conflicts with the whites, they actively adopted many aspects of white culture and society, such as writing a constitution, creating a written version of their language, and establishing a supreme court.[63]

When Georgia tried to confiscate their lands, they took their case all the way to the Supreme Court, which ruled in their favor. Despite this, Jackson decided to forcibly remove them to the west anyway, and to that end he ordered General Winfield Scott to round up and place them into internment camps. A military escort force marched them about 900 miles to Oklahoma during which 4,000 of the approximately 13,000 who went died, which is why the journey is known as the Trail of Tears. Like vultures, "white land speculators" grabbed and divvied up the lands the Cherokees had been forced to abandon.[64]

After the Civil War, the federal government set its sights on opening up the lands west of the Mississippi to white settlers. To do that, it needed to remove the native people living there. The commander of the U.S. Army, General William Tecumseh Sherman, placed General Philip H. Sheridan in charge of this task. The two came up with a plan similar to that which they had used during the Civil War: they would defeat the aboriginal people living on the Plains by starving them out. Since most Native Americans in this part of North America relied exclusively on buffalo herds for their livelihood, Sheridan encouraged hunters from England and America to come out and start shooting as many of them as they liked, with the U.S. Army sometimes giving them direct aid. The buffalo made this easier than other herd animals because they tend to remain together even when those standing around them fall over dead, making them easy targets. By the early 1880s they had nearly become extinct throughout the west.[65]

The starving Native Americans had no choice but to go onto reservations under the control of the all-powerful Indian Bureau. Utterly ruthless, no one, not even Congress, oversaw its activities. When Native Americans received U.S. citizenship in 1924, the government made them wards of the state. A 1928 *Nation* article written by John Collier reported that the Indian Bureau considered those under its control "essentially serfs," treating them like "half-animals." The Bureau took native children and placed them into boarding schools designed to wipe their culture out. Over the years, its officials repeatedly robbed them of their land and what little personal wealth they possessed.[66]

Although Native Americans have never received their own autonomous state—reservations being a cruel parody of that concept—the Armenians did. In 1919, Ottoman-born Armenian-American Vahan Cardashian started the American Committee for the Independence of Armenia with the support of Senator Henry Cabot Lodge of Massachusetts. Cardashian proposed the creation of an Armenian state that would span an area between the Mediterranean and the Black Sea. This became a reality with the signing of the Treaty of Sèvres on August 10, 1920, though it encompassed just a fraction of the area Cardashian had proposed. The next month the Turks invaded and took some of Armenia's new territory, forcing it to seek the protection of the Soviet Union by becoming one of its satellite states on December 2, 1920.[67]

7

Persia

Victim of the Great Game

Panic swept through the Urmia Plain in Persia on January 2, 1915, when the Russians announced their plans to evacuate the area in response to Enver's push into the Trans-Caucasus region, which threatened to cut off communications. After the Russians' departure, an Ottoman proxy force of Kurds invaded, prompting about 25,000 out of 32,200 to 33,000 mostly Assyrians and Armenians living on the plain to flee en masse toward the city of Tiflis just across the border in the Russian Empire. A vast chain of humanity made the journey, most of it on foot, "over frozen mountains and through half-frozen swamps" without shelter or food. Not all completed it, especially children and the elderly, who more easily succumbed to starvation or exposure.[1]

Anglican missionary Rev. J.D. Barnard reported from Tiflis: "As far as the eye could reach in both directions was a constant stream of refugees, sometimes so dense that the road was blocked. It was a dreadful sight and one I never want to see again." The city not only had to absorb the mostly Assyrians coming from the Urmia Plain, it also had to take in Armenians fleeing from the Ottoman Empire's *vilayet* of Erivan. In response to this human wave of suffering, the American Committee for Armenian and Syrian Relief said it needed $100,000 in donations for aid that would immediately go to Persia.[2]

Tabriz rose 4,400 feet above sea level and stood in the shadow of Mount Sahand, a 12,000 foot high dormant volcano. Surrounding the city were hardy almond trees capable of surviving hot summers and subzero winters plus the occasional earthquake. The Russians had a transportation depot here that ran "numbers of heavy motor trucks along the military road … [that took] … the place of rail communication" as well as a customs house and post office. The Ottomans wanted the city because it made a good strategic location from which to launch an attack against the undefended Russo-Persian border.[3]

The American consul in the city, Gordon Paddock, arranged for 600 Turks to peaceably enter Tabriz after the orderly departure of the Russians on January 5, 1915. He also convinced the Ottomans to keep their force of 25,000 Kurds they had brought with them away from the city. The Turks claimed they had come to "liberate" Persia from Russian occupation and to that end would allow an appropriate Persian official to rule there when he arrived.[4]

The city's Presbyterian mission took in 400 refugees, a number that included Armenians, Assyrians, Belgians, French, Swedes, Austrians, and Germans. Paddock placed it under his protection, which kept the Turks from molesting it, saying much about his mettle considering he had no means of communicating to outside world and could do nothing

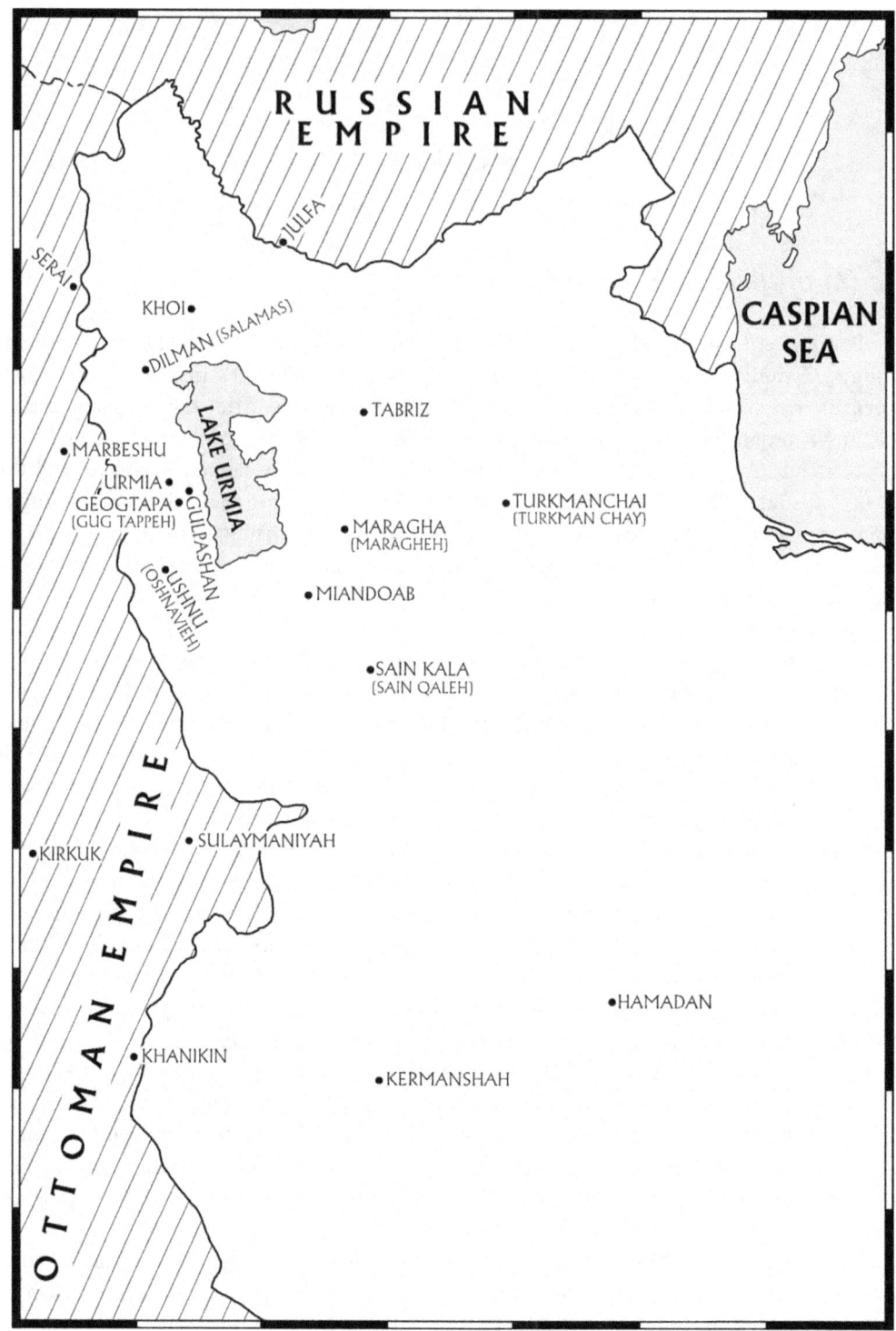

Persia (Iran). Map by the author based on one that appeared in *Persia and Afghanistan: Keith Johnston's General Atlas, Apr. 1912*. Edinburgh: W. & A.K. Johnston, 1912. David Rumsey Historical Map Collection.

had the Turks decided to overrun it anyway. Fortunately they departed on January 30 when the Russians arrived to retake the city, though they did not withdraw from the Urmia Plain.[5]

The Ottomans had long coveted the Urmia Plain, a parcel of land in the Persian province of Azerbaijan that spanned about 60 miles in length and 30 in width surrounded by the Zagros Mountains, which had long provided a natural barrier against invaders. A wide array of waterways irrigated its plentiful orchards of apricot, cherry, and almond trees as well as grain fields, vineyards, and other desirable crops. Water drained into Lake Urmia, the largest body of water in Persia and one of the world's saltiest. Those living here called it the Gate of Pleasure or the Paradise of Iran.[6]

Political weakness forced upon the Persian government by Russia and Britain had severely weakened its ability to defend itself against this Ottoman invasion. Called Iran by its inhabitants, it was a constitutional monarchy with limited independence because of Russian and British machinations. A treaty signed by both on September 23, 1907, guaranteed that neither Power would expand into Tibet or Afghanistan. It further allowed for economic interference in Persia when necessary, establishing the Russian sphere of influence in the north and British in the south. The treaty effectively ended the so-called "Great Game," the Russo-British struggle for domination and expansion into Southwest and Central Asia that played out for much of the nineteenth century. This rapprochement occurred because both Powers considered the rise of the German Empire a threat far more dangerous than one another. The treaty also gave the Russians permission to keep a garrison of several thousand on the Urmia Plain. Persia had no say in the matter, although in 1918 it would declare this unfair treaty null and void on its own authority.[7]

On November 1, 1914, Persia's prime minister, Mirza Hasan Mostofi al-Mamaleki, declared his nation officially neutral, though it did little good. Britain occupied its southwest region to protect the oil fields from Ottoman attacks. In 1915, Britain and Russia secretly divided the country in two, each planning to integrate their halves into their empires after the war. One contemporary British writer, Richard Hill, although surely unaware of the pact, wrote the following that succinctly expressed the imperialist justification for this action: "Persia is absolutely unfitted for self-government, incapable of understanding the elementary principles of autonomy. It seems but a question of a short time before she must succumb to those Powers that will give her a government firm and efficient." This about a people who had established and oversaw major empires throughout human history.[8]

Iran had lost much of its territory starting in 1799 after Russia started a series of wars against it as an excuse to gobble up parts of it. One of the consequences of these conflicts was the hated Treaty of Turkmenchay. Signed on February 28, 1828, it gave Russian and British subjects special rights in Persian lands and forced the Iranian government to pay a vast sum of reparations to Russia. These capitulations left the nation nothing more than a client state of both Powers so that by the end of the nineteenth century any important decisions its government made needed approval from either Russia or Britain.[9]

This weakness prompted the Ottomans to launch two incursions into Urmia Plain in late 1914. The first occurred between October 9 and 12 when a small raiding party consisting mainly of Kurds led by Turkish officers plundered a few villages. The second foray began on October 30 that consisted of about 400 mounted Kurds. In early December, the Kurds were finally defeated outside Urmia by a force of Cossacks reinforced by Russians with the aid of American Lewis machine guns and a surprise flanking movement.[10]

Ottoman Invasion

Yonan H. Shahbaz, a Baptist minister and naturalized American citizen who ran a mission in the Assyrian town of Geogtapa near the city of Urmia, knew there was trouble when he heard a gunshot as he sat down for breakfast. It signaled that a force of about 25,000 Kurds and several thousand Iranian Muslims had arrived in town. Shahbaz's American wife immediately raised the mission's U.S. flag, hoping it would protect them. Seeing it, villagers rushed into the mission's yard. Shahbaz suggested everyone there scatter and try to escape in smaller groups to make it harder for the Kurds to catch them. Many took refuge in the Russian church, which stood on Geogtapa's highest point. Well built and surrounded by thick walls, it would provide the best place for defense. Those within could hold off an armed force so long as it lacked cannons, which the Kurds did not possess. Unable to take the church, the Kurds retreated to and barricaded themselves in the southern part of town.[11]

While taking his family to the church, Shahbaz lost two-year-old Wilbert, one of his four sons. He went out find him but soon had to retreat to the church when someone took a shot at him. On January 4, 1915, he decided to lead his family, minus Wilbert, along with some friends and neighbors out of town to nearby Gulpashan with the hope of finding safety there. They had not gone far before 300 armed Kurds, many of them wearing kerchiefs to hide their faces from the neighbors they now attacked, opened fire upon them. Shahbaz told his wife to hide behind a wall to the west. She stopped and let out a terrible scream. There on the snowy ground lay two abandoned babies, which she picked up. The Kurds forced the Shahbaz party to split in two: half headed for the vineyards to the northwest near Gulpashan, and the others, including Shahbaz and his family, went due west.[12]

They climbed over a wall on the other side of which stretched a road, and down this came Shams-ul-la-Bek, an agent of the Persian governor headed for Urmia on horseback. Because he was a Persian official, Shahbaz figured the Kurds would leave him alone and to that end forced him to accompany them. Along the road they saw many horrors, including the rape of girls as young as seven or eight. Coming from the other direction rode a group of horsemen brandishing American and Ottoman flags that consisted of two Muslims, two Assyrians, and a medical doctor from the American Presbyterian mission in Urmia named Harry Phineas Packard. He told Shahbaz he had come to stop the Kurds from massacring those trapped in the church at Geogtapa.[13]

That a single American thought he alone could stop this sounds on the face of it like pure hubris, but Packard had a status few others could claim. Called Hakim Sahib, meaning "Sir Doctor," he had made it a point every year to head into the Zagros Mountains and there treat its population of Kurds and Assyrians, a dangerous thing to do because both groups distrusted outsiders. Packard had over the years befriended many Kurdish sheiks and, unlike most of his fellow American missionaries, rightly refused to damn all Kurds as a race of marauding monsters based on the actions of a few.[14]

Born in Illinois in 1874, he moved to Colorado in 1886, living there while attending high school, college, and medical school. In the summer of 1906, he, his wife Julia, and their one-year-old son, Hubert, headed to Urmia where Packard replaced Dr. Joseph P. Cochran, who had died of typhus. To effectively communicate with his patients, Packard learned Farsi, Syriac, and Kurdish. Fortunately he had a knack for picking up languages, as attested by the fact he already spoke English, German and Greek when he arrived.[15]

In his first few days, he removed cataracts from the eyes of a prominent Kurdish chief, Mirza Mohammad Agha, greatly increasing the esteem the Kurds had for him. This American doctor could cure the blind! On another occasion a Kurd burst into his examination room and demanded Packard come with him immediately to treat his father, a sheik, for a serious gunshot wound. Packard dropped everything and prepared for a trip that might last a day or two. Upon arriving, he cleaned and sewed up the sheik's wound, which caused this man to improve considerably by the next morning. As a mark of gratitude, the sheik gave Packard an honor guard for his trip home.[16]

During his journey to Geogtapa, Packard passed through a village in which its people were fighting with the Kurds. Despite bullets whizzing by, he found the Kurdish chief and convinced him to allow about 400 townspeople to head unmolested into Urmia. He reached Geogtapa just in time. Those held up in the church had nearly run out of ammunition. American flag in hand, he charged forward between the lines, making his way to the Kurdish sheiks leading the attack. He knew them all because he had treated them for ailments over the years, including the removal of kidney stones from one.[17]

Abdullah Beg Benari in particular kissed Packard on both cheeks out of real affection. He had not seen the American doctor since he had returned from his recent furlough in America. Packard asked Benari to stop the attack and allow the trapped townsfolk to go. The sheik replied, "They have fought and have killed and wounded a number of our men, and we must butcher them all to the last child one day old." Packard insisted he and the other chiefs reconsider.[18]

Although one of their number wanted to kill all those in the church and be done with it, the majority consented to allow the townsfolk to go on their way providing they gave up their firearms and ammunition as well as their houses and possessions. To this Packard agreed, but it led to another problem: how to stop the fighting? When the chiefs issued the command to cease attacking, their men ignored them. Packard wanted to go into the church to convince the townsfolk to surrender, but the Kurds would not allow it. They did not want his blood on their hands. An hour later the fighting settled down. Carrying an American flag, Ussher and a terrified Assyrian companion went to the church so he could inform those within about the deal he had made. The surviving 1,500 Assyrians walked five miles to the safety of Urmia and once there to the American mission compound.[19]

The Board of Foreign Missions had established its first Persian mission in 1834 and others thereafter, though in 1871 it handed control of these over to the Presbyterian Church. Because local law forbade missionaries from converting Muslims to Christianity, they turned their efforts towards the Nestorians, a Syriac-speaking Christian denomination that disliked the appellation "Nestorian," preferring to call themselves Assyrians. This sect had split from the mainstream Christian church in 431 C.E. when the Third Council at Ephesus condemned the opinions of Nestorius, the patriarch in Constantinople, prompting his supporters to found their own church based on his teachings. For the first 20 years the missionaries tried unsuccessfully to reform the existing church, which did nothing more than cause those who wished to follow the presbyterian rather than episcopal model of church structure to break off and form the Syrian Evangelical Church.[20]

The Presbyterians had most of their Persian stations in major towns and cities. They built hospitals, introduced modern medicine, and set up schools. Women dominated the missionary field because at this time it was one of the few career opportunities open to

"Assyrian Family Making Butter in Persia." Bain News Service. Creation date unknown. Library of Congress Prints and Photographs Division.

them. Most had university degrees and over half arrived at their stations unmarried. Those who did marry had to remain active in their work. They came as reformers who, as good Calvinists, saw wealth as a sign of the grace of God and, because of this philosophy, focused their efforts mainly on the elite.[21]

Thousands of Assyrians fled to the walled city Urmia for protection, the traditional birthplace of Zoroaster, the man who founded the religion named after him that inspired the Muslim practice of praying five times a day and who had supposedly prophesized that the three Magi of Biblical fame would begin their quest to see the Christ from here. The city's residents were mainly Turkish-speaking Muslims subject to Persian rule who lived in harmony with a Christian minority of about 35,000 as well as a small colony of Jews. Many refugees made went to the city's American mission compound.[22]

Overseeing this was William Ambrose Shedd, a Doctor of Divinity for whom the Kurds also had much respect. Born in Urmia on January 24, 1865, he lived there for five years until his parents and three siblings returned to America because of his mother's failing health. Although his family moved around, Shedd spent most of his time in the United States living in Marietta, Ohio, where at the age of 15 he began attending its college. He learned languages easily and spoke many: English, Syriac, Turkish, German and French.[23]

After the departure of the Russians, everyone looked to him as the person to oppose Ottoman oppression, a role he played for the next five months. Thousands of Christians who had fled to Russian territory entrusted the missionaries with their money for safekeeping with the proviso that they could borrow it without interest if the need arose. In addition to this, the Armenian representative of a local English bank asked Shedd to take into his care 10,000 Persian tomans of silver, this unit of money being worth a bit less than $1. In total the missionaries took in the equivalent of about $20,000. When the Ottomans tried to confiscate it as a legitimate prize of war, the missionaries refused to release it, and the Turks never tried to take it by force.[24]

The Americans displayed U.S. flags all around their compound walls—19 of them according to one account—with the hope they would keep the Turks out. To strengthen their position, they asked the relatively powerless Persian governor to persuade the Ottoman force to respect their neutrality. The governor also helped them relocate some of the refugees to other dwellings outside the compound and gave them Persian guards for protection.[25]

Beginning on January 3, around 20,000 people fled to Urmia to find refuge in its different missions, and somewhere between 10,000 and 17,000 squeezed themselves into the American compound in particular, although the missionaries had taken over the abandoned Anglican mission, giving them a total area of about six acres. The American compound proper covered about a block. Within its stone walls three feet thick and 20 feet high stood a variety of buildings including a church, school, printing office, and one- and two-story houses that served as residences for the Americans, who considered them subpar because they lacked modern conveniences. The local people, on the other hand, saw them as luxurious and saw the missionaries wealthy because they had servants and ate three good meals a day. The compound had two wells and a brook for water within its walls. The Americans shut and barred all its gates save for the one that opened to the busiest street. Because they considered their Persian guards unreliable, Hugo Arthur Muller, a clergyman and the mission's treasurer, set up an unarmed Assyrian force to keep a more diligent patrol of the walls. He also took charge of guarding the main gate.[26]

Conditions within the compound quickly deteriorated. A lack of a maternity ward led to the death of nearly all newborns. Sanitation became impossible, food scarce and expensive, and diseases, mostly measles and dysentery, spread, killing about 48 a day for a total of 4,000 by the time the Turks left. Feeding so many became one of the biggest struggles the missionaries faced. One eyewitness estimated they needed four tons of food a day. Although local Muslims donated some, it was not enough. The missionaries purchased bread in the form of thin wafers from the bazaar in the morning, reselling it to those who could pay for it in an attempt to stretch what funds they had. At night they gave the rest away to those who lacked the means to buy it. The money the mission had acquired from fleeing refugees and the local English bank quickly ran out, leaving it with a deficit of between $30,000 and $40,000 for the cost of food alone.[27]

To remedy this, Muller went to the bazaar and borrowed 1,000 tomans from a merchant, who paid it out in 2 kran silver pieces. These he put into a bag and gave to his porter, who slung it on his back. As he, Muller, and a Persian guard headed back to the compound, six well-armed Kurds surrounded them, hitting the money bag to verify its contents. Muller and the others ignored them and returned without being robbed.[28]

Among the refugees living in the compound were Shahbaz and his family. Shedd had given them a room, but they had to share with 23 others, forcing Shahbaz to sleep "under an office table." The day after their arrival, friends brought Shahbaz his missing son, but the ordeal had taken a toll on his little body and he died soon after. After a few weeks, Shahbaz feared the rampant disease in the compound might soon take the lives of his remaining family, so he determined to leave. Across the street lived a wealthy Russian

Christian he knew, Nazar Khan, and from him Shahbaz arranged to rent a room that he and his family occupied early the next dawn. Although it contained no furnishings or carpet, it would do. Khan then left the city altogether.[29]

Shahbaz's wife soon fell deathly ill. He dared not go out to find a doctor for fear of attracting the attention of the Turks or Kurds roaming the streets. Desperate, one night he traveled over the rooftops to reach a nearby physician he knew with whom he communicated through a window. The doctor came and his ministrations probably saved Shahbaz's wife. A few days later someone knocked on the gate door. Terrified, Shahbaz asked in Turkish: "Who is there?" The caller, a man, answered, "I am your friend."[30]

Suspicious that anyone who spoke Turkish had good intentions towards Christians, Shahbaz went to the roof to look down upon this visitor. Below he saw a Persian Muslim knew well, so he let him in. This man, who Shahbaz did not name in his memoir to protect him, was unsettled that Shahbaz and his family lived in an empty room that lacked even a rug for the floor. He returned in the afternoon with a Persian rug that fit the room perfectly. He also brought food and continued to do so daily for the next four months until the Russians returned to the city.[31]

Shahbaz had been wise to remain hidden and cautious. The Ottomans could and would execute those they deemed dangerous to their interests and cared little if this violated foreign sovereignty. Once, for example, about 70 soldiers invaded the American compound, snatched a hiding Russian Orthodox bishop and four priests, then hanged them all. In the fifth week of the occupation, Reghib Bey, the Ottoman official in charge of the city, demanded 6,000 tomans from Assyrians residents in exchange for leaving their houses and shops in peace, then gave the Persian governor 600 tomans to collect it. One missionary, Mary Lewis, had her doubts that the Turks would keep their word if the Assyrians paid.[32]

The Turks went into the French mission and there arrested about 100 Assyrian men. Imprisoning them, they built "a gallows with seven nooses" outside the city by the Kurdish Gate. Reghib demanded money for their release, adding insult to injury by charging visitors 2 krans (about 18 American cents) to see them. Reghib did not even bother to feed his prisoners; instead he asked the American missionaries to do that. A few weeks later he had the prisoners executed.[33]

On the Urmia Plain, Turks and Kurds killed males and raped females of all ages, one rapist boasting he had defiled 11 Christian girls under the age of seven. Eighteen men took one woman, raped her en masse, then released her. When she dragged herself to Urmia, local Persian officials did nothing about it. Turks and Kurds also took girls and women captive, forcing them to convert to Islam and marry Muslim men. Shedd would later rescue quite a few of them from this fate.[34]

Word of specific massacres got back to the missionaries. In one instance, 75 Christians were conscripted to fetch telegraph wire from the Ottoman town of Gawar, which was about 60 miles west of Urmia. As they returned, their guards herded them into a mountain valley and shot them all. Three victims faked their deaths, then returned to Urmia to report what had happened. About six months later a missionary led an expedition to search for the scene of the crime and there found the bodies—some in a nearly mummified condition—along with empty gun shells.[35]

Gulpashan, the town to which Shahbaz had wanted to take refuge and one of the wealthiest places in the district, had paid Ottoman officials and Kurdish chiefs for police protection against raiders, but it did little good. On the night of February 24, a party of Kurds, Turks, and Persian Muslims came to town and easily overcame police resistance. They demanded protection money as well as ropes for the war effort. They tied up all the town's males in groups of five, then took them to the graveyard outside of town and shot them. Next they executed all the old women and girls too young for marriage or sex, raped those left alive, then sold them into slavery. When word of this massacre reached Morgenthau, he protested to Talaat, who promised to protect Christians in Urmia.[36]

The Turks demanded from the city "ten thousand suits of shirts and pajamas for the army. Eight thousand were demanded from Moslem women, and two thousand from the Christian ... women." Since most of the Christians in Urmia lived inside the American compound, one of its missionaries, Lenore Russell Schoebel, handed out to them about "fifty-five bolts of calico." The women, sewing mostly by hand, soon produced 800 shirts despite their reluctance in making clothes for the people who had run them out of their homes and killed their kin.[37]

A couple of Turkish soldiers who entered the American compound had brought with them typhoid fever, which blossomed into an epidemic, sickening 18 American adults and nine of their children, including Shedd, his wife Louise, Dr. Packard, Margaret Wallace McDowell, Mary Lewis, and the compound's matron, Bernice Cochran. Both McDowell and Mrs. Shedd died. Packard became so ill those around him had little hope of his recovery, but he ultimately pulled through.[38]

On May 20, a Russian offensive pushed the Ottomans out of Urmia, and on the 24th they occupied the city. This force included a large number of Cossacks, a bogeyman in Eastern Europe parents used to scare their children but here greeted as heroes with the crowd shouting, "God bless those Cossacks!" With less than 1,000 houses still standing outside of the Urmia Plain's major cities, Shahbaz and his family could not return to Geogtapa. He decided to go home to America, though he had no money to do so, having spent it all either on survival or as charity to others.[39]

Desperate, he borrowed $30 at 100 percent interest. This he used to take his family to Tabriz in which he sought the aid of Paddock. After a month of waiting with no answer, he figured his American citizenship must have come into question, so he decided to take his family 100 miles to Russia on foot. Before departing, he left Paddock a note about his plans. Fortunately, the consul read it the next day and immediately sent a messenger to retrieve him and his family, who were about an hour outside of the city. A telegram had just come from America informing Paddock that the secretary of state would forward Shahbaz $500. With this he bought the first good meal his family had had in a long time, then hired a carriage to take them to Russia and from there home to America.[40]

Had Shahbaz decided to stay in Urmia, he would have not found conditions to his liking. A pamphlet issued by the American Committee for Armenian and Syrian Relief printed this report from Urmia's American missionaries:

> At the beginning of June, 1915, when the people emerged from our premises emaciated from sickness and malnutrition and crushed by the blow that had fallen upon them, they were confronted by a seemingly hopeless situation. Practically all their household furnishings and food supplies had been plundered; the same was true of their domestic animals on which they depended in large measure for their subsistence; their houses were without any doors and windows and probably a full third of them had been demolished. They were in terror of going back to their villages; they feared their Moslem neighbors

who had despoiled them of their property, outraged their wives and daughters, and killed many of their relatives.[41]

So much so that the American missionaries had to stop feeding them just to make them leave. They gave each family a week's worth of flour and sent them on their way to their homes, presuming they still stood. The missionaries had control of the aid coming from the Committee for Armenian and Syrian Relief, so for the next three months rather than give survivors of the Ottoman occupation food directly, they handed them "2,661 sickles and scythes, and 1,129 spades" so they could grow their own.[42]

August 5 brought with it a rumor that the Russians again planned to abandon the city. The missionaries decided that all save for a skeleton staff should move the station and its relief assets to a safer place. Packard, his wife, children, and three others volunteered to stay. Those who departed, including Shedd and two of his two daughters, left in carriages accompanied by horses and donkeys they had bought just two hours earlier. Word of a decisive Russian victory over an Ottoman force prompted them to turn around, only for them to reconsider when they came upon a clash between Kurds and Russians. At this point Shedd, his daughters, and one other missionary decided to continue back home to the United States for a furlough. The others returned to Urmia.[43]

Escape from Urmia

Not long after seizing power in November 1917, the Bolsheviks ordered the withdrawal of all Russian forces from Persia, which had swelled to about 75,000 in June when the Provisional Government launched a new offensive to capture several key Ottoman cities, including Mosul and Kirkuk. Though a few Russians stayed behind as mercenaries, the Assyrians scavenged most of the machine guns, ammunition and cannons left behind, allowing them to gain control of Urmia Plain. Some Muslims, fearing they would be the target of revenge, appealed to the missionaries for protection.[44]

On New Year's Day, 1918, Shedd, who had returned from his furlough, became an honorary American vice-consul, a position later made official, which gave him the authority he needed to keep the Christians and Muslims from killing one another. He reluctantly became an unofficial *cadi*, or judge, to resolve issues among them. His "court," nothing more than a simple chamber in which he sat on a chair in front of a table, met in the mornings. He used the foreign aid under his control to penalize those who did something illegal, such as selling wine to the Russians who in their drunkenness sometimes raped, robbed, and caused other troubles.[45]

On February 22, Persian Muslims attacked a contingent of Assyrians moving military equipment at the behest of Russian mercenaries. To make matters worse, Kurdish chief Ismail Agha Shikak (better known as Simko), assassinated the Assyrian patriarch, Mar Shimun XXI Benyamin, after pretending friendship. The Assyrians retaliated by massacring 500 Kurdish refugees in Urmia. Simko probably carried out the assassination at the behest of the Persian government, who feared Assyrian ascendency on the Urmia Plain, though he certainly had his own reasons. He doubted the weak Persian government could offer effective resistance against an attempt to carve a Kurdish homeland out of the region. By killing Mar Shimun, he had removed a major unifying figure among the Assyrians, lessening their chances to build their own permanent powerbase in the area.[46]

In March, Persia's foreign minister accused the American missionaries of arming Christians on the Urmia Plain with the aim of destabilizing the entire province of Azerbaijan, something the American government officially denied, though its ambassador to Persia, John Lawrence Caldwell, thought there might be some truth behind it. In April 1918, the Ottomans again recaptured Van, causing some 20,000 Armenians to flee. Raiding Muslim villages as they trekked towards Persia, a clash with a lingering Russian force in June caused many of them to head into Urmia Plain in an effort to escape. The region simply could not absorb this influx of humanity because it was already suffering from a severe shortage of food, a famine difficult for humanitarian agencies to relieve for lack of decent roads.[47]

On June 18, an Ottoman force occupied Tabriz. Paddock departed for Tehran, leaving the Spanish consul in charge of the American consulate and the American mission's hospital. The United States had by this time gone to war with Germany but had not done so with the Ottoman Empire. The Turks seized the American and British consulates, the latter having been under U.S. control. Because the Porte had broken off diplomatic relations with the U.S. government, the Wilson Administration asked the Swedish ambassador to see if the Empire had indeed attacked the U.S. consulate. He did so twice but received no answer. The U.S. government warned if this had occurred, it might consider the incident an act of war.[48]

The Ottomans tried to retake Urmia only to be stopped on three occasions by a local Assyrian force. Shedd, despite knowing the Turks blamed him for their failure to keep the city in 1915, decided to remain because he believed the British would come to Urmia's rescue, a notion they reinforced when one of their planes landed on July 8 to inform the missionaries of plans to send a squadron of Syrian and Armenian soldiers led by British officers to nearby Sain Kala. Armed with machine guns and ammunition, they would arrive in about three weeks. July 31 came and went, yet still they had not come. Another advance on Urmia by the Ottomans convinced Shedd to flee, although many of his fellow missionaries remained. About three hours after departing, the Turks arrived.[49]

Shedd and his wife became part of a much larger exodus of about 80,000 people fleeing south. As often happens when a mass of humanity moves without proper sanitization, an epidemic of cholera broke out. The refugees repaired to an abandoned small Russian port at the southern tip of Lake Urmia, and from here traveled five days to reach Miandoab. The next morning fighting erupted outside of the town. An Ottoman force had caught up with them. Shedd jumped onto a horse and raced to rally the defense while the majority of refugees made a frantic flight from the town. For the next few hours the Turks sniped at them as they traveled along the base of the mountains through which they passed. Then a squad of nine British soldiers armed with a Lewis machine gun arrived to "rescue" Shedd, whom they heard the Turks had taken prisoner.[50]

In the British camp in Sain Kala, Shedd reported that he did not feel well. Fearing that he had come down with cholera, Mary Lewis, now his wife, gave him calomel, a mercury purgative that failed to do anything useful. He had indeed come down with this dread disease and died of it on August 7 at the age of 53. Mary buried him on a remote hillside and continued on. Another 25 days of travel brought her to the city of Hamadan, which stood about 50 miles from Urmia, and from there she went to Baqubah. The war and its fallout prevented her from returning to recover her husband's body for another year. After having him exhumed, she took him to Tabriz for a memorial service.[51]

Upon reoccupying Urmia, the Turks repeated their usual pattern of looting, killing, and kidnapping girls for use as sexual slaves. This time they did not hesitate to target the American missionaries still in the city, including Mrs. Judith David. She along with her three children, a cousin, and a maid hid for eight days in the house of a Muslim woman who had once been a refugee living with David. The Turks robbed David's home, so she told the Ottoman commander-in-chief she would auction off her remaining possessions and donate the proceeds to a Turkish orphanage in exchange for protection. To this he agreed. She and the others moved in with the Persian governor, a good friend of hers. Though the Turks soon arrested him, one his servants continued to feed the guests. On October 8, the Turks arrested the remaining American missionaries and shipped them off to Tabriz at which they placed them under house arrest. One morning the Americans found the gate unlocked and the guards gone. The Turks had left in compliance with the Armistice of November 11, 1918.[52]

In early December, Simko "sacked and looted" Urmia. He destroyed the American compound, slaughtered both Persians and Assyrians, and cut down the gardens surrounding the city before the Persian government could send anyone to take control. Packard returned to Urmia several times in the next year, settling there with his family permanently in May 1919 at a time when tensions between the Persians and Kurds in and around the Urmia Plain had increased in part because a wave of Kurds who had come from other regions had occupied abandoned Christian villages.[53]

The Persian government then did something utterly stupid. Fearing Simko's machinations to create a Kurdish homeland from its territory, it mailed him a box of sweets in mid–May that, when opened, exploded, killing Simko's brother but not its target. The next day the Persian garrison in Urmia began attacking Kurds and Assyrians. Simko retaliated by laying siege to the city and cutting off its water supply. On May 24, a couple of Persian officials asked Packard to arbitrate the matter, but this peace only lasted a few hours. A force of Persian soldiers accompanied by irregulars drove the Kurds out of the city, then began looting it.[54]

A group of them, unarmed, targeted the American compound, but the missionaries drove them out and barred the gates. The looters soon returned with arms, forced their way in, and took "more than 5,000 bushels of food" neatly stored in 40 rooms plus grabbed just about anything else they could take off with, including books, money, and furnishings.[55]

Packard along with French missionary Father Antoine Clarys retreated with others into the main relief office. In time the invaders started dragging out those within and murdering them. One of the local governor's officers arrived and took Packard and Clarys to an adjoining room. He told them to sit down while he dealt with more looters coming up a stairs with the intent of killing all Christians. He beat them back by whacking the tops of their heads with the flat side of his dagger. Soon more of Packard's friends keen on rescuing him arrived, but even after he and Clarys escaped, safety eluded them. An angry crowd tried to route them to a secluded place where they could kill them, but fortunately Packard's old friend, the mullah Mirza Mohammad (from whom Packard once removed a cataract) saved them from this fate and made sure they reached the safety of the governor's residence. The governor had already retrieved Packard's wife and children from their residence at the missionary's hospital compound, which was about two miles outside the city.[56]

About 320 Christians reached the governor's yard, 100 or so wounded. Over the next few days a search party rescued 260 more. For 24 days, around 600 Christians remained trapped in the yard until word of their plight reached the ears of Paddock, who had returned to his station in Tabriz. Accompanied by volunteers Muller, Dr. Edward Mills Dodd, Sardar-i-Fateh, and an English chauffeur, they drove two cars on the long journey around Lake Urmia. While traveling through the Salmas region, Simko unexpectedly gave them an escort of 100 warriors.[57]

Paddock arranged for the departure of all those trapped at the governor's house. Packard and Dodd stayed behind to ready the sick for transportation, while Paddock took those capable of traveling on foot to Tabriz. He and Muller led the way with Packard's wife and children in the other car. Persian soldiers kept the people lining the streets intent on killing the parade of Christians at bay. Simko's men escorted them to the western shore of Lake Urmia. While going around this body of water made for a very long trek, sailing across did not always speed things up. Depending on conditions, a sailboat, the most likely mode of transport, could take from two to eight days to cross depending on the wind. And while a powered vessel would speed up the trip considerably, even that had to carefully negotiate the many salt marshes along the lake's shores. In this case the American refugees boarded two powered boats flying U.S. flags for the trip to the eastern side. They all made it safely to Tabriz.[58]

Little remained of the Urmia station save for the Muslim Boys' School and the house of one person. Looters had partially destroyed the Allen house and left all remaining structures empty, even stripping out some of their doors and windows. Packard and his family returned to Persia in 1921 but did not go back to Urmia since it lacked a hospital in which he could work. Instead they settled in a mission in the city of Kermanshah.[59]

Simko's effort to establish a Kurdish state ended when an Iranian force defeated him in 1922. He made a second attempt in 1926, but this failed as well, forcing him to go into exile in Iraq. In 1928, he traveled to Turkey because he thought the Turks were going to offer him a regiment of Kurdish cavalry as well as an estate along the Iranian border, but nothing came of it. Near the end of June 1929, the Persian government offered him amnesty and invited him to govern the city of Ushnu. During his trip to a meeting about this, he either became the victim of an assassination or died during firefight that had broken out.[60]

Chapter Notes

Databases (Abbreviations in parentheses)

Ancestry.com
California Digital Newspaper Collection (CDNC)
Cornell University: The Cornell Daily Sun Keith R. Johnson '56 Digital Archive (CDS)
EBSCO: Academic Search Premier (ASP)
EBSCO: MasterFILE Premier (MFP)
ESBCO: *Nation* Archive (TNA)
EBSCO: Religion and Philosophy Collection (RPC)
Gale Group: *Times* Digital Archive 1785–2007 (TDA)
JSTOR
Library of Congress: Chronicling America (CA)
Newsbank: *Cleveland Plain Dealer* Historical Newspaper (CPDHN)
ProQuest: Historical Newspapers: *New York Times*, 1851–2009 (HN:TNYT)
University of Oregon Libraries: Historical Oregon Newspapers (HON)

Prologue

1. Gordon Brook-Shepherd, *The Austrians: A Thousand Year Odyssey* (New York: Carroll & Graf Publishers, 1996), 6; Eric Roman, *Austria-Hungary & the Successor States: A Reference Guide from the Renaissance to the Present* (New York: Facts on File, 2003), 6.
2. Brook-Shepherd, *The Austrians*, 6.
3. Ibid., 11–12; Roman, *Austria-Hungary & the Successor States*, 6.
4. "Francis Joseph Dead: The Oldest Ruler," *Times* [London], November 22, 1916, 7, TDA; "Austrian Emperor Franz Joseph Dead: Remarkable Reign Filled with Domestic and Dynastic Tragedies Is Ended," *Sausalito News*, November 25, 1916, CDNC.
5. "How the Hapsburg Curse Has Been Fulfilled with Startling Exactness: 18 Misfortunes That Have Befallen Them Since the Countess Karolyi Shook Her Quivering Finger at Emperor Francis Joseph and Appealing to Heaven Said...," *Washington Times* [Washington, D.C.], November 17, 1918, CA.
6. Roman, *Austria-Hungary & the Successor States*, 74–75; Steven Ozment, *A Mighty Fortress: A New History of the German People* (New York: HarperCollins, 2004), 209.
7. Brook-Shepherd, *The Austrians*, 90–92.
8. John K. Cox, *The History of Serbia* (Westport, CT: Greenwood Press, 2002), 29–30, 40–41, 53; W.S. Chase, "The Berlin Congress," *Frank Leslie's Popular Monthly*, September 1878, 258, 262; Bernadotte E. Schmitt, "The Bosnian Annexation Crisis (I)," *Slavonic and East European Review* 9, no. 26 (December 1930): 312–313, JSTOR.
9. Schmitt, "The Bosnian Annexation Crisis (I)," 312; "The Hapsburg Monarchy and the Slavs," *Nation*, December 3, 1908, TNA.
10. Cox, *The History of Serbia*, 36, 57; Richard C. Hall, "Balkan Wars," *History Today* 62, no. 11 (November 2012): 36–37, RPC.
11. Hall, "Balkan Wars," 38.
12. "Plans Great New Empire? Heir to Austrian Throne Said to Be Arranging a Slav Confederacy," *New York Times*, December 27, 1912, HN:TNYT; Henry S. Pratt, "The Late Archduke Francis Ferdinand—His Pro-Slavic Sympathies—Serb Ambitions," *Nation*, July 30, 1914, 126–127.
13. "The Man of Mystery in the Balkan Crisis," *Current Literature*, January 1909, 42, 44–45: "whose women he...," 44; Catherine Radziwill, *The Austrian Court from Within* (London: Cassell and Co., 1916), 76; Ben Hurst, "The Crown Prince of Austria and the Heir Presumptive," *Donahoe's Magazine*, March 1908, 323–324; John van der Kiste, *Emperor Francis Joseph: Life, Death and the Hapsburg Empire* (Phoenix Mill, UK: Sutton Publishing, 2005), 146.
14. "How the Hapsburg Curse Has Been Fulfilled with Startling Exactness" *Washington Times*; "The Next Royal Attraction," *Roanoke Times* [Virginia], August 15, 1893: "tolerated and but...," CA.
15. Lavender Cassels, *The Archduke and the Assassin: Sarajevo, June 28th 1914* (New York: Stein and Day, 1984), 25; van der Kiste, *Emperor Francis Joseph*, 146.
16. "Still Another Royal Visitor: Archduke Franz Ferdinand D'este on His Way Here," August 13, 1893: "Arabia, Australia, India...," and "Austria's Crown Prince in Town: He Has Been Hunting in the West and also Visited the Fair," October 7, 1893, both in *New York Times*, HN:TNYT.
17. Arthur J. May, "The Archduke Francis Ferdinand in the United States," *Journal of the Illinois State Historical Society* (1908–1984), 39, no. 3 (September 1946): 335, 337, JSTOR: "him of obscure...," 337; "Ferdinand of Austria: The Detestable Prince Who Passed Through Seattle Last Week," *Seattle Post-Intelligencer*, September 11, 1893, CA.
18. May, "The Archduke Francis Ferdinand in the United States," 338–340; "Austria's Crown Prince in Town," October 7, 1893, *New York Times*.
19. "The Man of Mystery in the Balkan Crisis," *Current Literature*, 44–45; "The Archduke Franz Ferdinand D'este," *Times*, May 25, 1900, TDA; Radziwill, *The Austrian Court from Within*, 78.

20. van der Kiste, *Emperor Francis Joseph*, 173; "Aunt of Alfonso Dies in Budapest: Archduchess Isabella Was Wife of Friedrich of Hapsburg, Uncle of King of Spain," *New York Times*, September 6, 1931, HN:TNYT; Greg King and Sue Woolmans, *The Assassination of the Archduke: Sarajevo 1914 and the Romance That Changed the World* (New York: St. Martin's Press, 2013), 44–45.

21. Radziwill, *The Austrian Court from Within*, 75–76; "The Archduke Franz Ferdinand D'este," *Times*; van der Kiste, *Emperor Francis Joseph*, 173, 174: "cretins or epileptics," 174.

22. Irenæus Prime-Stevenson, "A Marriage—For Love?" *Independent*, August 9, 1900, 1963; Cassels, *The Archduke and the Assassin*, 46; "The Archduke Franz Ferdinand," *Times*, June 29, 1900, TDA; Radziwill, *The Austrian Court from Within*, 78, 80.

23. Tim Butcher, *The Trigger: Hunting the Assassin Who Brought the World to War* (New York: Grove Press, 2014), 24; Statement of Gavrilo Princip, 13 October, 1914, *The Sarajevo Trial*, vol. 1, translated by W.A. Dolph Owings, Elizabeth Pribic, and Nikola Pribic (Chapel Hill, NC: Documentary Publications, 1984), 81; David James Smith, *One Morning in Sarajevo: 29 June, 1914* (London: Phoenix, 2008), 10–11; Notes of Dr. Martin Pappenheim, quoted in "Confessions of the Assassin Whose Deed Led to the World War," by Hamilton Fish Armstrong, *Current History*, August 1927, 705.

24. Statement of Princip, 12 October, 1914, *The Sarajevo Trial*, vol. 1, 55; Butcher, *The Trigger*, 26; Armstrong, "Confessions of the Assassin Whose Deed Led to the World War," 702.

25. Armstrong, "Confessions of the Assassin Whose Deed Led to the World War," 700; Statement of Nedeljko Cabrinovic, 12 October, 1914, *The Sarajevo Trial*, vol. 1, 18–19, 31.

26. Statement of Princip, 12 October, 1914, 55, and statement of Nedeljko Cabrinovic, 12 October, 1914, 22–25, and statement of Trifko Grabez, 12 October, 1914, all in *The Sarajevo Trial*, vol. 1, 82, 88–89, 92; Armstrong, "Confessions of the Assassin Whose Deed Led to the World War," 700; International Conciliation, *The Austrian Red Book: Official Translation Prepared by the Austrian Government* (New York: American Association for International Conciliation, 1915), 52.

27. Smith, *One Morning in Sarajevo*, 76–77; Statement of Nedeljko Cabrinovic, 12 October, 1914, 25, and statement of Princip, 12 October, 1914, 57, 59, both in *The Sarajevo Trial*, vol. 1; International Conciliation, *The Austrian Red Book*, 51.

28. Statement of Nedeljko Cabrinovic, 12 and 14 October, 1914, 27, 151, and statement of Grabez, 13 October, 1914, 81, 93–94, and statement of Princip, 12 October, 1914, 59, all in *The Sarajevo Trial*, vol. 1; Butcher, *The Trigger*, 252–253; International Conciliation, *The Austrian Red Book*, 52.

29. Statement of Princip, 13 October, 1914, 79, and statement of Grabez, 13 October, 1914, 93–94, both in *The Sarajevo Trial*, vol. 1.

30. Smith, *One Morning in Sarajevo*, 86–87; Cassels, *The Archduke and the Assassin*, 121.

31. Smith, *One Morning in Sarajevo*, 83–84, 87; Cassels, *The Archduke and the Assassin*, 123.

32. Statement of Danilo Ilic, 13 October, 1914, *The Sarajevo Trial*, vol. 1, 113.

33. Statement of Ilic, 13 October, 1914, 113, 115–117, and statement of Vaso Cubrilovic, 13 October, 1914, 127–130, 137, and statement of Cvjetko Popovic, 13 October, 1914, 140–142, 146, all in *The Sarajevo Trial*, vol. 1.

34. International Conciliation, *The Austrian Red Book*, 52; Statement of Princip, 12 and 14 October, 1914, 59–60, 152, and statement of Cubrilovic, 12 October, 1914, 36: "a small calling…," and statement of Nedeljko Cabrinovic, 12 and 14 October, 1914, 36–38, 149, and statement of Grabez, 13 October, 1914, 94–95, all in *The Sarajevo Trial*, vol. 1.

35. Butcher, *The Trigger*, 255–256; Statement of Cabrinovic, 12 October, 1914, 38–39, and statement of Princip, 12 October, 1914, 61, and statement of Grabez, 13 October, 1914, 95, all in *The Sarajevo Trial*, vol. 1.

36. Statement of Grabez, 13 October, 1914, 95–96, *The Sarajevo Trial*, vol. 1.

37. Statement of Grabez, 13 October, 1914, 98–100, and statement of Veljko Cubrilovic, 14 October, 1914, both in *The Sarajevo Trial*, vol. 1, 153, 158–159, 161.

38. Statement of Mitar Kerovic, 15 October, 1914, 259, and statement of Nedjo Kerovic, 15 October, 1914, 279–280, and statement of Cvijan Stjepanovic, 15 October, 1914, 288, 291, all in *The Sarajevo Trial*, vol. 2.

39. Statement of Nedjo Kerovic, 15 October, 1914, 285, and statement of Stjepanovic, 15 October, 1914, 290, and statement of Veljko Cubrilovic, 14 October, 1914, 162–163, and statement of Misko Jovanovic, 14 October, 1914, 174, 181–182, all in *The Sarajevo Trial*, vol. 2; Statement of Grabez, 13 October, 1914, 99–101, and statement of Nedeljko Cabrinovic, 12 October, 1914, 40–41, both in *The Sarajevo Trial*, vol. 1.

40. Statement of Ilic, 13 October, 1914, 114–115, and statement of Grabez, 13 October, 1914, 101, both in *The Sarajevo Trial*, vol. 1; Butcher, *The Trigger*, 207; Statement of Jovanovic, 14 October, 1914, *The Sarajevo Trial*, vol. 2, 179.

41. Statement of Jovanovic, 14 October, 1914, *The Sarajevo Trial*, vol. 2, 184–186.

42. Statement of Grabez, 13 October, 1914, *The Sarajevo Trial*, vol. 1, 102–103.

43. Ibid., 103; Luigi Albertini, *The Origins of the War of 1914: The Crisis of 1914, from the Sarajevo Outrage to the Austro-Hungarian Mobilization*, vol. 1, translated and edited by Isabella M. Massey (Oxford: Oxford University Press, 1953), 35.

44. Statement of Nedeljko Cabrinovic, 12 October, 1914, *The Sarajevo Trial*, vol. 1, 41–45; Albertini, *The Origins of the War of 1914*, 35–36; King and Woolmans, *The Assassination of the Archduke*, 201: "rolled-down canvas…"

45. Statement of Princip, 12 October, 1914, 67; "Heir to Austria's Throne Is Slain with His Wife by a Bosnian Youth to Avenge Seizure of His Country: Francis Ferdinand Shot During State Visit to Sarajevo," *New York Times*, June 29, 1914, HN:TNYT: "Herr Burgermeister, it…"

46. Butcher, *The Trigger*, 273–275; "Heir to Austria's Throne Is Slain with His Wife by a Bosnian Youth to Avenge Seizure of His Country" *New York Times*, 1; King and Woolmans, *The Assassination of the Archduke*, 197, 206–207.

47. John Elliot, "The Browning FN Model 1910: The Gun That Killed 8.5 Million People," Gunswww, August

2, 2011, accessed August 9, 2014, http://www.guns.com/2011/08/02/the-browning-fn-model-1910-the-gun-that-killed-85-million-people.

48. Statement of Princip, 12 and 13 October, 1914, 68, 74, *The Sarajevo Trial*, vol. 1; Elizabeth J. Kopras, *Patty's Toxicology*, Sixth Edition, vol. 2, s.v. "Cyanide and Nitriles," edited by Eula Bingham and Barbara Cohrssen (Hoboken, NJ: Wiley, 2012), 945–946.

49. Statement of Grabez, 13 October, 1914, *The Sarajevo Trial*, vol. 1., 102–105.

50. Statement of Popovic, 13 October, 1914, *The Sarajevo Trial*, vol. 1, 142–145: "didn't have the...," and "in the basement...," 143.

51. Owings, Pribic, and Pribic, trans., xvii, and statement of Princip, 12 October, 1914, 54, 83, both in *The Sarajevo Trial*, vol. 1; Notes of Dr. Martin Pappenheim, 704.

52. Owings, Pribic, and Pribic, trans., *The Sarajevo Trial*, vol. 2, 527–528, 530.

53. Armstrong, "Confessions of the Assassin Whose Deed Led to the World War," 699; Martin Jay, "The Manacles of Gavrilo Princip," *Salmagundi* no. 106/107 (Spring–Summer 1995): 16, 18–19, JSTOR: "on the confluence...," 16; Albertini, *The Origins of the War of 1914*, 47.

54. Samuel R. Williamson, Jr., "The Origins of World War I," *Journal of Interdisciplinary History* 18, no. 4 (Spring 1988): 806–807, JSTOR.

55. Smith, *One Morning in Sarajevo*, 82, 89–91; International Conciliation, *The Austrian Red Book*, 52.

56. Albertini, *The Origins of the War of 1914*, 120; "Servia's Reply Accepted All Austria's Conditions Except Investigation of Servians by Austrians," *New York Times*, July 27, 1914, HN:TNYT; "Peace of Balkans in Serious Danger: Austria's Demand on Servia Imperious," *Morning Oregonian*, July 25, 1914, HON.

57. Williamson, Jr., "The Origins of World War I," 812–816; John Keegan, *The First World War* (New York: Vintage Books, 1998), 67–69.

58. James W. Garner, "Some Questions of International Law in the European War," *American Journal of International Law* 9, no. 1 (January 1915): 72–74, 79–80, JSTOR; Samuel R. Williamson, Jr., "The Origin of the War," in *The Oxford Illustrated History of the First World War*, edited by Hew Strachan (Oxford: Oxford University Press, 1998), 21–22.

59. Williamson, Jr., "The Origin of the War," 24–25; Keegan, *The First World War*, 29–30.

60. Henri Pirenne, *Belgium and the First World War*, translated by Vincent Capelle and Jeff Lipkes (Wesley Chapel, FL: Brabant Press, 2014), 44, 55; David Stevenson, "Battlefield or Barrier? Rearmament and Military Planning in Belgium, 1902–1914," *International History Review* 29, no. 3 (September 2007): 473–507, JSTOR.

61. Pirenne, *Belgium and the First World War*, 23; Max Hastings, *Catastrophe 1914: Europe Goes to War* (New York: Alfred A. Knopf, 2013), 160–162; Keegan, *The First World War*, 77–78: "between 1888 and...," 77; *Belgium and Holland Including the Grand-Duchy of Luxembourg: Handbook for Travellers* (Leipzig, Germany: Karl Baedeker, 1910), 247–247; Douglas Goldring, *Ways of Escape: A Book of Adventure* (New York: Duffield and Co., 1912), 4.

62. "Germans Fall in Masses at Liege Battle: Scene of Carnage Described by Tribune's Correspondent," *New York Tribune*, August 9, 1914; Hastings, *Catastrophe 1914*, 160–161, 164; "100,000 Germans Storming Liege; 11,000 Casualties: Crown Prince Heads the Invading Forces," *Washington Times*, August 6, 1914, CA: "two regiments of..."; Keegan, *The First World War*, 78; William Manchester, *The Arms of Krupp, 1587–1968* (Boston: Little, Brown and Company, 1968), 282.

63. Hastings, *Catastrophe 1914*, 164; Keegan, *The First World War*, 86–87; "100,000 Germans Storming Liege," *Washington Times*; Pirenne, *Belgium and the First World War*, 56.

64. "King Albert Falls to Death Climbing Peak Near Namur; Body Found, Wound in Head: Killed Instantaneously," *New York Times*, February 18, 1934, HN:TNYT: "toiled in a...," and "in the guise..."

65. Ibid.; "King of the Belgians Killed: Rock-Climbing Accident Near Namur," *Times*, February 19, 1934, TDA.

Chapter 1

1. Louise Townsend Nicholl, "Trapped in War-Stricken Europe," Chapter 1, *Day Book* [Chicago], August 29, 1914, CA.

2. Ibid., 13–14: "hot, crowded, hectic," 13; Lawrence H. Officer, "Exchange Rates Between the United States Dollar and Forty-one Currencies," *MeasuringWorth*, 2014, accessed January 19, 2014, www.measuringworth.com/exchangeglobal; *Northern France from Belgium to the English Channel to the Loire Excluding Paris and Its Environs: Handbook for Travellers* (Leipzig, Germany: Karl Baedeker, 1894), xi–xii.

3. Nicholl, "Trapped in War-Stricken Europe," Chapter 1 and Chapter 2 (August 31, 1914).

4. "An American Woman Flees from Paris," *Outlook*, September 2, 1914, 34–35.

5. Ernest Hamlin Abbott, "The Experiences of an American Refugee from Paris: Editorial Correspondence from Paris and London," *Outlook*, August 29, 1914, 1025.

6. Alexander Dana Noyes, *Financial Chapters of the War* (New York: Charles Scribner's Sons, 1916), 25–26, 34: "old stockings," "chimney-pieces," and "European statisticians estimated...," 26; Robert W. de Forest, "First Aid to Stranded Americans in Europe," *Survey*, September 12, 1914, 589; Letter from Henry Breckinridge to Lindley M. Garrison, 14 October 1914, *Report on the Operations of United States Relief Commission in Europe* by United States, War Department, Relief Commission in Europe (Washington, D.C.: Government Printing Office, 1914), 1.

7. Will Irwin, "The 'Glory' of War," *American Magazine*, December 1914, 54; Noyes, *Financial Chapters of the War*, 31, 34, 36.

8. Raymond Weeks, "Foreign Correspondence: An American in Paris—Declaration of War—Starting for the Front," *Nation*, August 27, 1914, 245, TNA.

9. "Notes of Tourists Trapped in Europe: Many Prepared to Face Trials Cheerfully If They Can Once Get on Shipboard," August 7, 1914, and "Mayor Plans to Aid Americans Abroad: President Thanks Mitchel for Offer to Co-operate with the National Government," August 4, 1914, both in *New York Times*, HN:TNYT.

10. "3 Refugee Ships in with 4100 More: Campania, Baltic, and St. Louis Bring Host of Americans from Eu-

ropean War," *New York Times*, August 23, 1914, CA; W.A. McLean, "Highway Legislation," *Good Roads*, July 4, 1914, 16.

11. Nicholl, "Trapped in War-Stricken Europe," Chapter 2.

12. Nicholl, "Trapped in War-Stricken Europe," Chapter 2 and Chapter 3 (September 1, 1914); Lilian Whiting, *Paris the Beautiful* (Boston: Little, Brown, and Co., 1909), 41.

13. Nicholl, "Trapped in War-Stricken Europe," Chapter 3.

14. John Horne and Alan Kramer, *German Atrocities, 1914: A History of Denial* (New Haven: Yale University Press, 2001), 150; Craig Robertson, *The Passport in America: A History of a Document* (New York: Oxford University Press, 2010), 186.

15. Robertson, *The Passport in America*, 192; Nicholl, "Trapped in War-Stricken Europe," Chapters 2 and 3.

16. Nicholl, "Trapped in War-Stricken Europe," Chapter 3; "French Air Fleet Repels Zeppelins," *Daily East Oregonian* [Pendleton, OR], August 6, 1914, CA.

17. "Battles in the Air to Be War Feature: Glenn H. Curtiss Tells of Russia's Surprising Strength in Fighting Aeroplanes," August 5, 1914, and "Glenn Curtiss Dies, Pioneer in Aviation: End Comes Suddenly in Buffalo Hospital During Convalescence from an Operation," July 24, 1930, both in *New York Times*, HN:TNYT.

18. "Battles in the Air to Be War Feature," *New York Times*; Hastings, *Catastrophe 1914*, 457–458.

19. Gelett Burgess, "How Fear Came to Paris," *Collier's Weekly*, October 17, 1914, 5; "Mayor Plans to Aid Americans Abroad," and "Gelett Burgess, Humorist, Is Dead: Author of the Famous 'Purple Cow' Verse Began Career as Railroad Draftsman," September 19, 1951, both in *New York Times*, HN:TNYT; *American National Biography* [hereafter *ANB*], vol. 3, s.v. "Burgess, Gelett," 937: "puzzled his neighbors…"; Helen Throop Purdy, *San Francisco as It Was, as It Is, and How to See It* (San Francisco: Paul Elder and Co., 1912), 45.

20. *ANB*, s.v. "Burgess, Gelett," 937; "Gelett Burgess, Humorist, Is Dead," *New York Times*; Frank Luther Mott, *A History of American Magazines*, vol. 4 (Cambridge: Harvard University Press, 1938, 1957, 1968), 308.

21. *ANB*, s.v. "Burgess, Gelett," 938; Burgess, "How Fear Came to Paris," 21, 23.

22. Burgess, "How Fear Came to Paris," 22; Justin D. Murphy, *Military Aircraft, Origins to 1918: An Illustrated History of Their Impact* (Santa Barbara, CA: ABC-CLIO, 2005), 104: "designed by Igo…"

23. Nicholl, "Trapped in War-Stricken Europe," Chapter 4, September 2, 1914.

24. *Ibid.*

25. *Ibid.*; Joel Cook, *England, Picturesque and Descriptive: A Reminiscence of Foreign Travel* (Philadelphia: Porter and Coates, 1900), 509–510.

26. Nicholl, "Trapped in War-Stricken Europe," Chapter 4.

27. Ernest Hamlin Abbott, "The Experiences of an American Refugee from Paris," *Outlook*, August 29, 1914, 1026; Hines to Woodrow Wilson, August 1914, 9, in *The Life and Letters of Walter H. Page*, vol. 1, by Burton J. Hendrick (Garden City: Doubleday, Page & Co., 1922), 304.

28. J. Ranken Towse, "Foreign Correspondence: Calm in England—Early Preparations for War—The Response to the Appeal for Recruits," *Nation*, August 27, 1914, 244, TNA.

29. *Ibid.*, 245; John Singleton, "Britain's Military Use of Horses, 1914–1918," *Past & Present* no. 139 (May 1993): 178, 184, JSTOR; Louis A. DiMarco, *War Horse: A History of the Military Horse and Rider* (Yardley, PA: Westholme, 2008) 318; Leger Tours, "The Old Contemptibles," Marc Hope, guide, May 18–May 22, 2015.

30. DiMarco, *War Horse*, 309–310, 327.

31. Singleton, "Britain's Military Use of Horses, 1914–1918," 186, 199.

32. *Ibid.*, 193.

33. "Britain in War Time: How Lancaster Faces Hard Times Ahead," *Times*, August 13, 1914, TDA.

34. Deian Hopkin, "Domestic Censorship in the First World War," *Journal of Contemporary History* 5, no. 4 (1970): 153–157, JSTOR.

35. Richard Harding Davis, "The Germans in Brussels," *Scribner's Magazine*, November 1914, 566; John M. McEwen, "Lloyd George's Acquisition of the Daily Chronicle in 1918," *Journal of British Studies* 22, no. 1 (Autumn 1982): 128, JSTOR.

36. Robert Crozier Long, "Struggling Toward Holy Russia," *Collier's Weekly*, October 3, 1914, 9.

37. Nicholl, "Trapped in War-Stricken Europe," Chapter 4; "3 Refugee Ships in with 4100 More," *New York Times*: "was practically … [an] …"

38. Nicholl, "Trapped in War-Stricken Europe," Chapter 5, September 3, 1914.

39. *Ibid.*

40. Melvin Maddocks, *The Great Liners* (Alexandria, VA: Time-Life Books, 1978), 60–62, 74: "a late luncheon…," 60.

41. *Ibid.*

42. Abbott, "The Experiences of an American Refugee from Paris," 1024; "Methodist Book Concern Is Insuring Lives of Employees: For Each of Its Workers Company Pays Premiums on Policies Equivalent to One Year's Full Salary; the Church Publishing House, Run by Ministers, Has Distributed $5,000,000 in Profits," July 25, 1914, and "Dr. Meyer Is Christian Leader, Prominent also as Statesman: London Clergyman Takes Rand as Dominant Force in Religious World; Declares a Significant Thing in Church Affairs Is Growth of Brotherhood Movement, to Unite for Common Good," August 1, 1914, both in *El Paso Herald*, CA; Joseph Frazier Wall, *Andrew Carnegie* (New York: Oxford University Press, 1970), 917, 920–922.

43. "$2,000,000 to Clergy Carnegie Peace Gift: Twenty-five Denominations Are Represented in Church Peace Union Which He Endows," *New York Times*, February 11, 1914, HN:TNYT.

44. Abbott, "The Experiences of an American Refugee from Paris," 1024–1026: "but the chance…," 1024.

45. Ona Brown, "American Woman Tells Her Experiences in Warzone: While Conducting a Party of Texan Girls Through Europe, She and Her Charges Suddenly Found Themselves in the Midst of Mobilizations, and Had No Little Trouble in Getting Home Unharmed," *New York Times*, August 23, 1914, HN:TNYT.

46. *Ibid.*

47. *Ibid.*

48. Mark Greenburg and the Editors of the Newsweek Book Division, *The Hague* (New York: Newsweek, 1982), 14, 124–125.

49. Albert R. Williams, "With the Germans in Belgium," *Outlook*, September 16, 1914, 139: "would save some...," and "miles of barbed..."; Hubert P. van Tuyll van Serooskerken, *The Netherlands and World War I: Espionage, Diplomacy and Survival* (Leiden, Netherlands: Brill, 2001), 22, 103, 105; *Belgium and Holland Including the Grand-Duchy of Luxembourg*, 453.

50. van Serooskerken, *The Netherlands and World War I*, 85–86.

51. Williams, "With the Germans in Belgium," 139; Ivan V. Hogg, *Historical Dictionary of World War I*, s.v. "Uhlans," (Lanham, MD: The Scarecrow Press, 1998), 187: "by their square-topped..."

52. Marc Frey, "Trade, Ships, and the Neutrality of the Netherlands in the First World War," *International History Review* 19, no. 3 (August 1997): 542–546, JSTOR: "cotton and grain...," 543; Greenburg, *The Hague*, 125.

53. Brown, "American Woman Tells Her Experiences in Warzone," *New York Times*.

54. *Ibid*.

55. "Dr. Henry Van Dyke Dies in 81st Year: Author, Diplomat, Clergyman, Educator and Poet Long Leader in Public Life," *New York Times*, April 11, 1933, HN:TNYT.

56. Brown, "American Woman Tells Her Experiences in Warzone," *New York Times*.

57. "The France Bringing 2,090 Refugees Home," *New York Tribune*, August 5, 1914, CA; Maurice Parmelee, "An American in Berlin," *Outlook*, September 2, 1914, 40.

58. "To Send Americans to Nearest Ports: Mobilization of Refugees First Step of Administration in Affording Relief," *New York Times*, August 9, 1914, HN:TNYT; Parmelee, "An American in Berlin," 39.

59. Irwin, "The 'Glory' of War," 54.

60. "American Refugees Report Adventures: Travel from the Warring Countries Presented Hardships and Some Indignities," *New York Times*, August 6, 1914; *ANB*, vol. 15, s.v. "Meyer, George Lengerke," 400–401.

61. "American Refugees Report Adventures," *New York Times*; M.A. DeWolfe Howe, *George von Lengerke Meyer: His Life and Public Services* (New York: Dodd, Mead and Co., 1919), 504, including an account of flight from Germany by Marian Alice Meyer, 504–505.

62. Meyer, account of flight from Germany, 505–506; *Southern Germany (Wurtenberg and Bavaria): Handbook for Travellers* (Leipzig: Karl Baedeker, 1907), 3.

63. Meyer, account of flight from Germany, 506.

64. Meyer, account of flight from Germany, 507–508: "a man dressed...," 507, and "and no sooner...," 508.

65. Meyer, account of flight from Germany, 506, 508–510.

66. "3 Refugee Ships in with 4100 More," *New York Times*.

67. *Ibid*.; *Belgium and Holland Including the Grand-Duchy of Luxembourg*, 247.

68. "3 Refugee Ships in with 4100 More," *New York Times*.

69. "Untitled," *New York Times*, August 24, 1914, HN:TNYT; Keith Hamilton and Richard Langhorne, *The Practice of Diplomacy: Its Evolution, Theory and Administration* (London: Routledge, 1995), 115–116.

70. "James W. Gerard, 84, Dies; Envoy to Germany 1913–17: Ambassador Before U.S. Entry into World War I Was Noted Lawyer," *New York Times*, September 7, 1951, HN:TNYT.

71. "*Ibid*.; James W. Gerard, *My Four Years in Germany* (New York: Grosset & Dunlap, 1917), 173–174: "I told him..."

72. "James W. Gerard, 84, Dies," *New York Times*; Gerard, *My Four Years in Germany*, 272; "General Count Von Montgelas," February 8, 1938, and "Count Johann Von Bernstorff," October 7, 1939, both in *Times*, TDA.

73. Gerard, *My Four Years in Germany*, 272–275: "Even if I..."

74. *Ibid*., 108–109.

75. *Ibid*., 109–110; George Weiss, *America's Maritime Progress: A Review of the Redevelopment of the American Merchant Marine, Together with Brief Biographies of Men and Companies Representative of the Shipping World* (New York: The New York Marine News Company, 1920), 195.

76. "Americans in Paris All Thank Herrick: To Give Testimonial to Ambassador, Who Has Worked for Their Protection," August 8, 1914, and "Americans Pack Trains to Paris: Endured Great Hardships in Getting Out of Germany and over the French Frontier," August 4, 1914, both in *New York Times*, HN:TNYT.

77. *Ibid*.

78. "Herrick Architect of His Own Fortune: Son of an Ohio Farmer, He Began by Peddling Miscellaneous Goods to Neighbors," *New York Times*, April 1, 1929, HN:TNYT; *ANB*, vol. 10, s.v. "Herrick, Myron Timothy," 665: "for widows, orphans..."

79. "Americans Under Fire While Fleeing to Liner to Take Refuge in Ditch: Finland's 1,082 Passengers Tell of Thrilling Adventures in Germany and Belgium—Former Wheat King's Experience," *Evening World* [New York City], August 19, 1914, CA: "wheat king of..."; *Austria-Hungary Including Dalmatia and Bosnia: Handbook for Travellers* (Leipzig: Karl Baedeker, 1905), 243–244; "James A. Patten Dies at Age of 76: Chicago 'Wheat King' and Philanthropist Succumbs to Pneumonia," *New York Times*, HN:TNYT: "born in Freeland..."

80. "Americans Under Fire While Fleeing to Liner to Take Refuge in Ditch," *Evening World*; *Belgium and Holland Including the Grand-Duchy of Luxembourg*, 275.

81. "Americans Under Fire While Fleeing to Liner to Take Refuge in Ditch," *Evening World*.

82. *Ibid*.: "nine stranded Americans"; International Mercantile Marine Company, *Facts for Travelers: Atlantic Transport Company, American Line, Dominion Line, Leyland Line, Red Star Line, White Star Line* (New York: American Bank Note Co., 1908), 41.

83. "Americans Under Fire While Fleeing to Liner to Take Refuge in Ditch," *Evening World*.

84. "Guard Neutrality, Mr. Straus Urges: Back from Warzone, He Sees Need That United States Be Ready to Talk Peace," *New York Times*, September 4, 1914, HN:TNYT; "Americans to Come Home: United Fruit Co.'s Ships to Sail from Bristol, Eng., to N.Y.," August 5, 1914, and "21 Steamers to Tourists' Rescue: Boats of Two Lines to Be Used for Bringing Home Americans," August 5, 1914, both in *New York Tribune*, CA; Marcelo Bucheli, *Bananas and Business: The United Fruit Company in Columbia, 1899–2000* (New York: New York University Press, 2005), 48.

85. "Americans in London: Citizen's Committee to Help the Stranded," August 6, 1914, and "Notice to American Travelers: S.S. 'The Viking,'" August 7, 1914, and "Shipping: Special Sailing to New York," August 18, 1914, all in *Times*, TDA; "Buys a Ship for Tourists: Syndicate

Offers Passages Under American Flag for $500 Each," August 6, 1914: "that the object…," and "Doubt Cast on Viking: Denied That the Chartered Vessel Has American Registry," August 8, 1914, and "206 More Vessels Seized or Sunk: State Department's Second List Shows a Large Majority of German Ships," September 24, 1914, all in *New York Times*, HN:TNYT.

86. Hines to Woodrow Wilson, 9 August 1914, in *The Life and Letters of Walter H. Page*, vol. 1, 303–305; 3; Breckinridge to Garrison, 14 October 1914, *Report on the Operations of United States Relief Commission in Europe*, 1; Ernest Hamlin Abbott, "Americans in the Warzone," *Outlook*, September 9, 1914, 83: "there would be…"

87. Abbott, "Americans in the Warzone," 83: "in the crowd…"; "Untitled," *Life*. March 30, 1893, 193: "It is a…"

88. Abbott, "Americans in the Warzone," 83: "probably not one…"; S. Standwood Menken, "The Work of the American Committee of London," *Survey*, September 12, 1914, 590.

89. "Theodore Hetzler, Banker, Dies at 70: Head of Fifth Ave. Institution; Began as Messenger Boy in 1891—Collector of Etchings," *New York Times*, August 14, 1945, HN:TNYT.

90. "The Savoy Hotel," *Times*, June 16, 1904, TDA.

91. Hines to Wilson, 9 August 1914, in *The Life and Letters of Walter H. Page*, vol. 1, 303; "Americans in London," *Times*, 3; Abbott, "Americans in the Warzone," 84; Menken, "The Work of the American Committee of London," 592: "immediately arranged that…"; American Bankers Association, *Proceedings of the Forty-fifth Annual Convention of the American Bankers Association and Annual Proceedings of the Trust Company Section, Savings Bank Section, Clearing House Section, National Bank Section, and Summary of Proceedings of American Institute of Banking and State Secretaries Sections* (New York: American Bankers Association, 1919), 68.

92. Abbott, "Americans in the Warzone," 85; Menken, "The Work of the American Committee of London," 592–593; American Citizens' Committee, *American Bulletin* [London], August 12, 1914.

93. "Theodore Hetzler, Banker, Dies at 70," *New York Times*.

94. George H. Nash, *The Life of Herbert Hoover: The Engineer, 1874–1914* (New York: W.W. Norton & Company, 1983), 560–561, 568, 573, 575.

95. Herbert Hoover, *The Memoirs of Herbert Hoover: Years of Adventure, 1874–1920* (New York: The Macmillan Company, 1951), 147; "Sioux Indians of Wild West Show Held as Spies," *El Paso Herald*, September 3, 1914, CA.

96. Hoover, *The Memoirs of Herbert Hoover*, 145; "Woman Refugee on Hunger Strike: Demanded First-Class Passage to American from London Relief Committee," *New York Times*, September 15, 1914, HN:TNYT.

97. Richard Harding Davis, *With the Allies* (New York: Charles Scribner's Sons, 1919), 159–160: "Thousands of Americans…," 159, and "On leaving Switzerland…," 160.

98. "To Send Americans to Nearest Ports: Mobilization of Refugees First Step of Administration in Affording Relief," *New York Times*, August 9, 1914, HN:TNYT; "3000 Americans to Go Home Via Paris: Ambassador Herrick Arranges Return of Refugees Through Fighting France," *Morning Oregonian*, August 25, 1914, HON; Letter from Henry Breckinridge to Lindley M. Garrison, 14 October 1914, *Report on the Operations of United States Relief Commission in Europe*, 1–3; "Plan for Tourist Relief Complete: Asst. Secretary of War and Army Officers to Establish Bureaus Abroad," *New York Tribune*, August 5, 1914, CA.

99. "Col. Henry Breckinridge Dies; Ex-Assistant Secretary of War: Wilson Cabinet Aide at 27—Was Intermediary in the Lindbergh Kidnapped," *New York Times*, May 3, 1960, HN:TNYT.

100. Nash, *The Life of Herbert Hoover: The Engineer, 1874–1914*, 9–10, and *The Life of Herbert Hoover: Humanitarian, 1914–1917* (1988), 10–12.

101. Hoover, *The Memoirs of Herbert Hoover*, 145; Breckinridge to Garrison, October 14, 1914, *Report on the Operations of United States Relief Commission in Europe*, 2; "War Refugees Who Haven't Paid: Government Gives Out List of Debts Against Those Aided in Europe," *New York Times*, November 1, 1915, HN:TNYT.

102. "The Homecoming of the Tourist's Trunk: How Two Thousand Pieces of Abandoned Baggage Have Been Collected and Brought to This Country," *Independent*, November 30, 1914, 319.

103. "President's Appeal for Impartiality and Restraint in Discussing War," August 19, 1914: "The United States…," and "Americans May Sell Anything to Europe: No Violation of Neutrality for Our Citizens to Furnish War Material to Belligerents," October 15, 1914, both in *New York Times*, HN:TNYT.

Chapter 2

1. Hugh Gibson, 5 and 8 August, 1914, *A Diplomatic Diary* (London: Hodder and Stoughton, 1917), 22, 39; E. Alexander Powell, *Fighting in Flanders* (New York: Charles Scribner's Sons, 1914), 45.

2. Richard Harding Davis, "The Germans in Brussels," November 1914, 566–568, and "'To Be Treated as a Spy,'" December 1914, 702, both in *Scribner's Magazine*; "R.H. Davis, Novelist, Dies at Telephone: Found by Wife in Library at Home, Suddenly Stricken with Heart Disease," *New York Times*, April 13, 1916, HN:TNYT; *ANB*, vol. 6, s.v. "Davis, Richard Harding," 224: "foppish wardrobe, complete…"; Joyce Milton, *The Yellow Kids: Foreign Correspondents in the Heyday of Yellow Journalism* (New York: Harper & Row Publishers, 1989), 111.

3. "R.H. Davis, Novelist, Dies at Telephone," *New York Times*; Emily Godbey, "Disaster Tourism and the Melodrama of Authenticity: Revisiting the 1889 Johnstown Flood," *Pennsylvania History* 73, no. 3 (Summer 2006): 275–276, JSTOR.

4. *ANB*, s.v. "Davis, Richard Harding," 224; "Tried to Bunco a Reporter: 'Sheeny Mike' Tackles an Evening Sun Young Man and Comes to Grief," *Sun* [New York City], November 3, 1889, CA

5. *ANB*, s.v. "Davis, Richard Harding," 225; "R.H. Davis, Novelist, Dies at Telephone," *New York Times*.

6. *ANB*, s.v. "Davis, Richard Harding," 224; "R.H. Davis, Novelist, Dies at Telephone," *New York Times*; Brand Whitlock, *Belgium: A Personal Narrative* (New York: D. Appleton and Co., 1919), 149; "Sam Browne," *New York Times*, September 23, 1917, HN:TNYT.

7. Powell, *Fighting in Flanders*, 7: "some of the…," and "a series of…"; Davis, "The Germans in Brussels," 567; Will Irwin, "Detained by the Germans," *Collier's Weekly*, October 3, 1914, 5.

8. Gibson, 19 August 1914, *A Diplomatic Diary*, 75; Arno Dosch, "Louvain the Lost," *World's Work*, October 1914, A–B; "Irvin S. Cobb," March 11, 1944, and "Irvin S. Cobb Dies; Humorist to Last: Wife at Bedside as Noted Writer Succumbs Here After Long Illness," March 11, 1944, and "John M'Cutcheon, Noted Cartoonist: Chicago Tribune Artist for 43 Years, Pulitzer Prize Winner, Dies—Covered Five Wars," June 11, 1949, all in *New York Times*, HN:TNYT.

9. Dosch, "Louvain the Lost," A, "Dosch-Fleurot, 72, Newsman, Is Dead: Correspondent in Madrid for Christian-Science Monitor—Once in Europe for World," April 17, 1951, and "Will Irwin Dead; Noted Journalist: Former War Correspondent, Biographer of Hoover, Gained Fame as Reporter, Author," February 25, 1948, both in *New York Times*, HN:TNYT; Byron Farwell, *Over There: The United States in the Great War, 1917–1918* (New York: W.W. Norton & Co., 1999), 122, 124–125.

10. Irwin, "Detained by the Germans," 6; Dosch, "Louvain the Lost," B–C; Gibson, 22 August, 1914, *A Diplomatic Diary*, 101.

11. Irwin, "Detained by the Germans," 23; Dosch, "Louvain the Lost," C–D.

12. Irwin, "Detained by the Germans," 23–24; Dosch, "Louvain the Lost," D.

13. Irwin, "Detained by the Germans," 24; Dosch, "Louvain the Lost," E.

14. Irwin, "Detained by the Germans," 26; Dosch, "Louvain the Lost," E.

15. Irwin, "Detained by the Germans," 26; Gibson, 22 August, 1914, *A Diplomatic Diary*, 99–101: "fifty centimes every…"

16. Gibson, 27 August, 1914, *A Diplomatic Diary*, 104; "Cobb Still Held; M'Cutcheon also: Ambassador Gerard's Secretary Brings News of Adventurous Correspondents to London," *New York Times*, September 27, 1914, HN:TNYT.

17. Gibson, 5 August, 1914, *A Diplomatic Diary*, 15–17.

18. *Ibid.*, 1–2; David A. Langbart, e-mail message to author, National Archives, January 15, 2014; "Hugh S. Gibson Dies at Geneva; Long a Diplomat and Relief Aide: Foreign Service Officer 30 Years, Head of Committee for Migration, Was 71," *New York Times*, December 13, 1954, HN:TNYT; Pirenne, *Belgium and the First World War*, 56.

19. ANB, vol. 23, s.v. "Whitlock, Brand," 271–272; "Brand Whitlock, Diplomat, Is Dead: War-Time Minister to Belgium Succumbs in Cannes After Second Operation," *New York Times*, May 25, 1934, HN:TNYT.

20. Gibson, 6 August, 1914, *A Diplomatic Diary*, 22–23; Whitlock, *Belgium: A Personal Narrative*, 82–83.

21. Whitlock, *Belgium: A Personal Narrative*, 114–116.

22. Whitlock, *Belgium: A Personal Narrative*, 117; "Burgomaster Max, Belgian Hero, Dies: As Municipal Head in Brussels Defied German Invaders in 1914, Finally Being Jailed," *New York Times*, November 7, 1939, HN:TNYT; Davis, "The Germans in Brussels," 569; Gibson, 20 August, 1914, *A Diplomatic Diary*, 78; Pirenne, *Belgium and the First World War*, 52.

23. Davis, "The Germans in Brussels," 568; Gibson, 20 August, 1914, *A Diplomatic Diary*, 79.

24. Davis, "The Germans in Brussels," 569–570: "a captain and…," 569; Gibson, 20 August, 1914, *A Diplomatic Diary*, 79; Arnold J. Toynbee, *The German Terror in Belgium: An Historical Record* (New York: George H. Doran Company, 1917), 18.

25. Robert Gils and Luc Schokkaert, editors, *Fort Liezele* [guidebook], translated by Alain Van Daele (Puurs, Belgium: Marc Van Reit/Stitching Fort Liezele vzw, 2001), 9; Pirenne, *Belgium and the First World War*, 57; Gibson, 9 August, 1914, *A Diplomatic Diary*, 38.

26. "Burgomaster Max, Belgian Hero, Dies," *New York Times*.

27. *Ibid.*; Gibson, 21 August, 1914, *A Diplomatic Diary*, 93–94; "The Bombardment of Antwerp: No Panic in the City," *Times*, October 2, 1914, TDA.

28. "The Bombardment of Antwerp," *Times*; "Belgian Banking Under German Rule," *Business Digest and Investment Weekly*, June 17, 1919, 782.

29. "Saw Burning of Louvain: American Under Fire with Germans When the City Was Destroyed," *New York Times*, September 7, 1914, HN:TNYT; Richard Ernsberger, Jr., "The 'Man of Force' Who Saved Belgium," *American History*, April 2014, 36: "imported three-quarters…"; Johan den Hertog, "The Commission for Relief in Belgium and the Political Diplomatic History of the First World War," *Diplomacy & Statecraft* 21, vol. 4 (December 2010): 596, ASP.

30. Ernsberger, Jr., "The 'Man of Force' Who Saved Belgium," 36–39.

31. *Ibid.*, 39–40.

32. "Forcing Belgians to Work in Germany: Governor General von Bissing's Explanation and Cardinal Mercer's Reply," *Current History*, December 1916, 478.

33. *Ibid.*, 479–480; Stevenson, "Battlefield or Barrier?" 473.

34. Horace Green, *The Log of a Noncombatant* (Boston: Houghton Mifflin Co., 1915), 18, 20: "rope and cordage," 20; "Attack of Belgians Drives Germans South: Termonde, Aerschot and Diest Reoccupied—Force Moving Toward France Is Harried," *New York Times*, September 11, 1914, HN:TNYT: "demanded $200,000."

35. "Germany Invades France at Five Different Points: French Troops Defeat Enemy at Cirey—Luxemburg Occupied," *Jasper Weekly Courier* [Indiana], August 7, 1914, CA; Louis Renault, *First Violations of International Law by Germany: Luxemburg and Belgium*, translated by Frank Carr (London: Longmans, Green and Co., 1917), 6; James Newcomer, *The Grand Duchy of Luxembourg: The Evolution of Nationhood, 963 A.D. to 1983* (Lanham, MD: University Press of America, 1984), 235.

36. Gibson, 6 August, 1914, *A Diplomatic Diary*, 21; Whitlock, *Belgium: A Personal Narrative*, 79–80.

37. *Ibid.*

38. Gibson, 6 August, 1914, *A Diplomatic Diary*, 22; Whitlock, *Belgium: A Personal Narrative*, 80–81: "If I'm violating…," 81.

39. E.J. Dillon, "Belgian Uniforms Targets for Foes: Garb Causes Heavy Mortality, Particularly Among Officers and Surgeons," *Cleveland Plain Dealer*, August 10, 1914, CPDHN; "Boy Scout, Keen as Savage, Honored by King Albert," *Sausalito News*, September 19, 1914, CDNC; "A Belgian Boy Scouts Success," *Times*, September 2, 1914, TDA.

40. "One Hundred German Spies are Executed in Belgium: War Minister Calls Upon All Austrians and Germans to Declare Themselves or Be Prepared to Meet Fate of Those Already Killed," *Hawaiian Gazette* [Honolulu],

August 11, 1914, and "Women Spies, Disguised as Nuns, Captured and Killed by Belgians," *Tacoma Times*, August 24, 1914, both in CA; E.J. Dillon, "Belgian Uniforms Targets for Foes," *Cleveland Plain Dealer*; Martin H. Donohoe, "Daring Exploits by German Spies: They Terrorize Belgium More Than the Presence of Invading Armies," *New York Times*, August 13, 1914, HN:TNYT: "The superheated imagination…"; "Mr. M.H. Donohoe," *Times*, January 21, 1927, TDA.

41. Donohoe, "Daring Exploits by German Spies," *New York Times*; "Mr. M.H. Donohoe," and "Dr. Charles Sarolea," March 12, 1953: "head of the…," both in *Times*, TDA.

42. Nicholas Hiley, "Counter-Espionage and Security in Great Britain During the First World War," *The English Historical Review* 101, no. 400 (July 1986): 637–638, JSTOR.

43. Nevil Monroe Hopkins, "What I Saw in Belgium While Under Arrest in the German Lines; and Later in Antwerp Just Before Its Fall," *World's Work*, January 1915, 278; "Dr. N.M. Hopkins, Inventor, Author: Descendant of Noted Colonial Leaders Dies at 71—Had Served in the Government," *New York Times*, March 27, 1945, HN:TNYT: "a super-submarine designed…"

44. Hopkins, "What I Saw in Belgium While Under Arrest in the German Lines," 278.

45. Ibid., 279.

46. Davis, "'To Be Treated as a Spy,'" 702; *Belgium and Holland Including the Grand-Duchy of Luxemburg*, 8.

47. Davis, "'To Be Treated as a Spy,'" 702–703.

48. Ibid., 703.

49. Ibid., 705–706.

50. Ibid., 706; Hastings, *Catastrophe 1914*, 202–204.

51. Keegan, *The First World War*, 98–100.

52. *Military Uniforms Visual Encyclopedia* (Bradley's Close, UK: Amber Books, 2011), 54, 55, 58, 62, 67; Roy R. Behrens, *Art & Camouflage: Concealment and Deception in Nature, Art and War* (Cedar Falls, IA, 1981), 41.

53. Davis, "'To Be Treated as a Spy,'" 706; Gibson, 27 August, 1914, *A Diplomatic Diary*, 124.

54. Davis, "'To Be Treated as a Spy,'" 708–709; *Belgium and Holland Including the Grand-Duchy of Luxemburg*, 7.

55. Davis, "'To Be Treated as a Spy,'" 710–711: "You might as…," 711.

56. Ibid., 711.

57. Ibid., 714; Whitlock, *Belgium: A Personal Narrative*, 149–150; Gibson, 27 August, 1914, *A Diplomatic Diary*, 125.

58. Albert R. Williams, "With the Spy Hunters in Belgium: A Story of Personal Adventure," *Outlook*, July 7, 1915, 553; "Albert Rhys Williams Is Dead; Author and Soviet Apologist, 78," *New York Times*, February 28, 1962, HN:TNYT.

59. Albert Rhys Williams, *In the Claws of the German Eagle* (New York: E.P. Dutton & Co., 1917), 13–16.

60. Ibid., 30–31: "a pass from…," 30, and "cards of introduction…," 31.

61. Ibid., 33–35; Mott, *A History of American Magazines*, vol. 4, 422–424, 430–431.

62. Williams, *In the Claws of the German Eagle*, 41–42.

63. Ibid., 84–85, 88.

64. Albert R. Williams, "With the Germans in Belgium," *Outlook*, September 16, 1914, 140; Toynbee, *The German Terror in Belgium*, 25.

65. Williams, "With the Germans in Belgium," 141; Toynbee, *The German Terror in Belgium*, 26–27; James Bryce Bryce and Great Britain, Committee on Alleged German Outrages, *Report of the Committee on Alleged German Outrages Appointed by His Britannic Majesty's Government and Presided over by The Rt. HON. Viscount Bryce, O.M, &c., &c., Formerly British Ambassador at Washington* (Ottawa: Government Printing Bureau, 1916), 12; "Germans Wipe Out Vise, a Belgian Town: Men Made Prisoners, Women Driven into Holland—Charge Firing from Houses," August 17, 1914, *New York Times*, HN:TNYT.

66. Williams, "With the Germans in Belgium," 141; Toynbee, *The German Terror in Belgium*, 26–27; Bryce, *Report of the Committee on Alleged German Outrages Appointed*, 12; Dowling, "Campaign of Hate," in *The Marshall Cavendish Illustrated Encyclopedia of World War I*, vol. 3, edited by Peter Young (New York: Marshall Cavendish, 1984), 792; Bryce, *Report of the Committee on Alleged German Outrages*, 10–12; Larry Zuckerman, *The Rape of Belgium: The Untold Story of World War I* (New York: New York University Press, 2010), 53.

67. Donohoe, "Daring Exploits by German Spies," *New York Times*; Zuckerman, *The Rape of Belgium*, 53; Dowling, "Campaign of Hate," 792; Horne and Alan, *German Atrocities, 1914*, 140.

68. Albert R. Williams, "From Liège to Holland," *Outlook*, September 30, 1914, 267–268.

69. Ibid., 268.

70. Ibid., 268–269: "Is it dangerous…," and "Yes, it is…," and "Go straight ahead…," 268.

71. Dowling, "Campaign of Hate," 789–790, 799.

72. "A Review of the World: The Clash of Nations and the Long Deadlock That Has Followed It," *Current Opinion*, November 1917, 302; "Publisher's Prefix" and Robert J. Thompson to William Jennings Bryan, undated, both in *England and Germany in the War: Letters to the State Department* (Boston: Chapple Publishing Co., 1915), 5, 95, 97, 99–100.

73. "E.A. Powell Dead; Explorer Was 78: World Traveler Wrote About Remote Areas of the Globe—Reporter and Soldier," *New York Times*, November 14, 1957, HN:TNYT: "Department of Agriculture…"; Powell, *Fighting in Flanders*, 27.

74. Powell, *Fighting in Flanders*, 23: "He was a…"; E. Alexander Powell, "Driven to Atrocities, German Commander Tells Correspondent," *North Platte Semi-Weekly Tribune* [Nebraska], September 25, 1914, 3, CA: "mouthpiece."

75. Powell, *Fighting in Flanders*, 110–112: "I am the…," 111.

76. Powell, "Driven to Atrocities," 3, and *Fighting in Flanders*, 110.

77. Powell, "Driven to Atrocities," 3: "a ghastly, blackened…"; "How German Troops Won Hot Fight at Aerschot," *Evening World*, August 20, 1914, CA; Bryce, *Report of the Committee on Alleged German Outrages*, 22; "Handfuls Held Thousands: Heroic Defense of Louvain and Aerschot by Belgians," *New York Times*, August 22, 1914, HN:TNYT.

78. Bryce, *Report of the Committee on Alleged German Outrages*, 22–24; Toynbee, *The German Terror in Belgium*, 61, 71.

79. "Saw Ruins of Aerschot: Correspondent Tells of a Church Wrecked and 161 Villagers Killed," *New York Times*, September 12, 1914, HN:TNYT: "is partly burned…"; Powell, "Driven to Atrocities," 3: "When we entered…"; Bryce, *Report of the Committee on Alleged German Outrages*, 23.

80. Powell, "Driven to Atrocities," 3.

81. Theodore Wesley Koch, *The University of Louvain and Its Library* (London: J.M. Dent & Sons, 1917), 9, 12, 15–16.

82. "Priceless Treasures Destroyed in Louvain's Library: For Centuries Scholars Have Flocked There from All over the World to Consult Rare Volumes," *New York Times*, October 4, 1914, HN:TNYT: "over 211,000 volumes," and "a series of…"; Bernard A. Cook, *Belgium: A History* (New York: Peter Lang, 2005), 95.

83. Toynbee, *The German Terror in Belgium*, 18, 59, 64–65; Anonymous, *An Eye-Witness at Louvain* (London: Eyre & Spottiswoode, 1914), 4.

84. Koch, *The University of Louvain and Its Library*, 21; Anonymous, *An Eye-Witness at Louvain*, 3–4; "Belgian Pictures Wreck of Louvain: University Professor, Charging System in Pillage, Calls It 'Highway Robbery,'" *New York Times*, September 29, 1914, HN:TNYT.

85. "Saw Burning of Louvain," and "Germany Defends Action at Louvain: Government Statement Says Priests Gave Arms to Civilians," August 30, 1914, both in *New York Times*, HN:TNYT; Powell, "Driven to Atrocities," 3: "revenge," and "Whenever civilians fire…"

86. Kevin A. Codd, "The American College of Louvain," *Catholic Historical Review* 93, no. 1 (January 2007): 63, 65, 69.

87. Anonymous, *An Eye-Witness at Louvain*, 6–7; Jon Thiem, "The Great Library of Alexandria Burnt: Towards the History of a Symbol," *Journal of the History of Ideas* 40, no. 4 (October–December 1979): 509–510, JSTOR.

88. Anonymous, *An Eye-Witness at Louvain*, 6; Whitlock, *Belgium: A Personal Narrative*, 154–155, 159: "a filthy cart"; Kevin A. Codd, "The American College of Louvain," *Catholic Historical Review* 93, no. 1 (January 2007): 71, JSTOR.

89. Gibson, 28 August, 1914, *A Diplomatic Diary*, 128–129: "hats, wooden shoes…," 129; "Saw Burning of Louvain: American Under Fire with Germans when the City Was Destroyed," *New York Times*, September 7, 1914, HN:TNYT.

90. Gibson, 28 August, 1914, *A Diplomatic Diary*, 127–128; "Saw Burning of Louvain," *New York Times*.

91. Gibson, 28 August, 1914, *A Diplomatic Diary*, 135–136, 140; "Saw Burning of Louvain," *New York Times*.

92. "Ruins of Louvain Visited by Crowds: City Slowly Coming to Life, with a Few Shops Doing a Brisk Business," *New York Times*, November 13, 1914, HN:TNYT.

93. Mary Boyle O'Reilly, "Eye-Witness Describes Ghastly Scenes on Liege Battlefield," *Day Book*, August 12, 1914, CA.

94. "300 War Refugees of Belgium Here: Rev. John B. De Ville of Chicago Brings Party He Gathered in the Stricken Land," *New York Times*, December 9, 1915, HN:TNYT.

95. Ibid.

96. "'British Lies' and American Sentiment," and Paul Darmstaedter, "The German Point of View," both in *Nation*, November 26, 1914, 621, 629, TNA.

97. Darmstaedter, "The German Point of View," 629.

98. John Lowe, *The Great Powers, Imperialism and the German Problem, 1865–1925* (London: Routledge, 1994), 166; "Kaiser's Speech: Utterances at Morocco May Cause Trouble," *Aberdeen Herald* [Washington], April 6, 1905, CA: "In an independent…"

99. Lowe, *The Great Powers, Imperialism and the German Problem, 1865–1925*, 169.

100. Edmund Morris, *Theodore Rex* (New York: The Modern Library, 2001), 440–441; Lowe, *The Great Powers, Imperialism and the German Problem, 1865–1925*, 173–174; "A Victory for France: Opinion in London—Future Trouble over Morocco Expected," *New York Times*, April 1, 1906, HN:TNYT.

101. Lowe, *The Great Powers, Imperialism and the German Problem, 1865–1925*, 175–176; Nigel Falls, "The Panther at Agadir," *History Today*, January 2007, 37–38, ASP.

102. Falls, "The Panther at Agadir," 38–39; Lowe, *The Great Powers, Imperialism and the German Problem, 1865–1925*, 180; Darmstaedter, "The German Point of View," 629.

103. Darmstaedter, "The German Point of View," 629; Geoffrey Wawro, *Warfare and Society in Europe, 1792–1914* (New York: Routledge, 2000), 192–193; C. Jay Smith, Jr., "Great Britain and the 1914–1915 Straits Agreement with Russia: The British Promise of November 1914," *American Historical Review*, 70, no. 4 (July 1965): 1017, JSTOR; David Stevenson, "War Aims and Peace Negotiations," in *The Oxford Illustrated History of the First World War*, 209.

104. Darmstaedter, "The German Point of View," 629; Zuckerman, *The Rape of Belgium*, 59; Martin Ewans, *European Atrocity, African Catastrophe: Leopold II, the Congo Free State, and Its Aftermath* (London: Routledge-Curzon, 2002), 105, 161, 164; Cook, *Belgium: A History*, 85; Guy Vanthemsche, *Belgium and the Congo, 1885–1980*, translated by Alice Cameron and Stephen Windross, revised by Kate Connelley (New York: Cambridge University Press, 2012), 22, 195; Robert G. Weisbord, "The King, the Cardinal and the Pope: Leopold II's Genocide in the Congo and the Vatican," *Journal of Genocide Research* 5, no. 1, March 2003: 36, ASP.

105. Ewans, *European Atrocity, African Catastrophe*, 163–164; Weisbord, "The King, the Cardinal and the Pope," 36.

106. Weisbord, "The King, the Cardinal and the Pope," 38–39; "White Savages," *Deseret Weekly* [Salt Lake City], May 9, 1891; Vanthemsche, *Belgium and the Congo, 1885–1980*, 26–27.

107. Darmstaedter, "The German Point of View," 629; Horne and Kramer, *German Atrocities, 1914*, 80; Max Egremont, *Forgotten Land: Journeys Among the Ghosts of East Prussia* (New York: Farrar, Straus and Giroux, 2011), 82–85; "In Thick of Battle at Tilsit, Prussia," *Logan Republican* [Utah], November 10, 1914, CA.

108. "In Thick of Battle at Tilsit, Prussia," *Logan Republican*.

Chapter 3

1. Gibson, 27 August, 1914, *A Diplomatic Diary*, 102.

2. *Ibid.*, 105–106; *Belgium and Holland Including the Grand-Duchy of Luxembourg*, 158.

3. Gibson, 27 August, 1914, *A Diplomatic Diary*, 106: "I was glad …"; "Saw Burning of Louvain," *New York Times*.

4. Gibson, 27 August, 1914, *A Diplomatic Diary*, 107–108; Toynbee, *The German Terror in Belgium*, 77; "Allies Halt Big Attack but Retreat in North: Combined Armies Check Teuton Onslaught in Vosges While Force in Belgium Moves Back, Paris War Office Reports," *Cleveland Plain Dealer*, August 27, 1914, CPDHN; "Malines-Louvain Battle: Germans in Great Strength Opposed the Sortie from Antwerp," September 15, 1914, and "Battle at Malines Is Fiercely Fought: Germans Reattacking, Dead Piled Up in City—Assailants Push on Toward Antwerp," August 27, 1914, and, "Saw Burning of Louvain," all in *New York Times*, HN:TNYT; Mike Croll, *The History of Landmines* (Barnsley, UK: Leo Cooper, 1998), 26.

5. Gibson, 27 August, 1914, *A Diplomatic Diary*, 110–112; *Belgium and Holland Including the Grand-Duchy of Luxembourg*, 165.

6. Gibson, 27 August, 1914, *A Diplomatic Diary*, 113–114; Powell, *Fighting in Flanders*, 51–52.

7. Gibson, 27 August, 1914, *A Diplomatic Diary*, 114, 117; Powell, *Fighting in Flanders*, 54–55; "Saw Burning of Louvain," *New York Times*, 1.

8. Powell, *Fighting in Flanders*, 58; "Germans Fall in Masses at Liege Battle: Scene of Carnage Described by Tribune's Correspondent," *New York Tribune*, August 9, 1914, CA; Hastings, *Catastrophe 1914*, 161; Cook, *Belgium: A History*, 93.

9. Gibson, 27 August, 1914, *A Diplomatic Diary*, 117–118; "Defends Zeppelins for Antwerp Raid: German Reservist Says Presence of King and Military Stores Laid City Liable," *New York Times*, August 29, 1914, HN:TNYT; "New Attack by Zeppelin Is Repulsed at Antwerp: King and Queen of Belgium Are Forced to Go in Hiding as a Result of the Bomb-Dropping Episode," *Evening World*, August 26, 1914, and "German Violations of Hague Convention Arouse World: Belgian Authorities Preparing to Protest Officially to All Powers Against Manner of Hostilities—Aerial Fighters Clearly Break Rules of Civilized Warfare—Committee of High Officials Investigate Zeppelin Bomb Dropping Episode," *Ogden Standard* [Utah], August 26, 1914, both in CA.

10. "Count Ferdinand Zeppelin: A Biographical Sketch," *Cassier's Magazine: An Engineering Monthly*, August 1910, 383; T.R. MacMechen and Carl Dienstbach, "All Aboard for the Airship!" *Hampton's Magazine*, May 1911, 552.

11. Guillaume de Syon, *Zeppelin!* (Baltimore: John Hopkins University Press, 2002), 16–20; "Count Ferdinand Zeppelin," *Cassier's Magazine*, 383.

12. MacMechen and Dienstbach, "All Aboard for the Airship!" 552–553; de Syon, *Zeppelin!* 26–30, 36, 56–57; "Explosion Destroys Zeppelin's Airship: Caught in a Violent Storm While Motor Is Being Repaired Near Echterdingen," August 6, 1908, and "Zeppelin's Airship Wrecked by a Gale: Fights Against Storm in Vain and Lies, Pierced by Tree Stems, in Teutoburgian Forest," June 29, 1910, both in *New York Times*, HN:TNYT.

13. *Nova*, Season 41, Episode 11, "Zeppelin Terror Attack," directed by Ian Duncan, aired on January 15, 2014, Windfall Films Ltd., 2015, television program, NOVA/WGBH Boston in association with Channel 4 and National Geographic Channels, 2014.

14. Martin L. Levitt, "The Development and Politicization of the American Helium Industry, 1917–1940," *Historical Studies in the Physical and Biological Sciences* 30, no. 2 (2000): 333–334, JSTOR.

15. Arnold D. Harvey, "'Against London': A Zeppelin Officer's Account," *Air Power History* 57, no. 2 (Summer 2010): 16, 18, 20, ASP.

16. Arthur Ruhl, "Up to the Front," *Collier's Weekly*, October 24, 1914, 5, 6; *Northern France from Belgium to the English Channel to the Loire Excluding Paris and Its Environs: Handbook for Travellers* (Leipzig, Germany: Karl Baedeker, 1894), 113.

17. Arthur Rulh, "The Germans Are Coming!" *Collier's Weekly*, September 26, 1914, 8; *Belgium and Holland Including the Grand-Duchy of Luxembourg*, 13–14.

18. *Belgium and Holland Including the Grand-Duchy of Luxembourg*, 55; Rulh, "The Germans Are Coming!" 9.

19. "Appeal of Ghent Reaches America: Major in Medical Corps Reserve Criticizes Germany in Letter to Germany," *Morning Oregonian* [Portland], September 10, 1914, HON.

20. Williams, *In the Claws of the German Eagle*, 105–106; "German Officers Shot in Ghent: One Killed and Another Wounded When They Enter the City After Agreeing to Stay Out," September 10, 1914, and "Shooting Spies in Ghent: Crowds Assemble at Dawn to See One Put to Death by Troops," October 12, 1914, both in *New York Times*, HN:TNYT; Powell, *Fighting in Flanders*, 106–108.

21. Powell, *Fighting in Flanders*, 109.

22. E-mail from Amy Garrett to author, Office of the Historian, U.S. Department of State, February 27, 2014; Green, *The Log of a Noncombatant*, 13: "a hair-trigger politician …"; Williams, *In the Claws of the German Eagle*, 32–33: "If you send …," 32.

23. "Ghent Yields Peacefully: Everyone Who Could Get Away Fled Before Germans Entered," *New York Times*, October 14, 1914, HN:TNYT; Toynbee, *The German Terror in Belgium*, 19; "U.S. Vice Consul Saved the Wounded at Ghent: Civilians, Fleeing at Approach of Germans, Took All Vehicles, So Official American Auto Was Used to Transport Helpless Man to Train," *New-York Tribune*, October 14, 1914, CA.

24. Cook, *Belgium: A History*, 102.

25. Arthur Ruhl, "The Fall of Antwerp," *Collier's Weekly*, November 14, 1914, 5: "awoke to the …"; Antwerp, *Antwerp Builds Bridges: 1914–2014* (Antwerp, Belgium: V redescentrum, 2014), 3–4, 9; "Tells Horror of Antwerp's Fall: Eyewitness's Story of Bursting Shells, Crumbling Forts, and Frightful Panic," *New York Times*, October 12, 1914, HN:TNYT.

26. Ruhl, "The Fall of Antwerp," 6; Powell, *Fighting in Flanders*, 31–33; Gils and Luc, ed., *Fort Liezele*, 9.

27. Toynbee, *The German Terror in Belgium*, 19; "Diary Tells of Fall of Antwerp: Eleven-Inch Howitzers Prove Superior to the World's Strongest Forts," *Caldwell Watchman* [Columbia, LA], October 16, 1914, CA; Powell, *Fighting in Flanders*, 31–33; Green, *The Log of a Noncombatant*, 6; Gils and Luc, ed., *Fort Liezele*, 9; "Tells Horror of Antwerp's Fall," *New York Times*.

28. Ruhl, "The Fall of Antwerp," 6–7.

29. Ibid., 7, 24, 26.

30. "Diary Tells of Fall of Antwerp," *Caldwell Watchman*; "Tells Horror of Antwerp's Fall," *New York Times*;

"Germans Press Advance on Ostend; 24 Antwerp Forts Still Holding Out; Allies and Invaders Both Claim Gains," *Sun*, October 13, 1914, CA; F. Tennyson Jesse, "A Woman in Battle: at Belgium's Last Stand," *Collier's Weekly*, November 14, 1914, 14, 33; Hastings, *Catastrophe 1914*, 448–450.

31. John Horne, *A Companion to World War I* (Chichester, UK, and Malden, MA: Wiley-Blackwell, 2010), 353–357; Roy Greenslade, "First World War: How State and Press Kept Truth off the Front Page," *The Guardian*, July 27, 2014, http://www.theguardian.com/media/2014/jul/27/first-world-war-state-press-reporting.

32. David Mould, "Donald Thompson: Photographer at War," *Kansas History: A Journal of the Central Plains* 5, no. 3 (Autumn 1982): 154, www.kshs.org/publicat/history/1982autumn_mould.pdf; Ancestry.com: Census Place: St Joseph Ward 4, Buchanan, Missouri, Roll: T625_907, Page: 3B, 1920, Enumeration District: 85, Image: 731, and California Death Index, 1940–1997, Provo, UT, USA, Operations Inc, 2000, and State of California, California Death Index, 1940–1997, Sacramento, CA, USA: State of California Department of Health Services, Center for Health Statistics; Powell, *Fighting in Flanders*, "a sunflower smile," 14, and "and blew into ...," 13.

33. "Arrest Bogus Army Officer: Is Alleged to Have Passed Valueless Checks," *Los Angeles Herald*, September 14, 1909, CDNC; "Untitled," June 6, 1911, and "Held on Fraud Charge: Man Who Impersonated Army Officer Is Given to Federal Authorities," September 19, 1909, both in *Cleveland Plain Dealer* [OH], CPDHN; "War Photographer Held as Swindler: Donald C. Thompson Taken for Impersonating Naval Officers and for Bad Checks," *New York Times*, June 6, 1923, HN:TNYT.

34. Donald C. Thompson, *Donald Thompson in Russia* (New York: The Century Co., 1918), xi: "their dastardly deed ..."; Powell, *Fighting in Flanders*, 15: "Three ... English, American ..."

35. Mould, "Donald Thompson: Photographer at War," 156; Thompson, *Donald Thompson in Russia*, vii; Powell, *Fighting in Flanders*, 14; "Sir Sam Hughes," *Times*, August 25, 1921, TDA.

36. Brian Coe, *Cameras: From Daguerreotypes to Instant Pictures* (New York: Crown Publishers, 1978), 88, 105; Thompson to Dot [Dorothy Thompson], 11 March, 1917, 64, and Introduction, vii–viii, xvii, *Donald Thompson in Russia*; Powell, *Fighting in Flanders*, 14–15.

37. Powell, *Fighting in Flanders*, 15–16; Mould, "Donald Thompson: Photographer at War," 165; Thompson, *Donald Thompson in Russia*, viii; "33,000 Canadians Land: Another Portion of Expeditionary Force Arrives at Plymouth," *New York Times*, October 15, 1914, TDA.

38. Thompson, *Donald Thompson in Russia*, viii; Mould, "Donald Thompson: Photographer at War," 157–158; "Paid a War Bribe in Cigar Coupons: D.C. Thompson Says Russian Woman Hid Film for Him for '$1,000,'" *New York Times*, November 16, 1914, HN:TNYT.

39. "Paid a War Bribe in Cigar Coupons," *New York Times*; Powell, *Fighting in Flanders*, 18–19; C.P. Russell, "What the United Cigar Stores Company Has Accomplished in Twenty Years: A History of What the Chain That Eliminated the Wooden Indian Has Done for the Tobacco Business," *Printer's Ink: A Journal for Advertisers*, May 19, 1901, 17–18.

40. Powell, *Fighting in Flanders*, 19–20; Mould, "Donald Thompson: Photographer at War," 158; Thompson, *Donald Thompson in Russia*, viii.

41. Powell, *Fighting in Flanders*, 21–22; Mould, "Donald Thompson: Photographer at War," 158; Thompson, *Donald Thompson in Russia*, viii–ix.

42. Thomson, *Donald Thompson in Russia*, ix–x; "Donald Thompson: Photographer at War," 158.

43. Green, *Log of a Noncombatant*, 91–94, 103; "Paid a War Bribe in Cigar Coupons,'" *New York Times*.

44. Thomson, *Donald Thompson in Russia*, xi; John M. McEwen, "The National Press During the First World War: Ownership and Circulation," *Journal of Contemporary History* 17, no. 3 (July 1982): 464, 466, 482, JSTOR; "Death of Lord Northcliffe: Peaceful End to Long Illness," and "Viscount Northcliffe: Maker of the Modern Press," both in *Times*, August 15, 1922, TDA.

45. "Viscount Northcliffe: Maker of the Modern Press," *Times*.

46. Thomson, *Donald Thompson in Russia*, xi; Mould, "Donald Thompson: Photographer at War," 162.

47. "Thompson Put Out by British Shell: Intrepid Kansas Photographer Finally Gets a Taste of Real War with Germans," *Omaha Daily Bee* [Nebraska], November 2, 1914.

48. *Ibid.*; *Belgium and Holland Including the Grand-Duchy of Luxembourg*, 47: "a quiet little..."; "Germans Capture Dixmude in Belgium," *Ogden Standard*, November 11, 1914, CA.

49. Stephen Pope and Elizabeth-Anne Wheal, *The Dictionary of the First World War*, s.v. "Yser, Battle of the" (New York: St. Martin's Press, 1995), 516; Pirenne, *Belgium and the First World War*, 58.

50. "Germans Would Soak Allies by Opening Dikes," *Weekly Times-Record* [Valley City, ND], November 19, 1914, CA.

51. "Thompson Put Out by British Shell," *Omaha Daily Bee*; "King Albert Falls to Death Climbing Peak Near Namur," *New York Times*.

52. Mould, "Donald Thompson: Photographer at War," 161–162; "Thompson Put Out by British Shell," *Omaha Daily Bee*; "Camera Men Back from War," *Coos Bay Times* [Marshfield, OR], December 8, 1914, HON.

53. Mould, "Donald Thompson: Photographer at War," 162; "Colonel Was Man of Many Careers: Known as a Military Expert and War Correspondent as Well as a Publisher," April 1, 1955, and "Major Papers Were Built up in McCormick's Press Empire: The Chicago Tribune and New York News Leaders in Circulation and Revenue—Times-Herald Was Sold in 1954," April 1, 1955, and "Publisher Active in G.O.P. Affairs: But Kept Independent View—Opposed Nomination of Dewey and Eisenhower," April 2, 1955, all in *New York Times*, HN:TNYT.

54. John Radzilowski, *A Traveller's History of Poland* (Northampton, MA: Interlinks Books, 2013), 130, 148; "Russians Take Key to Austria: Capture Przemysl After Six-Month Siege as Defenders Starve; Czar's Army of 120,000 Will Start Great Drive on Cracow," *Cleveland Plain Dealer*, March 23, 1915, CPDHN; Hastings, *Catastrophe 1914*, 400.

55. "Russians Take Key to Austria," *Cleveland Plain Dealer*; "Big Battle Under Way in Galicia: Two Million Men in Fierce Encounter," *Bemidji Daily Pioneer* [Vermont], September 22, 1914, CA.

56. "Russians Take Key to Austria," and "Przemysl

Troops to Escape Siberia: That Is Made Condition of Surrender of Garrison to Russians," March 25, 1915, both in *Cleveland Plain Dealer*, CPDHN; Mould, "Donald Thompson: Photographer at War," 163.

57. "Colonel Was Man of Many Careers," *New York Times*; Martin Gilbert, *The First World War: A Complete History* (New York: Henry Holt and Company, 1994), 165–166; Jutus D. Doenecke, *Nothing Less Than War: A New History of America's Entry into World War I* (Lexington: University Press of Kentucky, 2011), 98; Thompson, *Donald Thompson in Russia*, xiv; Mould, "Donald Thompson: Photographer at War," 164; "Servia's Distress: An Interview with George Macaulay Trevelyan," *Outlook*, April 28, 1915, 966

58. Jay Winter and Blain Baggett, *The Great War and the Shaping of the Twentieth Century* (New York: Penguin, 1996), 109–110, 112.

59. Mould, "Donald Thompson: Photographer at War," 165; Keegan, *The First World War*, 286, 289–290.

60. General Staff of Great Headquarters (German), "The Battle of the Somme in July," translation into English, *Journal of the Military Service of the United States* 59, no. 204 (November–December 1916): 423–425; Keegan, *The First World War*, 295; Mould, "Donald Thompson: Photographer at War," 165.

61. Thompson, *Donald Thompson in Russia*, xvi; Douglas Thompson, *War as It Really Is* (Donald C. Thompson Film Company and Leslie's Weekly Online at *FedFlix*, 1916), 35mm film, from FedFlix, National Archives, https://archive.org/details/gov.archives.arc.25045.r1.

62. Douglas Thomspon, *War as It Really Is*; Ledger Tours, "The Old Contempibles"; Lydia Monin and Andrew Gallimore, *The Devil's Garden: A History of Landmines* (London: Pimlico, 2002), 42.

63. Evan Hadingham, "The Hidden World of the Great War: The Lost Underground of World War I," *National Geographic*, August 2014, 122, 124–125, Ledger Tours, "The Old Contempibles."

Chapter 4

1. Thompson, *Donald Thompson in Russia*, xvi–xvii; Mould, "Donald Thompson: Photographer at War," 165, 167; Florence MacLeod Harper, *Runaway Russia* (New York: The Century Co., 1918), viii.

2. Thompson to Dot, 12 December, 1916, *Donald Thompson in Russia*, 3–4, 7: "I fear Japan …"; Frederick Hastings, "Sunday in the City of the Tsar," *Frank Leslie's Sunday Magazine*, July 1888, 34.

3. Timothy D. Saxon, "Anglo-Japanese Naval Cooperation, 1914–1918," *Faculty Publications and Presentations* 5 (2000), http://digitalcommons.liberty.edu/hist_fac_pubs/5/; Yone Noguchi, "The Impracticability of Sending a Japanese Army to Europe," *Nation*, November 4, 1915, 540, TNA.

4. Thompson to Dot, 5 and 22 January and 17 and February, 1917, *Donald Thompson in Russia*, 8, 11, 20; William Harman Black, *The Real Round-the-World Pocket Guide Book for Europe, the United States of America … Actual Diary and Expense Account of an Independent 100-Day Trip over the Northern Route via the Trans-Siberian Railway, and Full Particulars of an Eastward and a Westward Trip by the Southern Route Through the Suez and India…* (New York: Association for New York, 1915), 413–414, 420.

5. Steven G. Marks, *Road to Power: The Trans-Siberian Railroad and the Colonization of Asian Russia, 1850–1917* (Ithaca: Cornell University Press, 1991), 170, 174–178; United States, War Dept, Military Intelligence Division, *Siberia and Eastern Russia: General Description and Introductory Information*, part 1 (Washington, D.C.: Government Printing Office, 1918), 55.

6. Thompson to Dot, 8 February, 1917, *Donald Thompson in Russia*, 18; Harper, *Runaway Russia*, 4–7.

7. Thompson to Dot, 17, 24, and 26 February, 1917, *Donald Thompson in Russia*, 20–21, 24, 27; Harper, *Runaway Russia*, 8, 19; Stilton Jones, *Russia in Revolution: Being the Experiences of an Englishman in Petrograd During the Upheaval* (London: Herbert Jenkins, 1917), 163: "the largest and …"

8. Thompson to Dot, 5 March, 1917, *Donald Thompson in Russia*, 31–32.

9. "Starving Amid Plenty: Russia Suffers, London Hears, from Lack of Organization," *New York Times*, January 30, 1917, HN:TNYT; Richard Pipes, *A Concise History of the Russian Revolution* (New York: Alfred A. Knopf, 1995), 75; Christopher Read, *War and Revolution in Russia, 1914–22: The Collapse of Tsarism and Establishment of Soviet Power* (New York: Palgrave Macmillan, 2013), 51.

10. Pipes, *A Concise History of the Russian Revolution*, 75; Read, *War and Revolution in Russia, 1914–22*, 50; "Bread Shortage Leads to Revolt: Strikes at Russian Munitions Factories Followed by Raids on Food Shops," *Washington Times*, March 16, 1917, CA; "Hunger Causes Petrograd Riots: Military Chief Orders Troops to Use Arms Against Demonstrators—Cars Stopped," *New York Times*, March 12, 1917, HN:TNYT.

11. John Ure, *The Cossacks: An Illustrated History* (Woodstock, NY: The Overlook Press, 2002), 30–32; Frank Welsh, *The History of the World: From the Dawn of Humanity to the Modern Age* (London: Quercus, 2011), 324.

12. Pipes, *A Concise History of the Russian Revolution*, 77: "Down with the …"; Thompson to Dot, 10 March, 1917, *Donald Thompson in Russia*, 54, 57.

13. Arnold Dosch Fleurot, "Petrograd Troops Join Forces with Revolting People: Dreaded Cossacks Refuse to Unsling Rifles and Riots Are Raging," *Cleveland Plain Dealer*, March 18, 1917, CPDHN; "Bread Shortage Leads to Revolt," *Washington Times*; Ure, *The Cossacks*, 237–238; Pipes, *A Concise History of the Russian Revolution*, 77–78; "How the Bloodshed Started: Guards Fired on People, but Latter Showed no Animosity," *New York Times*, March 16, 1917, HN:TNYT.

14. Harper, *Runaway Russia*, 37–38; Zoe Bakeeff Petersen, "The Architectural Heritage of Leningrad," *American Slavic and East European Review* 4:3/4 (December 1945): 19; Fleurot, "Petrograd Troops Join Forces with Revolting People," *Cleveland Plain Dealer*; Thompson to Dot, 11 March, 1917, *Donald Thompson in Russia*, 64, 67; "How the Bloodshed Started," *New York Times*.

15. Harper, *Runaway Russia*, 38–39; Thompson to Dot, 11 March, 1917, *Donald Thompson in Russia*, 68–69.

16. Harper, *Runaway Russia*, 38, 40–41; Thompson to Dot, 11 March, 1917, *Donald Thompson in Russia*, 70–71.

17. Pipes, *A Concise History of the Russian Revolution*, 79; Thompson to Dot, 18 March, 1917, *Donald Thompson in Russia*, 91; "Guard Regiments Started Uprising: Other Troops Sent Against Them Joined Their Ranks and People Followed Suit," *New York Times*, March 17, 1917, HN:TNYT: "live hens."

18. "Tsar Abdicates; Michael Regent: Russian Minister Swept Out of Office," *Morning Oregonian*, March 16, 1917, HON; "People in Revolt Burn and Slay in Streets of Russia's Capital: Fashionable Hotel Riddled by Machine Guns When Pro-German Shoots at Crowd—Count Frederick's Home Set on Fire and Family Ill-Treated—General de Knorring Shot," *New York Times*, March 16, 1917, HN:TNYT; Jones, *Russia in Revolution*, 164; Edvard Radzinsky, *The Last Tsar: The Life and Death of Nicolas II*, translated by Marian Schwartz (New York: Anchor Books, 1993), 186–187.

19. Thompson to Dot, 18 March, 1917, *Donald Thompson in Russia*, 89–90: "I carried her …"

20. Jones, *Russia in Revolution*, 164–165.

21. Pipes, *A Concise History of the Russian Revolution*, 80–81; Alexander Rabinowitch, *The Bolsheviks in Power: The First Year of Soviet Rule in Petrograd* (Bloomington: Indiana University Press, 2007), 1; Alden Whitman, "Alexander Kerensky Dies Here at 89," *New York Times*, June 12, 1970, HN:TNYT.

22. Rabinowitch, *The Bolsheviks in Power*, 1; "Alexander Kerensky: Russian Leader Who Was Ousted by the Bolsheviks," *Times*, June 15, 1970, TDA; Whitman, "Alexander Kerensky Dies Here at 89."

23. "Alexander Kerensky: Russian Leader Who Was Ousted by the Bolsheviks," *Times*; Whitman, "Alexander Kerensky Dies Here at 89," *New York Times*.

24. Donald C. Thompson, *The Crime of the Twentieth Century* (New York: Leslie-Judge Co., 1918), 37, and Thompson to Dot, 9 March, 1917, *Donald Thompson in Russia*, 48.

25. Thompson to Dot, 22 and 26 March, 1917, *Donald Thompson in Russia*, 127, 131–132.

26. Harper, *Runaway Russia*, 78; "American Surgeon Has Made Record in Russia: Dr. Eugene Hurd Performed Three Thousand Operations in Past Year," *Cornell Daily Sun* [New York], February 1916, CDS.

27. Thompson to Dot, 5 June, 1917, *Donald Thompson in Russia*, 236; "Dr. Eugene Hurd: Operated on More Than 31,000 Soldiers in the World War," *New York Times*, May 21, 1941, HN:TNYT; "Doctor Weds Baroness: Physician Decorated for War Service in Russia," *Morning Oregonian*, September 16, 1920, HON.

28. "American Surgeon Has Made Record in Russia," *Cornell Daily Sun*.

29. Harper, *Runaway Russia*, 78–83; R. Scotland Liddell, *Actions and Reactions in Russia* (New York: E.P. Dutton & Co., 1918), 14; Thompson to Dot, 7 June, 1917, *Donald Thompson in Russia*, 241; "Teutons Strike from the Baltic to the Black Sea: Pursue Russians in Galicia on 155-Mile Line and Cross the Sereth," *New York Times*, July 25, 1917, HN:TNYT.

30. Harper, *Runaway Russia*, 83–87; "The Russian Red Cross," *British Medical Journal* 1, no. 2829 (March 20, 1915): 520, JSTOR; Eugene Hurd, "Russian Red Cross Is Best in World: America Praises Efficiency and Generosity in Handling of Wounded," *Sunday Oregonian* [Portland], April 30, 1916, HON; Thompson, *The Crime of the Twentieth Century*, and Thompson to Dot, 7 June, 1917, *Donald Thompson in Russia*, 243; Read, *War and Revolution in Russia, 1914–22*, 59, 63–65, 88.

31. Harper, *Runaway Russia*, 145, 147–148; George Orwell, *Animal Farm: A Fairy Story* (New York: Signet Classics, 1996), 26, 35.

32. Harper, *Runaway Russia*, 151–152.

33. *Ibid.*, 88–89; "Points to America's Duty in Russia: Mrs. Florence Harper Tells How That Country Can Be Saved," *New York Times*, May 11, 1918, HN:TNYT.

34. Thompson, *The Crime of the Twentieth Century*, 86–87, 165–167, and Thompson to Dot, 24 May, 1917, *Donald Thompson in Russia*, 207; Robert E. Cook, "The Mist That Rolled into the Trenches: Chemical Escalation in World War I," *Bulletin of the Atomic Scientists* 27, no. 1 (January 1971): 36–37, and Gerard J. Fitzgerald, "Chemical Warfare and Medical Response During World War I," *American Journal of Public Health* 98, no. 4 (April 2008): 611–612, both in MFP.

35. Cook, "The Mist That Rolled into the Trenches," 38; Fitzgerald, "Chemical Warfare and Medical Response During World War I," 611.

36. Thompson to Dot, 7 June, 1917, *Donald Thompson in Russia*, 241–242.

37. "Teutons Strike from the Baltic to the Black Sea," *New York Times*; G.J. Meyer, *A World Undone: The Story of the Great War* (New York: Delacorte Press, 2006), 484; "Fate of Russian Army Lies in Hands of Kerensky: War Minister Is Given Full Power to Act," *Bisbee Daily Review* [Arizona], July 24, 1917, and "Russians Battle on Along 120-Mile Line," *Washington Times*, July 12, 1917, and "Kerensky Leads in Russ Advance: Popular Head of Army Rides to Front Line in Big Move," *Cresco Plain Dealer* [Iowa], July 6, 1917, and "Russian Advance Is Led in Person by War Minister: Kerensky, at Head of Men on Firing Line, Gives Order to Attack," *Richmond Times-Dispatch* [Virginia], July 3, 1917, all in CA; "Rout Marks Long Front in Galicia: Demoralized Russian Army Continues Its Retreat on 140 Mile Front," *Rogue River Courier*, July 25, 1917, HON.

38. "Teutons Strike from the Baltic to the Black Sea," *New York Times*; Meyer, *A World Undone*, 484–485; Alexander F. Kerensky, *The Catastrophe: Kerensky's Own Story of the Russian Revolution* (New York: D. Appleton and Co., 1927; Krause Reprint Co., 1977), 210, 212–213.

39. "Leader of Russian Women's Battalion of Death on Her Way to Washington: Kerensky May Be Her Escort Camouflaged as an Aviator," *Washington Times*, May 26, 1918, CA; John W. Bookwalter, *Siberia and Central Asia* (London: C. Arthur Pearson, 1900), 147–148: "a huge, ugly …," and "a flourishing university …," 148; Melissa K. Stockdale, "'My Death for the Motherland Is Happiness': Women, Patriotism, and Soldiering in Russia's Great War, 1914–1917," *American Historical Review* 109, no. 1 (February 2004): 78, 84–85, 90, JSTOR; Thompson to Dot, 13 July, 1917, *Donald Thompson in Russia*, 266.

40. Meyer, *A World Undone*, 347: "knee-deep slush"; "Leader of Russian Women's Battalion of Death on Her Way to Washington," *Washington Times*.

41. "Leader of Russian Women's Battalion of Death on Her Way to Washington," *Washington Times*; Meyer, *A World Undone*, 351–352, 365–366.

42. "Leader of Russian Women's Battalion of Death on Her Way to Washington," *Washington Times*; "Presi-

dent of Last Russian Duma Dies: M. Rodzianko Informed Emperor, Then at Battlefront, That Will of People Must Prevail," *New York Times*, January 28, 1924, HN:TNYT; "Exiled President of the Duma: M. Rodianko's Career," *Times*, February 1, 1924, TDA; Stockdale, "'My Death for the Motherland Is Happiness,'" 79–80, 92, 98, 102; Harper, *Runaway Russia*, 168; Thompson, *The Crime of the Twentieth Century*, 97.

43. Stockdale, "'My Death for the Motherland Is Happiness,'" 93, 113; "Leader of Russian Women's Battalion of Death on Her Way to Washington," *Washington Times*.

44. Thompson to Dot, 13 July, 1917, *Donald Thompson in Russia*, 269; Harper, *Runaway Russia*, 167–168: "She walks and ...," 167.

45. Annette M.B. Meakin, *Russia: Travels and Studies* (London: Hurst and Blackett, 1906), 15; Israel Getzler, *Kronstadt, 1917–1921: The Fate of a Soviet Democracy* (Cambridge: Cambridge University Press, 1983), 1–2; Ruth Kedzie Wood, *The Tourist's Russia* (New York: Dodd, Mead and Company, 1912), 99; Read, *War and Revolution in Russia, 1914–22*, 60.

46. Getzler, *Kronstadt, 1917–1921*, 24–25; Thompson to Dot, 12 July, 1917, *Donald Thompson in Russia*, 264: "the worst wrecks ..."

47. "Russ Sailors Menace Petrograd, Demand Ex-Tsar Be Given to Them," *El Paso Herald* [TX], CA: "a smooth faced ..."; Getzler, *Kronstadt, 1917–1921*, 25–26, 33–34, 37–38, 55.

48. Getzler, *Kronstadt, 1917–1921*, 80–81; Harper, *Runaway Russia*, 195–196.

49. Getzler, *Kronstadt, 1917–1921*, 21, 24–25; Harper, *Runaway Russia*, 196–197: "This man was ..."

50. Harper, *Runaway Russia*, 200–201, 203: "It isn't pleasant ...," 203.

51. *Ibid.*, 205–206; Frances Fort Brown, "Latest News in the World of Books," *Chattanooga News*, May 22, 1918, CA; "Points to America's Duty in Russia," *New York Times*, HN:TNYT.

52. Harper, *Runaway Russia*, 214–215.

53. Thompson, *The Crime of the Twentieth Century*, 27; Harper, *Runaway Russia*, 217, 223; Charles Edward Russell, "Agents Defame U.S: Lies Spread by Germans," *Tacoma Times*, August 22, 1917, CA.

54. Carl J. Richard, *When the United States Invaded Russia: Woodrow Wilson's Siberian Disaster* (Lanham, MD: Rowman & Littlefield Publishers, 2013), 146; Leonard Schapiro, "The Rôle of the Jews in the Russian Revolutionary Movement," *Slavonic and East European Review* 40, no. 94 (December 1961): 148, JSTOR.

55. Herman Bernstein, "Horrors Worse Than Kishineff Charged Against Russia To-day: Unparalleled Conspiracy to Crush the Jews Alleged to Be Organized to Cover Up Defeats of Tsar's Troops—Torture and Massacre Declared to Be Rife in Hundreds of Towns," *Sun*, June 6, 1915, CA.

56. Bernstein, "Horrors Worse Than Kishineff Charged Against Russia To-day," *Sun*; "Russia's Expulsion of Jews: Horrors Wrought by a Decree That Forced 200,000 People at Short Notice to Leave Warzone," *New York Times*, August 15, 1915, HN:TNYT; Eric Lohr, "The Russian Army and the Jews: Mass Deportation, Hostages, and Violence During World War I," *Russian Review* 60, no. 3 (July 2001): 410–415, JSTOR.

57. "With Authors and Publishers," *New York Times*, February 17, 1918, HN:TNYT; Ruth Pierce to Mother and Dad, 30 June, 1915, *Trapped in "Black Russia": Letters, June–November 1915* (Boston: Houghton Mifflin Co., 1918), 10–11: "The men looked ...," 10.

58. Pierce to Mother and Dad, 20 and 30 July, and October 1915, *Trapped in "Black Russia,"* 24–25, 44, 53, 131–132: "Let's shut the ...," 25.

59. *Ibid.*, 30 July, 1915, and October 1915, 44–50: "They say the ...," 50.

60. *Ibid.*, August 1915, 66–67, 70–72; Frederic S. Zuckerman, *The Tsarist Secret Police in Russian Society, 1880–1917* (New York: New York University Press, 1996), 21–22.

61. Pierce to Mother and Dad, August 1915, *Trapped in "Black Russia,"* 70–71, 74, 76.

62. *Ibid.*, September 1915, 89–90.

63. *Ibid.*, September 1915, 90.

64. *Ibid.*, 91.

65. *Ibid.*, October and November 1915, 93, 95, 97, 120, 122, 147, 149–150; Frank H. Simonds, "The Russian Campaign from Dunajec to Dvina: A Review of the Attempt of the Central Powers to Repeat Napoleon's Gamble and Win," *New York Tribune*, September 26, 1915, CA; Anthony Arnoux, *The European War: September 1915–March 1916*, vol. 3 (Boston: Privately Printed, 1917), 70–73; "Kerensky Made Russian Premier as Lvoff Quits: New Chief Will also Retain Posts of War and Marine," *New York Times*, July 21, 1917, HN:TNYT.

66. Thompson to Dot, 15 July, 1917, *Donald Thompson in Russia*, 285–286; Getzler, *Kronstadt, 1917–1921*, 111, 117; "Martial Law Is Declared in Petrograd: Armed Cossacks Patrol the Streets Following Serious Riots," *New York Tribune*, July 19, 1917, CA.

67. "Martial Law Is Declared in Petrograd," *New York Tribune*; Anna Geifman, *Thou Shalt Kill: Revolutionary Terrorism in Russia, 1894–1917* (Princeton: Princeton University Press, 1993), 78; Manfred Hildermeier, *The Russian Socialist Revolutionary Party Before the First World War* (New York: St. Martin's Press, 2000), 125; Thompson to Dot, 16 July, 1917, *Donald Thompson in Russia*, 291; Harper, *Runaway Russia*, 260; Getzler, *Kronstadt, 1917–1921*, 111.

68. Thompson to Dot, 16 July, 1917, *Donald Thompson in Russia*, 292; Pipes, *A Concise History of the Russian Revolution*, 114–117; Rabinowitch, *The Bolsheviks in Power*, 2; "Points to America's Duty in Russia," and "Petrograd Riots Due to Germans, Says Kerensky: New Premier Declares Treason Has Brought Country to Brink of Ruin," both in *New York Times*, July 22, 1917, HN:TNYT.

69. Getzler, *Kronstadt, 1917–1921*, 119–121.

70. "Kerensky Made Russian Premier as Lvoff Quits," and, Whitman, "Alexander Kerensky Dies Here at 89," both in *New York Times*; Rabinowitch, *The Bolsheviks in Power*, 3, 5.

71. George C. Guins, "The Fateful Days of 1917," *Russian Review* 26, no. 3 (July 1967): 286, 294–295, JSTOR; "Kerensky Made Russian Premier as Lvoff Quits," *New York Times*.

72. "Kerensky Made Russian Premier as Lvoff Quits," *New York Times*; Harper, *Runaway Russia*, 287–288; Thompson to Dot, 15 August, 1917, *Donald Thompson in Russia*, 347.

73. Louis Edgar Browne, "How the Bolsheviki Seized the Reins of Power from Kerensky: Graphic Word Picture of Scenes in Petrograd Before and After Radical's Hours

of Triumph," *Sunday Star* [Washington, D.C.], November 11, 1917; "Bolsheviki Plans Cleverly Made: Had the Garrison's Pledges Before They Dealt Their Blow at Kerensky," *New York Times*, November 10, 1917, HN:TNYT.

74. Keegan, *The First World War*, 341–342.

75. "Alexander Kerensky: Russian Leader Who Was Ousted by the Bolsheviks," *Times*.

Chapter 5

1. Clarence D. Ussher and Grace H. Knapp, *An American Physician in Turkey: A Narrative of Adventures in Peace and in War* (Boston: Houghton Mifflin Company, 1917), 7, 221–223: "the premises were …," and "a few days…," 223; Grace Higley Knapp, *The Mission at Van in Turkey in War Time* ([S.I.]: Privately Printed, 1916), 12.

2. Ussher and Knapp, *An American Physician in Turkey*, 224–225, 229–233.

3. *Ibid.*, 2; William E. Strong, *The Story of the American Board: An Account of the First Hundred Years of the American Board of Commissioners for Foreign Missions* (Boston: The Pilgrim Press, 1910), 3, 6.

4. William T. Youngs, *The Congregationalists* (New York: Greenwood Press, 1990), 3–4, 7; John Otis Barrows, *In the Land of Ararat: A Sketch of the Life of Mrs. Elizabeth Freeman Barrows Ussher, Missionary to Turkey and a Martyr of the Great War* (New York: Fleming H. Revell Co., 1916), 85: "To give indiscriminately …"

5. Suzanne E. Moranian, "The Armenian Genocide and American Mission Relief Efforts," in *America and the Armenian Genocide of 1915*, edited by Jay Winter (Cambridge: Cambridge University Press, 2003), 187.

6. Ussher and Knapp, *An American Physician in Turkey*, 2–5: "any ignorant native …," and "a French-Canadian …," 3.

7. Ussher and Knapp, *An American Physician in Turkey*, 20, 38–39; George S. Herrick, "A Key Man in Constantinople: William W. Peet, Treasurer of American Missions in Turkey," *Missionary Review of the World*, March 1915, 183: "treasurer of the …"

8. Ussher and Knapp, *An American Physician in Turkey*, 71; Barrows, 49–50, and account by Elizabeth Barrows Ussher, quoted in *In the Land of Ararat*, 52.

9. Ussher and Knapp, *An American Physician in Turkey*, 39, 41–42; Robert C. Walton, "Trabzon: Russia Success in Turkey," in *The Marshall Cavendish Illustrated Encyclopedia of World War I*, vol. 3, 1308.

10. Ussher and Knapp, *An American Physician in Turkey*, 47–48, 50; Account by Elizabeth Barrows Ussher, quoted in *In the Land of Ararat*, 67–68.

11. Ussher and Knapp, *An American Physician in Turkey*, 50–52, 64–66.

12. *Ibid.*, 63–64, 66.

13. *Ibid.*, *An American Physician in Turkey*, 70.

14. *Ibid.*, 213–214, 216; "Armenian Victims Slain by Thousands: Turks Have Organized Most Effective Massacre World Ever Has Seen," *Richmond Times-Dispatch*, October 4, 1915, CA.

15. Caroline Finkel, *Osman's Dream: The Story of the Ottoman Empire, 1300-1924* (New York: Basic Books, 2005), 504–509; Vahakn N. Dadrian, "The Armenian Genocide: An Interpretation," in *America and the Armenian Genocide*, 58–59; Stanford J. Shaw and Ezel Kural Shaw, *History of the Ottoman Empire and Modern Turkey: Reform, Revolution, and Republic: The Rise of Modern Turkey, 1808-1975*, vol. 2 (Cambridge: Cambridge University Press, 1977), 266–267, 274.

16. Finkel, *Osman's Dream*, 504–509, 511–512, 523–524: "unpopular war in …," 506; Moranian, "The Armenian Genocide and American Mission Relief Efforts," 189; Dadrian, "The Armenian Genocide: An Interpretation," 58–59, 61–62.

17. John Haywood with Brian Catchpole, *Historical Atlas of the 19th Century World, 1783-1914* (New York: Barnes & Noble Books, 2002), 5.14–5.15; "Washington Accepts 'Istanbul' as Replacing 'Constantinople,'" *New York Times*, May 28, 1930, HN:TNTY; Selcuk Aksin Somel, s.v. "Mehmed V," "Sublime Porte," and "Vilâyet," *Historical Dictionary of the Ottoman Empire* (Lanham, MD: The Scarecrow Press, 2003), 275–276, 182, 320–321.

18. Moranian, "The Armenian Genocide and American Mission Relief Efforts," 190; E.G. Tabet, "Turkey's Subject Races and the Young Turks," *Nation*, March 9, 1916, 276–277, TNA; Dadrian, "The Armenian Genocide: An Interpretation," 60.

19. Ulrich Trumpener, "Turkey's Entry into World War I: An Assessment of Responsibilities," *Journal of Modern History* 34, no. 4 (December 1962): 369–371, JSTOR; John Stevenson, "Turkey Enters the War," in *The Marshall Cavendish Illustrated Encyclopedia of World War I*, vol. 2, 400.

20. Stevenson, "Turkey Enters the War," 400; Shaw and Shaw, *History of the Ottoman Empire and Modern Turkey*, 311.

21. Stevenson, "Turkey Enters the War," 369–370, 400; Trumpener, "Turkey's Entry into World War I," 369–370, 373; David Gaunt, Jan Bet-Sawoce, and Rochao Donef, *Massacres, Resistance, Protectors: Muslim-Christian Relations in Eastern Anatolia During World War I* (Piscataway, NJ: Gorgias Press, 2006), 62; Shaw and Shaw, *History of the Ottoman Empire and Modern Turkey*, 312.

22. Michael A. Reynolds, *Shattering Empires: The Clash and Collapse of the Ottoman and Russian Empires, 1908-1918* (Cambridge: Cambridge University Press, 2011), 117, 125.

23. Gaunt, Bet-Sawoce, and Donef, *Massacres, Resistance, Protectors*, 56–57.

24. Richard G. Hovannisian, "Simon Vratzian and Armenian Nationalism," *Middle Eastern Studies* 5, no. 3 (October 1969): 204, JSTOR; Gaunt, Bet-Sawoce, and Donef, *Massacres, Resistance, Protectors*, 56; Reynolds, *Shattering Empires*, 117; Donald Bloxham, "The Armenian Genocide of 1915-1916: Cumulative Radicalization and the Development of a Destruction Policy," *Past & Present* no. 181 (November 2003): 159–160, JSTOR.

25. Ussher and Knapp, *An American Physician in Turkey*, 234, 260: "past-master of …"; Henry Morgenthau, *Ambassador Morgenthau's Story* (Garden City, NJ: Doubleday, Page & Co., 1919), 296: "a man of …"

26. Moranian, "The Armenian Genocide and American Mission Relief Efforts," 186; Knapp, *The Mission at Van in Turkey in War Time*, 11: "a plateau bordered …"; Morgenthau, *Ambassador Morgenthau's Story*, 293; Great Britain, Foreign Office, "Narrative of Mr. Y.K. Rushdouni, Published Serially in the Armenian Journal 'Gotchnag' of New York," *The Treatment of Armenians in the Ottoman Empire: Documents Presented to Viscount Grey of Fallodon*,

Secretary of State for Foreign Affairs, edited by Arnold Toynbee (London: Hodder and Stoughton, 1916), 52, Ussher and Knapp, *An American Physician in Turkey*, 239.

27. Ussher and Knapp, *An American Physician in Turkey*, 239–244.

28. Knapp, *The Mission at Van in Turkey in War Time*, 13–14; Morgenthau, *Ambassador Morgenthau's Story*, 294; "Narrative of Mr. Y.K. Rushdouni," *The Treatment of the Armenians in the Ottoman Empire*, 61; "Report from Max Erwin von Scheubner-Richter to Hans Freiherr von Wagenheim, May 15, 1915, translated by Linda Struck," *The Armenian Genocide: Evidence from the German Foreign Office Archives, 1915–1916*, edited by Wolfgang Gust (New York: Berghahn, 2014), 177–177; Ussher and Knapp, *An American Physician in Turkey*, 237.

29. Letter from Elizabeth Barrows Ussher to home, 8 May, 1915, quoted in *In the Land of Ararat*, 128; "Revolt of Armenians Loses Van to Turkey: Ottoman Reign of 800 Years Brought to End in Province of 13,000 Square Miles," *Richmond Times-Dispatch*, August 15, 1915, CA; Knapp, *The Mission at Van in Turkey in War Time*, 16; "Armenians in Trenches Against the Turks," *Daily East Oregonian*, August 12, 1915, and "Ussher's Brother Wounded at Van," *Ashland Tidings* [Oregon], August 26, 1915, "extinguishing fires, reporting …," both in HON.

30. Dadrian, "The Armenian Genocide: An Interpretation," 52, 57; Simon Payaslian, *The History of Armenia: From the Origins to the Present* (New York: Palgrave Macmillan, 2007), 120; John Bulloch and Harvey Morris, *No Friends but the Mountains: The Tragic History of the Kurds* (New York: Oxford University Press, 1992), 83–84.

31. Ussher and Knapp, *An American Physician in Turkey*, 262; Knapp, *The Mission at Van in Turkey in War Time*, 17.

32. Ussher and Knapp, *An American Physician in Turkey*, 266–267: "little babies shattered," 266; Telegram from William Jennings Bryan to American Embassy in Constantinople, 27 April, 1915, and telegram from Bryan to George Bakhméteff, 28 April, 1915, both in *United States Official Records on the Armenian Genocide, 1915–1917*, compiled by Ara Sarafian (Princeton, NJ: Gomidas Institute, 2004), 18–19.

33. Ussher and Knapp, *An American Physician in Turkey*, 262; Knapp, *The Mission at Van in Turkey in War Time*, 274, Letter from Elizabeth Barrows Ussher to John Otis Barrows, quoted in *In the Land of Ararat*, 130.

34. Ussher and Knapp, *An American Physician in Turkey*, 274; *United States Diplomacy on the Bosporus: The Diaries of Ambassador Morgenthau, 1913–1916*, 8 May, 1915, compiled by Ara Sarafian (Princeton, NJ: Gomidas Institute, 2004), 220.

35. Letter from Elizabeth Barrows Ussher to John Otis Barrows, *In the Land of Ararat*, 131; Ussher and Knapp, *An American Physician in Turkey*, 278, 280–281; "Ussher's Brother Wounded at Van," *Ashland Tidings*; Knapp, *The Mission at Van in Turkey in War Time*, 26; Reynolds, *Shattering Empires*, 134.

36. "Record of an Interview with Roupen, of Sassoun, by Mr. A.S. Safrastian, Dated Tiflis, 6th November, 1915," *The Treatment of the Armenians in the Ottoman Empire*, 84.

37. Barrows, "Account of Elizabeth Barrows Ussher," *The Treatment of the Armenians in the Ottoman Empire*, 145–146; "Revolt of Armenians Loses Van to Turkey: Ottoman Reign of 800 Years Brought to End in Province of 13,000 Square Miles," *Richmond Times-Dispatch*, August 15, 1915, CA; Ussher and Knapp, *An American Physician in Turkey*, 290; Knapp, *The Mission at Van in Turkey in War Time*, 28.

38. Knapp, *The Mission at Van in Turkey in War Time*, 28; Edward Schumacher, "Alexandra Tolstoy Is Dead at 95; Author's Daughter Aided Refugees," *New York Times*, September 27, 1979, HN:TNYT.

39. Ussher and Knapp, *An American Physician in Turkey*, 294, 298–299; Victoria A. Harden, *The Cambridge Historical Dictionary of Disease*, s.v. "Epidemic Typhus," 352; Knapp, *The Mission at Van in Turkey in War Time*, 29; Barrows Ussher to home, 8 May, 1915, quoted in *In the Land of Ararat*, 129–130.

40. Ussher and Knapp, *An American Physician in Turkey*, 299–300; Knapp, *The Mission at Van in Turkey in War Time*, 30.

41. Ussher and Knapp, *An American Physician in Turkey*, 303–305.

42. *Ibid.*, 307–308: "a litter hung …," and "took turns walking," 307; Knapp, *The Mission at Van in Turkey in War Time*, 32–33.

43. Knapp, *The Mission at Van in Turkey in War Time*, 311; A.O. Sarkissian, "Genocide in Turkey," in *The Marshall Cavendish Illustrated Encyclopedia of World War I*, vol. 5, 1326; "Narrative of Mr. A.S. Safrastian, Dated Van, 2nd December, 1915, and Published in the Armenian Journal 'Ararat' of London, January, 1916," 74: "a waterless and …," and, "The Flight to the Caucasus: Dispatches to the Armenian Journal 'Horizons' of Tiflis, from Mr. Sampson Aroutounian, President of the Armenian National Committee in Tiflis, Who Went in Person to Meet the Refugees," 46, all in *The Treatment of the Armenians*.

44. Knapp, *The Mission at Van in Turkey in War Time*, 35; Ussher and Knapp, *An American Physician in Turkey*, 312; "Narrative of Mr. A.S. Safrastian," 74.

45. "The Flight from the Caucasus: Despatch [sic] from the Special Correspondent of the Armenian Journal 'Arev' of Bakou [Baku], *The Treatment of the Armenians*, 197.

46. Knapp, *The Mission at Van in Turkey in War Time*, 37–38; Ussher and Knapp, *An American Physician in Turkey*, 315.

47. Morgenthau, *Ambassador Morgenthau's Story*, 326–327; Bloxham, "The Armenian Genocide of 1915–1916, 140; Sarkissian, "Genocide in Turkey," 1325.

48. E. Briquet, "Zeitoun First Exodus," quoted in *The Diaries of Henry Morgenthau*, 30 May, 1915, 241; "Enclosure with Despatch [sic] No. 269, April 21, 1915, to American Embassy, Constantinople, 'Regarding Zeitoun and Other Villages: Information from Dr. [Caroline F.] Hamilton and Mr. [Dr. C.F.] Ranney,'" *United States Official Records on the Armenian Genocide*; Henry Wood, "Atrocities by the Turks on Helpless Armenians: Outrages Which Rival Those of Abdul Hamid Are Being Inflicted Upon Men, Women and Children of Country," *Daily Gate City* [Keokuk, IA], August 2, 1915, CA.

49. E. Briquet, "Zeitoun First Exodus," 241; Wood, "Atrocities by the Turks on Helpless Armenians," *Daily Gate City*; "Regarding Zeitoun and Other Villages: Information from Dr. [Caroline F.] Hamilton and Mr. [Dr. C.F.] Ranney," *United States Official Records on the Armenian Genocide*, 10–11.

50. E. Briquet, "Zeitoun First Exodus," 241; Letter from J.B. Jackson to Morgenthau, 12 May, 1915, *United States Official Records on the Armenian Genocide, 1915-1917*, 37: "between 4,300 and ..."

51. W.J. Childs, "Across Asia on Foot—IV," *Blackwood's Magazine*, May 1915, 643; United States, Department of Commerce, *Commerce Reports*, October 6, 1919, 105; E. Briquet, "Zeitoun First Exodus," 241.

52. Letter from William S. Dodd to Morgenthau, 6 May and 15 August, 1915, *United States Official Records on the Armenian Genocide, 1915-1917*, 37-38: "soldiers needed clothing ...," 38.

53. Dodd to Morgenthau, 15 August, 1915, *United States Official Records on the Armenian Genocide, 1915-1917*, 192-193.

54. Post to Morgenthau, 3 September, 1915, and Dodd to Morgenthau, 15 August, 1915, both in *United States Official Records on the Armenian Genocide, 1915-1917*, 197, 248; Morgenthau, *Ambassador Morgenthau's Story*, 337: "dull-witted and ..."

55. Dodd to Morgenthau, 15 August, 1915, *United States Official Records on the Armenian Genocide, 1915-1917*, 192; "H. Morgenthau Sr. Dies in Home at 90: U.S. Ambassador to Turkey Before First World War Was an Expert on Near East," *New York Times*, November 26, 1946, HN:TNYT.

56. "H. Morgenthau Sr. Dies in Home at 90," *New York Times*, 18; *ANB*, vol. 15, s.v. "Morgenthau, Henry," 862.

57. Post to Morgenthau, 3 September and 27 October, 1915, *United States Official Records on the Armenian Genocide, 1915-1917*, 247, 338-339.

58. Rouben Paul Adalian, "American Diplomatic Correspondence in the Age of Mass Murder: The Armenian Genocide in the U.S. Archives," in *America and the Armenian Genocide of 1915*, 157; 10 August, 1915, *The Diaries of Ambassador Morgenthau*, 299; Susan K. Blair, "Introduction," in *The Slaughterhouse Province: An American Diplomat's Report on the Armenian Genocide, 1915-1917* by Leslie A. Davis (New Rochelle, NY: Aristide D. Caratzas, 1989, 4, 14; "Report of Leslie A. Davis, American Consul, Formally of Harput, on the Work of the American Consulate at Harput Since the Beginning of the Present War," *United States Official Records on the Armenian Genocide, 1915-1917*, 611, 614.

59. Davis, "Work of the American Consulate at Harput Since the Beginning of the Present War," 614-615; Letter from Davis to Morgenthau, 30 December, 1915, *United States Official Records on the Armenian Genocide, 1915-1917*, 611, 470-471.

60. Report from Leslie A. Davis to Morgenthau, 11 August, 1915, quoted in *The Diaries of Ambassador Morgenthau*, 300: "without exception," and "A more pitiable ..."; Adalian, "American Diplomatic Correspondence in the Age of Mass Murder," 159.

61. Bulloch and Morris, *No Friends but the Mountains*, 198; "Turkey's Holy War: How the Savage Kurds Have Been Turned Loose on the Persian Christians, Have Assaulted American Missionaries, Hanged Bishops and Priests, Tortured Men, Women, Children and Massacred Thousands," *Richmond Times-Dispatch*, May 9, 1915, CA.

62. Bulloch and Morris, *No Friends but the Mountains*, 75-76, 78-82; *Historical Dictionary of the Ottoman Empire*, s.v. "Vilâyet," 320-321.

63. Bulloch and Morris, *No Friends but the Mountains*, 84-85; Reynolds, *Shattering Empires*, 78; Gaunt, Bet-Sawoce, and Donef, *Massacres, Resistance, Protectors*, 55: "rich but immoral ..."; David McDowall, *A Modern History of the Kurds* (London: I.B. Tauris, 1996), 105.

64. *Historical Dictionary of the Ottoman Empire*, s.v. "Talaat Pasha," 288; "Talaat's Career: Extermination of the Armenians," *Times*, March 16, 1921, TDA.

65. "The Late Talaat Pasha: An Engaging Villain," *Times*, March 17, 1921, TDA.

66. Morgenthau, *Ambassador Morgenthau's Story*, 331: "He's English, isn't ...,"; 10 May, 1915, *The Diaries of Ambassador Morgenthau*, 227-228.

67. Morgenthau, *Ambassador Morgenthau's Story*, 337-339; Joseph B. Treaster, "Insurer to Pay Armenian Massacre Claims," *New York Times*, April 12, 2001, HN:TNYT.

68. Ibid.

69. *Historical Dictionary of the Ottoman Empire*, s.v. "Enver Pasha," 85; "Enver Pasha," *New York Tribune*, August 19, 1922, CA.

70. August, 1915, *The Diaries of Ambassador Morgenthau*, 295-296.

71. Morgenthau, *Ambassador Morgenthau's Story*, 370.

72. Ibid., 373-374; "H. Von Wangenheim, Diplomatist, Dead: German Ambassador Was Credited with Bringing About the Turko-German Alliance," *New York Times*, October 26, 1915, HN:TNYT; "Report from Hans Freiherr von Wagenheim to Theobald von Bethmann Hollwegg, May 8, 1915, translated by Linda Struck," *America and the Armenian Genocide of 1915*, 176.

73. Gust, "Overview of the Armenian Genocide," 105; "Letter, dated Aleppo, 8th October 1915, from Four Members of the German Missions Staff in Turkey to the Imperial Minister of Foreign Affairs at Berlin," *The Treatment of the Armenians*, xxxii-xxxiii: "Out of 2,000 ...," xxxii.

74. Morgenthau, *Ambassador Morgenthau's Story*, 375-376; "Overview of the Armenian Genocide," *The Armenian Genocide: Evidence from the German Foreign Office Archives, 1915-1916*, 105; "Capt. Hans Humann, War Veteran, Dead: Was Credited With Helping to Induce Turkey to Side with Central Powers," *New York Times*, October 8, 1933, HN:TNYT.

75. Telegram from Morgenthau to Secretary of State, 11 August, 1915, *United States Official Records on the Armenian Genocide, 1915-1917*, 37; Robert L. Daniel, "The Armenian Question and American-Turkish Relations, 1914-1927," *Mississippi Valley Historical Review*, 46, no. 2 (September 1959): 256, JSTOR.

76. Morgenthau, *Ambassador Morgenthau's Story*, 339-340; "Queen Eleanore of Bulgaria Dies: Second Wife of King Ferdinand Succumbs at Sofia in Her 58th Year," September 13, 1917, and "Mrs. Morgenthau Home from Turkey: Ambassador's Wife in Constantinople Heard the Russian Guns," October 15, 1915, both in *New York Times*, HN:TNYT; "Queen Eleonore of Bulgaria: Life of Womanly Devotion," *Times*, September 13, 1917, TDA.

77. Morgenthau, *Ambassador Morgenthau's Story*, 340-342; Richard C. Hall, "Bulgaria in the First World War," *Historian* 73, no. 2 (Summer 2011): 303, ASP.

78. Morgenthau, *Ambassador Morgenthau's Story*, 385; "Morgenthau Quits as Envoy to Turkey: Will Take Active Part in President Wilson's Campaign for Re-election," *New York Times*, April 26, 1916, HN:TNTY; "Elkus Slated

as Ambassador to Turkish Empire," *Rogue River Courier*, April 2, 1916, CA; Adalian, "American Diplomatic Correspondence in the Age of Mass Murder," 152; Abram I. Elkus, *The Memoirs of Abram Elkus: Lawyer, Ambassador, Statesman* (Princeton, NJ: Gomidas Institute, 2004), 50, 89–90: "a trained lawyer," 50.

Chapter 6

1. George E. White, *Adventuring with Anatolia College* (Grinnell, IA: Herald Register Publishing Co., 1940), 83–84; "Conditions in Marsovan," 26 June, 1915, and Frances C. Gage, "Report of Difficulties in Armenia, December 22, 1915," 26, both enclosed with a letter from Henry Morgenthau to Secretary of State [Lansing], *United States Official Records on the Armenian Genocide, 1915–1917*, 141, 407; Keith David Watenpaugh, "The League of Nations' Rescue of Armenian Genocide Survivors and the Making of Modern Humanitarianism, 1920–1927," *American Historical Review* 115, no. 5 (December 2010): 1315, 1318, MFP.
2. Watenpaugh, "'The League of Nations' Rescue of Armenian Genocide Survivors and the Making of Modern Humanitarianism, 1920–1927," 1324; "Armenian Women Put up at Auction: Refugee Tells of the Fate of Those in Turkish Hands," *New York Times*, September 29, 1915, HN:TNYT.
3. "Girls Freed from Turkish Harems Tell Stories of Atrocities: Many of Them Turned into Streets with Babies Are Found Crazed by Starvation and Exposure," *Harrisburg Telegraph*, June 2, 1919, 11, CA.
4. White, *Adventuring with Anatolia College*, 84; Gage, "Report of Difficulties in Armenia, 408; Childs, "Across Asia on Foot," 169.
5. Gage, "Report of Difficulties in Armenia," 409–413: "We found no …," 411; Childs, "Across Asia on Foot," 342; Elizabeth Wilson, *The Road Ahead: Experiences in the Life of Frances C. Gage* (New York: The Womans Press, 1918), 98–99: "Sivas an hour …," 99.
6. Aurora Mardiganian, *Ravished Armenia or "The Auction of Souls": The Story of Aurora Mardiganian, the Christian Girl Who Survived the Great Massacres*, interpreted by H.L. Gates (New York: International Copyright Bureau, 1919), 29–33, 47: "who wanted to …," 47.
7. Ibid., 38–40, 55–56.
8. Ibid., 56.
9. Ibid., 57, 74, 76, 80.
10. Ibid., 81–82, 86–89; "Like a Story in the Fairy Books: Herded in the Desert by Turks, Little Aurora, the Christian Girl Refugee, from Ravished Armenian, Greeted Like a Princess on a Triumphal Trip Across the Country to California," *Washington Times*, January 5, 1919.
11. Mardiganian, *Ravished Armenia*, 90, 92–95, 105–106.
12. Ibid., 106–108.
13. Ibid., 116–118: "into the desert …," 116.
14. Ibid., 124–128.
15. Ibid., 128, 132–133; Mark Sykes, *Dar-ul-Islam: A Record of a Journey Through Ten of the Asiatic Provinces of Turkey* (London: Bickers & Son, 1904), 112–117: "a miserable place," 117.
16. Mardiganian, *Ravished Armenia*, 139–142: "screamed and pushed …," 140.

17. Ibid., 145–146, 152–153, 156–157, 159; *Palestine and Syria with the Chief Routes Through Mesopotamia and Babylonia*, 4th edition (Leipzig: Karl Baedker, 1906), 400.
18. Mardiganian, *Ravished Armenia*, 160–161, 163–167.
19. Ibid., 170–173, 177.
20. Ibid., 170–173, 184–187.
21. Ibid., 187–190.
22. Ibid., 191–192, 195, 203–206.
23. Ibid., 211–214.
24. Ibid., 214–220.
25. Ibid., 220–222.
26. Ibid., 223, 226–229.
27. Ibid., 230–233: "My eyes see …," 233.
28. Ibid., 235–238.
29. Ibid., 239–245: "Ahmed Bey had …," 240, and "highlands of grass," 242.
30. Ibid., 247–249 "and fell at …," 248.
31. "'Miss Graffam's Own Story,' Taken Stenographically by Dr. Richard's Secretary," Box 28, ABC 1-91 Collection, American Board of Commissioners for Foreign Missions Archives, Biographies, Houghton Library, Harvard University, Massachusetts, 1; "Kaiser's Land For Mission: Woman Relief Worker's Unique Career in Turkey and Armenia," *New York Times*, January 23, 1921, HN:TNYT.
32. "Miss Graffam's Own Story," 1–2, 4–5; Letter from Mary L. Graffam to William Peet, enclosed with a Letter from Henry Morgenthau to the U.S. Secretary of State, 7 August, 1915, *United States Official Records on the Armenian Genocide, 1915–1917*, 240, 244; "Kaiser's Land For Mission," *New York Times*: "two ox carts …"
33. Graffam to Peet, 7 August, 1915, 240–242.
34. "Kaiser's Land for Mission," *New York Times*; "Miss Graffam's Own Story," 3–4.
35. "Kaiser's Land for Mission," *New York Times*: "rented houses and …"; "Miss Graffam's Own Story," 4–5.
36. "Walter Mackintosh Geddes," *Yale Forest School News*, January 1, 1916, 11.
37. "Memorandum [signed] by Walter M. Geddes, Enclosed with a Letter from George Horton to Secretary of State, November 8, 1915," *United States Official Records on the Armenian Genocide, 1915–1917*, 380.
38. Ibid., 381.
39. Ibid., 382–383; Adalian, "American Diplomatic Correspondence in the Age of Mass Murder, 180.
40. Anonymous, "Report on the Armenian Question," enclosed with a letter from George Horton to Secretary of State Robert Lansing, 15 January, 1916, *United States Official Records on the Armenian Genocide, 1915–1917*, 450; "Rev. Francis H. Leslie, of Oorfa [Urfah]," *Missionary Herald at Home and Abroad*, January 1916, 18–19.
41. "Letter Dated Ourfa [Urfah], 14th June, 1915, from Mr. K.: Communicated by the American Committee for Armenian and Syrian Relief," 528–529, and "Postscript to a Memorial (Doc. 141) by a Foreign Witness from Aleppo: Communicated by the American Committee for Armenian and Syrian Relief," 532, both in *The Treatment of the Armenians*; Anonymous, "Report on the Armenian Question," 450.
42. Anonymous, "Report on the Armenian Question," 450–451.
43. First deposition of Ethel Marston Agazarian, enclosed with a letter from Abram L. Elkus to the U.S. Sec-

retary of State, 17 November, 1916, *United States Official Records on the Armenian Genocide, 1915–1917*, 562.

44. First deposition of Ethel Marston Agazarian, 563.
45. *Ibid.*, 564.
46. *Ibid.*, 564; Elkus, *The Memoirs of Abram Elkus*, 66.
47. Elkus, *The Memoirs of Abram Elkins*, 69.
48. "Report from a Foreign Resident at Damascus: Dated 20th September, but Containing Information up to the 3rd October, 1915; Communicated by the American Committee for Armenian and Syrian Relief," 558–560, and "Exiles on the Euphrates: Record, Dated Erzeroum [*sic*] June, 1915, by M. Henry Barby, of an Interview with Dr. H. Toroyan, an Armenian Physician Formerly in the Service of the Ottoman Army; Published in 'Le Journal,' of Paris, 13th July, 1916," 563–564, both in *The Treatment of Armenians in the Ottoman Empire*; Sarkissian, "Genocide in Turkey," 1323.
49. Eric Bogosian, *Operation Nemesis: The Assassination Plot That Avenged the Armenian Genocide* (New York: Little, Brown and Company, 2015), 98–99; Guenter Lewy, "Revisiting the Armenian Genocide," *Middle East Quarterly* 12, no. 4 (Fall 2005): 4; ASP; "Talaat Pasha Slain in Berlin Suburb: Armenian Student Shoots Former Turkish Grand Vizier, Held Responsible for Massacres," *New York Times*, March 16, 1921, HN:TNYT; Elie Kedourie, "The End of the Ottoman Empire," *Journal of Contemporary History*, 3, no. 4 (October 1968): 19–20, JSTOR; Shaw and Shaw, *History of the Ottoman Empire and Modern Turkey*, 311.
50. Michelle Tusan, "The Armenian Genocide and Foreign Policy," *Phi Kappa Phi Forum* 94, no. 2 (Summer 2014): 14–15, ASP.
51. "Djemal Pasha, Fugitive, Assassinated in Tiflis; Condemned as Author of Armenian Massacres," *New York Times*, July 26, 1922, HN:TNTY; "Last of the Three Bloody Pashas," *Sunday Oregonian*, August 22, 1922, HON; Walter Duranty, "Enver Pasha Slain by Soviet Force: Turks' War Leader Is Left Dead on the Field After Desperate Fight in Bokhara," *New York Times*, August 18, 1922, HN:TNYT; "Enver Pasha," *New York Tribune*, August 19, 1922, CA.
52. "Talaat Pasha Slain in Berlin Suburb: Armenian Student Shoots Former Turkish Grand Vizier, Held Responsible for Massacres," *New York Times*, March 16, 1921, HN:TNYT; "Assassin Kills Talaat Pasha, Turk War Lord: Ex-Vizier, Accused of Ordering Massacres, Shot to Death in a Berlin Suburb by Armenian," *New York Tribune*, March 16, 1921, CA.
53. "Talaat Slayer Acquitted in Berlin Court: Armenian Boy, Who Laid Murder to Vision of Mother in Dream, Is Freed on Insanity Plea," *New York Tribune*, June 4, 1921, CA: "could not be …"; Bogosian, *Operation Nemesis*, 97–99, 123.
54. Bogosian, *Operation Nemesis*, 98; "I have placed …" was quoted and translated by Louis P. Lochner in *What About Germany?* (New York: Dodd, Mead & Co., 1943), 2.
55. Stanley Goldman, "Prologue: The Man Who Made Genocide a Crime: The Legacy of Raphael Lemkin," *Loyola of Los Angeles International & Comparative Law Review* 34, no. 3 (Spring 2013): 296–297, ASP.
56. Lewy, "Revisiting the Armenian Genocide," 3–4; Republic of Turkey, Ministry of Foreign Affairs, "The Armenian Allegation of Genocide: The Issue and the Facts," accessed February 14, 2016, http://www.mfa.gov.tr/the-armenian-allegation-of-genocide-the-issue-and-the-facts.en.mfa; Letter from Davis to Morgenthau, 30 December, 1915, *United States Official Records on the Armenian Genocide, 1915–1917*, 474.
57. Bloxham, "The Armenian Genocide of 1915–1916," 140; "Armenian Victims Slain by Thousands," *Richmond Times-Dispatch*; Sarkissian, "Genocide in Turkey," 1325.
58. "Information Regarding Events in Armenia, Published in the 'Sonnenaufgang' (Organ of the 'German League for the Promotion of Charitable Work in the East), October 1915; and in the 'Allegemeine Mission-Zietschrisft,' November 1915," 25, and "Letter from an Authoritative Source, Dated Constantinople, 15th [and] 28th June, 1915, Published in the New York Journal 'Gotchnag,' 28th August, 1915," 6, both in *The Treatment of the Armenians in the Ottoman Empire*; "Armenian Victims Slain by Thousands," *Richmond Times-Dispatch*.
59. Mark Malkasian, "The Disintegration of the Armenian Cause in the United States, 1918–1927," *International Journal of Middle East Studies* 16, no. 3 (August 1984): 350, JSTOR; Daniel, "The Armenian Question and American-Turkish Relations, 1914–1927," 253; Rouben Paul Adalian, "Near East Relief and the Armenian Genocide," Armenian National Institute, accessed August 12, 2016, http://www.armenian-genocide.org/ner.html.
60. "'Ravished Armenia' in Film: Mrs. Harriman Speaks at Showing of Turkish and German," *New York Times*, February 15, 1919, HN:TNYT; Alin K. Gregorian, "Scholar Captures Tragedy, Miracle of Aurora Mardiganian's Life Story," *Armenian Mirror-Spectator* (Watertown, MA), March 24, 2014, accessed February 1, 2016, http://www.mirrorspectator.com/2014/03/24/scholar-captures-tragedy-miracle-of-aurora-mardiganians-life-story; Anthony Slide, "Introduction," in *Ravished Armenia and the Story of Aurora Mardigian* (Lanham, MD: The Scarecrow Press, 1997), 6–7.
61. "'Ravished Armenia' in Film," *New York Times*; Slide, "Introduction," 7–8; Gregorian, "Scholar Captures Tragedy, Miracle of Aurora Mardiganian's Life Story"; "Turk Barbarity Is Shown in Picture," September 8, 1919, and May Ridgway, "Child Victim of the Turks Completes Plea for Aid," January 10, 1919, both in *Los Angeles Evening Herald*, CDNC; "Ravished Armenia: How Little Aurora, the Rescued Waif, Helped to Raise the Armenian Relief Fund to Save the Remnants of Her Persecuted People," *Washington Times*, March 9, 1919, CA.
62. Gregorian, "Scholar Captures Tragedy, Miracle of Aurora Mardiganian's Life Story"; "Girl Who Fled Turks Finds Uncle Here: Last Words of Slain Mother Only Clew [*sic*] in American's Search for Relatives," *Los Angeles Evening Herald*, November 14, 1918, CDNC; Vartan Matiossian, "The Quest for Aurora: On 'Ravished Armenia' and its Surviving Fragment," April 15, 2014, accessed February 2, 2016, http://armenianweekly.com/2014/04/15/aurora.
63. Bettina Drew, "The Great Amnesia," *Southwest Review*, 99, no. 4 (2014): 557–558, ASP: "1780s to the …"; "Marion Blackburn, "Return to the Trail of Tears," *Archaeology*, March/April 2012, 56, ASP.
64. Drew, "The Great Amnesia," 558–559; Blackburn, "Return to the Trail of Tears," 53–54: "White land speculators," 53; Ronald Wright, *Stolen Continents: The "New World" Through Indian Eyes* (Boston: Houghton Mifflin, 1992), 201, 215.

65. David D. Smits, "The Frontier Army and the Destruction of the Buffalo, 1865–1883," *Western Historical Quarterly* 25:3 (Autumn 1994): 314–315, 317, 337–338, JSTOR; Smithsonian Institution, Board of Regents, *Annual Report of the Board of Regents of the Smithsonian Institute Showing the Operations, Expenditures, and Condition of the Institution for the Year Ending June 30, 1887*, part 2 (Washington D.C.: Government Printing Office, 1889), 465–46, 469.

66. Alex Alvarez, *Native Americans and the Question of Genocide* (Lanham, MD: Rowman & Littlefield, 2014), 147; John Collier, "The Vanquished Indian," *Nation*, January 11, 1928, 38–39, TNA: "essentially serfs," 38, and "half-animals," 39.

67. Malkasian, "The Disintegration of the Armenian Cause in the United States, 1918–1927," 351–352, 354.

Chapter 7

1. "Statement of the Rev. William A. Shedd, D.D., of the American (Presbyterian) Mission Station at Urmia; Communicated by the Board of Foreign Missions on the Presbyterian Church in the U.S.A.," *The Treatment of the Armenians in the Ottoman Empire*, 101; Abraham Yohannan, *The Death of a Nation, or the Ever Persecuted Nestorians or Assyrian Christians* (New York: G.P. Putman's Sons, 1916), 120–121; Richard Hill, "The Nations at War: I—What About Persia?" *Outlook*, November 17, 1915, 670; "World-wide Missionary News: Moslems in Asia," *Missionary Review of the World*, October 1915, 781; Robert E. Speer, "Help Needed in Persia," *Wisconsin Presbyterian*, April 1916, 11.

2. "Christians Suffer from War Horrors: More than 50,000 Offenceless Ones in Persia Exiled," *Guthrie Daily Leader* [Oklahoma], March 12, 1915: "As far as …"; E. Briquet, "First Exodus from Urmia, January, 1915," 105–106; Speer, "Help Needed in Persia," 11.

3. Letter from William B. Lake to Harry W. Wilson, quoted in "Almonds in Northwestern Persia," *Pacific Rural Press*, October 16, 1915, 374, CDNC; William Warfield, *The Gate of Asia: A Journey from the Persian Gulf to the Black Sea* (New York: G.P. Putman's Sons, 1916), 358–360: "numbers of heavy …"; "Teutons Win as Turks Aim Fresh Drive: Germans Gain Decisive Victories over French Near Soissons in Western Battle Zone," *Cleveland Plain Dealer*, January 14, 1915, CPDHN.

4. "Turks Take Tabriz," *Independent*, January 25, 1915, 117; Yonan H. Shahbaz, *The Rage of Islam: An Account of the Massacre of Christians by the Turks in Persia* (Philadelphia: The Roger Williams Press, 1918), 67; "Letter Dated Tabriz, 17th March, 1915, from the Rev. F.N. Jessup; Communicated by the Board of Foreign Missions of the Presbyterian Church in the U.S.A.," *The Treatment of Armenians in the Ottoman Empire*, 113.

5. "Letter dated Tabriz, 17th March, 1915, from the Rev. F.N. Jessup," 114; "Christians Suffer from War Horrors," *Guthrie Daily Leader*.

6. Gaunt, Bet-Sawoce, and Donef, *Massacres, Resistance, Protectors*, 89; Shahbaz, *The Rage of Islam*, 3, 57; A.V. Williams Jackson, *Persia Past and Present: A Book of Travel and Research* (New York: Macmillan Co., 1906), 63–67.

7. William Walker Rockwell, *The Pitiful Flight of the Assyrian Christians in Persia and Kurdistan Described from the Reports Eye-witnesses* (New York: American Committee for Armenian and Syrian Relief, 1916), 15; Yohannan, *The Death of a Nation*, 117; "Control of Persia: 'Sphere of Influence' Convention Ratified," *Evening Star* [Washington, D.C.], September 23, 1907, CA; "Persia Annuls Treaty: Notifies The Hague That It Won't Recognize Russo-British Compact," *New York Times*, May 4, 1918, HN:TNYT; Peter Hopkirk, *The Great Game: The Struggle for Empire in Central Asia* (New York: Kodansha International, 1992), 518–522.

8. Mohammad Gholi Majd, *Persia in World War I and Its Conquest by Great Britain* (Lanham, MD: University Press of America, 2003), 31, 37, 39, 69; Hill, "The Nations at War," November 17, 1915, 670, 672: "Persia is absolutely …"

9. Homa Katouzian, *Iran: A Beginner's Guide* (London: Oneworld Publications, 2013), 65–67, 76.

10. Rockwell, *The Pitiful Flight of the Assyrian Christians in Persia and Kurdistan Described from the Reports Eye-witnesses*, 15; Shahbaz, *The Rage of Islam*, 57, 59–60; "Persia Country of Hunger and Disease: Mrs. E.T. Allen Arrives Here from Storm Center," *Morning Oregonian*, November 4, 1918, HON; "Dr. Coan Penned in the Warzone: Missionary, Who Talked in Market Square Church, Marooned in Constantinople," *Star-Independent* [Harrisonburg, PA], December 4, 1914, and "Battle Fought Around Mission: Kurd Tribesmen Rise in Persia Against the Cossacks," *The Washington Herald* [Washington, D.C.], December 9, 1914, both in CA; McDowell, *A Modern History of the Kurds*, 104.

11. Shahbaz, *The Rage of Islam*, x, 76, 79–82; "Yonan H. Shahbaz," *Bennington Evening Banner* [Vermont], March 2, 1907, CA; Mary Lewis Shedd, 9 January, 1915, *The War Journal of a Missionary in Persia*, edited by Mary Schauffler Platt (New York: Board of Foreign Missions of the Presbyterian Church in the U.S.A., [1915?], 6.

12. Shahbaz, *The Rage of Islam*, 82–88, 90–91.

13. *Ibid.*, 92–95; Harry P. Packard, "Hallelujah—The Hakim Sahib Has Come!" *Missionary Review of the World*, August 1921, 644.

14. Shedd, 9 January, 1915, 6, *The War Journal of a Missionary in Persia*; Margaret Packard Aro, *Hakim Sahib, "Sir Doctor": The Great Adventure Story of a Missionary Surgeon and Sometimes Diplomat to Persia, Dr. Harry P. Packard, 1874–1954* (Colorado Springs, CO: Out of the Box Publications, 2003), 27–28, 37–38; Paul Shimmon and Harry P. Packard, letter to the editor, "The Plight of Assyria: Needs of Christian and Kurd in That War-Ravaged Country," *New York Times*, September 18, 1916, HN:TNYT.

15. Aro, *Hakim Sahib, "Sir Doctor,"* 16–17, 22, 24.

16. *Ibid.*, 27, 36–37.

17. "Persian Christians Massacred by Moslems," *Literary Digest*, April 10, 1915, 809; Packard, "Hallelujah—The Hakim Sahib Has Come!" 644–645; Aro, *Hakim Sahib, "Sir Doctor,"* 30.

18. Packard, "Hallelujah—The Hakim Sahib Has Come!" 645.

19. *Ibid.*, 645–646; Shedd, 9 January, 1915, *The War Journal of a Missionary in Persia*, 7.

20. William A. Shedd, "How a Mission Saved a Community," *Southern Workman*, April 1916, 454; Yohannan, *The Death of a Nation*, 4, 11–12, 819; Mary Lewis Shedd,

The Measure of a Man: The Life of William Ambrose Shedd, Missionary to Persia (New York: George H. Doran Co, 1922), 30–31; "Statement of the Rev. William A. Shedd, D.D., of the American (Presbyterian) Mission Station at Urmia," 101; Rockwell, *The Pitiful Plight of the Assyrian Christians in Persia and Kurdistan Described from the Reports of Eye-witnesses*, 7, 10.

21. Michael P. Zirinsky, "Harbingers of Change: Presbyterian Women in Iran, 1883–1949," *American Presbyterians* 70, no. 3 (Fall 1992): 173–176, JSTOR.

22. Jackson, *Persia Past and Present*, 88; Katouzian, *Iran: A Beginner's Guide*, 89, 102; Andrew Lawler, "Edge of an Empire," *Archaeology*, September/October 2011, 46.

23. Shedd, *The Measure of a Man*, 37–39, 41, 43, 45–51; William T. Ellis, "The Yankee Cadi," *Century Illustrated Magazine*, February 1919, 569, 571.

24. Shedd, *The Measure of a Man*, 25, 176, and February 5, 1915, *The War Journal of Missionary in Persia*, 24; "Urmia After Its Evacuation by the Turks and Kurds: Letter Dated Urmia, 20th May, 1915, from Mrs. J.P. Cochrane to Friends in the United States; Communicated by the Board of Foreign Missions of the Presbyterian Church in the U.S.A.," *The Treatment of the Armenians in the Ottoman Empire*, 152; Jackson, *Persia Past and Present*, 46.

25. "Statement of the Rev. William A. Shedd, D.D., of the American (Presbyterian) Mission Station at Urmia," 102; Shahbaz, *The Rage of Islam*, 103; Shedd, "How a Mission Saved a Community," 458–459.

26. Shedd, 9 January, 1915, *The War Journal of a Missionary in Persia*, 7, and *The Measure of a Man*, 144, 146, 148, 189; "Statement of the Rev. William A. Shedd, D.D., of the American (Presbyterian) Mission Station at Urmia," 102; William T. Ellis, "15,000 Refugees Saved from Turk Massacre: Syrians and Armenians Besieged in Six-Acre Missionary Compound for Five Months with Single Guard and Old Glory at Gate; Typhus Takes 4,000 Victims Despite Heroic Efforts," *New York Tribune*, February 3, 1918, 4, CA; Yohannan, *The Death of a Nation*, 122; Shahbaz, *The Rage of Islam*, 104; Zirinsky, "Harbingers of Change," 175.

27. Shedd, *The Measure of a Man*, 146, 176–178, and 13 January and 5 February, 1915, *The War Journal of a Missionary in Persia*, 10, 21; "Urmia After Its Evacuation by the Turks and Kurds," 152, 154; Ellis, "15,000 Refugees Saved from Turk Massacre," 4; "Extracts from the Annual Report (for the Year 1915) Presented by the Medical Department at Urmia to the Board of Foreign Missions of the Presbyterian Church in the U.S.A.," *The Treatment of the Armenians in the Ottoman Empire*, 161.

28. Shedd, 29 March, 1915, *The War Journal of a Missionary in Persia*, 44–45.

29. Shahbaz, *The Rage of Islam*, 98–99, 109–111: "under an office …," 109.

30. *Ibid.*, 111–113: "Who Is It?" and, "I am your …," 112–113.

31. *Ibid.*, *The Rage of Islam*, 113–114.

32. "Turkey's Holy War: How the Savage Kurds Have Been Turned Loose on the Persian Christians, Have Assaulted American Missionaries, Hanged Bishops and Priests, Tortured Men, Women, Children and Massacred Thousands," *Richmond Times-Dispatch*, May 9, 1915, CA; Yohnanan, *The Death of a Nation*, 133; Shedd, 12 February, 1915, *The War Journal of a Missionary in Persia*, 23.

33. Shedd, 17 and 23 February, 1915, *The War Journal of a Missionary in Persia*, 23–24, 27; "Turkey's Holy War," *Richmond Times-Dispatch*.

34. "Extracts from the Annual Report (for the Year 1915)," and "Statement of the Rev. William A. Shedd, D.D., of the American (Presbyterian) Mission Station at Urmia," 103–104, and "Extracts from the Annual Report (for the Year 1915) Presented by the Medical Department at Urmia to the Board of Foreign Missions of the Presbyterian Church in the U.S.A.," 161, all in *The Treatment of the Armenians in the Ottoman Empire*.

35. Yohhanan, *The Death of a Nation*, 135–136.

36. Shahbaz, *The Rage of Islam*, 120–121, 122–124; "Hundreds Killed in Persian Town; American Beaten: Kurds Shoot All Men in Gulpashan and Hang Refugees Taken from Missions," *Webster City Freeman* [Iowa], March 30, 1915, and "Presbyterian Mission Sorely Pressed," *Bryan Daily Eagle and Pilot* [Texas], March 25, 1915, and "Turk Grand Vizier Orders Protection: Tells Subordinates to Look After Safety of Thousands in Persia," *Harrisburg Telegraph* [Pennsylvania], March 27, 1915, all in CA; "U.S. Flag Halts Bloody Massacre: Turkish Troops Massacreing [sic] Assyrians; 15,000 Refugees in American Mission," *Sausalito News* [California], April 3, 1915, CDNC.

37. Shedd, 18 March, 1915, *The War Journal of a Missionary*, 38–39: "ten thousand suits …," and "fifty-five bolts …," 38.

38. "Urmia After Its Evacuation by the Turks and Kurds," 153; Shedd, *The Measure of a Man*, 178–180, and 16 and 18 March, and 6 April, 1915, *The War Journal of a Missionary in Persia*, 36, 37, 48–49; Presbyterian Church of the United States of America, *The Seventy-ninth Annual Report Board of Foreign Missions of the Presbyterian Church of the United States of America* (New York: [Publisher unidentified], 1916), 300.

39. Shahbaz, *The Rage of Islam*, 152–153: "God bless those …," 153.

40. *Ibid.*, 108, 154–161, 163, 167; "World-wide Missionary News," *Missionary Review of the World*, 782.

41. "Fourth Bulletin of the American Committee for Armenian and Syrian Relief, *Report of Relief Distribution in the Urumia* [sic] *Plain, June 1, 1915, to January 1, 1916*," quoted in Rockwell, *The Pitiful Plight of the Assyrian Christians in Persia and Kurdistan Described from the Reports of Eye-witnesses*, 22.

42. *Ibid.*

43. "Letter Dated Tabriz, 20th August, 1915, from Mr. Hugo A. Muller (Treasurer of the American Mission Station at Urmia); Communicated by the Board of Foreign Missions to the Presbyterian Church in the U.S.A.," *The Treatment of the Armenians in the Ottoman Empire*, 182–183; Shedd, *Measure of a Man*, 202.

44. Majd, *Persia in World War I and Its Conquest by Great Britain*, 151; F.G. Coan, "The Present Moment in Persia," *Woman's Work*, December 1918, 245–246.

45. Shedd, *The Measure of a Man*, 221; Ellis, "The Yankee Cadi," 568–569, 571–572.

46. Aro, *Hakim Sahib*, *"Sir Doctor,"* 75; Paul Shimmon, "The Martyrdom of a Great Prelate," *Spirit of Missions*, July 1918, 489; Morris, *No Friends but the Mountains*, 199; Augusta Gudhart, "The Blood of Martyrs," *Atlantic*, July 22, 1922, 116; McDowell, *A Modern History of the Kurds*, 216; Kerim Yildiz and Tanyel B. Taysi, *The Kurds in Iran: The Past, Present and Future* (London: Pluto Press, 2007), 11: "chief of the …"

47. Majd, *Persia in World War I and Its Conquest by Great Britain*, 213; Shedd, *The Measure of a Man*, 221; "Mohammedans Fight Assyrian Christians," *Sunday Star*, April 14, 1918, CA.

48. "Turks Occupy Tabriz, Second Persian City: In Order to Protect Their Caucasian Front, Says an Official Statement," *New York Times*, June 18, 1918, HN:TNYT; "U.S. Insists on Answer from Turkey: Third Inquiry Regarding Tabriz Affair May Lead to Declaration of War," *New York Tribune*, June 26, 1918, CA.

49. Shedd, *The Measure of a Man*, 242, 248, 253–255, 257–258.

50. *Ibid.*, 262–265.

51. *Ibid.*, 268–269; Jackson, *Persia Past and Present*, 144–145; Coan, "The Present Moment in Persia," 247; "'From the Front'—Asia: Death of W.A. Shedd, D.D.," *Assembly Herald*, October 1918, 490; Presbyterian Church in the U.S.A., Board of Foreign Missions, *The Eighty-third Annual Report of the Board of Foreign Missions of the Presbyterian Church in the United States of America* (New York: [Publisher Unidentified], 1920, 56.

52. Judith Davis, "The Simple Tale of Heroic Fidelity," *Continent*, June 15, 1922, 771–772; Aro, *Hakim Sahib, "Sir Doctor,"* 96–97; "Turks and Kurds Destroy Property of Missions Supported by Harrisburg," *Harrisburg Telegraph*, December 12, 1918, CA.

53. Gudhart, "The Blood of Martyrs," 116: "sacked and looted"; Aro, *Hakim Sahib, "Sir Doctor,"* 102–103.

54. McDowell, *A Modern History of the Kurds*, 216; Aro, *Hakim Sahib, "Sir Doctor,"* 107.

55. Aro, *Hakim Sahib, "Sir Doctor,"* 106; David, "The Simple Tale of a Heroic Fidelity," 772.

56. Aro, *Hakim Sahib, "Sir Doctor,"* 107–109.

57. *Ibid.*, 109–110; David, "The Simple Tale of a Heroic Fidelity," 772; Robert E. Speer, "Affairs in Persia," *Woman's Work*, December 1919, 254–255.

58. Warfield, *The Gate of Asia*, 353–354; "Christians Suffer from War Horrors," *Guthrie Daily Leader*; Aro, *Hakim Sahib, "Sir Doctor,"* 114–117; David, "The Simple Tale of a Heroic Fidelity," 772; Robert E. Speer, "Affairs in Persia," *Woman's Work*, December 1919, 255.

59. Aro, *Hakim Sahib, "Sir Doctor,"* 141; Presbyterian Church in the U.S.A., *The Eighty-third Annual Report of the Board of Foreign Missions of the Presbyterian Church in the United States of America*, 325.

60. McDowell, *A Modern History of the Kurds*, 220–221; Nader Entessar, *Kurdish Politics in the Middle East* (Lanham: Lexington Books, 2010), 17; Yildiz and Taysi, *The Kurds in Iran*, 12.

Bibliography

Newspapers

Aberdeen Herald (WA)
American Bulletin (London)
Armenian Mirror-Spectator (Watertown, MA)
Ashland Tidings (OR)
Bemidji Daily Pioneer (VT)
Bennington Evening Banner (VT)
Bisbee Daily Review (AZ)
Bryan Daily Eagle and Pilot (TX)
Caldwell Watchman (Columbia, LA)
Chattanooga News
Cleveland Plain Dealer (OH)
Coos Bay Times (Marshfield, OR)
Cornell Daily Sun (NY)
Cresco Plain Dealer (IA)
Daily East Oregonian (Pendleton, OR)
Daily Gate City (Keokuk, IA)
Day Book (Chicago)
Deseret Weekly (Salt Lake City)
El Paso Herald (TX)
Evening Star/Sunday Star (Washington, D.C.)
Evening World (New York City)
Guthrie Daily Leader (OK)
Harrisburg Telegraph (PA)
Hawaiian Gazette (Honolulu)
Jasper Weekly Courier (IN)
Logan Republican (UT)
Los Angeles Herald
Morning Oregonian/Sunday Oregonian (Portland)
New York Times
New York Tribune
North Platte Semi-Weekly Tribune (NE)
Ogden Standard (UT)
Omaha Daily Bee (NE)
Richmond Times-Dispatch (VA)
Rogue River Courier (Grants Pass, OR)
Sausalito News (CA)
Seattle Post-Intelligencer
Sun (New York)
Tacoma Times
Times (London)
Washington Times (Washington, D.C.)
Webster City Freeman (IA)
Weekly Times-Record (Valley City, ND)

Periodicals

Air Power History
American History
American Magazine
Archaeology
Armenian Weekly
Assembly Herald
Atlantic
Blackwood's Magazine
Business Digest and Investment Weekly
Cassier's Magazine: An Engineering Monthly
Century Illustrated Magazine
Collier's Weekly
Continent
Current History
Current Literature
Current Opinion
Donahoe's Magazine
Frank Leslie's Popular Monthly
Frank Leslie's Sunday Magazine
Good Roads
Gunswww
Hampton's Magazine
History Today
Independent
Life
Literary Digest
Missionary Herald at Home and Abroad
Missionary Review of the World
Nation
National Geographic
Outlook
Pacific Rural Press
Printer's Ink: A Journal for Advertisers
Scribner's Magazine
Southern Workman
Spirit of Missions
Survey
Wisconsin Presbyterian
Woman's Work
The World's Work
Yale Forest School News

Scholarly Journal Articles

Bloxham, Donald. "The Armenian Genocide of 1915–1916: Cumulative Radicalization and the Development of a Destruction Policy." *Past & Present* no. 181 (November 2003): 141–191.

Codd, Kevin A. "The American College of Louvain." *Catholic Historical Review* 93, no.1 (January 2007): 47–83.

Cook, Robert E. "The Mist That Rolled into the Trenches: Chemical Escalation in World War I." *Bulletin of the Atomic Scientists* 27, no. 1 (January 1971): 34–38.

Daniel, Robert L. "The Armenian Question and American-Turkish Relations, 1914–1927," *Mississippi Valley Historical Review* 46, no. 2 (September 1959): 252–275

den Hertog, Johan. "The Commission for Relief in Belgium and the Political Diplomatic History of the First World War." *Diplomacy & Statecraft* 21, no. 4 (December 2010): 593–613.

Drew, Bettina. "The Great Amnesia." *Southwest Review* 99, no. 4 (2014): 556–569.

Fitzgerald, Gerard J. "Chemical Warfare and Medical Response During World War I." *American Journal of Public Health* 98, no. 4 (April 2008): 611–625.

Frey, Marc. "Trade, Ships, and the Neutrality of the Netherlands in the First World War." *International History Review* 19, no. 3 (August 1997): 541–562.

Garner, James W. "Some Questions of International Law in the European War." *American Journal of International Law* 9, no. 1 (January 1915): 72–112.

General Staff of Great Headquarters (German). Trans. into English. "The Battle of the Somme in July." *Journal of the Military Service of the United States* 59, no. 204 (November–December 1916): 423–429.

Godbey, Emily. "Disaster Tourism and the Melodrama of Authenticity: Revisiting the 1889 Johnstown Flood," *Pennsylvania History* 73, no. 3 (Summer 2006): 273–315.

Goldman, Stanley. "Prologue: The Man Who Made Genocide a Crime: The Legacy of Raphael Lemkin." *Loyola of Los Angeles International & Comparative Law Review* 34, no. 3 (Spring 2013): 295–300.

Guins, George C. "The Fateful Days of 1917." *Russian Review* 26, no. 3 (July 1967): 286–295.

Hall, Richard C. "Balkan Wars." *History Today* 62, no. 11 (November 2012): 36–42.

———. "Bulgaria in the First World War." *Historian* 73:2 (Summer 2011): 300–315.

Hiley, Nicholas. "Counter-Espionage and Security in Great Britain During the First World War." *The English Historical Review* 101, no. 400 (July 1986): 635–670.

Hopkin, Deian. "Domestic Censorship in the First World War." *Journal of Contemporary History* 5, no. 4 (1970): 151–169.

Jay, Martin. "The Manacles of Gavrilo Princip." *Salmagundi* no. 106/107 (Spring-Summer 1995): 14–21.

Kedourie, Elie. "The End of the Ottoman Empire." *Journal of Contemporary History* 3, no. 4 (October 1968): 19–28.

Levitt, Martin L. "The Development and Politicization of the American Helium Industry, 1917–1940." *Historical Studies in the Physical and Biological Sciences* 30, no. 2 (2000): 333–347.

Lewy, Guenter. "Revisiting the Armenian Genocide." *Middle East Quarterly* 12, no. 4 (Fall 2005): 3–12.

Lohr, Eric. "The Russian Army and the Jews: Mass Deportation, Hostages, and Violence During World War I." *Russian Review* 60, no. 3 (July 2001): 404–419.

Malkasian, Mark. "The Disintegration of the Armenian Cause in the United States, 1918–1927." *International Journal of Middle East Studies* 16, no. 3 (August 1984): 349–365.

May, Arthur J. "The Archduke Francis Ferdinand in the United States." *Journal of the Illinois State Historical Society* (1908–1984) 39, no. 3 (September 1946): 333–344.

McEwen, John M. "Lloyd George's Acquisition of the Daily Chronicle in 1918." *Journal of British Studies* 22, no. 1 (Autumn 1982): 127–144.

———. "The National Press During the First World War: Ownership and Circulation." *Journal of Contemporary History* 17, no. 3 (July 1982): 459–486.

Mould, David. "Donald Thompson: Photographer at War." *Kansas History: A Journal of the Central Plains* 5, no. 3 (Autumn 1982): 154–168. www.kshs.org/publicat/history/1982autumn_mould.pdf.

Petersen, Zoe Bakeeff. "The Architectural Heritage of Leningrad." *American Slavic and East European Review* 4, no. 3/4 (December 1945): 18–34.

Richard G. Hovannisian. "Simon Vratzian and Armenian Nationalism." *Middle Eastern Studies* 5, no. 3 (October 1969): 192–220.

"The Russian Red Cross." *British Medical Journal* 1, no. 2829 (March 20, 1915): 520.

Saxon, Timothy D. "Anglo-Japanese Naval Cooperation, 1914–1918." *Faculty Publications and Presentations* 5 (2000). http://digitalcommons.liberty.edu/hist_fac_pubs/5.

Schapiro, Leonard. "The Rôle of the Jews in the Russian Revolutionary Movement." *Slavonic and East European Review* 40, no. 94 (December 1961): 148–167.

Schmitt, Bernadotte E. "The Bosnian Annexation Crisis (I)," *Slavonic and East European Review* 9, no. 26 (December 1930): 312–334.

Singleton, John. "Britain's Military Use of Horses, 1914–1918." *Past & Present* no. 139 (May 1993): 178–203.

Smith, C Jay, Jr. "Great Britain and the 1914–1915 Straits Agreement with Russia: The British Promise of November 1914." *American Historical Review* 70, no. 4 (July 1965): 1015–1034.

Smits, David D. "The Frontier Army and the Destruction of the Buffalo, 1865–1883." *Western Historical Quarterly* 25, no. 3 (Autumn 1994): 312–338.

Stevenson, David. "Battlefield or Barrier? Rearmament and Military Planning in Belgium, 1902–1914." *International History Review* 29, no. 3 (September 2007): 473–507.

Stockdale, Melissa K. "'My Death for the Motherland Is Happiness': Women, Patriotism, and Soldiering in Russia's Great War, 1914–1917." *American Historical Review* 109:1 (February 2004): 78–116.

Thiem, Jon. "The Great Library of Alexandria Burnt: Towards the History of a Symbol." *Journal of the History of Ideas* 40, no. 4 (October–December 1979): 507–526.

Trumpener, Ulrich. "Turkey's Entry into World War I: An Assessment of Responsibilities." *Journal of Modern History* 34, no. 4 (December 1962): 369–380.

Tusan, Michelle. "The Armenian Genocide and Foreign Policy." *Phi Kappa Phi Forum* 94, no. 2 (Summer 2014): 13–15.

Watenpaugh, Keith David. "The League of Nations' Rescue of Armenian Genocide Survivors and the Making of Modern Humanitarianism, 1920–1927." *American Historical Review* 115, no. 5 (December 2010): 1315–1339.

Weisbord, Robert G. "The King, the Cardinal and the Pope: Leopold II's Genocide in the Congo and the Vatican." *Journal of Genocide Research* 5, no. 1, March 2003: 35–45.

Williamson, Jr., Samuel R. "The Origins of World War I." *Journal of Interdisciplinary History* 18, no. 4 (Spring 1988): 795–818.

Zirinsky, Michael P. "Harbingers of Change: Presbyterian Women in Iran, 1883–1949." *American Presbyterians* 70, no. 3 (Fall 1992): 173–186.

Personal Correspondence

Bors, Lisa. Director of the Annual Fund. The Ambrose Swasey Library. Colgate Rochester Crozer Divinity School. E-mail to author. February 5, 2015.

Garrett, Amy. Office of the Historian. U.S. Department of State. E-mail to author. February 27, 2014.

Langbart, David A. National Archives. E-mail to author. January 15, 2014.

Government Documents

Antwerp. *Antwerp Builds Bridges: 1914–2014*. Antwerp: V redescentrum, 2014.

Bryce Bryce, James, and Great Britain. Committee on Alleged German Outrages. *Report of the Committee on Alleged German Outrages Appointed by His Britannic Majesty's Government and Presided Over by The Rt. HON. Viscount Bryce, O.M, &c., &c., Formerly British Ambassador at Washington*. Ottawa: Government Printing Bureau, 1916.

Great Britain. Foreign Office. *Treatment of Armenians in the Ottoman Empire: Documents Presented to Viscount Grey of Fallodon, Secretary of State for Foreign Affairs*. Edited by Arnold Toynbee. London: Hodder and Stoughton, 1916.

Gust, Wolfgang, ed. *The Armenian Genocide: Evidence from the German Foreign Office Archives, 1915–1916*. New York: Berghahn, 2014.

International Conciliation. *The Austrian Red Book: Official Translation Prepared by the Austrian Government*. New York: American Association for International Conciliation, 1915.

Owings, W.A. Dolph, Elizabeth Pribic, and Nikola Pribic, trans. *The Sarajevo Trial*. Vols. 1 and 2. Chapel Hill, NC: Documentary Publications, 1984.

Republic of Turkey. Ministry of Foreign Affairs. "The Armenian Allegation of Genocide: The Issue and the Facts." http://www.mfa.gov.tr/the-armenian-allegation-of-genocide-the-issue-and-the-facts.en.mfa.

Sarafian, Ara, compiler. *United States Official Records on the Armenian Genocide, 1915–1917*. Princeton, NJ: Gomidas Institute, 2004.

Smithsonian Institution. Board of Regents. *Annual Report of the Board of Regents of the Smithsonian Institute Showing the Operations, Expenditures, and Condition of the Institution for the Year Ending June 30, 1887*. Part 2. Washington, D.C.: Government Printing Office, 1889.

United States. Department of Commerce. *Commerce Reports*. October 6, 1919.

———. Relief Commission in Europe, 1914. *Report on the Operations of United States Relief Commission in Europe*. Washington, D.C.: Government Printing Office, 1914.

———. War Dept. Military Intelligence Division. *Siberia and Eastern Russia: General Description and Introductory Information*. Part 1. Washington, D.C.: Government Printing Office, 1918.

Diaries, Letters, Manuscripts and Memoirs

Anonymous. *An Eye-Witness at Louvain*. London: Eyre & Spottiswoode, 1914.

Davis, Leslie A. *The Slaughterhouse Province: An American Diplomat's Report on the Armenian Genocide, 1915–1917*. New Rochelle, NY: Aristide D. Caratzas, 1989.

Davis, Richard Harding. *With the Allies*. New York: Charles Scribner's Sons, 1919.

Elkus, Abram I. *The Memoirs of Abram Elkus: Lawyer, Ambassador, Statesman*. Princeton, NJ: Gomidas Institute, 2004.

Gerard, James W. *My Four Years in Germany*. New York: Grosset & Dunlap, 1917.

Gibson, Hugh. *A Diplomatic Diary*. London: Hodder and Stoughton, 1917.

Green, Horace. *The Log of a Noncombatant*. Boston: Houghton Mifflin Co., 1915.

Harper, Florence MacLeod. *Runaway Russia*. New York: The Century Co., 1918.

Hendrick, Burton J. *The Life and Letters of Walter H. Page*. Vol. 1. Garden City: Doubleday, Page & Co., 1922.

Hoover, Herbert. *The Memoirs of Herbert Hoover: Years of Adventure, 1874–1920*. New York: The Macmillan Company, 1951.

Hopkirk, Peter. *The Great Game: The Struggle for Empire in Central Asia*. New York: Kodansha International, 1992.

Jones, Stilton. *Russia in Revolution: Being the Experiences of an Englishman in Petrograd During the Upheaval*. London: Herbert Jenkins, 1917.

Katouzian, Homa. *Iran: A Beginner's Guide*. London: Oneworld Publications, 2013.

Kerensky, Alexander F. *The Catastrophe: Kerensky's Own Story of the Russian Revolution*. New York: D. Appleton and Co., 1927; Krause Reprint Co., 1977.

Knapp, Grace Higley. *The Mission at Van in Turkey in War Time*. [S.I.]: Privately Printed, 1916.

Mardiganian, Aurora. *Ravished Armenia or "The Auction of Souls": The Story of Aurora Mardiganian, the Christian Girl Who Survived the Great Massacres*. Interpreted by H.L. Gates. New York: International Copyright Bureau, 1919.

"Miss Graffam's Own Story," Taken Stenographically by Dr. Richard's Secretary. Box 28. ABC 1—91 Collection. American Board of Commissioners for Foreign Missions Archives. Biographies. Houghton Library. Harvard University. Massachusetts.

Morgenthau, Henry. *Ambassador Morgenthau's Story*. Garden City, NJ: Doubleday, Page & Co., 1919.

———. *United States Diplomacy on the Bosporus: The Diaries of Ambassador Morgenthau, 1913–1916*. Compiled by Ara Sarafian. Princeton, NJ: Gomidas Institute, 2004.

Pierce, Ruth. *Trapped in "Black Russia": Letters, June–November 1915*. Boston: Houghton Mifflin Co., 1918.

Powell, E. Alexander. *Fighting in Flanders*. New York: Charles Scribner's Sons, 1914.

Rockwell, William Walker. *The Pitiful Plight of the Assyrian Christians in Persia and Kurdistan Described from the Reports of Eye-witnesses.* New York: American Committee for Armenian and Syrian Relief, 1916.

Shahbaz, Yonan H. *The Rage of Islam: An Account of the Massacre of Christians by the Turks in Persia.* Philadelphia: The Roger Williams Press, 1918.

Shedd, Mary Lewis. *The War Journal of a Missionary in Persia.* Edited by Mary Schauffler Platt. New York: Board of Foreign Missions of the Presbyterian Church in the U.S.A., [1915?].

Thompson, Donald C. *The Crime of the Twentieth Century.* New York: Leslie-Judge Co., 1918.

_____. *Donald Thompson in Russia.* New York: The Century Co., 1918.

Thompson, Robert J. *England and Germany in the War: Letters to the State Department.* Boston: Chapple Publishing Co., 1915.

Ussher, Clarence D., and Grace H. Knapp. *An American Physician in Turkey: A Narrative of Adventures in Peace and in War.* Boston: Houghton Mifflin Company, 1917.

White, George E. *Adventuring with Anatolia College.* Grinnell, IA: Herald Register Publishing Co., 1940.

Whitlock, Brand. *Belgium: A Personal Narrative.* New York: D. Appleton and Co., 1919.

Williams, Albert Rhys. *In the Claws of the German Eagle.* New York: E.P. Dutton & Co., 1917.

Books

Albertini, Luigi. *The Origins of the War of 1914: The Crisis of 1914, from the Sarajevo Outrage to the Austro-Hungarian Mobilization.* Vol. 1. Translated and edited by Isabella M. Massey. Oxford: Oxford University Press, 1953.

Alvarez, Alex. *Native Americans and the Question of Genocide.* Lanham, MD: Rowman & Littlefield, 2014.

American Bankers Association. *Proceedings of the Forty-fifth Annual Convention of the American Bankers Association and Annual Proceedings of the Trust Company Section, Savings Bank Section, Clearing House Section, National Bank Section, and Summary of Proceedings of American Institute of Banking and State Secretaries Sections.* New York: American Bankers Association, 1919.

American National Biography. 24 vols. Edited by John A. Garraty and Mark C. Carnes. New York: Oxford University Press, 1999.

Arnoux, Anthony. *The European War: September 1915–March 1916.* Vol. 3. Boston: Privately Printed, 1917.

Aro, Margaret Packard. *Hakim Sahib, "Sir Doctor": The Great Adventure Story of a Missionary Surgeon and Sometimes Diplomat to Persia, Dr. Harry P. Packard, 1874–1954.* Colorado Springs, CO: Out of the Box Publications, 2003.

Austria-Hungary Including Dalmatia and Bosnia: Handbook for Travellers. Leipzig: Karl Baedeker, 1905.

Barrows, John Otis. *In the Land of Ararat: A Sketch of the Life of Mrs. Elizabeth Freeman Barrows Ussher, Missionary to Turkey and a Martyr of the Great War.* New York: Fleming H. Revell Co., 1916.

Behrens, Roy R. *Art & Camouflage: Concealment and Deception in Nature, Art and War.* Cedar Falls, IA, 1981.

Belgium and Holland Including the Grand-Duchy of Luxembourg: Handbook for Travellers. Leipzig, Germany: Karl Baedeker, 1910.

Black, William Harman. *The Real Round-the-World Pocket Guide Book for Europe, the United States of America ... Actual Diary and Expense Account of an Independent 100-Day Trip Over the Northern Route via the Trans-Siberian Railway, and Full Particulars of an Eastward and a Westward Trip by the Southern Route Through the Suez and India....* New York: Association for New York, 1915.

Bogosian, Eric. *Operation Nemesis: The Assassination Plot That Avenged the Armenian Genocide.* New York: Little, Brown and Company, 2015.

Bookwalter, John W. *Siberia and Central Asia.* London: C. Arthur Pearson, 1900.

Brook-Shepherd, Gordon. *The Austrians: A Thousand Year Odyssey.* New York: Carroll & Graf Publishers, 1996.

Bucheli, Marcelo. *Bananas and Business: The United Fruit Company in Columbia, 1899–2000.* New York: New York University Press, 2005.

Bulloch, John, and Harvey Morris. *No Friends but the Mountains: The Tragic History of the Kurds.* New York: Oxford University Press, 1992.

Butcher, Tim. *The Trigger: Hunting the Assassin Who Brought the World to War.* New York: Grove Press, 2014.

Cassels, Lavender. *The Archduke and the Assassin: Sarajevo, June 28th 1914.* New York: Stein and Day, 1984.

Coe, Brian. *Cameras: From Daguerreotypes to Instant Pictures.* New York: Crown Publishers, 1978.

Cook, Bernard A. *Belgium: A History.* New York: Peter Lang, 2005.

Cox, John K. *The History of Serbia.* Westport, CT: Greenwood Press, 2002.

Croll, Mike. *The History of Landmines.* Barnsley, UK: Leo Cooper, 1998.

de Syon, Guillaume. *Zeppelin!* Baltimore: John Hopkins University Press, 2002.

DiMarco, Louis A. *War Horse: A History of the Military Horse and Rider.* Yardley, PA: Westholme, 2008.

Doenecke, Jutus D. *Nothing Less Than War: A New History of America's Entry into World War I.* Lexington: University Press of Kentucky, 2011.

Egremont, Max. *Forgotten Land: Journeys Among the Ghosts of East Prussia.* New York: Farrar, Straus and Giroux, 2011.

Ewans, Martin. *European Atrocity, African Catastrophe: Leopold II, the Congo Free State, and Its Aftermath.* London: RoutledgeCurzon, 2002.

Farwell, Byron. *Over There: The United States in the Great War, 1917–1918.* New York: W.W. Norton & Co., 1999.

Finkel, Caroline. *Osman's Dream: The Story of the Ottoman Empire, 1300–1924.* New York: Basic Books, 2005.

Gaunt, David, Jan Bet-Sawoce, and Rochao Donef. *Massacres, Resistance, Protectors: Muslim-Christian Relations in Eastern Anatolia During World War I.* Piscataway, NJ: Gorgias Press, 2006.

Geifman, Anna. *Thou Shalt Kill: Revolutionary Terrorism in Russia, 1894–1917.* Princeton: Princeton University Press, 1993.

Getzler, Israel. *Krondstadt, 1917–1921: The Fate of a Soviet Democracy.* Cambridge: Cambridge University Press, 1983.

Bibliography

Gilbert, Martin. *The First World War: A Complete History.* New York: Henry Holt and Company, 1994.

Gils, Robert, and Luc Schokkaert, ed. *Fort Liezele.* Translated by Alain Van Daele. Puurs, Belgium: Marc Van Reit/Stitching Fort Liezele vzw, 2001.

Goldring, Douglas. *Ways of Escape: A Book of Adventure.* New York: Duffield and Co., 1912.

Gould, S. Baring. *A Book of the Rhine from Cleve to Mainz.* London: Methuen & Co., 1906.

Greenburg, Mark, and the Editors of the Newsweek Book Division. *The Hague.* New York: Newsweek, 1982.

Hamilton, Keith, and Richard Langhorne. *The Practice of Diplomacy: Its Evolution, Theory and Administration.* London: Routledge, 1995.

Hastings, Max. *Catastrophe 1914: Europe Goes to War.* New York: Alfred A. Knopf, 2013.

Haywood, John, with Brian Catchpole. *Historical Atlas of the 19th Century World, 1783–1914.* New York: Barnes & Noble Books, 2002.

Hildermeier, Manfred. *The Russian Socialist Revolutionary Party Before the First World War.* New York: St. Martin's Press, 2000.

Hogg, Ivan V. *Historical Dictionary of World War I.* Lanham, MD: The Scarecrow Press, 1998.

Horne, John. *A Companion to World War I.* Chichester, UK, and Malden, MA: Wiley-Blackwell, 2010.

_____, and Alan Kramer. *German Atrocities, 1914: A History of Denial.* New Haven: Yale University Press, 2001.

Howe, M.A. DeWolfe. *George von Lengerke Meyer: His Life and Public Services.* New York: Dodd, Mead and Co., 1919.

Jackson, A.V. Williams. *Persia Past and Present: A Book of Travel and Research.* New York: Macmillan Co., 1906.

Keegan, John. *The First World War.* New York: Vintage Books, 1998.

King, Greg, and Sue Woolmans. *The Assassination of the Archduke: Sarajevo 1914 and the Romance That Changed the World.* New York: St. Martin's Press, 2013.

Kiple, Kenneth F., ed. *The Cambridge Historical Dictionary of Disease.* Cambridge: Cambridge University Press, 2003.

Koch, Theodore Wesley. *The University of Louvain and Its Library.* London: J.M. Dent & Sons, 1917.

Kopras, Elizabeth J. *Patty's Toxicology.* Sixth Edition. Vol. 2. Edited by Eula Bingham and Barbara Cohrssen. Hoboken, NJ: Wiley, 2012.

Liddell, Scotland. *Actions and Reactions in Russia.* New York: E.P. Dutton & Co., 1918.

Lochner, Louis P. *What About Germany?* New York: Dodd, Mead & Co., 1943.

Lowe, John. *The Great Powers, Imperialism and the German Problem, 1865–1925.* London: Routledge, 1994.

Maddocks, Melvin. *The Great Liners.* Alexandria, VA: Time-Life Books, 1978.

Majd, Mohammad Gholi. *Persia in World War I and Its Conquest by Great Britain.* Lanham, MD: University Press of America, 2003.

Manchester, William. *The Arms of Krupp, 1587–1968.* Boston: Little, Brown and Company, 1968.

Marks, Steven G. *Road to Power: The Trans-Siberian Railroad and the Colonization of Asian Russia, 1850–1917.* Ithaca: Cornell University Press, 1991.

McDowall, David. *A Modern History of the Kurds.* London: I.B. Tauris, 1996.

Meakin, Annette M.B. *Russia: Travels and Studies.* London: Hurst and Blackett, 1906.

Meyer, G.J. *A World Undone: The Story of the Great War.* New York: Delacorte Press, 2006.

Military Uniforms Visual Encyclopedia. Bradley's Close, UK: Amber Books, 2011.

Milton, Joyce. *The Yellow Kids: Foreign Correspondents in the Heyday of Yellow Journalism.* New York: Harper & Row Publishers, 1989.

Morris, Edmund. *Theodore Rex.* New York: The Modern Library, 2001.

Mott, Frank Luther. *A History of American Magazines.* Vol. 4. Cambridge: Harvard University Press, 1938, 1957, 1968.

Murphy, Justin D. *Military Aircraft, Origins to 1918: An Illustrated History of Their Impact.* Santa Barbara, CA: ABC-CLIO, 2005.

Nash, George H. *The Life of Herbert Hoover: Humanitarian, 1914–1917.* New York: W.W. Norton & Company, 1988.

_____. *The Life of Herbert Hoover: The Engineer, 1874–1914.* New York: W.W. Norton & Company, 1983.

Newcomer, James. *The Grand Duchy of Luxemburg: The Evolution of Nationhood, 963 A.D. to 1983.* Lanham, MD: Texas Christian University, 1984.

Northern France from Belgium to the English Channel to the Loire Excluding Paris and Its Environs: Handbook for Travellers. Leipzig, Germany: Karl Baedeker, 1894.

Noyes, Alexander Dana. *Financial Chapters of the War.* New York: Charles Scribner's Sons, 1916.

Orwell, George. *Animal Farm: A Fairy Story.* New York: Signet Classics, 1996.

The Oxford Illustrated History of the First World War. Edited by Hew Strachan. Oxford: Oxford University Press, 1998.

Ozment, Steven. *A Mighty Fortress: A New History of the German People.* New York: HarperCollins, 2004.

Palestine and Syria with the Chief Routes Through Mesopotamia and Babylonia. 4th edition. Leipzig: Karl Baedeker, 1906.

Payaslian, Simon. *The History of Armenia: From the Origins to the Present.* New York: Palgrave Macmillan, 2007.

Pipes, Richard. *A Concise History of the Russian Revolution.* New York: Alfred A. Knopf, 1995.

Pirenne, Henri. *Belgium and the First World War.* Translated by Vincent Capelle and Jeff Lipkes. Wesley Chapel, FL: Brabant Press, 2014.

Pope, Stephen, and Elizabeth-Anne Wheal. *The Dictionary of the First World War.* New York: St. Martin's Press, 1995.

Presbyterian Church of the United States of America. *The Eighty-third Annual Report of the Board of Foreign Missions of the Presbyterian Church in the United States of America.* New York: [Publisher Unidentified], 1920.

_____. *The Seventy-ninth Annual Report Board of Foreign Missions of the Presbyterian Church of the United States of America.* New York: [Publisher unidentified], 1916.

Purdy, Helen Throop. *San Francisco as It Was, as It Is, and How to See It.* San Francisco: Paul Elder and Co., 1912.

Rabinowitch, Alexander. *The Bolsheviks in Power: The First Year of Soviet Rule in Petrograd.* Bloomington: Indiana University Press, 2007.

Radzilowski, John. *A Traveller's History of Poland.* Northampton, MA: Interlinks Books, 2013.

Radzinsky, Edvard. *The Last Tsar: The Life and Death of Nicolas II.* Translated by Marian Schwartz. New York: Anchor Books, 1993.

Radziwill, Catherine. *The Austrian Court from Within.* London: Cassell and Co., 1916.

Read, Christopher. *War and Revolution in Russia, 1914–22: The Collapse of Tsarism and Establishment of Soviet Power.* New York: Palgrave Macmillan, 2013.

Renault, Louis. *First Violations of International Law by Germany: Luxemburg and Belgium.* Translated by Frank Carr. London: Longmans, Green and Co., 1917.

Reynolds, Michael A. *Shattering Empires: The Clash and Collapse of the Ottoman and Russian Empires, 1908-1918.* Cambridge: Cambridge University Press, 2011.

The Rhine, Including the Black Forest & The Vosges: Handbook for Travellers. Leipzig, Germany: Karl Baedeker, 1911.

Richard, Carl J. *When the United States Invaded Russia: Woodrow Wilson's Siberian Disaster.* Lanham, MD: Rowman & Littlefield Publishers, 2013.

Robertson, Craig. *The Passport in America: A History of a Document.* New York: Oxford University Press, 2010.

Roman, Eric. *Austria-Hungary & the Successor States: A Reference Guide from the Renaissance to the Present.* New York: Facts on File, 2003.

Shaw, Stanford J., and Ezel Kural Shaw. *History of the Ottoman Empire and Modern Turkey: Reform, Revolution, and Republic: The Rise of Modern Turkey, 1808-1975.* Vol. 2. Cambridge: Cambridge University Press, 1977.

Shedd, Mary Lewis. *The Measure of a Man: The Life of William Ambrose Shedd, Missionary to Persia.* New York: George H. Doran Co, 1922.

Slide, Anthony. *Ravished Armenia and the Story of Aurora Mardiganian.* Lanham, MD: The Scarecrow Press, 1997.

Smith, David James. *One Morning in Sarajevo: 29 June, 1914.* London: Phoenix, 2008.

Somel, Selcuk Aksin. *Historical Dictionary of the Ottoman Empire.* Lanham, MD: The Scarecrow Press, 2003.

Southern Germany (Wurtenberg and Bavaria): Handbook for Travellers. Leipzig: Karl Baedeker, 1907.

Strachan, Hew, ed. *The Oxford Illustrated History of the First World War.* Oxford: Oxford University Press, 1998.

Strong, William E. *The Story of the American Board: An Account of the First Hundred Years of the American Board of Commissioners for Foreign Missions.* Boston: The Pilgrim Press, 1910.

Sykes, Mark. *Dar-ul-Islam: A Record of a Journey Through Ten of the Asiatic Provinces of Turkey.* London: Bickers & Son, 1904.

Toynbee, Arnold J. *The German Terror in Belgium: An Historical Record.* New York: George H. Doran Company, 1917.

Ure, John. *The Cossacks: An Illustrated History.* Woodstock, NY: The Overlook Press, 2002.

van der Kiste, John. *Emperor Francis Joseph: Life, Death and the Hapsburg Empire.* Phoenix Mill, UK: Sutton Publishing, 2005.

Vanthemsche, Guy. *Belgium and the Congo, 1885–1980.* Translated by Alice Cameron and Stephen Windross. Revised by Kate Connelley. New York: Cambridge University Press, 2012.

van Tuyll van Serooskerken, Hubert P. *The Netherlands and World War I: Espionage, Diplomacy and Survival.* Leiden, Netherlands: Brill, 2001.

Wall, Joseph Frazier. *Andrew Carnegie.* New York: Oxford University Press, 1970.

Warfield, William. *The Gate of Asia: A Journey from the Persian Gulf to the Black Sea.* New York: G.P. Putman's Sons, 1916.

Wawro, Geoffrey. *Warfare and Society in Europe, 1792–1914.* New York: Routledge, 2000.

Weiss, George. *America's Maritime Progress: A Review of the Redevelopment of the American Merchant Marine, Together with Brief Biographies of Men and Companies Representative of the Shipping World.* New York: The New York Marine News Company, 1920.

Welsh, Frank. *The History of the World: From the Dawn of Humanity to the Modern Age.* London: Quercus, 2011.

Whiting, Lilian. *Paris the Beautiful.* Boston: Little, Brown, and Co., 1909.

Wilson, Elizabeth. *The Road Ahead: Experiences in the Life of Frances C. Gage.* New York: The Womans Press, 1918.

Winter, Jay, ed. *America and the Armenian Genocide of 1915.* Cambridge: Cambridge University Press, 2003.

_____, and Blain Baggett. *The Great War and the Shaping of the Twentieth Century.* New York: Penguin, 1996.

Wood, Ruth Kedzie. *The Tourist's Russia.* New York: Dodd, Mead and Company, 1912.

Yildiz, Kerim, and Tanyel B. Taysi. *The Kurds in Iran: The Past, Present and Future.* London: Pluto Press, 2007.

Yohannan, Abraham. *The Death of a Nation, or the Ever Persecuted Nestorians or Assyrian Christians.* New York: G.P. Putman's Sons, 1916.

Young, Peter, ed. *The Marshall Cavendish Illustrated Encyclopedia of World War I.* 12 vols. New York: Marshall Cavendish, 1984.

Youngs, William T. *The Congregationalists.* New York: Greenwood Press, 1990.

Zuckerman, Frederic S. *The Tsarist Secret Police in Russian Society, 1880-1917.* New York: New York University Press, 1996.

Zuckerman, Larry. *The Rape of Belgium: The Untold Story of World War I.* New York: New York University Press, 2010.

Index

Numbers in ***bold italics*** indicate pages with illustrations

Aarschot 69–70
Abbott, Ernest Hamlin 33
Ada Bazar 118
Admiralty (Britain) 31, 88, 111
The Adoration of the Lamb 79
Adrianople 7, 120
Afghanistan ***144***, 144–145
Afium Karahissar 133
Agadir 74
Agazarian, Bagdasar 135–136
Agazarian, Ethel Marston 135–137
agha 120
Ahmed Bey 131–132
Albania 7, 111
Albany 36
Albert (son of Rudolf I) 3
Albert I 19, ***21***, 21–22, 53, 57, 60, 82, 84, 85–86; death 22
Albert, Charles Marie Pierre, Count de Broqueville 55–56
Aleksandrovich, Grand Duke Michael 93
Aleppo 122, 133–134 ***134***, ***135***, 137
Algeciras 74
Allies 36, 47, 64, 70, 75, ***81***, 87–88, 96
Alsace-Lorraine 74
Alsace-Lorraine Railway 60
Alt Wien (World Columbia Exhibition) 10
Amasia 126–127
American Board of Commissioners for Foreign Missions 105
American Bulletin 46
American Citizens' Committee 45–48; Herbert Hoover takes over 46; policy for issues tickets on liners 46
American College (Louvain) 71–72
American Committee for Armenian and Syrian Relief 140, 143, 151–152
American Committee for Relief in the Near East 140
American Committee for the Independence of Armenia 141–142
American Express 23, 26, 27–28, 30, 34, 46
American-Hamburg Line 32
American Line 23, 30, 36, 44
American National Biography 29

American Olympic Fencing Team 47
American Relief Clearing House 42
American Society of Mechanical Engineers 63
Amiens 84
Anatolia 108, 119, 127, 132
Andover Theological Seminary 105
Andrew (the Meyers' valet) 38
Anichkov Palace (Petrograd) 92
Animal Farm 96
Anitab 108
Anna (fiancée of Henry Fin) 73
Annunciata of Naples 9
Antwerp 19, 44, 47, 57, 58, 61, 62, 63, 65, 66, 76–77 80–81, ***81***, 82, 84–86; 19, 57, 66, 77, 80, 82; German attack on 80–82; national redoubt 80
Apis 13, 18–19
Appel Quay (Sarajevo) 15–17
Arabia 9, 133
Arabkir 129
Arc de Triomphe 27
Armenian 108
Armenian Apostolic Church 108
Armenian Genocide 119, 122, 132–134, ***134***, 135–136, ***136***, 137, 138–142; Adolf Hitler uses as justification to deport Jews 139; deaths due to starvation and thirst 118, 122, 133–134, ***134***; mass killings 122, 126, 130, 136, ***136***, 137–138, 139, 140; Ottoman plan for 132, 139; robbery 129, 132, 140; sale of possessions 128, 132; use of conscription to round up Armenian men 136, 139; *see also* slavery in the Ottoman Empire
Armenian National Bureau 112
Armenian Plateau 122
Armenians 108, 109–110, 111, 112–114, 115, 117–118, 119, 120, 121–125, 126–132, 133–134, ***134***, 135, ***136***, 136–137, ***137***, 138–143, 148, 153; gain a homeland 141–142; repeated persecution of in the Ottoman Empire 113; *see also* Armenian Genocide
Armistice of Mudros 138

Army Air Service, Russian 28
Army Headquarters, Russian 101
army, Russian 28, 90, 95, 96, 97–98, 99, 101–102, 103–104, 112, 114, 115, 139, 143, 145, 151, 152, 153; last offensive of the war 97; rounding up of Jews in Galicia 101
Army, U.S. 68, 90, 141
Asia 68, 89, 90, 91, 145
Asia Minor 9, 107, 133–134, 138
Assembly of Delegates 99
Associated Press 68
Assyrians 143, 146–147, ***148***, 149–155
Astoria Hotel (Petrograd) 90, 93, 100
Ath 58, 63–64
atrocities 66–72, 73–75, 84, 87, 101–102, 119; committed by Germany against the Belgians 66–71, ***71***, 72–75, 84; committed by Russia 101–102; debate over by Americans 68; fake stories (propaganda) 68
The Auction of Souls 140–141
Australia 9, 31
Austria 3, 6–7, 9–10, 17, 19, 23, 26, 33, 46, 87, 98
Austro-Hungarian Bank (Sarajevo) 15
Austro-Hungarian Empire 3, ***4–5***, 7, 9, 11, 12, 15 17–19, 29, 33, 55, 73–74, 86–87, 102
Avtovac 13
Axis Rule in Occupied Europe 139
Azerbaijan 145, 153

Babenberg family 3
Bad Kissingen 38
baggage abandonment and recovery 48
Baldzhuan (modern Tajikistan) 138
Balkan League 7
Baltic Fleet, Russian 99
Baltic Sea 90
Banja Koviljaca 14
Baquhah 154
Barman, Capt. Thomas J. 44
Barnard, J.D. 143
Barrows (later) Ussher, Elizabeth

Index

Freeman 108–110, 114–115; death 115
Barrows, John Otis 108
Barton, James L. 108, 140
Battalion of Death 98
Battle of Kosovo 7
Battle of Mons 78
Battle of the Frontiers 64
Battle of the Marne 64
Battle of the Somme 88
Battle of the Yser 85–86
battlefield tourism 72–73
Batumi 119
Bavaria 6, 38, 40
Bayamo 44
Bayern, Sophie Friederike von 6
Bazar de la Charité (Paris) 7
Becker, Jules de 71–72
Bekran Agha 131
Belgian Congo 74–75
Belgium 19–20, 21–22, 32, 35, 39, 40, 43, 49, **50**, 51, 52–54, 55–58, **59**, 60, 61–64, 65, 66, 67–73, 74–75, 76, 77, 79, 80, 81, 82, 83, 84, 85, 86, 88, 102, 143; German pretense for invading 19; resistance to German invasion 19–20, 21; preparedness for possible war 19
Belgrade 7, *11*–13, 19
Beloeil 64
Benari, Abdullah Beg 147
Bendimahi River 116
Benevolent and Protective Order of the Elks 83
Bennet, James O'Donnell 68
Benyamin, Mar Shimun XXI 152
Bergri 116
Berlin 36–37, 39–40, 42, 47, 70, 121
Bernstein, Herman 101
Bernstorff, Johann Heinrich von 40
Bethmann Hollweg, Theobald von 59, 122
Beyens, Baron Eugène-Napoléon 60
Beyerlinck, Laurentius 70
Bismarck, Otto von 6
Bissing, Moritz Ferdinand von 60
Bitlis 114
Black Hand 12–18
Black Sea 88, 91, 97, 111, 142
Blount, Daniel Lynds 72, 76–77
Bochkareva, Maria Leontievna 97–98
Boehn, Gen. Hans Matthias von 68–70; justifies German atrocities 69
Boer War 73
Bogosian, Eric 139
Bohemia 3, 6, 7, 42
Bolimów 96
Bolsheviks 96, 98–99, 103–104, 112, 152
Bolton (friend of Florence Harper) 90
Boma 75
Bon Marché (Paris) 23

Bond, Louise 109
Bonus Army 46
Bordeaux 42
Boris (interpreter for Donald Thompson) 90, 93–94, 99, 100, 102–103
Bosnia 7, 12–14
Boston 51, 101, 105, 108
Boulogne 83
Boy Scouts (Belgium) 62
Boys' School (American mission, Van) 105
Boys' School, Muslim (American mission, Urmia) 155
Brabant 58
Bratislava Castle 10
Braun, Baron Émile 79
Breckinridge, Henry 47–48
Breslau 111
Brialmont, Gen. Henri-Alexis 20
British Expeditionary Force (BEF) 49, 64, 83
British West African Field Force 64
Broadway Tabernacle (New York City) 33
Brooklyn 22, 85, 90, 118
Broqueville, Charles de 19, 55
Broussi 95
Brown, Grant Hugh 44
Brown, Ona 33–34, 36
Browning FN Model 1910 (gun that killed Franz Ferdinand) 12–13, 17
Bruges 57, 79, 85
Brusilov, Gen. Aleksei 97–98
Brussels 19, 39, 44, 49, 52–58, 60, 62–66, 69, 72–73, 76–77, 79, 85; German occupation of 57–58
Bryan, Williams Jennings 37, 114, 118
Bucharest 87
Budapest 89
buffalo (American bison) 141
Bulgaria 7, 87, 101–102, 125
Bülow, Gen. Karl von 64
Burgess, Gelett 29
Butcher Regiment 112, 114

Cabrinovic, Nedeljko 11–15, 17–18
cadi 152
Cady, Hamilton Perkins 78
Caldwell, John Lawrence 153
California 29, 46, 95, 121, 140
camouflage 64, 80
Canada 73, 105
Canadian Expeditionary Force 83
Capital 82
Cardashian, Vahan 141–142
Carinthia 3
Carlton (London) 47
Carnegie, Andrew 33, 35
Carpathian Mountains 98
Carrick Theater (Los Angeles) 140
Cartier Centenary 83
Casement, Roger 75
Caspian Sea 91
Castle Rock (Van) 112

Cathedral of St. Michael and St. Gudula (Brussels) 58
Catholic University of Louvain *see* University of Louvain
Caucasus 68, 112, 122, 138, 143
Celtic 32
censorship 31, 82, 88, 101, 117–119
Central Committee of Soviets 103
Central Powers 125
Central Reality Bond Company 119
Champs Elysées, Avenue des (Paris) 27
Charlemagne 3
Charleroi Canal (Hal) 63
Charles the Bold, Duke of Burgundy 3, 6
Charles V, Holy Roman Emperor 6, 70
Charlottenburg 139
Cherbourg 47
Chernov, Viktor Mikhailovich 103
Cherokees 141
Cheytanian, Setrak 121
Chicago 10, 40, 43, 47, 51, 73, 94
Chicago (ship) 30
Chicago Herald 55, 73
Chicago Tribune 52, 84, 86
Chimishguezek 127–128, 131
China 9, 89
Chinese Eastern Railway 89
chlorine gas 96
cholera 114, 153
Christian Science Monitor 52
Chronicle of Utrecht 70
Church Peace Union 33
Churchill, Winston 82, 88, 111
Ciganovic, Milan 12–13, 17–18
Cirque Royal (Brussels) 55
Civil Guard (Brussels) 57
Civil War, U.S. 31, 77, 141
Clark, Cecil 51
Clarys, Antoine 154
Cleveland, Grover 9
Cobb, Irvin S. 52, **52**, 54
Cochran, Bernice 151
Cochran, Joseph P. 146
Cogswell, Henry 29
Collier, John 141
Collier's Weekly 78
Cologne 39, 43, 48, 77
Colorado 146
Columbia Law School 118
Columbus, Ohio 82
Commission for Relief in Belgium (CRB) 60
Committee of Seven 110
Committee of Union and Progress (CUP) 110, 111, 120
Committee on Public Information 52
Conan Doyle, Arthur 75
Congo Museum (Tervuren) 52
Congregationalist Church 65, 105, 108
Congress, U.S. 47, 141
Constance 33
Constantinople 74, 87–88, 108–111,

114, 117, 120, 122, 125, 129, 136, 147
Constitutional Democrats (Kadets) 94
Contich 63
Cossacks 91, *91*, 92, 103, 116, 145, 151
Cotton Exchange (Manchester, England) 42
Council of Ministers (Belgium) 77
Creel, George 52
Crépy-en-Valois 78
Crimea 137
Croatia 13, 46
Croy, Archduchess Isabella von 10
Croy, Maria Christina von 10
Cuba 45, 51
Cubrilovic, Vaso 13, 18
Cubrilovic, Veljko 14, 18
Cumurija Bridge (Sarajevo) 15
Cumurija Strauss (Sarajevo) 17
Cunard Line 44
Curtiss, Glenn H. 28
cyanide 13, 15, 17–18; as means of suicide 17
Czech Republic 18

Daily Chronicle 62
Daily Mail 68, 84–85; brief history 85
Daily Observer 85
Dallas 33
Damascus 133, 137
Danube River 13
Dardanelles Strait 88, 111
Darmstaedter, Paul 73–75
Dashnaktsutyun (Armenian Revolutionary Federation) 113
David, Judith 154
Davis, Leslie A. 119, 139; brief biography 119
Davis, Richard Harding 31, 46–47, 49, *51*, 57, 63–65; biographical details 49, 51; detained as a spy 63–64
Day Book 73
Democratic Finance Committee 118
Democratic Party 40
Denmark 47
Department of Agriculture, U.S. 68
Department of the Navy, U.S. 62
Dersim, *vilayet* of 132
The Devil in the White City 10
de Ville, John B. 73
Diarbekr 130; *vilayet* of 140
Dieppe 27, 29–30
Dimitrijevic, Col. Dragutin *see* Apis
Dixmude 85–86
Djemal, Ahmed 111, 137–138, *138*
Djukic, Lazar 13
Doboj 15
Dodd, Edward Mills 155
Dodd, William S. 118
Donohoe, Martin H. 62, 67
Dosch-Fleurot, Arno 52

Dover 44
Drina Front 12
Drina River 14
Duma 93–94, 98, 100, 103
Dupiéreux, Eugène 71–72
Dvinsk Front 95
Dvinsk-Vilna Railroad 97

East Africa 31
East Gat (Belgium) 44
Edinburgh University 62
Eger River 18
Egin 129
Egypt 111, 119
Eiffel Tower 29
Eindhoven 65
Elbe River 18
Elder & Fyffes Line 44
Elisabeth (wife of Franz Joseph) 6
Elkus, Abram I. *124*, 125, 136–137; brief biography 125
Ellis Island 32, 140
embassy, American (Petrograd) 90
Empress of Russia 89
Enghien 63
Engineering Corps, German 77
England 23, 26–27, 29–30, 33, 36, 39, 42, 47, 58, 60, 83, 104, 111, 141
English Channel 29, 39, 44
Enver, Ismail 110–112, 122, *123*, 129, 137, 138–139, 143; brief biography 122; death 138
Eppegem 76
Equitable Life of New York 121
Erivan, *vilayet* of 143
Erzerum 108–109, 112, 115, 119, 130, 132; *vilayet* of 138
Erzingan 119
espionage *see* spies and spying
Etrich, Igo 29
Europe 3, 7, 22, *24–25*, 26–28, 31, 35–36, 38, 45–48, 52, 55, 61, 70, 83, 89, 104, 110, 112, 125, 139
Evening Sun 49
Evert, Alexei 97
Everybody's Magazine 68
Executive Committee 99

Falmouth 47
Fatimah (Armenian woman) 128
February Revolution, 1917 89–104
Ferdinand (Sophie Friederike's uncle) 6
Fes 74
Fifth Avenue Hospital (New York City) 45
Fin, Henry 73
Finland 44
First Balkan War 11, 12
First Hague Peace Conference 35
First New York National Guard 45
First Regiment of Machine-gunners 103
Flanders 60
Flower Hospital (New York City) 45
Foca 13

Fontanka Canal (Petrograd) 92, *92*
Foreign Mission Board of the Reformed Episcopal Church in India 105
Foreign Office (German) 40
Foreign Service, U.S. 54, 119
Fortress of St. Peter and Paul (Petrograd) 92
Fourth Army, Austrian 98
franc-tireurs 70
France 3, 19, 23, 26–27, 28, 31, 32, 33, 36, 40, 42, 47, 55, 57, 58, 60, 64, 73–74, 83, 88, 89, 104; war aims 3, 74
La France (ship) 30
Francqui, Émile 58
Frankfurt 39
Frankfurter Zeitung 122
Franz Ferdinand, Archduke 3, 7, *8*, 9–10, 11–16, *16*, 17–18, 38; marriage 10; plan for the Serbs 8, 9; trip across the United States 9–10; *see also* plot and assassination of Franz Ferdinand
Franz Joseph 3, *6*, 6–7, 9, 10, 18
Franz Joseph Strauss (Sarajevo) 16, 17
Free Synagogue (Manhattan) 118
Freeland Corners 42
French, John 64
French Congo 74
French Revolution 70
Friedrichshafen 77

Gabon 74
Gage, Frances C. 127
Galicia 86, 95, 97, 98, 101
Galway 62
Garden City (Van) 112
Gare de l'Est (Paris) *26*, 29
gas masks 96
Gaston, Edward Page 48
Gate of Pleasure *see* Urmia Plain
Gates, Henry Leyford (H.L.) 140
Gawar 150
Geddes, Walter Mackintosh 133
General Staff, German 19, 88
Geneseo 40
Geneva 6
genocide 119, 132, 139
Geogtapa 146–147, 151
George, Lloyd 60
Georgia 141
Gerard, James W. 40, *41*, 42
German Confederation 6
Germantown 36
Germany 3, 7, 18, 19–22, 23, 26, 27, 28–29, 30, 33, 35–39, 40, 42–44, 46, 48, 49, 52–54, 55, 57–58, 60–61, 62–73, 74–75; employs slave labor 60, 67; looting of occupied territories 58, 60, 66–67, 69, 78–79; war aims 3, 73–74
Ghafour, Hadji 130
Ghent 57, 66, 68, 79–80; unofficial peace with the Germans nearly broken 79

Gibson, Hugh 54, **55**, 58, 61, 69, 72, 76–77; trip to Antwerp 76–77; trip to Louvain 72
Girls' School (Merzivan) 126
Girls' School (Van) 108
Goeben 111
Goldring, Douglas 20
Gottingen 73
Gottshalk, A.L. 119
government, U.S. 47–48, 52, 125, 141, 153
Grabez, Trifko 12–15, 17–18
Graffam, Mary Louise 132–133
Grand-Hôtel (Antwerp) 77
Gray 135
Grbic, Rade 13
Great Britain 3, 10, 19, 23, 26, 28, 30–31, 33, 35, 42, 44–45, 57, 58, 60, 62, 63, 64, 69, 72, 74, 78, 79, 81, **81**, 82, 83, 85–86, 88, 89, 96, 100, 102, 104, 111, 137, 138, 145, 153; Americans trapped in 44–46; war aims 3, 19, 145
Great Depression 46
Great Game 143, 145
Greece 7
Greek Orthodox Church 12, 86, 91, 108
Green, Horace 79, 84
Grodno 95
Gulf of Finland 98
Gulpashan 146, 150
Gutmann, Herbert 40, 42
Gwazim 127

Haber, Fritz 96
Hadzici 11
Hague 33, **34**, 34–35
Hague Convention 72, 77
Haidar Pasha 131
Haig, Gen. Douglas 88
Haimhausen, Edgar Haniel von 37–38
Hal 63, 65
Halim, Said 122
Hamadan 153
Hamburg 32, 46
Hamid II, Sultan Abdul 113
Hamidiyé 113
Hapsburg family 3, 7, 18
Harassa 135–136
Harbin 89–90
Harmsworth, Sir Alfred Charles William *see* Northcliffe, Lord
Harper, Florence MacLeod 89–90, 92, 94–96, 98, 99–100, 103, 104; massacre by Petrograd police 92–93; trip to Kronstadt 99–100; work as a Sister of Mercy 95–96
Harput 108, 109, 119, 130, 136, 139
Harrington, Wellesley 36
Harvard Law School 48
Hauptmann, Bruno Richard 48
Havenstein, Rudolf 40
Hebrew Technical School for Girls (New York City) 125
helium 78
Henry Morgenthau Company 118

Herbesthal 43
Herrick, Myron T. 42, **43**, 83
Herwaerts, Major Hans von 72
Herzegovina 7, 11, 12
Hetzler, Theodore 45–46
High Command, German 59, 67; confiscates food from occupies territories 59
Hill, Richard 145
Hindenburg 78
Hitler, Adolf 3, 139
Hochstetter, Nella von 95
Holland 35, 42
Holland-American Line 36, 42
Holocaust 139
Holy Roman Empire 3, 6
Home Office (Britain) 31–32
Honduras 51
Hong Kong 89
Hooge Château 88
Hook of Holland 39
Hoover, Herbert 46, 48, 52, 58, 60
Hoover, Lou 46
Hopkins, Nevil Monroe 62–63
horses (for war) 27, 30–31, 69, 87
Hosts *see* Cossacks
Hot Springs Hotel (Yellowstone National Park) 10
Hôtel de la Banniere 78
Hotel de la Poste 80
Hôtel de Ville (Brussels) 65
Hôtel de Ville (Louvain) 53
Hôtel des Mille Colonnes (Louvain) 54
Hotel Regina (Paris) 33
Hôtel St. Antoine (Antwerp) 77
Hudson Bay Company 29
Huffman, Lieutenant D.C. 82
Hughes, Sam 83
Humaan, Lt. Cmdr. Hans 122–123
Hungarian Diet 7
Hungary 6–7, 18
Hunter, Edward C. 75
Huntington Township (Ohio) 42
Hurd, Eugene 95–97
Hussein Pasha 127

Igdir 115–116
Ilic, Danilo 11, 13–15, 17–18
Ilic, Stoja 11
Illinois 55, 146
Illustrated London News 84
De Imitatio Christi (*Imitation of Christ*) 70
Imperator 38
Imperial Army, German 19, 38, 39, 55, 60, 64, 66–72, 73–75, 77, 79; burns Louvain 70–71; commits atrocities 66–72, 73–75; justifications for atrocities 69–70; looting 60, 66–67, 69, 79
Imperial Bank 40
Imperial Bridge (Sarajevo) 15
Imperial Medical College (Constantinople) 108
India 9, 52, 105
Indian Bureau 141
Indian Removal 141

International Women's Day 91
Iowa 55
Iran *see* Persia
Iraq 111, 155
Ireland 62, 83
Iris River 126
Irwin, Richard William 47
Irwin, Will 52–54
Isakovic's Island 14
Islam 119, 120, 126–132, 150
Istanbul *see* Constantinople
Istria 3
Italy 9, 19, 36, 38, 87
Itchen River 30

Jackson, Andrew 141
Jackson, J.B. 117
Jagow, Gottlieb von 39
Janchu (son of Marie, Ruth Pierce's friend) 101
Janissaries 7
Jansen, Mr. 73
Japan 9, 42, 51, 73, 89, 90; aid to the Royal Navy 89
Jarotzky, Maj. Gen. Thaddäus von 58
Javert (alias for unnamed German intelligence officer) 65–66
Javert (character in *Les Misérables*) 65
Jefferson, Charles E. 33
Jevdet Bey 112–114, 131
Jewish Ladies' Benevolent Society 101
Jews 94, 100–101, 120, 125, 139, 148; alleged participation in the February Revolution 100–101; persecution by the Russians 100–102
Johnstown Flood 49
Joseph II (Austrian emperor) 18
journalists 13, 31, 33, 35, 49, 51–52, 54, 56, 62, 65, 68, 78, 80, 82, 84, 86, 101; and credentials 49
Jovanovic, Misko 14–15, 18

Kaisariel 109
Kaiserin Elizabeth 9
Kamerun 74
Kâmil, Mehmed 111
Karl Ludwig (brother of Franz Ferdinand) 9
Karlsbad 42
Karlsruhe 38
Kavana Bosna (Tuzla) 14
Kemal Effendi 128–129
Kempis, Thomas à 70
Kent, Fred I. 45
Kerenskii, Aleksandr Fedorovich 94, 97–98, 103–104
Kerovic, Mitar 14
Kerovic, Nedjo 14, 18
Khan, Nazar 150
Kiev 101–102; German advance towards 102
Kitchener, Lord Horatio Herbert 85
Kleve 39
Kluck, Gen. Alexander von 64
Knapp, Grace 105, 115

Komuna (Commune) 11
Konak (Sarajevo) 17
Konya 118–119, 133
Kornilov, Gen. Lavr Georgievich 104
Kosovo 7
Kotlin 98
Kragujevac 12
Kronstadt 98–100, 103
Kronstadt Committee of the Movement 99
Kurdish Gate (Urmia) 150
Kurds 113, 116, 119–120, 126, 128–129, 130, 131, 132, 133, 143, 145–147, 148, 149, 150–151, 152, 154–155; desire for a homeland 120, 152, 154–155
Kuropotkin, Gen. Alexei 97

Lacerda, Felix Cavalcanti de 61
Ladies' Home Journal 51
laissez-passer 49, 63, 84
Lake of Starnberg 6
Lake Urmia 145, 153, 155
Lake Van 112, 113, 116
Lamanov, Anatoli 99
Lansing, Robert 48, 118, 124–125
La Panne 86
Lark 29
Larson, Erik 10
Law XII 7
League of Nations 33, 126
Leavenworth 82
Leefdael 53
legation, German (Brussels) 54, 61
legation, U.S. (Brussels) 54–55, 60–61, 65, 66, 76; search for hidden telegraph on German legation's roof 61; takeover of German legation 54
Le Havre 30, 57
Leman, Gen. Gérard 21
Lemberg 97
Lemkin, Raphael 139
Lenin, V.I. 94, 102–104
Leopold II (king of Belgium) 21, 52, 74–75
Leslie, Francis H. 134–135
Leslie's Weekly 89
Lewis (journalist) 54
Lewis (Shedd), Mary 150, 151, 153
Leysen, Georges 62
Library of Alexandria 71
Liège 19–20, **20**, 21, 22, 39, 44, 66, 67, 72–73, 77; forts 19–21, 44
Life 45
Life of Charles V 70
Ligne, Prince 64–65
Limburg 35
Lindbergh, Charles 47–48
Lisbon 40
Liverpool 32, 44, 83
Lodge, Henry Cabot 142
Lolla, Panna 102
London 7, 29, 31, 32, 33, 44–47, 48, 51, 58, 68, 78, 79, 83, 84, 86, 104; Americans stranded in 45–47

London Daily Telegraph 49
Long, Robert Crozier 31–32
Long, Steve 140
Loomis, Estelle 28
looting 58, 60, 69, 72, 79, 154
Lorelie 137
Los Angeles 83, 121, 140
Louvain 52–53, **53** 53–54, 57, 62, 65, 70–72, 73
Louvre 29, 34
Loznica 13
Ludendorff, Gen. Erich 97, **97**
Ludwig II (king of Bavaria) 6
Lusitania 40, 46
Lüttwitz, Gen. Walther von 72, Luxembourg, Grand Duchy of 19, 36, 60; occupation by Germans 60
Lvov, Georgii Evgevevich 93, 103

MacArthur, Gen. Douglas 46
MacCallum, F.W. (Frederick William) 132
Macedonia 7, 110, 125
Madrid 52
Magi 148
Magyars (ethnic group) 7, 9
Maine 62, 135
Malatia 129, 133
Mali Zvornik 14
Malines 53, 62, 70, 76, 85
al-Mamaleki, Mirza Hasan Mostofi 145
Mamuret-al-Aziz, *vilayet* of 140
Manchester 31, 42
Manchuria 89
Manila 52, 89
Mannheim 118
Marash 117
Marchfeld 3
Mardiganian, Arshaluys (Aurora) 127–128, **128**, 129–132; arrives in the United States 140; makes *The Auction of Souls* 140; watches death of family 129, 131
Mardiganian, Ipranos 131
Mardiganian, Lusanne 127, 129
Mardiganian, Paul 127–128
Maria Teresa da Imaculada 10
Maria Theresa (mother of Joseph II) 18
Marie (Meyers' maid) 38
Marie (Ruth Pierce's friend) 101–102
Marietta 148
Marne River 64, 79
Marootian, Martin 121
Marseillaise 92
Martin V, Pope 70
Mary (daughter of Charles the Bold) 3, 6
Massachusetts 38, 47, 105, 142
Massachusetts Institute of Technology 29
Mauretania 44
Max, Adolphe Eugène Jean Henri 56–57, **57**, 58, 76
Maximalists 103

Maximilian (emperor of Mexico) 6
Maximilian I, Holy Roman Emperor 3
Mayerling 9
McAndrews and Forbes 133
McClure's 52
McCormick, Robert R. 86
McCoy, Elizabeth Genevieve 51
McCutcheon, John 52–54
McDowell, Margaret Wallace 151
McFarland, David F. 78
McFarland, Lt. Earl 82
McKinley, William 38
Mclaren, Grisell 129
Medical Corps, U.S. 79
Mediterranean Sea 74, 88, 142
Medz Yeghern (Great Crime) *see* Armenian Genocide
Mehmed V, Sultan 111, 119
Mehmedbasic, Mehmed 13, 17
Melle 80
Mensheviks 94
Mercantile Marine (Paris) 23, 28
Merchant's School (Sarajevo) 11
Merizzi, Col. Erich Edler von 15–16
Merzivan 108, 126–127
Metropole (hotel in Brussels) 66
Meuse River 20, 22, 35
Mexican Revolution 51
Mexico 6, 68
Meyer, George von Lengerke **38**, 38–39
Meyer, Julia 38–39
Meyer, Marion Alice Appleton 38–39
Miandoab 153
Michigan 134
Miliukov, Pavel Nikolaevich 94
Miljacka River 15
Milosevic, Obren 14
Milovic, Jakov 14
Ministry of Foreign Affairs (Belgium) 49
Ministry of Foreign Affairs (Turkey) 139
mission, American (Merzivan) 108, 126
mission, American (Urmia) 146, 147–151
mission, American (Van) 105, 108, 112–115; attack on 113, 114; problem with sanitation and disease 114, 115
mission, Anglican (Urmia) 149
mission, Baptist (Geogtapa) 146
Mississippi River 141
Mohammad Agha, Mirza 147
monetary policy and money 23, 26–27, 28, 34, 36, 40, 42 45–47; hoarding of hard currency and gold 26–27; refusal to accept letters of credit or traveler's checks 23, 26
Mons 58, 64, 78, 83
Mons-Condé Canal 64
Montagua 44

Montenegro 7, 9, 17
Montgelas, Count Max von 40
Montreal 83
Mora Bey 132
Moravia 3
Morgan, Gerald 49, 63
Morgenthau, Henry 112, 114, 117, 118–119, 120–124, *124*, 125, 127, 140, 151; brief biography 118; resigns ambassadorship 125
Morgenthau, Josephine 125
Moritz Schiller's delicatessen 16
Moroccan Crises 74
Morocco 74
Mortimer, George "Sheeny Mike" 51
Moscow 98
Mosul 140, 152
Mouland 35, 66, 68
Mount Sahand 143
Muller, Hugo Arthur 149, 155
Musa Bey 128–129
Mush 131
mustard gas 96

Namur 57
Napoleonic Wars 31
Narod (People) 12
Narodna odbrana (National Defense) 11
Natamos Consolidated of California 46
Nation 27, 73, 141
National Bank (Belgium) 58
Native Americans 46, 141
Naval Cathedral of Saint Nicholas (Kronstadt) 100
Naval Investigation Prison (Kronstadt) 99
Nazim (son of Ahmed Bey) 131
Nâzim, Hüseyin 111
Neckar River 38
Nestorians *see* Assyrians
Nestorius 147
Netherlands 6, 19, 33–36, 39, 42, 43, 47, 66–68, 80; plans for possible invasion 35
Nevsky Prospekt (Petrograd) 92
New Amsterdam 36
New England 108
New York (state) 36, 40, 43, 44, 45, 52, 68, 119, 121
New York City 32, 44, 48, 49, 52, 84, 125
New York Daily News 86
New York Life 121–122
New York State Supreme Court 40
New York Times 9, 39, 62, 69
New York Tribune 122, 138
Nicholas II, Tsar 35, 91–93, 95, 97; abdication 93
Nicholl, Louise Townsend 23, 27–28, 29–30, 32–33
Nieuport 85–86
Nikolaev, Major General 115
Ninth Corps (German Imperial Army) 68
Non-Party 99

Noordeinde Palace (The Hague) 35
Norfolk 82
North America 73, 141
North Carolina 141
USS *North Carolina* 47
North Sea 36, 44
Northcliffe, Lord (Sir Alfred Charles William Harmsworth) 84–85
Northfield Seminary and Women's College 108
Norway 35, 47
Nôtre, André le 64
Notre Dame (Aarschot) 69
Notre Dame (Hal) 63
Novelty Theater (Topeka) 86
Nuremberg 42

Oberlin College 132
Obljaj, Herzegovina 11
October Revolution 104
Odessa 102, 111
Ohio 42, 55, 82, 132, 148
Ojalvo, Vital 109
Okhrana 93, 102
Oklahoma 141
Olympics 47
One Morning in Sarajevo: 29 June, 1914 18
Ontario 83
Operation Nemesis: The Assassination Plot That Avenged the Armenian Genocide 139
O'Reilly, Mary Boyle 73
Orwell, George 96
Oslo 140
Osmanieh 133
Ostend 42, 57, 79, 80, 82, 84, 85
Ottokar II 3
Ottoman Empire 7, 105, *106–107*, 108, 109–112, 113–114, 115, 117, 118, 119, 120, 121, 122, 125, 126–127, 131, 132, 133, 135–137, 138, 139–140, 141, 143, 145, 146, 148, 149, 150, 151, 152, 153, 154; Committee of Union and Progress' takeover 110–111; relationship with Britain sours 111; secretly allies itself with Germany 111; war aims 111–112
Ottoman Freedom Society 110
Ottoman War Crimes Tribunals 138
Ourthe River 20
Outlook 66

Packard, Harry Phineas 146–147, 151, 152, 154–155; brief biography 146; saves Geogtapa 147
Packard, Hubert 146
Packard, Julia 146
Paddock, Gordon 143, 151, 153, 155
Page, Walter Hines *47*, 48, 58
Pakarich, Nerkin 138
Palais de Justice (Louvain) 54
Pale 14
Palestine 30

Panther 74
Pappenheim, Martin 18
Paradise of Iran *see* Urmia Plain
Parchevskii, Tovarish 99
Paris 6, 20, 23, *26*, 26–29, 30, 33–34, 38, 42, 47, 54, 67, 77, 78, 83, 85; German air attack 28–29
passports 7, 14, 27, 28, 29, 31, 40, 49, 52, 62, 64, 83, 85, 102, 136–137
Patten, James A. 42–44
Patterson, Joseph Medill 86
Paul, Saint 92, 117
Pavlovskii Guard Regiment 92
Peace Palace (Vredespaleis) (The Hague) *34*, 34–35
Peage, rue de (Antwerp) 84
Peet, William W. 108
Peking 89
Pennsylvania 36, 49
permis de séjour 49
Persia 119, 139, 143, *144*, 145, 146–148, *148*, 149–155; reason for political weakness 145; Russo-British plan to divide it after the war 145
Petar (king of Serbia) 13, 18
Peter the Great 92
Petrograd 40, 89–92, *92*, 93–94, 95, 98, 99, 103, 104, 117, 125; food riots 90–93; invasion of from Kronstadt 98–99
Petrograd Soviet 94, 103
Philadelphia 105
Philadelphia (ship) 23, 30, 32
Philadelphia Record 49
Philippines 82
pickelhuabe 64
Pierce, Ruth 101–102
Pijemont 12
Pilgrims 63, 105
Place de Meir (Antwerp) 84
Poids Public (Antwerp) 77
poison gas 88, 96
Poland 7, 86, 96, 139
Popovic, Cvjetko 13, 17–18
Popovic, Capt. Rade 13
Porter, Bruce 29
Portland (Maine) 62
Portland (Oregon) 52
Post, Wilfred M. 118
Powell, E. Alexander 68–71, 77, 82, 84; interview with General Boehn 69–71
Presbyterian Church 36, 143, 146, 147–148
Press Bureau (Britain) 31
Preston, Andrew W. 44
Priboj 14
Princeton 36
Princip, Gavrilo 11–18; carries out assassination of Franz Ferdinand 17; formulates plot to assassinate Franz Ferdinand 12
Princip, Jovo 11
propaganda 12, 52, 68, 70, 100–101
Prosvjenti Savjet (Cultural Council) (Sarajevo) 17

Protopopov, Aleksandr Dmitrievich 91
Provisional Government 93–94, 98, 99, 102–104, 152
Prussia 6, 19, 29, 39, 40, 43, 74, 75, 77, 86, 101
Prvanovic, Capt. Joca 13
Przemysl 86–87, **87**; Russian siege of 86–87
Puntigam, Anton 17
Puritans 105

Queen's Hotel (Antwerp) 84

Race for the Sea 85–86
Ramadan 120
Raskolnikov, Fedor 103
Rasputin 87
Ravished Armenia 140
Red Crescent 132
Red Cross 62, 80, 94, 95, 101, 105, 115–116, 118, 125
Red Sea 9
Red Star Line 44
Red Sultan *see* Hamid II, Sultan Abdul
refugees 23, 27–30, 32, 33, 34, 36–40, 42–48, 47, 52, 55, 113–114, 115, 116, 117–118, 119, 126–137, 139, 141, 143, 146–148, 149; American 23, 27–30, 32, 33, 34, 36–40, 42–48; Armenian 113–114, 117–118, 119, 126–134, **134**, 135–137, **137**, 139, 143; Assyrian 143, 146–148, 149
Régent, boulevard du (Brussels) 57
Reghib Bey 150
Regulation 27 32
Rescue Movement 126
Reuss-Köstritz, Tsarina Eleonore 125
Revolutionary Socialists 103
Reynolds, George C. 109
Reynolds, Mrs. 116–117
Rhine River 38
Ritz (London) 47
Ritz (New York City) 32
Rivne Fortress 102
Rodzianko, Mikhail Vladimirovich 98
Roehampton (London) 32
Roermond 35
Roman Catholic 86, 91, 119
Romanus, Jacques 70
Rome 47
Roos, Marcel 68
Roosevelt, Franklin D. 40, 82
Roosevelt, Theodore 52, 66, 74
Rosenfeld, Morris 44
Rotterdam 36, 39, 44, 48, 73
Rouen 23
Royal Army Veterinary Corps 31
Royal Military Canal (England) 78
Royal Navy 58, 89, 111
Rudolf (son of Rudolf I) 3
Rudolf I, Holy Roman Emperor 3
Ruhl, Arthur 78–82

Rupert of Hentzau (alias for unnamed German officer) 63, 64
Rupert of Hentzau (villain in *The Prisoner of Zenda*) 63
Russia 3, 19, 28, 31, 33, 35, 38, 65, 74, 86–88, 89–94, 95–98, 99–102, 103–104, 105, 111–112, 114–117, 119, 122, 132, 139, 143, 145, 146, 148, 149, 150, 151–153; anti-Semitic activities 100–102; ends participation in the war 104; war aims 3, 75; *see also* Soviet Union
Russian Hill (San Francisco) 29
Russian Revolution, 1905 90, 103
Russo-Japanese War 51, 73, 125

Saavedra y Vinent, Rodrigo de, Second Marqués de Villalobar 55
Sabac 13, 87
Sabit Bey 119
Sadovaia (Petrograd) 92
Sain Kala 153
St. Isaac's Cathedral 93
Saint-Lazare train station (Paris) 29
Sairt 114
Salmas 155
Sam Browne belt 51
San Francisco 9, 29, 52
San Guglielmo 44
San River 86
Sarajevo 11, 12, 13, 14–16, 17
Sardar-i-Fateh 155
Sarikamis 112
Saroléa, Charles 62
Savoy (London) 45, 83
Scheldt River 79, 80, 84
Schlieffen, Alfred Graf von 19
Schlieffen Plan 74
Schoebel, Lenore Russell 151
School of Languages (Louvain) 54
Schwarz, David 78
Science, rue del la (Brussels) 54
Scotland 23
Scott, Gen. Winfield 141
Scribe, rue (Paris) 23
Scribner's Magazine 68
Sea of Japan 90
Seaforth 32
Seaman, Major Louis L. 79
Seattle 9–10, 95
Seattle-Post Intelligencer 10
Second Balkan War 51
Second Hague Peace Conference 35
Secret Service, U.S. 82
Seine River 63, 76
Selfridges (London) 46
Selig, William N. 140
Sempstad 69
Seraing 21
Serbia 6–7, 11–15, 18–19, 23, 33, 55, 73, 74, 87, 125; answer to ultimatum issued by Austro-Hungarian Empire 19; invasion by Austro-Hungarian Empire 19; struggle for independence 7, 9

Serbian National Bank 13
Serbs 3, 7, 9, 87
Shahbaz, Wilbert 146
Shahbaz, Yonan H. 146, 149–150, 151
Shams-ul-la-Bek 146
Shanghai 89
Shattakh 113
Shedd, Louise 151
Shedd, William Ambrose 148–149, 150, 151–153; brief biography 148; death 153; on furlough 152; work as *cadi* 152
Sheppard, William Henry 75
Sheridan, Gen. Philip H. 141
Sherman, Gen. William Tecumseh 141
Sherman Antitrust Act 42
Shikak, Ismail Agha (Simko) 152, 154, 155; assassination attempt upon 154; death 155
ship, passenger 23, 30, 32–33, 36, 38, 44–45, 46; classes of accommodations 32–33
Siberia 87, 97, 101, 102
Simbirsk (now Ulyanovsk) 94
Sioux (members of a Wild West troupe) 46
Sisters of Mercy 94
Sivas 126–127, 132–133
Sketch 29
slavery in the Ottoman Empire 119, 126, 127, 129–132, 137, 151, 154
Slavs 7, 13, 74
Sleicher, John 89
Small Fortress (Theresientstadt) 18
Smith, David James 18
Smith, F. Willoughby 117
Smyrna 108, 123, 133
Société générale de Belgique 58
Sofia 125
Soignies 63
Soldiers' Committee 95
Songhua River 89
Sophie Maria Josephine Albina, Duchess of Hohenberg 10, 12, 13, 17, 18
South America 31, 54
South Bend 79
South Carolina 141
Southampton 23, 30, 32
Southern Pacific Railroad 28
Soviet of Military Deputies 99
Soviet of Workers' Deputies 99
Soviet Union 65, 138, 142
soviets 94, 99
Spain 35, 74
Spanish-American War 40, 45, 51, 52
Spanish flu 140
spies and spying 15, 32 36, 39, 46, 54, 55, 60, 61–62, 63, 64, 65, 77, 80, 82, 84, 85, 89, 101, 133; paranoia about 61–62, 63
Stanford University 52
State Department, U.S. 28, 68, 73, 119, 125, 137

Stjepanovic, Cvijan 14
Strand (London) 45
Strauss, S.W. 40
Stuttgart 38
Styr River 98
Styria 3
Sublime Porte **110**, 111
submarine warfare, Germany declaration of unrestricted 40
Sudan 68
Suez Canal 9, 138
Sun 140
Superior Court of Massachusetts 47
Supreme Court, U.S. 141
Sweden 35, 47
Switzerland 3, 34, 36, 38, 39, 42, 47, 55, 103, 138
Sykes, Mark 129
Syracuse 68
Syria 111, 137, 138
Syrian Desert 126
Syrian Evangelical Church 147

Tabriz 143, 151, 153, 154, 155
Taft, William Howard 42
Talaat, Mehmed 111, 114, 117, 120–121 **121**, 125, 129, 137, 138, 151; assassination 138; brief biography 120
Tangier 73–74
Tankosic, Maj. Vojin 12, 13
Tarnopol 97
Taube 29
Taurida Palace (Petrograd) 103
Taurus 117
Tehlirian, Soghomon 138–139
Tehran 153
Tennessee 141
USS *Tennessee* 47
Termonde 60
Tervuren 52, 71
Test River 30
Theresientstadt (Terezín) 18
Third Army, Ottoman 110–112, 122
Third Army, Russian 101
Third Council at Ephesus 147
Thirteenth Corps (German Imperial Army) 38
Thompson, Donald C. 68–69, 82–86, 87–88, 89–90, 92–94, 96–97, 98, 99–100, 102–103, 104; biographic details 82; escapes from French authorities 83; massacre by Petrograd police 92–93; trip to Kronstadt 99–100
Thompson, Robert J. 68–69
Thompson's Fort (Antwerp) 84
Thrace 117
Tibet 145
Tiflis **116**, 117, 139, 143
Tigris River 114, 130, 140
Tilsit 75
Times (London) 31, 120
Tirlemont 52
Tisza, István 18
Toledo 55
Toledo Blade 55

Tolstaya, Countess Alexandra 115
Tolstoy, Leo 115
Tomsk 97
Topcider 12
Topeka 82, 86
Town Hall (Sarajevo) 15, 16
Trail of Tears 141
Trans-Caucasus region 143
Trans-Siberian Railway 89–90
traveler's checks 23, 26, 36
Treasury Department, U.S. 47, 48
Treaty of Ghent 79
Treaty of London 7
Treaty of Madrid 74
Treaty of Sèvres 142
Treaty of Turkmenchay 145
Treaty of Versailles 3
trench warfare 31, 35, 76, 83, 86, 88, 97; and mining 88
Trevelyan, George Macaulay 87
Trieste 9, 46
Triple Entente 74
Trogvinski Glasnik 13
Trotskii, Leon 103–104
Tuileries Garden (Paris) 33
Turkey (modern) 28, 108, 111, 138–140, 155; *see also* Ottoman Empire
Tuzla 14–15
Twain, Mark 75
Twenty Ninth "Grodno Nobility" Flying Column 95
Tyndale, William 76
typhoid fever 151
typhus 101, 115, 116, 125, 132, 146
Tyrol 3

Ujedinjenje Ili Smrt (Union or Death) *see* Black Hand
Ukraine 102
Ulhans 35
Ulianov, Vladimir Ilich *see* Lenin, V.I.
Ulster Orangemen 83
Umar I, Caliph 71
United Cigar Stores 84
United Fruit Company 44
United Kingdom *see* Great Britain
United States 1, 9, 27–28, 31, 33, 35–36, 39–40, 42, 45–48, 49, 52, 68, 73, 75, 78, 79, 98, 101, 102, 104, 125, 129, 139, 140–141, 148, 152, 153
United States Relief Committee 47
University of California Berkley 28–29
University of Chicago 94
University of Ghent 80
University of Kansas 78
University of Louvain 70–71, **71**; destruction of library 70, **71**
University of St. Petersburg 94
Urbana, Ohio 55
Urfah 130–131, 132, 134–135; Armenian rebellion against deportation 134–135
Urmia Plain 143, 145–146, 150–154; Ottoman incursions 145; Ottoman occupation 143, 145, 150–151, 154
Urmia 145–147, 148–152, 153–155; attacked by Simko 154–155; occupation by the Turks 151
Ushnu 155
Ussher, Clarence D. 105, 108–109, 112–117, 129, 140, 147; comes down with typhus 115; escapes the Ottomans 115–117
Ussher, Neville 115

vâli 105, 111, 112, 118, 119, 127, 131, 132, 133
Van 108–109, 112–115, 122, 153; siege of the Armenian quarter 112–114; *vilayet* of 120
van Calck, William 79
Vancouver 89, 95
van Dyke, Henry 36, **37**, 66
van Eyck, Jan 79
van Hee, Julius 66, 68–69, 79–80
Vartabed (friend of Arshaluys Mardiganian) 132
Vartessarian, Arousiag 130
Vaterland 32, 46
Velno 35
Venus de Milo 29
Versailles 64
Verviers 39, 44
Vesdre River 39
Vichy 27
Vienna 3, 9, 18, 47
Viking 44
vilâyets 111, 120, 140
Vilna 97
Vilvorde 76
Vinaigriers, rue de (Paris) 29
Viren, Vice-admiral Robert Nikolaevich 99
Visé 35, 66–67
Vladivostok 90, 95
Vlajnic's sweet shop 15
Volga River 94, 97

Wagenheim, Baron Hans Freiherr von 111, 122–123
Waizfelder, G.P. 39, 47
Waizfelder, Mrs. G.P. 39
Waldorf Hotel (London) 45
Walsenburg, Capt. August 130
War As It Really Is 88
war horses *see* horses (for war)
war mobilization 19, 23, 27, 29–30, 38, 39, 43; in Britain 19, 30; in France 19, 23, 27, 29–30; in the Netherlands 35
War of 1812 79
War Office, British 31, 83
War Office, French 83
Washington, D.C. 46
Washington Times-Herald 86
Waterloo, boulevard du (Brussels) 57
Watts, Ethelbert 52
Webb, Charlotte 127
Weeks, Raymond 27

Index

Weitz, Paul 122
Welkenraedt 39
Wesleyan College 105
Western Front 30, 64, 82, 85, 97
Whelan, George J. 84
White, George E. 126–127, *127*
White Star Line 32
Whitlock, Brand 52, 54–55, *56*, 56–57, 58, 61, 64–65, 66, 72; biographic details 55
Wiart, Count Henri Carton de 60–61, *61*
Wild West troupe trapped in Europe 46
Wilhelm II, Kaiser 38, 73–74, 103, 125, 133
Wilhelmina, Queen (Netherlands) 35
Wilhelmstrausse (Berlin) 40
William II, Count (Holland) 35
Williams, Albert Rhys 35, 65–68; arrested as spy 65–66; trip to Liège 67
Williams, George Washington 75
Wilson, Virginia 108–109
Wilson, Woodrow 28, 36, 38, 40, 42, 47, 48, 55, 68, 79, 118, 125; issues statement of U.S. neutrality 48
Wilson Administration 124, 153
Windsor Hotel (Niagara Falls) 9
Winter Palace (Petrograd) 104
"A Wise Economist Asks a Question" 52
Wislecenus, Otto 77
With the Allies 46–47
With the Russians at the Front 87
World 52, 84
World Columbia Exhibition 10
World War I 3, 6, 26, 31, 78; armistice 104, 138, 154; blame 3, 18, 73; cascade of war declarations 19; causes 3
World War II 3
World's Work 52
Würtemberg 38
Wurth, Maj. Alfred 64–65

xylyl-bromide 96

Yale Forest School News 134
Yale Forestry School 133
Yale University 139
Yaras, Jack 43–44
Yarrow, Ernest A. 105, 114
Yellowstone National Park 10
Yemen 111
Yenikhan 127
Yokohama 89
Young Turks 110, 128
Young Women's Christian Association 127
Ypres 88, 96
Yser (River) 85–86, 88

Zagros Mountains 145, 146
Zeitoun 117, 122, 134
Zemun 17
zeppelin (dirigible) 21, 28, 77–78; difficulty in shooting down 78
Zeppelin, Ferdinand von 77–78
Zilan, Sheik 131
Zimmerman, Arthur 40
Zinovev, Grigorii Eveevich 103
Znamenskaya Square 91
Zoroaster 148
Zuider Zee (Netherlands) 36
Zurich 103

www.ingramcontent.com/pod-product-compliance
Lightning Source LLC
Chambersburg PA
CBHW080805300426
44114CB00020B/2841